Reviews of Clyde N. Wilson's Works

Clyde Wilson had been ploughing the ground
long before many of us came to plant.
—**Donald Livingston**

Clyde Wilson is a national treasure.
—**Alice Teller**

Clyde Wilson shows great ability in the field of intellectual history.
—***American Historical Review***

Clyde Wilson exhibits the rarest kind of courage—intellectual courage.
—***The State Newspaper***

Clyde Wilson is certainly the biggest intellectual
heavyweight with the neo-Confederate scene.
—**Southern Poverty Law Center**

…a mind as precise and expansive as an encyclopedia.…
These are the same old preoccupations given new life and meaning by a real mind
—as opposed to what passes for minds in the current intellectual establishment.
—**Thomas H. Landess**

This generous collection of Clyde Wilson's essays …places him on the same level
with all the unreconstructed greats in modern Southern letters: Donald Davidson,
Andrew Lytle, Frank L. Owsley, Richard Weaver, and M.E. Bradford.
—**Joseph Scotchie**

Clyde Wilson is an obstreperous soldier in the great
Jacobin wars that have plagued the nation.
—**Robert C. Cheeks**

Professor Clyde N. Wilson's latest book is remarkable in many ways.
At one and the same time it is richly variegated and philosophically sound,
while its style and form are consistently elegant.
—**Jack Kershaw**

That man's willing to say in print what most folks are afraid to THINK"
—**Reader Comment**

"... the silver-tongued voice of the New Right..."
—**Chilton Williamson,** *National Review*

"*Carolina Cavalier* is the best biography of a figure of the war to have been written in memory."
—*Southern Partisan*

"... masterful interpretation.."
—*North Carolina Historical Review*

"Well-researched, flawlessly accurate, deeply thought out, well-written, and timely...."
—**James E. Kibler,** *Florida Historical Quarterly*

"... a careful scholar who has thought hard and deep about his beloved South.... Wilson is, in short, an exemplary historian who ... displays formidable talent."
—**Eugene D. Genovese,** *Chronicles*

"Here we find magisterial intellectual history ... clearly one of the best of his generation of historians." —**M. E. Bradford,** *National Review*

"Perceptive critics have called Carolina Cavalier 'outstanding, "most impressive,' magisterial intellectual history.' With such evaluations I concur." —**Grady McWhiney,** *Southwestern Historical Quarterly*

"... lucid prose and sharp analysis..." —***Blue & Gray Magazine***

"Professor Wilson, the very model of a scholar and a gentleman."
—**Thomas Dilorenzo**

It is hard to do justice to Clyde Wilson's work.... Suffice it to say that there is good, powerful writing here, where an understanding of the value of genuine aristocratic leadership is mixed with the practical wisdom of the plain folk of the South. I have long been waiting for a collection of Wilson's essays and, having seen it, I can say that it is well worth careful and repeated reading.
— **Joseph R. Stromberg**

DEFENDING DIXIE

Defending Dixie

Essays in Southern History and Culture

Clyde N. Wilson

Defending Dixie: Essays in Southern History and Culture
Copyright© 2006, 2025 by Clyde N. Wilson

Notice: The information in this book is true and complete to the best of his knowledge. It is offered without guarantee on the part of the author.

ALL RIGHTS RESERVED. No part of this publication may be reproduced, distributed, or transmitted in any form or by any means, including photocopying, recording, or other electronic or mechanical methods, or by any information storage and retrieval system without the prior written permission of the publisher, except in the case of very brief quotations embodied in critical reviews and certain other non-commercial uses permitted by copyright law.

Produced in the Republic of South Carolina by
SHOTWELL PUBLISHING LLC
Post Office Box 2592
Columbia, So. Carolina 29202
www.ShotwellPublishing.com

Cover: *The Flag of Sumter, October 20, 1863* by Conrad Wise Chapman.

ISBN: 978-1-963506-46-4

SECOND EDITION

10 9 8 7 6 5 4 3 2 1

To all the Usual Suspects.

You make me proud and give me hope.

Contents

Publisher's Note xv

Introduction by Thomas H. Landess xvii

Acknowledgements xxiii

Recovering Southern History
American Historians and Their History 1
Recovering Southern History 16
Cracks in the Treasury of Virtue 25
Two Heroes and a Poet 29
The Mind of the Old South 34
The Southern Cavalier Revisited 38
Crackers and Roundheads 42
An Obscene Carnival 49
Continuity in Southern History 53
Scratching the Fleas:
American Historians and Their History 55

The War—My Myth or Yours?
The Greatest Sacrifice 63
The War—My Myth or Yours? 66
General Richard Taylor 84
Tar Heels' Revenge 91
Blue Grass Belligerents 94
High Tech Hunley 97
The War Lover 99
Thank Heaven for the "Amateurs" 108
A Comment on Cold Mountain 112
Confederate Connections 114
American Iliad 124

The Bloody Banner—Long May It Wave

The Flag in South Carolina: An Unofficial History 129
Scholars' Statement in Support of the Confederate Flag 144
Maurice Bessinger's Stand 151
Confederate Memorial Day Address 155
Southern Heritage Then and Now 159
The Pledge of Allegiance 164
What is Patriotism? 166

State Rights Revisited

War, Reconstruction, and the End of the Union 169
Our First President 183
Our Second Constitution 186
The Consent of the Governed Revisited 190
Albert Taylor Bledsoe 193
Devolution 198
DiLorenzo and His Critics 202
Inventing the New Nation 207

The Other Southerners

The Redeemable South 213
Black Confederates 217
Black Confederates Reconsidered 220
Spielberg's Amistad 223
Race and Community 229
Returning Home 231
On Reparations 232

The Upper Right Corner

Yankee Slavers 235
The Yankee Problem in American History 242
The Yankee Problem, Again 252

    The Enemy Up Close 256
    The Flight of the Kiwis 262
    Royal Teddy 265
    Ambrose Bierce's War.. 268
    Scorcese's Gangs of New York 274
    Will They Never Learn?.. 277
    Yankee Wars 278

A Mirror for Artists
    New England Against America.. 279
    Literature in the Old South 286
    The True Fire Within... 298
    Thomas Nelson Page 300
    Cleanth Brooks on Faulkner... 309
    Faulkner and Thomas Wolfe 314
    Homage to George Garrett 319
    A Bow to the Ladies 333
    Tom Wolfe: Two Between the Ribs 341
    Bernard Cornwell's Starbuck Chronicles 344
    Styron's Bad Example.. 347

The Agrarian Vision
    Up From Menckenism... 351
    Uncle Sam's Other Province 354
    Andrew Lytle... 359
    Allen Tate... 361
    Family Reunion 363
    French Agrarian Cinema 365
    James Kibler.. 367
    Russell Kirk's "Southern Valor".. 370
    Belloc as Historian... 376
    Their Children's Children 378

In Justice to So Fine a Country

- What is a Southerner? 383
- The Rev. Mr. Longstreet and the Nine Dwarfs 390
- Harvard Goes South 393
- Keeping Up with the Joneses (Southern Style) 396
- Confederate Rainbow 398
- The Assault on Tobacco 401
- In the Land of Cotton 403
- Dixie Dystopia 410
- Tar Heel Dead 416
- South and West 422
- The South and the American Empire 424
- Lost Causes Regained: The Works of M.E. Bradford 428
- What to Say about Dixie? 436
- Confessions of a Neo-Confederate 441

About the Author 443

Publisher's Note

ORIGINALLY PUBLISHED IN 2006, *Defending Dixie* has established itself as essential reading in the study of the South.

During the years this book has been out of print, copies could be obtained only at very high prices. Persistent interest, evidenced by numerous inquiries regarding its availability, has persuaded Shotwell to republish this Southern classic.

The current edition is a newly produced version that maintains the original content of the first publication but differs in format from the original. A companion volume, *From Union to Empire*—the initial book in Dr. Wilson's two-volume series—will be released subsequently.

We wish to acknowledge Christopher Sullivan, former editor of the late *Southern Partisan* magazine, along with others whose efforts facilitated the production of this new edition for contemporary readers.

It is our sincere hope that readers will find value in this indispensable work, as so many have over previous years.

October 2025

INTRODUCTION

By Thomas H. Landess

Thirty years ago, Southern colleges and universities were alive with scholars who understood and defended the strong conservative strain in the American tradition, a strain quintessentially Southern. These professors taught in a number of academic departments, though mostly in History, Political Science, and English. You found a few moles in the soft sciences: Sociology and Psychology; but these disciplines by their very nature are antithetical to traditions of any sort.

During this era, conservative scholars were never in the majority; and liberal administrators, like greedy bears, tried to stop them as they swam upstream. But a number survived and provided the academy with a healthy dialogue on issues of importance. Today most are gone—dead, retired, or banished to remote offices and assigned remedial courses. Historian Clyde Wilson is an exception to this generalization. Currently, he is still teaching at the University of South Carolina, where for years he has been editing the works of John C. Calhoun and subverting the brighter graduate students. He is the last pterodactyl, soaring close to the sun, casting a long, cold shadow over the politically correct landscape.

This volume, a sequel, provides Wilson's growing readership with more of his observations on an astonishing variety of subjects: historiography, political philosophy, literature, art, and popular culture, to name but five. All of these concerns are worried over by a mind as precise and expansive as an encyclopedia. Many of the selections—some lengthy, some no more than a few paragraphs—are reviews of books that are less important than what Wilson has to say about them and the issues they raise.

There are three basic types of reviews. The first is little more than a description of the book's contents, with an advisory sentence or two at the end: read; don't read. The second type, favored by the *New York Times*, is an essay on the subject matter covered by the book, with little or no commentary on the book itself. The third is the kind Clyde Wilson writes: information on the book's content, combined with sufficient commentary to place the work in a larger intellectual, historical, or political context. The third type is the most difficult to write, first because it requires reviewers to read the books they review, and second because it demands sufficient intelligence and knowledge to understand what's just been read.

The chapters in Wilson's book are organized around specific topics; but they all derive from a commanding intelligence that organizes them into ranks and files and gives them their marching orders. Thus, *Defending Dixie* is a coherent volume rather than a patchwork collection of random and unrelated essays. No later than halfway through the book, the reader should awaken to the subtle unity in which all its parts participate. This is a study of the intellectual heritage of the South and how it has been ignored or distorted by a new generation of ersatz scholars and popular commentators.

This heritage is the lost key to the front door of America, or rather the Old Republic that was once America. As Wilson demonstrates, Southern intellectual history encompasses the thought of 18th century Federalists like James Madison, anti-Federalists like Patrick Henry, and in-betweeners like Thomas Jefferson. It also includes the Vanderbilt Agrarians, historians like Ulrich B. Phillips and Francis B. Simkins, and contemporaries like M.B. Bradford and Thomas DiLorenzo. And he traces common threads through all of it: a distrust of Big Government, a robust skepticism of political abstractions like equality, and a rejection of the idea that folks are innately good at heart.

Particularly impressive are Wilson's discussions of historiography. In the opening section of his book, he provides the reader with a clearly defined anatomy of contemporary historians and histories, acknowledging the inevitable fallibility of both while establishing solid guidelines for assessing their ultimate credibility. These discussions are particularly valuable in an era when ideologues of the Left are rewriting Southern history in an effort to destroy the remaining vestiges of a distinctly regional sensibility that stands in the path of a collectivist, globalist future.

Wilson likewise addresses the omnipresent historical question of the War Between the States—its origins, its meaning, its tragic consequences. At the beginning of the last century, Southerners knew why the

Introduction

War was fought and regarded its outcome as an unmitigated tragedy. By the end of the century, they were not so sure. Small wonder! During the second half of the 20th century Yankee historians created a rigid orthodoxy that reduced the War to a simplistic morality play with the South as swarthy villain and the Union as blond, blue-eyed hero. In this chapter Wilson provides a powerful corrective for such wrong-headed misrepresentation and provides corrective instruction.

Wilson was personally involved in the fight to keep the Confederate battle flag flying over the South Carolina capitol dome, so his lengthy commentary on this struggle is doubly significant—as primary history and as the testimony of an eyewitness and participant in history. With this dual perspective, he devotes a significant section of his book to the flag controversy and to the question of the flag's place in contemporary Southern society.

From the beginning of the nation's history—prior to the ratification of the Constitution—the question of State Rights was central to the making of America. The anti-Federalists articulated the position of most Southerners: that centralized government was the ultimate danger the "more perfect union" faced, that the already-existent rights of the states had to be protected in the new Constitution, and that without such protection the 13 colonies would be better off remaining under the loose Articles of Confederation to which they subscribed. In his well-argued discussion called "War, Reconstruction, and the End of the Union," Wilson shows how quickly and how thoroughly Lincoln, and his party scuttled the Old Republic—and with what disastrous consequences. In this chapter he also offers an in-depth analysis of the historical Lincoln along with a defense of Thomas DiLorenzo, Lincoln's most formidable contemporary critic.

In a chapter called "The Other Southerners," he takes up the delicate and multifaceted subject of the region's blacks: slavery, their service in the Confederate Army, and their recent return to the South. The most interesting segment is his ruthless review of Steven Spielberg's movie *Amistad*, which turns a complicated historical event into an anti-Southern morality play.

Wilson's dissection of this Hollywood travesty is worth the price of the book.

Having tackled the question of blacks, he then addresses a more adversarial relationship, that of Southerners to those who live in the "upper right-hand corner"—i.e., New Englanders. He begins with a look at the pro-slavery sentiment in Yankeeland, and the degree to which it has been swept under the rug or else misrepresented by contemporary historians. In a brilliant essay called "The Yankee Problem in American History," he gives the reader a dazzling display of erudition while discussing in clear and entertaining prose the image of the Yankee in history and literature. Finally, he looks at two New England families—the Beechers and the Adamses—and hangs out their dirty laundry for Southerners to see and enjoy.

In addition to being a student of history, Wilson knows a great deal about Southern literature and has written extensively on the subject. His perspective is that of a Southern historian who nonetheless knows good poetry and fiction when he reads it and can approach it with all the resources of a literary critic. In a lengthy chapter, he discusses such diverse figures as William Gilmore Simms, the humorists of the old Southwest, Confederate poet Henry Timrod, Thomas Nelson Page, William Faulkner, Thomas Wolfe, George Garrett, and several lesser knowns.

In his discussion of the Agrarians, Wilson doesn't attempt an in-depth analysis of *I'll Take My Stand* or the tenets of Agrarianism. In short essays he deals with Andrew Lytle, Allen Tate, and their spiritual and intellectual allies: Russell Kirk, James Kibler, and Hilaire Belloc. He also makes short work of a couple of social historians who misunderstand and consequently denigrate the Agrarian tradition.

The final chapter in Wilson's rich and variegated book is a smorgasbord of essays that do not fit easily into the previous categories. A list of several titles suggests why: "What Is a Southerner?" "Harvard Goes South," "The Assault on Tobacco," and "The South and the American Empire." In this chapter, he discusses the demographics of the South, Southern plantation life as revealed in the letters of a War-era Georgia family, various ethnic groups that have blended into the Southern community, and the history of Cotton.

The importance of this book lies in its originality, which derives from the operation of Clyde Wilson's creative intellect on disparate and wide-ranging bodies of knowledge. These are the same old preoccupations given new life and meaning by a real mind—as opposed to what passes for minds in the current intellectual establishment.

The book is a joy to read for one more reason: it's clear and imaginative prose. Most historians write like sociologists—bogged down in the passive voice, addicted to jargon and clichés, each sentence more pedestrian than the last. Wilson writes like a good novelist. His language is precise and highly functional; at the same time, it contains the kind of verbal surprise that engages a literate reader as well as one interested in the subject matter. *Defending Dixie* is the kind of book whose prose you can read for sheer pleasure.

Finally, be forewarned. If you hate the South and don't like to hear good things about the region, you might want to skip this book and pick up a copy of anything Southern that's favorably reviewed by the *New York Times*. As measured and objective as his arguments may be, Clyde Wilson is always the good Southerner. William Faulkner once recalled an important lesson from Sherwood Anderson: "'You have to have somewhere to start from: then you begin to learn,' he told me. 'It don't matter where it was, just so you remember it and ain't ashamed of it.'" Wilson knows exactly who he is and where he came from. More to the point, he is totally, unequivocally without shame.

Thomas H. Landess
Columbia, South Carolina
September 6, 2005

ACKNOWLEDGEMENTS

Defending Dixie: Essays in Southern History and Culture can be considered a companion to *From Union to Empire: Essays in the Jeffersonian Tradition*, which was published by the Foundation for American Education in 2003. Like the previous work, the book in hand collects writings that first appeared in many different places over a period of more than thirty years. For *Defending Dixie*, as for *From Union to Empire*, thanks are due to Charles Hamel, President of FAE, for his generosity in making publication possible. Likewise, to Christopher M. Sullivan for sponsoring and forwarding the project. Without the extraordinary dedication and labor of Tim Manning, Jr., this book would never have made it into your hands. Tim is the last but not least of the Usual Suspects who have immeasurably enriched my teaching career—and my life.

These writings are concerned with the South. They rest on some basic assumptions that I described a quarter century ago in *Why the South Will Survive*: Dixie is real (even though its essence may be intangible); its sons and daughters and friends must make sure that it continues to thrive; and all civilized folk have an obligation to give it fair credit. Given the ongoing barbarization of American society, high and low, the continued flourishing of the South as an alternative America is more necessary than ever. Dixie may fall short in many of the predominant American characteristics—wealth, optimism, and self-righteousness—but she has much to offer the 21st century. More importantly, there are plenty of good people who love her still.

I am honored that Tom Landess, the most gifted man of letters I know, has supplied some generous introductory lines. Truth to tell, it is really his collected essays that should be published rather than mine. I grew up to be a pretty good historian. However, most of what I know about literature and its importance, I learned from Jim Meriwether in unofficial late afternoon seminars sponsored by the folks at Jack Daniels. I have never properly thanked him until now.

The bulk of the pieces in *Defending Dixie* were first published in 1) *Chronicles: A Magazine of American Culture*; 2) on www.lewrockwell.com; and 3) in the Intercollegiate Studies Institute journals *Continuity, Intercollegiate Review,* and *Modern Age*. All have given permission for republishing material herein. Tom Fleming, editor of *Chronicles*, has for years been generous in publishing my fulminations, as has Lew Rockwell. Other pieces first appeared in books by Maurice Bessinger, Jim Kibler, and Mike Tuggle; books published by Fletcher and Fletcher, Gates of Vienna Books, and J.S. Sanders and Company; and *The Costs of War*, edited by John V. Denson, Transaction Publishers. Other items appeared in *Southern Partisan, Boston Review, South Carolina Review, National Review, World & I, Southern Patriot, II Domenicale,* and www.southerncaucus.org.

Clyde N. Wilson
Carolina, September 2005

Chapter One

Recovering Southern History

American Historians and Their History

To deliver examples to posterity, and to regulate the opinion of future times, is no slight or trivial undertaking; nor is it easy to commit more atrocious treason against the great republic of humanity, than by falsifying its records and misguiding its decrees.
  —Samuel Johnson, Rambler No. 136

In no society that ever existed has historically-oriented activity been a larger enterprise than in modern America. Consider the percentage of the GNP consumed by the teaching of history at every level of the education system; by the support of thousands of professional historians, museums, archives, and national historical parks; and by the publishing of historical books, journals, and films. And that is not even to account for the importance of history in providing symbols and frameworks of deliberation for public affairs. But it is also true that no major society has ever had a less real sense of history, including its own, and been more ambivalent about what history is for. This is partly because the American spirit is predominantly pragmatic and present-oriented. However, there is considerably more to the American confusion about history than our characteristic disdain for theoretical consistency that so often leaves Europeans uneasy. There is an ambiguity bordering on self-deception in most of the public activity and consciousness of history among Americans.

To understand my outrageous point, let us first consider what history is. There are three legitimate aspects in which history, as a deliberate activity, can be viewed. The first and most important of these has to do with the philosophy of history, or universal history, with those realms where history becomes a part of philosophy and theology. I do not propose to deal with this at all, but to consider American historical activity in two of its practically apparent aspects.

First, history involves the elaboration of a commonly shared mythology that provides part of the cohesion of a national or cultural group through the celebration of common ancestors. I mean mythology in the highest sense, not in a trivial sense. I do not mean that such history is the opposite of factual, but that it is true in a sense that transcends the merely factual. It is an ethical and aesthetic symbolization that serves the purpose of social unity.

Gerhart Niemeyer described such history well in his chapter, "The Ethics of Existence," in *Between Nothingness and Paradise*. We all participated in history of this kind when we watched the pageantry of the wedding of the Prince of Wales and Lady Diana Spencer. Without even being Englishmen and despite the ignorant babble of the television commentators, we were able to participate in a historic symbolism which has a tremendous binding power over a cultural community widely divided by time, space, and political boundaries.

The second legitimate aspect of historical activity has to do with the establishing of an accurate record of historical fact. It is part of the enterprise of organized knowledge, of the exercise of our disciplined curiosity about the world. In America since the late 19th century most historians have claimed to be, and sometimes even have been, primarily engaged in historical activity of this second sort. Often this activity has sought to lift itself to the status of "social science," to assert that there was a degree of scientific rigor and conclusiveness in its endeavors analogous to the "hard" sciences.

The identification of history with science assumed several things and implied some others. It assumed that history was an objective search for "facts" governed by a rigorous methodology. Nobody really believes this anymore, though some may pretend in the hope of having rub off on them, or on their "findings," some of the prestige that attaches to science. Of course, historical writing is not and cannot be objective in the sense of the "hard" sciences, which indeed may not be themselves as "objective" as they were once thought to be.

Another assumption governing history as social science was that it was cumulative. But this is at best doubtful. We do not so much add new knowledge to old as we throw away old knowledge for new or convert it to new uses. In the wake of the civil rights revolution of the 1960s, for instance, the history of Reconstruction was rewritten. But this was not because the discovery of new historical knowledge required the revising of previously erroneous views. Rather, it was because the emergence of new attitudes required the formulation of a new interpretation. It is doubtful that present historians of Reconstruction "know" any more about it than writers of the derided school of William A. Dunning. In fact, present writers, in many cases, know considerably less. They simply measure Reconstruction by a different scale of values. And since they reject old views rather than incorporate them with new ones into a more inclusive synthesis, there is no cumulative effect. (But in denying any cumulative aspect to the pursuit of historical knowledge I am being too severe. In fact, I think our knowledge is cumulative, but only a very small part of historical effort contributes to the slow accretion of real knowledge.)

One of the implications of the social science approach was its melioristic cast. While it was asserted that its chief characteristic was an objective search for truth, it was simultaneously implied, often in disguised fashion, that such objectively derived findings, like those of science, might have large social implications and substantive social utility. A little of this notion still clings to history, though less so than to other "social sciences."

Despite the collapse of scientific pretensions, there remains a legitimate sphere of historical activity relating to the establishment of an accurate, objective historical record. If complete ideal objectivity is unobtainable, a functional degree of objectivity is still possible. We are left with simply the old-fashioned standard of the decent, honest, dispassionate observer who cannot entirely free himself from those human passions and prejudices that distort reason, but who can with moral effort see both sides of a question. (I take for granted a minimal level of ability and professional "expertise.") It is exactly the same capacity that justifies our reliance on juries to determine guilt or innocence or to arrive at a just settlement of disputes. We should bear in mind here the observation of a wise historian of the last generation, Howard K. Beale, in assessing the literature on the Civil War, that those historians who assert objectivity for themselves are invariably the most biased, while those who are aware of their own prejudices make the nearest approach to fairness.

Let me complicate the argument further at this point by asserting that the two types of historical activity that I have distinguished, symbolization and objective record, cannot be completely disentangled in practice. It is even arguable that they should not be disentangled, in that the greatest historians are those who synthesize the two separate functions. The most successful and useful historian is the one who works within the restraint of the objective record, but is still able to cast his work into a form that serves the purpose of socially constructive symbolization. Recent examples of successful practice in this regard are

Shelby Foote's *The Civil War: A Narrative* and Daniel Boorstin's *The Americans: The Democratic Experience*.

It is possible, then, though not necessarily easy or common, to practice both types of history simultaneously. And this simultaneity applies both to motive and execution. A great historian may be guided by the purpose of establishing a reliable historical record. That does not exclude him from serving at the same time the purpose of social myth-making, of providing his society with symbolizations that will enhance its unity and inspire its civic life. Put another way, there is no necessary conflict between patriotism and objectivity.

In fact, by this calculation, no such thing as history that is both great and trans-cultural is possible. The "social scientist" assumed that his work was impartial, but he bootlegged in all sorts of social implications. The great historians of the pre-social science past, on the other hand, admitted their social purposes. Prior to the 19th century, indeed, there was hardly any conception of history other than "philosophy teaching by example." In this, as in much else, after a long and destructive detour into the cul-de-sac of "progress" and "enlightenment," we must, if we are to prosper, somehow recapture the old truth that was cast away as outmoded.

It is, then, neither possible nor necessary to disentangle the two varieties of history, and in the mind of a great historian they are subsumed in a whole. To hold both modes in mind is one thing. Not to be able to tell the difference is another. It is my contention that a great part of the history being produced in America today confuses the two modes in a way that causes it to fail both as objective record and as social inspiration.

The most apparent, though not the most important, evidence of this confusion is in the behavior of professional historians as a group. Most of us claim to be practitioners of the second sort of history, but in our observed behavior we pay obeisance to the first sort. As a group we often submit meekly to social symbolization that does not meet the requirement of working within the objective record. The failure to mount any effective criticism on historical grounds of the popular pseudo-historical melodrama "Roots" is an example. Historians, as a group, tacitly decided that what they perceived as the social utility of "Roots" overrode its serious failings as history. This is what I mean by confusion of modes. Given the sensational popularity of this vehicle and the importance of its subject, one can hardly imagine an occasion that called more appropriately for historians to come forth with corrective data in their role as objective investigators.

Another example. The highest paid and best-known historian in the United States today is Arthur M. Schlesinger, Jr. Schlesinger's contributions have not been to "original research" and to the establishment of a factual historical record, but to mythmaking. With great skill and success, he has provided plausible ancestors for new phenomena and tendencies in American society. In regard to several topics, the nature of Jacksonian politics and intellectual life and the meaning of the New Deal, for instance, he has succeeded in establishing the bounds of discussion even for those who disagree with his conclusions.

Schlesinger's symbolic imagination is impressive, although it has not kept close enough to the objective historical record to make his books into great works of history. My point, however, is not to criticize Schlesinger, who is indeed to be admired for his power in making history relevant to our current concerns. My intent is to indicate the way in which history is carried on in America. It is not, contrary to our self-serving professional image, that a body of historians has accumulated knowledge that has led them naturally to a particular interpretation. It is rather that an attractive interpretation has been set forth, and then numerous ranks of scholars have provided means to support (or to oppose, or to qualify) the interpretation. The interpretation itself is not a result of the search for knowledge about the past, but is a work of imagination put at the service of a will-to-power for a certain ideological perspective of the present. Most historians are not working toward new knowledge, but are serving an established or aspiring orthodoxy, an orthodoxy that succeeds more by political utility than by objective soundness or cumulative persuasiveness.

Another peculiar aspect of American history, one that almost guarantees its failure at any single moment as a synthesis of fact and symbol, is the periodic destruction and reconstruction it has undergone. This "refounding" accounts for the phenomenon observed by Cleanth Brooks, a keen observer of American culture, in his conversations with Robert Penn Warren (*The Possibilities of Order: Cleanth Brooks and His World*, p. 64): Americans in the mass have no sense of their history. The generally accepted expressions of American history never rise above the level of costume drama, of a present-centered manipulation of images relevant to the amusement of the recipient. There is a degree of abstractness in the relation of Americans to their past that is true of no other people to the same degree.

By a "refounding" I do not mean that occasional revision that occurs in any history by the acquisition of new knowledge or from the appearance of new perspectives with changing times. Nor do I mean the inevitable dilution of tradition that occurs as a result of the passage of time. What I mean is the actual destruction or suppression of old views, and their replacement by others newly manufactured for social purposes rather than as a consequence of knowledge.

I will point to two major examples of what I consider "refoundings." The first of these was an inevitable result of the Civil War, which in one aspect at least was the climax of a protracted struggle between Virginian and New England modes of interpreting the symbolic and social significance of the American past and of the American future. Richard Taylor, a Confederate general, recorded in his memoirs (aptly titled, for my purposes, *Destruction and Reconstruction*) a striking incident that occurred at the end of the Civil War. It was Taylor's painful duty to surrender the last Confederate forces in the Gulf area. Having made contact with the Union commander nearby, he crossed the lines at dawn under a white flag to complete the formalities and surrender his sword. This accomplished, Taylor gratefully accepted the invitation of federal officers to join them for breakfast. Most of the officers, in consideration for Taylor's feelings, steered the conversation away from war and politics. But one Union officer, a German-American, insisted on lecturing the defeated Rebel. In broken English he informed Taylor that "Now that the war is over, we will teach you Southerners what democracy is all about." The man to whom this statement was addressed was the son of a President of the United States and the grandson of a Virginia officer of the Revolution. One can hardly find a better symbol for the discontinuities introduced into American history, for the willful destruction and reconstruction of historical understandings that followed upon the Civil War.

What I mean is not the obvious fact that as a result of the outcome of the war, America was to take a new course. I am concerned with the understanding of history. The outcome of the war called not only for a new future but for a new past. What was involved was more than a change of direction, or a new perspective, or the loss of tradition through the passage of time. There are many senses in which a modern Englishman, for example, can no longer identify with George III or Henry VIII or Alfred the Great. But the German's comment goes beyond this; it indicates an abrupt and willed alteration of the social import of the symbols of the past.

What the refounding did in the wake of the Civil War was to cut off the inherited aspect of the American Revolutionary past, and to turn a living tradition into an abstract allegiance. The virtue and purpose of this was that it made it possible for society to validate symbolically its decision to take in more people and become more open towards new members and new elements whose allegiance could not be, in the beginning, inherited. A new historical understanding also made American tradition much more flexible in terms of what it legitimated in government action. In effect we had a new Constitution. It was the same document, but its meaning was transformed by virtue of the victory of one alternative conception of it and the alchemy of the Fourteenth Amendment. It was made to mean a great number of new things.

The very point of the Civil War was to decide between two alternative ways of understanding the meaning of America. Otherwise, there would have been no point to the war. But the nature of the war as a contest of alternative social symbolizations meant that history would have to be orchestrated to support the winning side. The losers must not only be conquered on the field of battle and disenfranchised in the body politic, but they must be discredited. The competitive legitimacy of their alternative view must be suppressed. If history is not so reconstructed, the victor must argue, it will fail in its mission of providing symbols for social cohesion for the new regime. In terms of historical understanding, the new regime must be given a justification. This means that history has to be written to establish the new regime as the only legitimate possibility within the accepted social symbols. All this is what was long ago generally diagnosed as Whig history—the assumption that the good guys always win. But it is Whig history with a vengeance. The losers must not only lose and be fated to lose; they must be misrepresented and traduced as well.

This effort is, then, perhaps inevitable and necessary. A certain amount of willful distortion of inherited symbols, a refounding, is the sine qua non of a new regime when cohesion is achieved by conquest rather than consent. The old understandings cannot be left intact to disturb the new settlement. So that the refounding of American history by the Civil War is accepted implicitly as a basic premise of American historiography. To do otherwise would render the accepted understandings too ambivalent to be useful as social symbols for the mass. That is why, for instance, some political scientists are committed to a verbalistic and ahistorical interpretation of the Declaration of Independence as a piece of universal egalitarian revelation, abstract and infinitely expandable.

They insist that the interpretation fixed on it by the outcome of the Civil War is not only the interpretation we must accept now (which is perhaps a defensible position), but they wish to obliterate even the recognition of the possibility that there ever was any other legitimate interpretation. The historical and contextual understanding of the Declaration as the document a particular people constructed for a particular purpose cannot be allowed, since that would raise the question of inherited tradition instead of abstract allegiance.

I have said that this kind of refounding is an inevitable accompaniment of a political revolution, but this may be overstated. Misrepresentation of the conquered foe is not inevitable, but a function of a certain kind of mind in intellectual or actual combat. There is, however, an alternative. That alternative is chivalry, the capacity to respect one's enemy and to represent his position fairly, even when disagreeing with it, and especially after he is defeated. But chivalry does not seem to have much to do with contemporary American symbolic struggles.

Even if the reorchestration of historical symbols is inevitable, as historians we must examine the peril it imposes upon the successful functioning of history, either as objective record or as a force for social cohesion. We must also consider the difficulties that it poses for that successful synthesis of the two described above as great history. In such circumstances, a synthesis that is at the same time an objective record and a source of inspiration would require a rare and remarkable skill. It would take a historian of immense power and magnanimity, probably assisted by events that transcended old categories, to make a true synthesis out of our history after the Civil War. The manipulation of the understanding of the Declaration of Independence seems to me a perfect example of what is not a successful merging of the factual and symbolic modes of history, of the ambiguity and mixture of modes that I have said was the characteristic failing of the practice of American history.

Because the success of the social symbol depends upon a false and forced and too abstract rendering of the objective record rather than a harmonious fit with it, the social symbol is in the long run bound to prove intellectually unsatisfactory and productive not only of bad history but of social conflict more than consensus.

To the extent that we accept a distorted record we divorce ourselves from the possibility of truly participating in early American history, of grasping our tradition in its fullness. If we are not allowed to understand what American history once was, but only what it now must be, we have introduced a distortion into our relationship with our past that will render inadequate our attempts to identify with it. But the success of history as civic inspiration rests upon the ability of a young person just becoming aware of the world to make a genuine and convincing identification between his own history and that of his country, an identification more intimate than the level of abstraction. The young person must be able to make his nation's history his own, make it a history of his own "fathers," just as was done, until a generation or so ago, by thousands of young men who sincerely modeled themselves on Abraham Lincoln or Daniel Webster or Theodore Roosevelt.

Although a failure as objective history, a symbolic distortion (such as that of reading an ahistorical universalism into the American Revolution) may succeed superficially as social mythmaking. But it will fail in the long run as consensus building, assuming that the defeated side is to be brought into a consensus rather than annihilated. Social mythmaking fails if it fails to go beyond the immediate victory it symbolizes and to achieve a higher and more inclusive mediation. If he is neither annihilated nor brought into a higher consensus, the loser has only one alternative aside from permanent resistance.

He can accept a conscious burden of destroying and reconstructing himself. A Southerner, for instance, may tactfully pretend to see or persuade himself that he does see virtues in Abraham Lincoln that are not really apparent to him. But this requires a degree of self-conscious detachment or ironic distance from the social symbols that make it impossible for him to identify fully with the consensus. This might be good for the Southerner as a historian. It might give him just enough objectivity about the symbols of the prevailing side to make him a keen observer. One might cite the examples of C. Vann Woodward, David M. Potter and other Southern historians in making original observations about the American mainstream.

The highest history would go further, however. It would reconcile new and old understandings, objective record and social symbol, into a higher synthesis. That is far better than doctoring the facts to fit the new understanding. It is even better than ironic detachment, no matter how brilliantly perceptive. It is my contention that as a result of the symbolic manipulation necessary to justify the outcome of the Civil War, American historians have nearly cut themselves off from grasping what American history was before that war. Let me give a few examples.

From the historical viewpoint the vast literature in recent years that has fought heatedly over Jefferson's racial views and sex life has been carried on in an atmosphere of complete unreality. The unexamined root assumption of all this literature has been that Jefferson was either like us in his attitudes toward black people, or if he was not he should have been and was a hypocrite for not having been. This is so much nonsense. It proceeds on the assumption that Jefferson was essentially a 20th century middle-class American rather than an 18th century Virginia planter. This is not simply the common mistake of reading the present into the past. It is a pervasive intellectual confusion that runs unchecked and unrecognized through both our popular and academic history. A false Jefferson has been created and fought over. We are emotionally and intellectually unwilling to see Jefferson in his own context.

If we did so, we would be forced to admit that American history, including some of its grandest symbols, incorporates elements that we cannot readily reconcile with the picture of our present selves that we cherish. Jefferson seen in his own context, that is, historically, perfectly understandable. But to see him in that context would be to admit that he was not what we want him to be.

Therefore, we must forever agonize over those facts that are incongruous with his refounded image, the refounded image which seems necessary for our national amour propre. We should admit that the appropriation we have made of Jefferson as a symbol is not consonant with the objective record. We may get away with that if we require only a vague symbol for the hustings, but we should not be allowed to get away with it as historians.

Let me cite a few more examples to support my argument that our unconscious assumptions, made as a result of the Civil War adjustment, distort the historical record. One of the episodes in the popular "Adams Family Chronicles" on public television concerned the acquisition of Florida. All the main characters in the story except for John Quincy Adams himself were Southerners and slaveowners—James Monroe, Andrew Jackson, William H. Crawford, Henry Clay, and John C. Calhoun. But Calhoun was the only one obviously portrayed as a Southerner. The producers of the show acted out an unconscious and false assumption. Good antebellum Southerners, those who have favorable or useful symbolic images, are really no different in behavior, beliefs, and outward characteristics from upper-middle-class residents of Columbus, Ohio, in 1982.

Only bad Southerners, e.g., Calhoun, are identifiably "Southern." I am not complaining that the show was told from Adams's viewpoint, which was only natural. I am saying that the context was distorted to perpetrate an unconscious and pleasing deception about the nature of Adams's times. To portray antebellum American history as it was in 1818, with an accurate context showing the Southern predominance at the time, would have meant that the victor of the Civil War had deprived himself of one of the fruits of his victory—the right to tell the story in a way flattering to himself and supporting the plausibility of his victory's moral justification.

Take a tour through Mount Vernon or Monticello and listen to the questions and comments of the typically garrulous visitors. You will see how disingenuously the subject of slavery is skirted around. In the Americans' minds, Mount Vernon is not an 18th century plantation, it is a midwest farm that happens to be situated in Virginia. Or get down your child's encyclopedia, turn to the table of Presidents, and look under "Occupation." George Washington is a "surveyor," Thomas Jefferson is a "lawyer," Andrew Jackson is a "soldier." The American consciousness is unable to admit to itself that eight of our first twelve Presidents were Southern plantation owners, not only as their chief occupation but in their primary social identity. On the one hand, the national mythology requires the stipulation that slavery was such a horrible evil that a crusade to wipe it out was one of the high marks of our national experience. On the other hand, the favorable associations of such symbols as Washington and Jefferson cannot be made compatible with the antislavery mythology.

This kind of ambivalence and self-deceit strikes deep wounds in our capacity to understand the past as a whole, to reconcile social symbols and objective record into a truly successful synthesis. What we do instead is doctor the old symbols and experiences to make them conform to later ideas of respectability. Then, after we have spread this middle-class American neatness over our history, some equally self-deceiving radical comes along, discovers that aspects of the past reality do not coincide with our convenient images, and runs to an equally distorted extreme of muckraking and repudiation. A true history would feel the need neither to disguise nor to lament the fact that George Washington was a slaveholder.

A true history is interested in making something of the past as a whole that will be both true and useful. Yet we feel that if we admit that Jefferson thought that blacks were probably inferior to whites, it will somehow undermine our position of tolerance and equality today. But should not history be more sophisticated than that? Perhaps we now face the inevitable distortions of our Civil War "refounding," which prevents us from seeing the truth. That refounding necessarily involved a shift from tradition to ideology, and from history as a search for antecedents to history as an unfinished agenda: i.e., from things as they were to things as one might have wished them to be, from the living community and its real experiences to a hypothetical community and its fictitious past.

The "nationalist" historiography which I have broadly described, and which followed the Civil War long furnished the matrix for American historical writing. The "Turner thesis" and the "Progressive" historiography of the early 20th century provided variations on the theme but did not alter the underlying assumptions. I would like to suggest, however, that our prevailing nationalist symbology is at the moment being undermined, that it stands a fair chance of being "refounded" itself and replaced with a new symbology. This refounding began about fifty years ago, gathered great momentum in the last few years, and is now poised for takeover.

As the first refounding was related to a change of power, the Civil War, so the second is related to another such development. The mainstream American, after ousting Southerners from the putative American consensus, is now in danger of being himself supplanted. The main theme of American history is being shifted from national unity and national achievement to what might be called ethnic multiplicity and ethnic achievement. I am not referring here to how we understand the American present. I am concerned with our understanding of the American past. What is under way is a refounding, not simply a shift in interpretation or an admission of new knowledge. Essential to this enterprise is establishing a whole new basis for American history, a further shift from inherited tradition to the abstract and protean use of the past.

The transformation of American history from an account of the building of a new nationality to the celebration of an ethnic collage is not a result of the discovery of new knowledge. We have as historians, we are told, only recently discovered the existence and great contributions of various minority groups in early American history. The implication of this questionable assertion is that such presence and contributions had been previously suppressed or ignored.

But this alteration in American history does not result from new knowledge. It involves, rather, a reformulation of the meaning of America and therefore of what American history includes. One vivid example of this changed attitude is the change in recent years in our commemorative postage stamps. While they once honored George Washington, Daniel Boone, and Thomas Edison, they now celebrate Benjamin Banneker and Frances Perkins. It is often asserted that the old history was white man's or WASP history (it could more accurately be called Northeastern WASP history) and that therefore it was false and that it deliberately suppressed the accomplishments of minorities, including that great non-minority, women.

This seems to me rather a misleading statement of the case. The old history was not ignorant of the existence of blacks, Indians, etc. History was written, as to the facts and the symbols, broadly speaking and quite properly, as the history of English-speaking Americans because that is whose history it was. It was, of course, itself divided by various conflicts: East/West, North/South, farmer/capitalist, and others.

I am not contending that minority or ethnic history is not a part of American history or unworthy of attention, or that interesting things have not been learned in recent years in this area. But I am seeking to point out that we have not merely found new knowledge, we have made a new symbolic departure in the meaning of American history. There is a vast difference between the writing of an American history that is a synthesis of the history and experiences of the various groups which have participated in the life of this continent, and presenting the central theme of American history as the mixing of these groups.

It is analogous to the difference between equality before the law and affirmative action. It is one thing to note the rather considerable contribution of Spaniards and Mexicans to the early exploration, settlement, and social structure of what is now the American Southwest. It is quite another to reconstruct American history as "Chicano" history. The one is an admission of new knowledge and new perspectives. The other is a shift of basis reflecting a shift or a would-be shift of power.

In my opinion, our new departure in ethnic history has not succeeded as history in the sense of objective record. The greater part (certainly not all) of what has been put forth in recent years as minority history does not seem as sound, as genuine, or as rigorously tested as the old WASP history, as self-serving and inadequate as the latter often was. The new history, that is to say, is a lot closer than the old to the line that divides propaganda from history. It lacks for the most part the objectivity that we described; it represents a will-to-power rather than a will to historical knowledge or even a will to social consensus. In stating this I am by no means asserting perfection for the old history, I am merely saying that on balance it had considerably higher critical standards than the emergent variety.

We historians, as a group, have surrendered our critical standards when faced with the question of minority contributions to American history. What are we to make of my child's fourth grade textbook, which identifies Thomas Jefferson and Frederick Douglass as the greatest Americans of the early 19th century? Please note: I am not saying that Douglass is unworthy of attention. I am pointing to proportion, or rather lack of it. And what about my child's seventh grade textbook which describes a civilization of "Old Africa" which, before being desecrated by white slave-catchers, was the equal of Greece, Rome, Egypt, and Western Europe?

Again, I am not saying that minority history is unworthy of attention, nor that the contributions and sufferings of all groups should not be noted. I am voicing my suspicion that what we are getting is not so much scholarly attention bestowed on neglected parts of history as a distorted and contrived past.

The new history has employed the poetic license of mythology without its healing and reconciling motives. It has assumed the prestige of objective, "scientific" history without abiding by its standards. We are now governed by the idea that American history is to be doled out like political patronage. We must consider before it is too late what this means to history—as the body of myths that inspire our society, as objective record, and in terms of our hope to produce truly great works.

The new history is not only politically inspired to a degree that the old nationalistic historiography, a natural product of American experience, was not; it is also government-subsidized to a degree that no previous history has been. It is a product of the state and not of the culture. Ethnic collage history is an officially promulgated and enforced history. Its rise coincides with a great rise in government support and supervision of the production of history. It has made its way by subsidy and bureaucratic directive. In the past, among historically conscious Americans, there has always been an evolution or at least a cycle of views. New views were introduced, and old views reassessed. But the effects of government subsidy and directive tend to discourage the possibility of new views developing. Original views of history that do not conform to the officially promulgated and subsidized liberal interpretations will have a harder time emerging in the future. History as one of the higher activities of Western man may even wither. There has been for a long time a liberal hegemony in the universities, which was preceded by a New England Puritan-Republican hegemony. This began to be transformed in the 1960s from genteel liberal bias to the hint at least of violent suppression of dissenting views by militant leftists and organized minority groups, if not indeed by the federal government itself.

The second refounding is inextricably bound up with the Marxist élan which has invaded a good part of the professional historical community. This has promoted an attitude of critical hostility towards elements and causes not favored by fashion, coupled with a romantic indulgence of those that are favored. This is the critical problem in the survival of history as a discipline. I do not think that minority history necessarily reflects Marxist elan and totalitarian attitudes. The first promoters of black history in this century, the Carter G. Woodson school, for instance, were careful scholars who sought not to undermine the American consensus, but to establish a place for the black American within it. But I think that minority history is currently a vehicle for leftist propaganda. A leftist world view, rather than old-fashioned standards of intellectual discourse, controls the organized discipline—in the selection of manuscripts for publication, in the hiring and advancement of faculty members, in the reviewing of books, in the selection of projects for government subsidy.

We have by no means reached bottom on the import of the new refounding. It is, undoubtedly, a silent shift of America symbolically out of Western civilization, an attempted divorce of American history from that culture which used to be referred to as Christendom, into a formless universalism. This shift is quite different from the Revolution, which involved a son of Europe setting up as his own man. In the new history he disowns his paternity.

Most certainly, American historical writing is, on the whole, growing more and more alienated from American culture. I do not think the average bright student of today can easily identify with his textbook. And I do not think that if the man in the street can identify with his history as it is being commonly presented to him, it will in any way make him a more earnest or a happier citizen. I do know that our historical writing, even at its best, fails ever more to convey the genuine rich diversity of America—its regions, its classes, its ethnic groups, and its great personalities—America as it is portrayed in the best of our creative literature. (1982)

Recovering Southern History

Introduction to a special issue of *Continuity: A Journal of History.*

Every historian has a viewpoint, shaped by his own background, values, and perception of the present. The relationship between background and viewpoint is not necessarily simple. As in the case of Supreme Court nominees, one cannot always predict in advance in what direction a historian's background, modified by research and thought, will lead. At any rate, we properly measure a historian's value, not by the degree to which he conforms to our own viewpoint, but rather by his observance of the canons of evidence and honest debate, and by his imaginative insight. Thus, to acknowledge that U.B. Phillips grew up in post-Civil War Georgia is a relevant datum in assessing his work as a historian of American slavery. However, it does not, as some seem to feel, constitute an all sufficient indictment of that work, any more than the fact that Kenneth M. Stampp grew up in the 20th century in a German community in Wisconsin necessarily guarantees him superior objectivity and insight as a historian of slavery.

If history teaches anything at all, it is that there is more than one side to a question. In fact, it has always seemed to me that the chief functional value and social utility of the study of history (not that it needs such justification) is that it can make more tolerant and foresighted citizens by disabusing us of the shallow, deterministic ideas that are a characteristic intellectual error of the modern age and especially of Americans. Such determinism creates social havoc by substituting ideological combat for moral struggle and denies human existence its ennobling contingency. Rather than appeal to preordained forces, honorable historians openly acknowledge that they have values in conflict and pursue the conflict frankly, if possible keeping it within the bounds of mutually acknowledged rules. If they do so, they can hope to construct a history that will be useful and instructive over a long range to the thoughtful, whether they share the viewpoint or not.

By contrast, the ineluctable penchant of the ideologue is for a sneak attack that obliterates the enemy in advance of declared hostilities. The ideologue is not interested in drawing understanding or inspiration from history, but in the manipulation of unreflected symbols for a quick, present-centered victory. Disagreement, or different values, become, in his book, a manifestation of evil, an incitement to extermination. The close relation of this attitude to those totalitarian deformations of reality that mark our age is evident, even when the practitioner goes under the guise of a "democrat." By such an attitude, the ideologue, usually but not always in our time the devotee of a progressivist program, not only proves himself incapable of historical thinking. He also poisons the wells of honest deliberation that are essential, as the Southerner John C. Calhoun long ago pointed out, to social comity and the process of consensus formation in a democracy. The factor of mind that closes out a free historical debate on the causes and meaning of the Civil War, by an appeal to inevitability or a sloganeering oversimplification of the moral issues involved, is exactly the same factor that makes electronic journalists incapable of a fair statement of the public questions of the day.

Nowhere has the power of ideological convention and presentism to choke off the examination of evidence and honorable debate been more persistent and pervasive than in regard to the issues surrounding the Civil War and Reconstruction and the "peculiar" history of the Southern region. This closure of debate is a critical defect in our self-understanding as a people because the great sectional conflict of the 19th century, despite all that has passed since, is still the central episode of our history as Americans. Slavery and the position of the black minority in American society; industrialization, centralization and modernization; the meaning of the Constitution; the bounds of government authority and individual liberty; the claims of tradition and innovation, social reality and social ideals; the nature of majority rule and consensus—there is no basic issue, except possibly our international role, for which the Civil War does not contain the fundamental knot of debate.

Despite the vast resources devoted to historical investigation, the American mind has never been fully liberated from the conventions that were formed to justify the new settlement that accompanied the victory in battle. (Professor Ludwell Johnson has written persuasively on the persistence of such conventions.) The Civil War still cannot be acknowledged as an honest disagreement, or viewed with the historical detachment with which a good English historian, say, can view his civil war. The ideologues sense that to grant the chivalrous concession of a fair argument of the merits of the losing side is to fatally compromise the scenario of leftward inevitability that constitutes their fundamental and unexaminable scheme of the course of American history.

Thus, the South, though it is hard to imagine any part of America more original or authentic, must be held at arm's length, explicable only as a peculiarity. Thus, the ideals formulated in the 17th century on Massachusetts Bay are America, by premise; those formulated at the same time on the Chesapeake Bay (though they may have had an equal or greater and possibly a more constructive role in the formation of America) are at best an interesting, at worst a malevolent, deviance. The Civil War must remain a contest of good America over bad America, of the mainstream over the deviant, even though, in terms of the larger experience of mankind, it is the mainstream that may be perceived as "peculiar."

Historiographically, my point is proved by the present reputations of James G. Randall and Avery O. Craven. Randall was an Illinoisan who devoted a scholarly career of great skill and dedication to elucidating Lincoln. Craven was an Iowa Quaker who made the most profound, thorough, and objective study of sectional conflict ever undertaken. Both are at this writing largely relegated to the historiographical dustbin as "pro-Southern" and therefore unworthy of attention. In fact, neither was in the least pro-Southern. (Jefferson Davis would have considered them incurably anti-Southern.) They represented the viewpoint, rather, of moderate Northerners, a viewpoint embodied, at least part of the time, by Lincoln himself, a viewpoint which has perhaps always represented the largest, though not the most aggressively argued, segment of American opinion toward the Civil War and Reconstruction.

As historians Randall and Craven did not close out the case in advance by appeal to the inevitability of conflict of good and evil, but rather sought to comprehend the course of events for a larger understanding. Randall's Lincoln is designed to emphasize his oneness with the moderate rather than the radical North. Craven was even able to comprehend why those who sought radical change in society and who demonized their opponents were in some sense responsible for conflict, rather than all the guilt belonging to those who merely wished to preserve what was lawful and familiar and to which no constructive alternative was offered. By the reigning canons of historiography, a historian must be committed, not only to a Northern position, but to a Radical Republican one, or be conclusively dismissed as "pro-Southern."

How much more difficult, then, for a historian who cannot, at least not without hypocrisy, escape an authentic Southern viewpoint. Whatever his scholarly integrity or imaginative power, such a historian has a hard row to hoe. Professor Grady McWhiney's account of the careers of two such, Francis Butler Simkins and Frank L. Owley, is a significant contribution to the self-understanding of American historians. It is also an important contribution to the self-understanding of American conservatism. As historians, Simkins and Owley are indispensable to the construction of any counter-leftist scenario of American history.

Simkins's great point was a rejection of the totalist notion that America had to be all one thing or all the other: that the South, indeed, had often preferred to be different and had a perfect right to do so. It was a modest and indeed a wholly democratic proposition. Is it not exceedingly strange in a society that prides itself on its pluralism and hunts out and celebrates every conceivable minority, that the most important minority by far in American history, the South (whether considered by geography, population, culture, or historical import), remains untolerated? Owley even more fundamentally threatened the reigning progressivist scenario. His *Plain Folk of the Old South*, which has been often attacked but never refuted, is a key document in any conservative (not consensus) account of American history. Simply put, his point is that the Old South was not an evil oligarchy that had to be suppressed because by its nature it was a threat to mainstream American democracy. Rather, the Old South was an essentially consensual society that provided a legitimate alternative version of American democracy.

No more fundamental challenge than Owley's has ever been offered to the Liberal conception of American history, for this always reduces, at bottom, to a scenario in which presidential Lone Rangers gallop in to save democracy from the dark forces of reaction; that is, the progressive scheme draws its persuasiveness from an appeal to the necessity of the righteous suppression of a rightward enemy who prevents the realization of the next, inevitable and higher, stage of progress. Deprive the forces of "progress" of their diabolized enemy and they lose much of their momentum.

Owsley and Simkins are conspicuous examples of historians who never repudiated their identity as Southerners. (Indeed, it is difficult to imagine a valuable historian who is not in some sense a patriot.) But there were many others who have enriched American historiography. One who might receive equally illuminating treatment is E. Merton Coulter, who turned out a steady stream of able and still useful monographs and surveys on many aspects of the history of the Old South, and who successfully combined professionalism and piety. Also worthy of similar attention is Douglas Southall Freeman, who memorialized the heroes of the War for Southern Independence in works that are masterpieces of American historical writing. Freeman was the only unequivocally Southern historian to enjoy wide acclaim, through the historical accident that his works appeared during the World War II era when the record of authentic American heroism seemed, for the moment, to be relevant and expedient.

It is rather clear to the thoughtful Southerner that the South has symbolically played the role of scapegoat for mainstream America. Southern history, rather than being understood on its own terms, has been a kind of colonial resource, from which raw materials have been drawn when needed. At various times, the liberal and conservative poles of mainstream America have joined to execrate the South as an obstacle to national imperatives. At other times one or the other has looked to the South for convenient allies. Put in a more positive light, this makes, as Calhoun observed, the South the indispensable balance wheel of the Union, which prevents centrifugal pressures from exploding the whole machine.

This tendency to use the South as a convenient resource has created curious conventions in American historiography. A conservative who dislikes Jefferson, for instance, points out that he was after all a Southern slaveowner, and therefore naturally had corrupt and debased ideas of the just commonwealth. If one wants to use Jefferson as a positive figure, one skips over, as lightly as possible, the same fact that he was, in his primary social identity, a Virginia planter. Or, in a more sophisticated version of the game, one suddenly finds Jefferson inconsistent and hypocritical, discovering that he was not what one wanted him to be. But the inconsistency is in the viewpoint of the beholder, not in Jefferson, who was what he was. A similar game was played recently in the obituaries of Senator Sam Ervin. Commentators were unable to reconcile the constitutionalist of Watergate with the opponent of liberal notions of civil rights. But the combination is far more authentically American than that of the commentators, and, from the standpoint of tradition, thoroughly consistent. Such games strike deep wounds in our ability to grasp the integrity of the past. Or, if one dislikes some of the social characteristics of the Southwest, they are, of course, "Southern." If one likes them, then they, of course, could not be

"Southern" but must be "Western." In fact, the phenomenon in question is both, the one ingredient as indispensable as the other. The division that is made is an empty semanticism. To the extent that the American West exists as something more than a place to raise cattle, it exists as the frontier sphere of the Southern ethos. One only has to note that our most famous Western characterization in fiction, after all, has as its hero *The Virginian*, or to scrutinize with some cultural sensitivity the difference between Texas and South Dakota.

The most glaring example that occurs to me of the colonialist attitude is in the conduct of the mandarins of the Washington liberal establishment. Though they have no more firmly held and consistently pursued idea than hatred of the South and all its effects, they flock, whenever possible, to the ancient Southern townhouses of Georgetown or Alexandria, there to bask in the reflected glory of the interiors, and sometimes of the very family portraits, of departed and derided Southern planters. Able to generate no respect not dependent upon the direct application of money and power, they derive vicarious respectability from a class whose influence on the formation of America, by their own belief, was wholly baneful. In all the replete annals of social hypocrisy, few tales surpass this.

It is easy to understand why the privileged liberal desires to close out consideration of the possible positive role of the South in American history, for his position depends upon a pose as the defender of the oppressed. But for self-declared conservatives to do so strikes the Southerner as extremely peculiar, though this is exactly what has routinely happened. Professor M.E. Bradford, who as a scholar undertook to point out to American conservatives (irrefutably on the evidence) some of the mischief in Lincoln's historical and constitutional views, was read out of the conservative camp by a born-again conservative newspaper columnist who had, only a few years previously, been an advocate of McGovernism. Straussian political scientists, thought to be a conservative force, have made strenuous efforts to equate the Old South with Nazi Germany. If anyone attempts to show the historical merits and conservative usefulness of the Southern view of the Constitution and the meaning of American society, he is invariably attacked by the Straussians, who keep a flying squad on alert for this purpose, as an amoral "historicist" who gives precedence to circumstance over ideal. Apparently the only moral approach to the meaning of America is allegiance to a verbalistic exegesis of certain selected phrases of certain documents, which in some mysterious unhistoricist way contain the revealed meaning of America, however much the revelation may be contradicted by actual life and tradition.

To the Southerner, such efforts seem perverse and self-defeating, if the goal is to establish a persuasive conservative genealogy. To him it is self-evident that any viable American conservatism must incorporate the South. (And therefore, that the readers of a professedly conservative historical journal will be interested in a recovery of some of the elements of Southern history.) Just as a practical matter, one might argue, the first conservative President of the century owes much of his conservatism to the residue of state rights and laissez-faire beliefs in the Democratic Party which formed him rather than to the energetic, Hamiltonian traditions of the Republican Party in which history has forced him to work out his destiny. Most certainly the core of his original grassroots support, as opposed to the vast legions which joined him during the progress of his success, was, in terms of its inheritance, as much Southern-tinged as it was traditionally Republican.

In a newly conservative climate, the effort to exclude the South from the emergent establishment creates some intellectual fashions that seem exceedingly odd to the historically minded. One may discuss the restoration of strict construction, limited government, and *laissez-faire*, for instance, as if they were discovered yesterday and without noticing even in passing the historic embodiment of those principles in the South. In fact, the political history of the Old South is very largely concerned with an effort to prevent tariffs, internal improvements, currency manipulation, pensions, and subsidies, which effort was condemned as legalistic obscurantism by the pragmatic, conservative business interests at the time.

Or one may plump for a recovery of aristocratic ethics or classical education or a sense of family, without even a moment's reflection that the South held onto these notions long after they had been derided elsewhere as hopelessly behind the times and unprogressive. Or one may reject utopian solutions to social problems and moral imperialism, and yet also reject the Old South as fascist or irrelevant for having done just that in the most authentic and conspicuously sustained effort in American history.

No one is likely to accept the Southern tradition whole cloth today, but for those who are searching for a genuine American conservatism to condemn its historic embodiment in the South while postulating a conservative ideology that is as abstract and flawed as its progressivist counterpart, will seem to many of us, to whom tradition and historical experience are central to the conservative idea, to be a strangely compromised endeavor. It is not only inexpedient, but it requires a celebration of theory over experience that negates the concept of conservatism.

There are underway at the present a variety of historical efforts that, without any deliberate concert, are making possible a recovery of important aspects of Southern history. Professors McWhiney and Forrest

McDonald have described, in a number of works, a "Celtic" South. By this I take them to mean that the South has enjoyed a way of life that received its formative values from a different part of British culture than did that strange amalgam of abstract moralism and ruthless utilitarianism, inexactly labeled Puritanism, that dominated Massachusetts and ultimately was taken to stand for the American mind Raimondo Luraghi, an Italian, has pointed to the existence of a "seigneurial" society in the Old South which differed in significant ways from the world of the bourgeoisie. The lively Marxist Eugene Genovese has portrayed an authentic paternalistic tradition in the slave South.

In American historiography there is a growing and sophisticated body of literature on "republicanism," aimed at recovering the actual beliefs and Weltanschauung of the Founders. This emphasis has naturally led to a realization of the persistence of "republicanism" in the outlook of the South. This realization has inevitably led further to a rediscovery of the complexity of Southern political thought, long dismissed as a simplistic defense of an outdated regime. Along with this rediscovery has gone a revisionist appreciation of the intellectual life of the South, which is most conspicuous in the works of Richard Beale Davis and Michael O'Brien.

Most recently, and from unexpected quarters, has come a new attention to the hallowed western tradition of chivalric honor as a lasting influence in the South. Even though, as Dr. Thomas Fleming has pointed out, the scholar who has taken on this topic has hopelessly confused two different phenomena—aristocratic ethics and community conformity. The absence of one in current American society explains low standards of political and intellectual ethics. The absence of the other accounts for massive moral breakdown. But perhaps the confusion of the two is not entirely unhappy, for both have perversely endured in the South, to the extent that the South has resisted or modified "modernization." (Honor was much better defined by Burckhardt—"that enigmatic mixture of conscience and egotism.")

The persistence of traditional folkways and attitudes, including orthodox Christian belief, in the South has been widely documented, most articulately in the works of the humanist sociologist John Shelton Reed. Finally, there is always with us the historical vision of Southern literature. Even the black experience is coming to be seen as not so wholly antagonistic to Southern history nor so wholly compatible with Northern as was once thought, as is evidenced by such recent works as John Boles's *Black Southerners*. This exhibits some of the possibilities of revisionist and restorative views of Southern history, though it by no means exhausts the possibilities.

These different approaches are not necessarily antagonistic alternatives. It can be argued that they are all compatible and are essentially apprehensions of different aspects of the same historical reality. This reality is also compatible with that phenomenon eloquently described by Russell Kirk in *The Conservative Mind* as "The Valor of the South." The reality in many ways runs athwart the course of mainstream America. Yet the reality is an authentic component of America and of American history, if America is something more than a protean abstraction that is to be made to mean anything that is desired. Just to the extent that we are dissatisfied with contemporary America, we ought to be impelled to reconsider an older and better version, which is, in some senses at least, a persistent feature of the history of the American South. (1984)

Recovering Southern History

Cracks in the Treasury of Virtue

A review of *Division and Reunion: America, 1848-1877,*[1] by Ludwell H. Johnson, New York: John Wiley and Sons, 1978, 301 pages; and *The Secret Six: John Brown and the Abolitionist Movement*, New York: Times Books, 1979, 375 pages.

It was Flannery O'Connor who remarked, in one of her short essays, that people will believe anything about the South as long as it is strange enough. She was speaking of the obstacles to acquiring a proper understanding of fiction with a Southern setting, but she could just as well have been referring to Southern historical writing. There is probably no subject under the sun that has spawned a greater amount of nonsense.

People who would never dream of passing judgment on contemporary Uganda or Elizabethan poetry without years of study feel no hesitation in passing sweeping judgments on the South. They embody their "knowledge" and conclusions not only in TV epics but in works of serious history.

This is an old phenomenon, one that has made us aware of the peculiar uses to which the South has habitually been put in the psychological life of non-Southern Americans. The non-Southern American has been repeatedly tempted, since the 17th century, to employ the South as a scapegoat in a peculiarly Puritan technique of self-gratification. Northerners of a certain type have used hostility to the South as a means of establishing their own identities, even of asserting their own heroic virtue. That the South is the center and embodiment of all evil, that it is a pollution of which America must be purged, has been a recurrent theme. These attacks, of the kind Edmund Burke condemned as "an indictment of a whole people," have been made upon a region which has done the attacker little or no harm. But attacks on the South typically have nothing to do with the evils and ills of our section, serious as they may be. It is extremely rare that we have received constructive criticism as opposed to blanket condemnation.

There has been a variation of sorts, whereby Northerners, for their own purposes, have projected favorable images upon the South. After the Civil War, the South was romanticized by Northerners who had

---

[1] *Division and Reunion* has been republished by the Foundation for American Education as *North Against South: The American Iliad, 1848-1877*.

become disgusted with the world they had created. Ironically, when this treatment went out of fashion, other Northern writers chalked it up as just one more sin of the South. Southerners' penchant for romanticizing their past, it was said, made them an absurd, dangerous people whose fantasies prevented them from coping with their own defects and problems.

Another peculiar permutation on the theme is that anything Southern that is to be praised—George Washington, for instance, or Davy Crockett, or country music—is discovered to be not really "Southern" after all. Anything American to be condemned (social disintegration and racial strife in Northern big cities, for example) is discovered somehow to be a result of the South's sins. In fact, one of the chief motivating factors for the great batch of books on slavery in the last few years has been the desire to find a way of blaming the long dead planters of the Old South for the inhumanity and hypocrisy of urban American life. This enterprise becomes more and more suspect as sociological evidence accumulates that black people in the South suffer less from crime, unemployment, and broken families than in the great liberal cities of other regions.

But the point is, all this historical investigation has not so much to do with determining the truth about the Old South as it does with an implicit self-gratification for the critic, a process which Robert Penn Warren denominated the "Treasury of Virtue" some years ago in a neglected masterpiece, *The Legacy of the Civil War*. The critical defect in much of the literature about the South, even much that is intelligently and responsibly done, is the Implied Comparison.

The South is always found wanting by the investigator, always found to fall short of his standards. But the standards are never stated. One may deplore inequality of wealth in the Old South, for instance, without ever being required to look into the question of whether such inequality was any greater (or even as great) as in the North or Europe. One may investigate and condemn violence or militarism in the Old South endlessly, without ever having to say how it compared with the like elsewhere. The virtue of the "Elsewhere," by comparison, is simply assumed. To vindicate it is the chief motive for the investigation, not to discover the facts.

The standard, really, is the Treasury of Virtue, the writer's self-congratulation on being one of the elect, on not being a sinner such as they.

The virtue of the two books under consideration is that they constitute part of the long-overdue investigation of the Implied Comparison.

They examine the motives and conduct of Northerners during the Civil War era. *Division and Reunion* is a collegiate survey of the period by a professor of history of the College of William and Mary. *The Secret Six* is an effort by a Northern conservative writer to come to grips with one element of the sectional conflict. Both works are assiduously researched and eloquently written. Their success is to be judged by the fact that Johnson's carries a foreword warning that it is "controversial" and that "learning begins with provocation" and that Scott's was reported out of print shortly after publication and is no longer obtainable.

Rather than assuming that the Civil War is explained by a completely understandable desire of virtuous Northerners to wipe out a wicked and indefensible South, Johnson has told the story even-handedly. He has examined the motives, policies, and behavior of Northern politicians, soldiers, and citizens with the rigor and candor that is usually reserved for the South. The picture that emerges is not a pretty one, but the focus is instructive, alike for the student seeking both sides of the story and for the Southerner seeking a better understanding of his forebears.

Scott devotes himself to the John Brown episode and examines Brown's life and exploits in scrupulous detail. There cannot be the slightest doubt that Brown was a hypocrite, a liar, a swindler, and a petty tyrant, in addition to being a mass murderer. Charles Manson and the Rev. Jim Jones, remember, justified their deeds as service to high political ideals.

But more interesting and instructive than Brown by far are the "secret six," the half-dozen wealthy, intelligent, and respectable New Englanders who clandestinely aided and abetted Brown's murderous activities in Kansas and at Harpers Ferry. These include Gerrit Smith, the richest man in the U.S. and a reformist crank; Theodore Parker, a noted Biblical scholar and pastor of the biggest church in Boston, also a secret enemy of religion; Samuel Gridley Howe, a brave soldier and true benefactor of mankind in the education of the disadvantaged, also a cruelly unscrupulous exploiter of women, including his wife, who wrote the venomous words of the "Battle Hymn of the Republic;" and others of similar ilk.

These people are examined in detail and largely through their own records. Clearly, their interest in the South, about which they knew little and understood nothing, bad as it might have been, was a convenient outlet for hatred and destructiveness. Even more important, for Brown and the others, was the way in which their hatred of the South, their desire to wipe out its civilization, provided for them a cover and excuse for their own individual sins. Thus Brown, a repulsive human being by every known standard, could become in the minds of many a martyr and saint. His friends could excuse their own lying, cheating, vindictiveness, irresponsibility, and betrayal on the grounds of their participation in the noble cause of South-hating. The South was evil, therefore its enemies good, the more relentless and irresponsible the better. And all this had only a superficial relationship to the actual existence and welfare of the black slave, as repeatedly emerges from Scott's evidence. On the other hand, the evidence shows that Southerners, even when subjected to the greatest provocation and while being denounced by a lying press as murderous barbarians, actually behaved with gentlemanly restraint and fair play.

Scott's careful portrayal is not just a historical exercise, as useful and honest as it is, as such. The phenomenon it probes is a recurrent one in American history and is as pertinent to understanding the 1960s as the 1860s. It is especially pertinent for the new conservatives who seem to be in the ascendant. Few of them have dealt honestly with the South and its enemies—Russell Kirk being a notable exception. They will never establish a viable American conservatism until they do.

There has always been a counter-current, of varying strength, set up by Northerners who did not participate in the fashionable gang-up against the South. The story of that is largely unwritten. In fact, anywhere one goes in the civilized world one encounters a considerable amount of sympathy and interest in the South and its history.

Despite all the heavily subsidized disapproval of the media and official history, there is some integrity and authenticity, some real glamour and heroism in the history of the South that continues to attract admirers even when Southerners themselves, it sometimes seems, have ceased to care. (1981)

Recovering Southern History

Two Heroes and a Poet

We have sung of the soldiers and sailors, but who shall hymn the politicians? —Herman Melville

Books reviewed: *Nathan Bedford Forrest: A Biography*, by Jack Hurst, New York: Alfred A. Knopf, 1993, 434 pages; *Richard Taylor: Soldier Prince of Dixie*, by T. Michael Parrish, Chapel Hill: University of North Carolina Press, 1992, 570 pages; and *The Civil War World of Herman Melville*, by Stanton Garner, Lawrence: University of Kansas Press, 1993, 544 pages.

The great classicist and poet A.E. Housman once wrote that the work of a scholar in the humanities is not like that of a scientist examining specimens under a microscope—it is more like the work of a dog searching for fleas. Housman thus punctured the scientific pretensions of some humanists and made an appeal for the old-fashioned virtues of painstaking work, common sense, and humble judgment. As another great British scholar, Veronica Wedgwood, put it: "History is an art—like all the other sciences."

It follows, and is indeed a truism, that all historians are biased. None escapes entirely the effects of his allegiances and preoccupations. But it is also true that some historians are more competent—and more honest—than others. Yet another great English historian, Sir Herbert Butterfield, suggested that it is best to trust those historians who are aware of and admit their own biases and who, as much as possible, separate the scholarly task of determining what happened and why from a personal moral judgment of these events—and that it is well to suspect and discount those historians who are eager to make sweeping moral condemnations, forgetting not only that there are at least two sides to every question but that we have all of us been exhorted to "judge not, that ye be not judged."

In regard to the Great Unpleasantness in the middle of the last century, which is still the central event in American history, good history continues to be written by serious and honest scholars, despite the reign of an official dogma which casts that great and complex happening in the most simplistic and misleading moralistic terms, as a righteous crusade for the suppression of wickedness. (What Robert Penn Warren called the national "Treasury of Virtue" with respect to the Civil War is very obviously the parent of political correctness.) The authors of the present literary selections are creatures of our time; their political values correct and unexceptional. But their honesty and competence as historians allow them to tell stories that are unfashionably true, though sometimes they do it a little too apologetically.

Unlike the other recent biography of Bedford Forrest by Brian S. Wills, so neatly and justly skewered by J.O. Tate in *Chronicles* ("Lastest with the Leastest," December 1992), Hurst's is a real contribution despite the fact—or perhaps because of the fact—that he is not a professional academic. Wills's biography contributed nothing new in data or in idea except to deconstruct the fascinating story of Forrest according to the canons of political correctness and psychobabble. Hurst, by contrast, has developed new material pertaining to the obscurities of Forrest's antebellum and postbellum life, and the more familiar history of the incredible campaigns he has retold clearly and well. Moreover, he is able to put Forrest in the perspective of his times, which is what a historian should do, rather than merely invoking labels. As Hurst points out, the American figure Forrest most resembles is his fellow Tennessean of a generation earlier, Andrew Jackson. The difference between them was that courageous, quick-witted, self-made Southerners could not play the same national role in Forrest's time as in Jackson's. Among the most interesting parts of the book are its presentations of Forrest's relation with black people after the war—another exceedingly complex historical situation that has been misrepresented by sloganeers. Hundreds of black people attended Forrest's funeral, and during Reconstruction he was berated by a Union officer from Connecticut for not working his plantation laborers hard enough

In a private conversation with an Englishman after the war, R.E. Lee is supposed to have been asked who was the greatest soldier produced by the American war and to have unhesitatingly replied: Forrest. Richard Taylor won fewer victories than Forrest, but those he did win exhibited a similar ability to triumph by skill and will against long odds. In the Red River Campaign in Louisiana in the spring of 1864, Taylor, with vastly outnumbered and under-equipped forces, defeated a huge federal military-naval expedition. (Of course, the federals had the misfortune to be commanded by one of many Republican political generals, "Commissary" Banks of Massachusetts.) After Forrest, Taylor may have been the best nonprofessional general produced by the war, though the South Carolinian Wade Hampton is also a contender.

Together, Taylor and Forrest represented extremes of Southern society: Taylor the well-educated, wealthy, cosmopolitan son of a President; Forrest the unpolished, self-made son of a frontier blacksmith. The two men, at such times as they collaborated, got along famously. Taylor had the respect for Forrest that all good soldiers had, and Forrest is reported to have said of Taylor: "He's the biggest man in the lot. If we'd had more like him, we would have licked the Yankees long ago." Both gave their all (which was a great deal) to their cause, and both ended the war shattered in health and fortune.

Taylor's biographer is clearly not sympathetic with the conservative, aristocratic values and way of life that his subject followed, but he is able to examine them with judicial impartiality. For the terrible simplifiers of American racial history, such impartiality complicates the evidence: Union forces devastated Taylor's plantation, thereby incidentally turning his slaves out to starve.

(They also nailed the family pets to a barn.) And consider the remarks of Sherman, then a Louisiana college president acquainted with Taylor, just before the war: "If they [Southerners] design to protect themselves against negroes and abolitionists, I will help; if they propose to leave the Union on account of a supposed fact that the northern people are all abolitionists... I will stand by Ohio and the Northwest."

Stanton Garner's *The Civil War World of Herman Melville* shifts our attention from the soldiers of the South to the civilian North: a dense and detailed (perhaps too dense and detailed) account of Melville's life, art, and mind in relation to the war. The book is an original contribution, with many virtues. It is not only literary history, but social and intellectual history as well.

In 1861 Melville was a literary has-been, living in genteel poverty and chiefly remembered as the author of *Typee*. *Moby Dick*, published ten years earlier, had been a complete critical and commercial failure, its author barely tolerated by the controlling Boston mafia of American literature. Melville had, seemingly, already consigned himself to oblivion when the war revived his literary aspirations and he undertook to record and interpret it in poetry, the result being *Battle-Pieces*, a collection published in 1866. This work has generally been regarded as unimportant, the work of an author emotionally disengaged from his subject, lost in his own fantasies. To the contrary, Garner contends that it is the most important body of poetry produced by an American about the war and by a writer deeply engage—an argument for which he makes a strong case.

One problem, of course, was that Melville's book was too profound for its time, when popular Northern war poetry consisted largely of sentimental jingles and blasphemous pseudo-hymns. Though Gamer does not put it exactly this way, another problem was that the work was politically incorrect: Melville refused to believe that God took sides in war and regarded the conflict between the American states as an immense tragedy bearable only when understood as part of the partially unknowable plan of divine providence. The outcome, for Melville, was foreordained and providential, a fact that did not however abrogate the ambiguity and pain of human action, decision, and suffering. ("O, much of doubt in after days / Shall cling, as now, to the war. / Of the right and wrong they'll still debate." "Power unanointed may come—/ Dominion (unsought by the free) / ... But the Founders' dream shall flee.") Consider these lines, reflecting on the employment of powerful artillery against the civilians of Charleston:

> Who weeps for the woeful City
> Let him weep for our guilty kind;
> Who joys at her wild despairing
> Christ, the Forgiver, convert his mind.

Garner's book has many incidental virtues. Its author treats Melville, as indeed a 19th century American should be treated, as a member of an extended family, not as an alienated artist of the modern type. Garner understands that Melville needs to be seen in relation to a huge circle of siblings, aunts and uncles, cousins, and in-laws whose viewpoints and experiences must be recognized as part of his creative material.

One advantage of this approach is that it forces the author to recognize and come to terms with the existence of the forgotten millions of Northerners who preferred McClellan's civilized and limited war to Sherman's terrorism against civilians; who resisted and resented Lincoln's incipient dictatorship and destruction of the Constitution (Melville was probably kept under surveillance by military spies in New York); and who regarded defeated Southerners as erring fellow countrymen, better treated with magnanimity than malice. This makes for some very interesting, neglected history. Garner also keeps tabs on other Northern writers in the course of his study of Melville: Whitman, who saw much of the war firsthand but was largely unable to rise above subjective experience; Hawthorne, whose views resembled Melville's but who was in sorrowful decline; gentle Whittier, who, nearly unique among abolitionists, hated the sin of slavery but not the slaveholding sinner; Emerson, the morally irresponsible, egotistical, nasty, self-serving prototype of the American liberal intellectual.

It is a measure of our low contemporary estate that Reconstruction, the most corrupt and shameful episode of the whole of our national history, is now regarded as a great achievement, faultable only because it did not go far enough. Yet Melville was so appalled by the onset of Radical Reconstruction, following a brief period of civility at the end of the war, that he literally stopped the presses to revise his book, adding a long poem, "Lee in the Capitol," and a prose "Supplement," both pleas to the North for magnanimity and moderation. These wise documents should be read by all decent Americans concerned with understanding regional and racial conflicts.

Melville's apprehension of the war as a tragedy in which no sweeping self-congratulation was justified by either side, though premature, was prophetic: it was the view that most decent Americans, North and South, came to have of the war when passions had finally died away. Melville thus anticipated what came to be a kind of national consensus in the late 19th and early 20th centuries regarding the American Civil War. This consensus, worked out in countless veterans' gatherings and public orations, went something like this: Southerners would acknowledge that they were glad that the Union had been preserved and slavery abolished. They would be, moreover, good citizens ever after. In return, Northerners would acknowledge that Southerners, though in error, had fought courageously and honorably in the war and would promise to respect their history and its symbols. This agreement held for a long time, until 1993 in fact, when the United States Senate violated it by its churlish action against the United Daughters of the Confederacy, although Southerners have faithfully kept their part of the agreement. Even more repulsive than the Senate majority's action was the historical ignorance it displayed and the vulgarity of the accompanying remarks. The senators should be reminded of the warning given by Melville's fictional Lee, when he was called before the Reconstruction Committee of the Senate:

> Push not your triumph; do not urge
> Submissiveness beyond the verge.

The historical Lee had been more prudent and reticent. (1994)

The Mind of the Old South

A review of *All Clever Men, Who Make Their Own Way: Critical Discourse in the Old South*, edited with an introduction by Michael O'Brien, Fayetteville: University of Arkansas Press, 1982, 456 pages.

    The intellectual history of the South is yet to be written. This assertion bootlegs two assumptions that do not go unchallenged. The first is that there is something called the South distinct enough to have a history. There are those who, from a variety of standpoints, dispute this premise. Some seem to feel that the South is evil and that therefore it is best treated as spurious and unreal, a kind of temporary aberration from the norm of a progressive democratic universe. For others, the South is intangible, dubiously quantifiable, and therefore we should concern ourselves with other things about which we can make more reliable, scientific generalizations. These challenges would seem to be overruled by common sense. The South must be in some sense a historical reality—millions have for generations acted as though it were, and even today, hundreds of presumptively sane people throughout the globe are devoting careers to studying it.

    The second bootlegged premise is that this phenomenon of the South, if admitted to be real, had a life of the mind sufficient to justify an intellectual history. Here we find it more difficult to secure assent. It will perhaps be admitted by many that Richard Beale Davis's three volumes established that there was intellectual and cultural activity in the colonial South significant enough for historical attention and distinct enough to be understood as Southern. (That is, distinct enough from the mind of New England which since the middle of the 19th century has been assumed to be equivalent to the mind of America.) As we can make some headway on good authority towards assent in regard to the colonial era, so, too, can we with modern times. Few would dispute that there has been in the 20th century literary and intellectual activity which could reasonably be called Southern, and which has been of significance, some would even say of world significance.

    Thus, if the intellectual history of the South has not been written, some pieces of it have been patched together in a preliminary sort of way. The great lacuna is the 19th century. Here, according to accepted notions, to the extent that Southerners exercised their intellects at all, it was merely in a sterile, reactionary, unreflective defense of the evil, obsolete and defective ideas of slavery and state rights. These having been justly thrust into the wastebasket of history, nothing was left but an equally sterile and reactionary romanticization of a delusionary Lost Cause, up until the time (placed by different authorities at different points in time and for some still in the future) when the South was forced to "join the 20th century." (Union with the 20th century is, today, not universally considered so unmixed a blessing as it was just a few years ago.)

Yet, it is inherently implausible that the interval between, say, Jefferson and Faulkner, could have been empty of anything of interest in its content or movement. Until very recently, this inherently implausible account of history has gone nearly unchallenged. Presumably, one would not expect to find anywhere in 19th century America the Athenian Academy, or even the intellectual concentration and standards of Oxford or Berlin in their best days. However, were there in the Old South men and women who were intelligent, widely read and traveled, interested in and abreast of the world of ideas past and current, and capable of formulating their thoughts creatively and communicably? Did the Old South, in other words, exhibit an intellectual culture in the best sense of that term rather than merely journalists and orators concerned with an apologia for their vested interests?

One way of answering this question, yes, which has been pursued and developed by scholars in the last few decades, but which has not yet been fully consummated, is literary. The more one understands the components of the literary achievement of figures like Faulkner and the Agrarians, the more apparent it becomes to the reasonably perceptive that such creation must rest upon historical roots, must have literary forebears. Thus, the creative literature of the Old South is very gradually being uncovered and assessed in context. A different and somewhat more direct answer is given in *All Clever Men*, the first book published by the University of Arkansas Press. The volume presents fourteen representative essays from the journals and books of the Old South. They are selected so as to show a variety of good minds at work on subjects related to the mainstream of Western culture as it was understood at the time.

All are unconcerned with narrow apologetics. All are by persons who no more would have rejected the description of Southern than Emerson would have denied he was a New Englander or Carlyle that he was a Scotsman. The selections are prefaced by an introductory essay that is a masterful description of the intellectual terrain of the Old South, its relation to the map of the world, and of the reasons why that terrain has gone uncharted and largely unknown. The author's insistence upon the significance of Southern mental activity is all the more persuasive in that he is not in the least interested in defending the Old South per se, but is interested in correcting and perfecting the record in regard to the larger intellectual history and historiography of the period.

This book has received some attention, but less or more perfunctory attention than it merits. This is partly because the British born and educated editor deals with his materials in a manner that is at the same time so broadly erudite and so playful that it is off-putting to earnest American scholars. Too few American scholars does it occur that their own intellectual foibles, conventions, and blind spots can be subjected to the same kind of detached critical appraisal that they as a matter of course mete out to others. Another reason for the relative neglect of *All Clever Men* is that suggested by O'Brien as responsible for the neglect of his subject matter heretofore: one of the conventions of American intellectuals is that intellectual and cultural activity and achievement are coexistent with progressivist social and political views. Where progressive views are absent, there could not possibly, therefore, be significant intellect at work. Thus, it is simply unthinkable that an antebellum Southerner, like George Frederick Holmes, could have been thoroughly familiar with European philosophy, art, and science since he drew from it an entirely different conclusions than Emerson.

Likewise, it is unthinkable (though true) that the greatest of American classicists, Basil Gildersleeve, received his training in antebellum Charleston and remained to the end of his days a fervent Confederate. And such a person as Louisa Cheves McCord, a plantation mistress who was quite a skilled poet and dramatist, but who also wrote eloquently against feminism and in defense of a traditional view of the role of women, could not possibly have existed. But indeed, such persons did exist, and in abundance. The assumption that intellectual achievement and adherence to the latest of leftist fashions are inseparable is, in the long view of history, a ludicrous convention pasted together a half century or so ago.

But, assuming that scholarship as actually practiced is indeed cumulative and self-correcting, the main reason for the relative neglect and misreading of the nature and quality of mental activity in the Old South is simply a matter of logistics. The primary sources have been too scattered and unknown and the task of assessing and drawing the proper conclusions from them too arduous. This book and another edited by O'Brien and David Moltke-Hansen on the intellectual life of antebellum Charleston provide the wherewithal to correct simplistic views of the Southern, and thus of the American mind. (1994)

The Southern Cavalier Revisited

A review of *The Rise and Fall of the Plantation South*, by Raimondo Luraghi, New York and London: Franklin Watts (New Viewpoints), 1978, 191 pages.

The South presents a problem for American conservatives. This is true even though the problem was recognized and a brilliant solution adumbrated in the writings of Russell Kirk early in the modern conservative intellectual movement—a solution which has been ignored. The South is, or should be, conservative. It is the least secular, the most traditional, the most resistant to modern ideologies of any of the major cultural formations that make up America. Yet one suspects that the South has often disappointed mainstream conservatives. The expectations of conservatives have been, perhaps, somewhat colonialist. In this they have differed little from liberals. Both have felt free to take what they found useful in the South without any obligation to take the whole. Both have tended to find in the South what they wanted or needed at a particular moment—a convenient ally or scapegoat. At various times, the mainstream right and left have joined to execrate the South as the center of all national evil. At other times each has based its strategy and hopes on the South. Each has had its Southern heroes and its Southern demons.

In the middle of the 19th century, as Raimondo Luraghi might formulate it, the North, seized by economic and ethnic transformations and egalitarian drives which necessitated a new view of the Constitution and the good society, carried its program by a crusade to put down the alleged innovations of the South. Men as diverse as John Brown and John Quincy Adams, Cornelius Vanderbilt and Charles Sumner, Henry David Thoreau and William T. Sherman were united on the necessity of wiping out the pernicious influence of the South—a drag on national upward imperatives. Yet, as soon as the war was won, there began a movement back toward the Southern view of the Constitution, and prescient thinkers began to mourn the national loss involved in the perishing of the aristocratic virtues of the Old South.

More recently, liberals and conservatives both ran against Wallace, while surreptitiously stealing planks from his platform. While there are numerous good reasons for President Carter's unpopularity, one can't help but suspect that he would have an easier time if he were not a Southerner. Neither left nor right trusts him. Liberals find Kennedy more "compassionate," and conservatives found Ford more "competent," factually dubious propositions in both cases. Yet the liberals would have lost the election without Carter, that is, if left to themselves; nor could conservatives get along without their Southern strategy, not to mention Southern leadership in Congress. Could it be that these phenomena tell us more about the minds of the beholders than about the South? Though it was not part of his purpose, Professor Luraghi of the University of Genoa, a leading European historian of America, provides us with a vantage point from which to solve the conundrum. He stands at that point where the Tory and the radical—he is a bit of both himself—meet to condemn the bourgeois. From that point the similarities of the middle class right and left are more striking than the differences, and the oft-noted paradoxes and peculiarities of the South are less bewildering.

According to the author, the Old South was part of a unique civilization, a civilization which he names "seigneurial" and strives to put into the context of Western history. The American Civil War was a struggle between that civilization, the dynamic of which was honor and ethics—that is, the ideal of the gentleman—and modern capitalist civilization derived from English Puritanism, the dynamics of which were rationalism, equality, and material productivity. Though the South's regime was destroyed, the cultural residues have not ceased to reverberate through American history.

To make his point, Luraghi takes us on a tour of forbidden territory. Long ago it was believed that our war was a contest between Cavalier and Puritan, that it in some sense or other recapitulated the issues of the English Civil War. Both sides subscribed to this notion. But in this century debunking scholars made the startling discovery that most Southerners were not descended from dukes and earls. Even though nobody had ever thought they were, except for a few romancers whose works were read mainly by Northern matrons, "modern wisdom" had proved, we were told, the notion of Puritan and Cavalier to be romantic nonsense, simply another of the dangerous delusions by which Southerners evaded reality. The finding seemed conclusive, especially to those who are unable to conceive of any other mainspring of human behavior than greed. For seventy-five years the very idea of the Southern cavalier has been sufficient to draw guffaws from educated audiences and has survived only in furtive corners occupied by patriotic societies of little old ladies.

It is interesting that a European scholar, whose main interests have been economic, industrial, and military history, chooses to begin the twelve graceful essays in which he interprets the Old South with a study of the idea of the gentleman in the Italian Renaissance, followed by an examination of the English expression of that idea in the person of Sir Walter Raleigh. The lesson is that, if we understand the Cavalier-Puritan conflict in a manner a little less literal-minded than "modern wisdom" dictates, we may recapture the germ of truth in it. (Here, unfortunately, Luraghi stands to lose nine-tenths of the American intelligentsia, who are nothing if not literal-minded.)

It was not always the destiny of America to embody material and egalitarian values. From the 16th to the 19th centuries America, in fact, gave a new lease on life to the obsolescent European ideal of the landed gentle-man—an individual who played out his life and liberty according to a code of personal honor and social responsibility. This was the "Newe Worlde" of Raleigh, and of Shakespeare. During these centuries there flourished a civilization unique to the Americas—the seigneurial, plantation, or hacienda society, neither feudal nor capitalist. It could be found in French Canada and Louisiana, in parts of Spanish and Portuguese America, and in its most articulated form in the Southern part of British America. It was a society whose economic bases, social organization, and vision of the good life differed from both feudal Europe and bourgeois Europe and America.

This description slights the sophistication of Luraghi's analysis. It is important to note that he is not spinning daydreams here. He might be just another sentimentalist, entrapped as many have been before by the romantic dream of the Old South, but these essays are the culmination of a lifetime of rigorous research in primary sources. He has previously written a two-volume history of the American war, celebrated in Europe, and a meticulous study of the industrialization of the South during the Civil War. He knows his subject as only a true scholar can, and is at some pains to draw out unfamiliar and telling illustrations from the history of the Old South. Note, too, that his findings are not incompatible with what Kirk had to say several decades ago about the South.

These findings show that the regime of the South was not egalitarian, that it was genuinely and responsibly paternalistic. Further, it achieved the highest maturity that can be expected of any society: it was able to produce a leadership class that was truly ethical and farseeing, with the ability to devote itself selflessly to the welfare of its people and to the realization of its highest impulses. The Confederate States of America thus was not an aberration or an error but a deliberate gamble to forestall an extinction that was probable in any case but certain without the gamble. The supreme political act of the planter class was the offer by the Confederate government late in the war of emancipation in exchange for foreign help. It was perhaps the most selfless act ever performed by a ruling class, which literally proposed to disinherit itself for national survival.

This reviewer cannot help but recall here Joseph Schumpeter's warning that capitalism carries within it the seeds of its own destruction in its inability to produce leadership, that its political salvation can only come from non-capitalist strata. If it is true that the only alternative to an ethical and foresighted leadership is coercion, then the cultural inheritance represented by the idea of the gentleman, best if not exclusively preserved in the South, may be all that stands between us and uniformitarianism of the right or left. It is worth pondering. (1984)

Crackers and Roundheads

A review of *Cracker Culture: Celtic Ways in the Old South*, by Grady McWhiney, Tuscaloosa and London: University of Alabama Press, 1988, 290 pages.

Despite all that has passed since, the Civil War is still at the center of American history. No one has ever doubted this in the South, where every native is a not-too-remote descendant of Confederate soldiers, or of slaves. In my native state (North Carolina) and my adopted state (South Carolina) the Civil War killed a quarter of the white men. There is nothing even remotely approaching this degree of sacrifice and devastation anywhere else in the American experience.

The late great Unpleasantness is not so direct a memory north of the Potomac and the Ohio, not to mention west of the Missouri. (In fact, one gets the impression that Pancho Villa, Trotsky, Gandhi, and Patrice Lumumba are more remembered and honored up there than Grant and the boys in blue. I hope not, but I fear so.) Nevertheless, the Civil War remains the critical core of American experience, not only because of its immense scale and revolutionary impact, but because it is the Gordian knot of our history.

The Civil War presents all of the major issues and fundamental conflicts of America in their starkest form: the meaning of the Constitution; the nature of majority rule and consensus; the benefits and burdens of industrialization, modernization, and centralization; governmental authority versus individual liberty; the claims of innovation and tradition, social ideals and social reality; the position of the black minority in American society. (It even molds our international role, because every subsequent war and extraterritorial objective of the U.S. has been defined psychically and rhetorically in imitation of the winning side in the Civil War.)

And despite the convention among ignorant and unthinking commentators that the war represented a simple struggle of good (freedom and Union) against evil (slavery and disunion), it does not present these issues in any conveniently simplistic manner. It presents them instead in tremendously complicated and ambivalent ways, which is why that experience will always remain of the most compelling interest to any American capable of historical imagination and understanding.

(For instance, was Lincoln a liberator or a tyrant? Or possibly both? Was the South fighting for freedom or for slavery? Or possibly both? What relative proportions did benevolence, racism, and economic self-interest have in the opposition to slavery? Was John Brown a heroic revolutionary, a dangerous subversive, or merely a mental case? The questions are without end.) In the earliest postwar period, when it could be simply declared that the war was a crusade to suppress wickedness, understanding was not much of a problem. As time passed, as the world became more complicated, as the ambiguities of victory and progress became more apparent to the thoughtful, and as more was learned about the sheer complexity of the war, this would not do.

Then for a long time the question of the cause or causes of the Civil War fascinated historians. Unfortunately, posing the blank question of "why" was bound to lead to abstraction, bad reasoning, and artificial disputes. In history, as in every other field of human knowledge, finding the right answers is far less important and difficult than asking the right questions. (My friend Ludwell Johnson, a Civil War historian, has written how it came home to him that we historians were on the wrong track some years ago, when, to the standard essay exam question "Why, the Civil War?" a student returned the philosophically flawless answer, "Why not?")

Such analytical dead ends suggest that the old-style history, which attempted to tell a story or to describe a past era, teaches us more than any amount of abstraction over "causes." History is not an expression of abstract laws, or the record of progress. It is a description of the actions of men, of life, which in turn is an expression of the (partly unknowable) mind of God. A historian who does an honest and competent job of narrative or description has created something permanently useful to everyone, whether they agree with him or not. The historian who claims to have found the final explanation is a fraud. You and I may agree in our description of a historical phenomenon or epoch, but disagree in values, as to whether we like or not what we have described, or whether we regard it as good or bad. You and I may agree that the New Deal was not really very revolutionary. I may be glad of the fact, and you may be sorry. Or you may think that it really was revolutionary when I don't. If we are both honest and competent it does not matter, we will learn from each other. The historian who recognizes and declares his viewpoint up front is much more objective and unbiased than the one who thinks that he is simply purveying the universal truth.

Professor McWhiney has produced one of those permanently valuable works of historical description. You may value the distinctiveness of the South, as Professor McWhiney and I do, or you may want it wiped out. Either way, and even if you disagree with his answers, you can respect his accomplishment for its solidity, originality, and contribution to understanding.

In *Cracker Culture*, McWhiney makes a quantum leap in understanding the South. He enhances our knowledge of what was at issue and what imperatives fueled the gigantic 19th century sectional conflict. Thus, by asking some of the right questions, he contributes toward the advance on the big answers. McWhiney's ideas have been gathering momentum for several years in preliminary works, and are here brought into fully developed maturity.

To understand what this book signifies, one has to understand what a Cracker is in McWhiney's lexicon. He is not simply, as we used to think, a somewhat benighted native of an area of poor soil in South Georgia and North Florida. A Cracker is an American of a particular ethnic heritage: the ethnic descendant of Celtic Britain, transferred to this continent in the 18th century, where he underwent an entrenchment and adaptation in the congenial environment of the American frontier and became a major component of American culture—became, that is, what has been known as the Southerner.

The Cracker is in part what we used to understand as a Scotch-Irishman, though one of McWhiney's strengths is that he gives the concept of Celticness in America much greater depth and breadth. The Cracker can perhaps be most readily grasped as the mythological Southern redneck, in an ethnic contrast to an American of Puritan Brit descent, epitomized in the mythological image of industrious, psalm-singing New Englanders. That the largest ethnic rift in American history took place between two different types of Brits will be a difficult point to grasp, perhaps, for those later-comers who think that all WASPs look alike.

Let us assume as a model a feudal, later a modern, England, developing over many centuries along the lines of intensive agriculture, commerce, and orderly communal life. By contrast, consider the outer fringes of Britain, not only Wales, Scotland, and Ireland, but the north and west of England herself, existing over several millennia (until the 19th century) with an economy based upon stock grazing and a much looser social structure, more tribal than feudal or commercial—with all the differences in manners, attitudes, and ways of life that these differences in ethnic origin, economy, and social structure entail. Both these models were implanted in America in the colonial period and both underwent development here, according to the large historical scheme that is postulated and vigorously filled in by McWhiney, with the aid of Forrest McDonald in the prologue.

A Cracker is not simply a backward fellow. Crackers come in all classes with all levels of education and in a variety of religious denominations. Though I have a doctor's degree and have published a few books, I don't mind telling you that I am a Cracker, at least by descent. Nor do I think Professor McWhiney will mind too much if I call him one as well. Perhaps the most conspicuous Cracker in American history was our seventh president, General Andrew Jackson. I would even argue, though McWhiney does not make this point, that Abraham Lincoln was a Cracker. Certainly, that was his background, though he worked hard and with only partial success to assimilate himself to a Puritan model as his political career progressed. After his death, the New Englanders simply appropriated him as a Puritan, as they have done everything else in American history that they wanted to control. (I wish you had been there when I tried to explain to the lady guide at Plymouth Rock that we were not on the scene of the first English colony. Talk about stonewalling!)

Where earlier historians have been interested in the aristocracy of the South, whether they admired it or deprecated it, McWhiney believes the distinctiveness of the South is in its redneckery, so to speak, and he gives that phenomenon historical depth by an examination of similarities and continuities ranging over many centuries of Celtic Britain and the American South—similarities in customs, attitudes, recreation, social roles, ideas of family and individual honor, combativeness, and skepticism of progress in its urbanized, Puritanical form. The marshaling of the evidence for similarity and continuity, ranging over millennia but concentrated in the 18th and 19th centuries, is the core of the book.

Explanations of Southern distinctiveness have been one of the most creative fields of American historical writing, calling forth the ingenuity of U.B. Phillips, C. Vann Woodward, David M. Potter, Professor McWhiney's mentor Francis Butler Simkins, and a host of others. McWhiney's is the best explanation because it is the most inclusive. It covers the greatest time period and the largest range of phenomena.

U.B. Phillips's postulate of white supremacy as the central theme of Southern history can be seen here from its positive side, as the Southerner's assertion and protection of his own identity among the peoples of the world. Those who before, during, and after the Civil War thought that what they regarded as the violence and unprogressiveness of the South was a product of slavery will, if they are honest, have to explain why nearly identical characteristics appeared with the Celt in ages and climes far from the African bondsman of the antebellum South.

As with any work of history, it is possible to pencil in a few reservations at the margins. What is described is a very real historical phenomenon. To label it "Celtic," however, perhaps raises more questions than it answers, and requires a considerable exegesis. Another reservation I have is that the description of the Celt and the Cracker relies necessarily and primarily on the observations of unsympathetic outsiders, resulting inevitably in a negative stereotyping which the author accepts a little too readily at face value. Such descriptions often tell us more about how the modernizing, urbanizing, Puritan observer thought than about what the Celt-Cracker was really like. The Puritan is by his very nature interested in condemning. He draws much of his sense of identity and importance from what he rejects, from feeling himself better than others. The Cracker, on the other hand, simply wants to be himself. He is hardly aware of the Puritan's existence until directly threatened.

To say that the Cracker is lazy or violent is to make a partisan value judgment, not an objective description. The Cracker does not lack concepts of work, law and order, and propriety. It is just that his concepts are different, and adapted to a different situation. To understand him better, one will have to go to Celtic and Southern literature and song.

We Crackers do have our virtues. The American frontiersman and the Cracker are synonymous. We have certainly provided more than our fair share of the loyalty that has sustained American society in crisis—the kind of loyalty that goes into combat without thought of profit and without need of folderol about saving the world for democracy. It is not for nothing that the British referred to the American air arm in World War II as the "Royal Texas Air Force," and that the Japanese shouted "To Hell with Roy Acuff" before a charge. They knew who their real enemy was. It is also true, I think, that us Crackers have provided nearly all of the color and creativity of American speech and literature. Billy Faulkner was one of our boys, just to name the head of a long list. Without us Crackers, American speech would be the flattest, dullest, and least interesting of any known variety of that magnificent tongue, English.

My last and largest reservation is that, while *Cracker Culture* goes a long way toward defining one aspect of the identity of the South, it does not quite finish the job. In a way, *Cracker Culture* is an improvement on the old story of explaining the Civil War as a contest of Roundheads and Cavaliers, substituting the Cracker for the Cavalier. However, the essential point about the Old South, it seems to me, is that it was a highly viable synthesis of both the Cracker and the Cavalier. Having established the descent and the importance of the Cracker culture, McWhiney needs next to examine the synthesis. Both components—in distinction from the Puritan—preferred honor to utility.

Washington, Jefferson, and Lee, after all, were not Crackers, though they were heroes to nearly all Southerners. John C. Calhoun, William Gilmore Simms, and Jefferson Davis were not Crackers either, though all of them had Celtic fathers. They were a synthesis of what the Celt had brought to the South and of the Cavalier inheritance of the Southern colonial tidewater that has remained characteristic into much later times. (I think of Harry Byrd, Richard Russell, and Sam Ervin.)

I hasten to assure you that I am aware that historians long ago proved that the "Cavalier South" was a fraud, that most Southerners were not descended from dukes and earls and did not live in tidewater mansions. Still, it is a matter of record that a substantial portion of the early settlers of Virginia, and to a lesser extent the other Southern colonies, were younger sons of the gentry and higher bourgeoisie of England (something that can be of little interest to a society that prides itself on being made up of the wretched refuse of the earth). But, of course, nobody ever did think that most Southerners were descended from Royalist nobility, except for romancers whose works were mainly read by Northern matrons, and unimaginative historians looking for a straw man to knock down. The idea of the Southern Cavalier and the Northern Roundhead was not meant as a photographic reality on either side, but as a metaphor for certain values and principles and tendencies in conflict.

Having given us the Cracker in his full glory, McWhiney ought now to describe for us the process of amalgamation between the Cracker and that even earlier Southern culture, that colonial tidewater whose social ideals were determined not by the Celtic fringe but by the gentry ethics and ideals of the Southern English counties. The distinctive elements of the Southern accent also came more from this source than from the Celts (or the Africans). All the real authorities agree on this.

The synthesis of Cracker and Cavalier culture has had many results, one of which is that the South has been at the same time more aristocratic and more populist than any other part of America. It thus has remained an incomprehensible problem for those whose imaginations are circumscribed by urban middle-class proprieties. This includes nearly all American historians, many of whom flunked marketing and civil engineering because they lacked the necessary imagination and so turned to scholarship. (The single greatest shortcoming of American historians, in general, is an excess of literal-mindedness in dealing with ideas. The second greatest shortcoming is a lack of sufficient literal-mindedness in dealing with documentary evidence.)

These reservations about *Cracker Culture* I intend not as criticism but as addenda and commentary on a stimulating work. Persecuted minority that we are, us Crackers will have to stick together. At least we no longer have to worry about the Roundheads. The few of them that are left have their hands full on other fronts. (1988)

An Obscene Carnival

The obscene carnival of digging up an American hero who died 141 years ago has come to an end. No arsenic was found in Zachary Taylor's remains, proving that he was not poisoned, which any competent and sensible historian could have told you without this grotesque and impious exercise. (Even if significant traces of arsenic had been found, it would, in fact, have meant nothing. Arsenic was an ingredient in many medicines and embalming fluids in common use in 1850, and its presence would not have proved conspiracy and poisoning.)

We did not learn anything about American history before the Civil War from this business. There was never the slightest possibility that we would do so. The affair tells us a lot, however, that will never be acknowledged, about our intellectually and ethically degraded present; more specifically, it reveals that what passes for the official view of earlier American history is not only ignorant but warped. No society has ever devoted more resources to historical study than modern America, and no society has ever so wantonly cut itself off not only from understanding but from identification with its own past.

This foolish exercise should never have been permitted by Taylor's descendants. There used to be better standards. It is little known, but in the early 19th century there was an effort by John Quincy Adams to remove George Washington's remains from Mount Vernon to the Capitol. It was quietly but firmly refused by the family, backed by overwhelming Virginia public opinion. It would have been an unseemly and unrepublican spectacle, an invasion of privacy that would have made Washington's tomb hostage to whatever band of politicians happened to get control.

It was alleged that President Taylor's symptoms at the time of death suggested poisoning, doubtless by pro-slavery advocates. Any historian familiar with the period knows the imprecision of medical data and records from that era, and would be extremely cautious in drawing any conclusions from them, especially one so drastic as a presidential assassination. But what gave a fraudulent plausibility to the story was something that is in the air: the belief, or rather faith, on the part of vast hordes of petty intellectuals that any and all evils and enormities, real and imagined, must be traced back to Southerners, and particularly to Southern slaveholders.

The issues that were current in 1850 were quite complicated. It would take several pages to explain them fully, and even then it would be beyond the intellectual capacity of a television news anchor or congressman to understand. But, broadly speaking, they did not involve being for or against slavery, contrary to what the media have repeated *ad nauseum*, for in fact almost no one respectable was against slavery, except in mild and marginal ways. The differences involved the political and economic balance of power between the North and South in regard to the future of the new territory acquired in the Mexican War, further complicated by the efforts of two political parties to maneuver for advantage while muddling and compromising the issues, as American politicians always do.

There was a wide variety of viewpoints. Though a Southerner and a slave-holder, Taylor was a conservative Whig who took a moderately Northern stand on the issues, as indeed did many Southern Whigs. The differences involved were quite heated, but hardly clear-cut enough to provoke assassination. An assassination theory is only given plausibility by anti-Southern paranoia: the belief that Southerners killed people who disagreed with them. The Old South produced some tough and violent customers, including Old Rough and Ready himself, but they were not the kind that went around poisoning people. It would have been totally out of character. The abolitionists, not the slaveholders, produced the John Browns and Edwin Stantons. Congressman Brooks of South Carolina publicly thrashed Charles Sumner, who had unquestionably slandered his state and his family, because he knew Sumner was too cowardly to accept a challenge. Brooks would have scorned a clandestine assault.

Taylor himself, a genuine and heroic soldier though a naive politician, would have repudiated the hysteria of a "slave power conspiracy." Anyone with any sense of context can see the absurdity of the assassination business. Would Taylor's family have had no suspicions? Within a little over a decade Zach Taylor's son-in-law was president of the Confederate States and his son one of its best generals, yet his death is used to slander Southerners. And an ideological phantasm becomes not only a historical interpretation but the cause of legal and scientific actions.

This incident fits a very familiar pattern. Whenever economic, social, and psychic tensions grow in "mainstream" America, there is a clamor of anti-Southern hysteria. It has happened over and over again. As racial hatred and social pathologies intensify in northern cities, it is utterly predictable that establishment intellectuals will escalate their war against Southerners and Southern history.

This is illustrated to perfection by William Freehling's recent book, *The Road to Disunion*, Vol. 1, which purports to be a new history of the coming of the Civil War, and which is a sort of background cover for the nasty Taylor business. This book was hyped for twenty years while in preparation, something that is almost unprecedented in academic circles. Its publication immediately catapulted the author from an already prestigious position at Johns Hopkins to an endowed chair at SUNY-Buffalo. While the book is well researched and even slightly original in marginal ways, and not without a certain cleverness, it is, substantially, as a work of history, an absurd cartoon. It literally reeks and drips with poisonous and near-paranoiac hatred not of slavery but of Southern whites, and, indeed, of almost all of American history. Even the academic historians have kept some distance and not been entirely persuaded by the book's pretension to be major and classic history. This so-called narrative is full of 1960s slang. The portraits of antebellum American statesmen are at best quarter-truths, but even what truth there is in them has been said a thousand times before by a thousand different writers. The book tells us exactly less than nothing about its subject, in the sense that a quarter-truth is worse than nothing at all.

The success of this book and the Taylor autopsy, which are both based upon a common and false interpretation of history, do tell us that the liberal intellectuals are under terrific pressure. Faced with a moral and social wasteland in modern America, what could be more convenient than to blame the old Southern slave-holding class for all our ills? It gives one such a nice and safe feeling of superiority and freedom from the necessity of any real thought or decision. Whatever the evils of past states of society, which are always easy to find, it is a fact that the Southern planter class of the 18th and 19th centuries provided the preponderance of the most able and honorable Founders and nourishers of the American Republic, and that American society has gone downhill in every way except material wealth since they were destroyed

If, as the Kerner Commission has made a convention, the Old Southern system of slavery is the cause of all the ills of modern American society, why is it that the further away we get from the plantation, in time and space, the worse the pathologies grow? Or, to put it another way, why, a century and a quarter after the end of the Civil War, is racial hatred, not to mention crime, illegitimacy, and drugs, worse in Chicago than in South Carolina?

In the meantime, we Southerners need an anti-defamation league, though that is not our style. We have learned the hard way the value of patience and a half loaf, and the danger of pushing points of honor too hard, and we have a primitive loyalty to this country, under the foolish delusion that it is still ours. A vastly disproportionate share of the reservists called up for the late Arabian adventure were from the Southeastern States. Everyone wants representation on the Supreme Court. Southerners, the people who more than any other founded the country and wrote the Constitution, have a representation on the Supreme Court of zero, even though we make up a third or more of the people. Yet, still, we Southerners allow a smirking Yalie to gull us out of our votes by a pretense of fellowship with Baptist ministers and country singers. It speaks well of our hearts but not of our heads. (1991)

Continuity in Southern History

A review of *Liberty and Slavery: Southern Politics to 1860*, by William J. Cooper, Jr.; New York: McGraw-Hill, 1983, 309 pages.

The past decade and a half has seen the publication of many innovative studies of particular aspects of the history of the Old South. What antebellum Southern history has lacked has been a good survey that incorporated old wisdom and new insights into a reasonable and judicious account that makes the "peculiarities" of that history understandable to the general reader. Insofar as political history is concerned, Cooper has gone a long way toward fulfilling the need. His succinct overview incorporates the growing and sophisticated body of literature on republicanism and ideology in the 18th and 19th centuries.

Liberty and Slavery cogently portrays the basic continuity of Southern values from early colonial times to the Confederacy. The political instincts, interests, and ideals of white Southerners remained fundamentally constant, revolving always about the positive and negative poles of Liberty and Slavery. Liberty meant individual independence and honor, conceived in a highly tangible and militantly masculine way, and, as a necessary corollary, the freedom of the community and state from outside control. Slavery meant, in terms of the English and Revolutionary "republican" inheritance, the loss and absence of Liberty. While the ideas did not, in the first instance, relate to the question of plantation slavery, the presence in Southern society of a conspicuous continuing illustration of the meaning of the loss of Liberty gave the ideas a particular edge and the course of Southern history a different path. The maintenance of Liberty, through a not uncommon historical irony, was inextricably bound up with the maintenance of the illustration.

While the South's basic values and orientation did not change from early colonial times to the Confederacy, two things did change. National politics, responding to the changing economy, ideology, and ethnic composition of the North, changed. This brought forth a change in emphasis and tactics from the leaders of the South. Secondly, Southern politics evolved in a democratizing direction; that is, its constituent base broadened, and its style became more mass-oriented. Contrary to what many have either hoped or assumed, this strengthened rather than undermined the consensual basis of the whole. *Liberty and Slavery*, far from a false consciousness imposed by an elite, was the democratically-based worldview of Southern society.

Cooper's overall thesis of consensus and continuity in the South is not new and is undoubtedly correct, but in *Liberty and Slavery* it has been brought up to date by the incorporation of newer scholarly perspectives and restated in a well-written and effectively-argued account that constitutes, as far as it goes, as good a general history of the Old South as has appeared in many years. Cooper's political history is wide enough to include economic and social developments and a considerable attention to ideas. Yet, limited as it is to politics, it does not, except in that respect, supplant earlier survey texts such as Clement Eaton's *The History of the Old South* or Francis Butler Simkins's and Charles P. Roland's *A History of the South*. The former rests upon an unsurpassed knowledge of primary sources, and the latter is a literary masterpiece that has left many permanently valuable and brilliantly formulated insights into Southern history. (1984)

Recovering Southern History

Scratching the Fleas: American Historians and Their History

Speech delivered to the John Randolph Club in San Antonio, Texas, on November 13, 2004, after receiving the first John Randolph Club Award.

There is no group I would rather receive recognition from than the John Randolph Club. I want to thank my valued comrade-in-arms Tom Fleming for this occasion. Tom is the truly indispensable man. Can you imagine a world without Tom Fleming and *Chronicles*? It would be immeasurably more intellectually, culturally, and morally impoverished than it already is. I would not be here to receive the first John Randolph Award without the opportunities Dr. Fleming has given me to say my piece. Our association began, Providentially, more than a quarter century ago in a rundown bar on the outskirts of the University of South Carolina. The rest, as they say, is history, which brings us to the subject for the evening.

For this occasion, I am instructed to reflect on the career of an historian, on "your view of the historian's task" along with "your views on the American republican tradition. "To consider historianship and the republican tradition can be a gloomy undertaking—examining two things apparently suffering through terminal illness. I will try not to make it too gloomy.

First, let me use this bully pulpit to talk about that shrine of heroism nearby that we have all visited this weekend. This is an indirect way of getting into my subject. How should we think about it, or rather, what is wrong with the way most Americans do think about it? We are taught to see the Alamo as one of the great exhibits of American valor. I beg to differ. It depends on what you mean by "American." The Alamo is an exhibit of Texan valor and Southern valor. If we call it "American" we might start to think about the U.S. Army and then of the U.S. government, neither of which deserves any credit for the Alamo. Soon we have conflated the heroes of the Alamo with the U.S. government soldiers so eloquently eulogized by Lincoln, who destroyed the "Union" and founded the "nation" at Gettysburg. When we have slipped into this way of thinking we have falsified the central story of American history by erecting a fake nationalist continuity of struggles for liberty. We have perverted the meaning of the Alamo, whose heroes sacrificed for the liberty of their land and their posterity.

The forces that triumphed at Gettysburg were still in the making at the time of the Alamo. But already, a significant segment of Northern Americans (the Blue counties of the last election, if you wish) were denouncing the heroes of the Alamo, their fellow countrymen, as enemies—as violent frontier barbarians and pirates engaged in spreading the sin of slavery and stealing from the harmless Mexicans. These people kept Texas out of the "Union" for ten years. Texas finally was allowed to join the Union, wisely reserving in her accession the right of secession. Fifteen years after Texas entered the Union, these same Northern forces mobilized two million men, a fourth of them foreigners, to destroy the liberty of Texas and keep it captive, as they openly boasted at the time, for the North's economic benefit. At the same time, triumphant New England pundits and German Forty-Eighters used the victory to convert American history from what had been a story of constitutional republican liberty into the story of a Redeemer Nation leading the march of humanity into an ideal future of Massachusetts-writ-large.

So, let's be careful to know what we mean when we say, "American history," lest we misrepresent both history and the republican tradition. Unless we are careful as to what is meant by "American history" we might even end up, God forbid, equating the heroes of the Alamo with imperial wars against remote foreign peoples and the ignorant, vulgar demagogues of the media who support such "battles for freedom." While I am at it, let me point out the nationalist trick of adopting from the South as "American" anything that is favorably regarded, while only disfavored things are described as "Southern." Thus, we have books on "Celtic" valor to avoid discussing the disproportionate contribution of Southerners to American heroism. We have "country" music rather than Southern music. We have Texas, when it is in good favor, denominated as "Western" and "not Southern." In fact, historic Texas has been what it has been because and only because it is the offspring of Dixie. The Texans of song and story are Southerners on a new and bigger landscape. Otherwise, Texas would be just another Kansas or South Dakota of sodbusters, land speculators, and Yankee schoolmarms.

After almost a lifetime of considering what historianship is, I am satisfied that what it is or should be is storytelling. Assuredly it can't be a scientific experiment, nor a logical proposition, nor the illustration of a theory. History is about human beings, and human beings do not live as a scientific experiment, nor a logical proposition, nor an ideological exhibit. Our existence is a drama, that is, a story, taking place in the mind of God. Through history we have our only knowledge of the mysterious drama of our existence beyond what has been granted us as Revelation.

I like the delightful saying of the English historian Veronica Wedgwood: "History is not a science—it is an art, like all the other sciences." Even better, one by the great English poet and classicist A.E. Housman: "A historian is not like a scientist examining a specimen under a microscope. He is more like a dog searching for fleas."

Or, more seriously, we can make the same point by calling on John Lukacs's perfect definition: "History is a certain kind of memory, organized and supported by evidence." With emphasis on the evidence. In asserting that history is not certainty, I don't deny that there are varying degrees of honesty and competence in the handling of evidence that allow us to judge the quality of a historian's work.

If history is best understood as a story, at least two things follow. First, a story-like that of the Alamo—is somebody's story—it is not everybody's story as is claimed by those with an agenda, whether they be nationalist ideologues or multiculturalists. Everybody can learn from a story, but if it is to be real and valid, it is some people's story. It follows that America in our time cannot have a real history because America today does not have a real people. There was a time, peaking in the World War II era, when the inhabitants of this vast and diverse nation-state almost mingled into one people. That opportunity is now past. The inhabitants of the United States are corralled under the same territorial monopoly of force and exploitation; they share the same bread and circuses. They are not a people, only the motley subjects of an empire. Aggregations of Oprah watchers, sports fans, and mall shoppers do not make a people. After Augustus, the story of Rome ceases to be the story of a heroic and patriotic people. The Roman people pass from sight. The history of Rome becomes only an account of more or less evil emperors and a chaos of peoples without stories. Such is America in the era of Bush. The future history of the last national election can be written only as a meaningless contest in which the jocks barely beat out the nerds for possession of the imperial palace.

What is a poor historian to do if there is no core people whose story is to be told? For certain, we cannot turn to the academy. Most of the work of academic historians today can portray the American story in no other terms except as an abstract fantasy of oppressors and oppressed. No society has ever had more professional historians and devoted more resources to historical work of all kinds than modern America—or produced so many useless, irrelevant, and downright pernicious products. I know a historian who teaches that the great Virginians of the American Revolution were like the Taliban. Presumably because they carried weapons and were not feminists. This is to reduce human experience to a paltry and partial perspective, to remove from it everything that is worthwhile and ennobling, usable and true. But this is what academic historians mostly do these days. Secondly, if we accept that a historian's task is to tell somebody's story, it follows also that all stories may be told from more than one perspective—historians should not be engaged in categorical political and moral judgments. A historian should be trying to say something true and useful about human beings, and doing so modestly and cautiously. No historian can discover an indisputable truth, at least not about anything important. But that is what historians are claiming to do these days by reducing the drama of human experience to abstract, supposedly universal theory.

Now, because I am arguing the immutable variability of human perspectives on human experience, please don't accuse me of being a relativist or a deconstructionist. My text here is not Foucault. It is Scripture: "Judge not, that ye be not judged."

If time allowed, I could cite enough chapter and verse supporting my case about the evil tenor of today's historianship to keep us here till Christmas. The American Historical Association recently gave its grandest prize to a politically correct work that was later shown to be based on fabricated evidence. Then there is Eric Foner. Professor Foner at the time of the fall of the Soviet Union was organizing public statements urging Russian leaders to save the noble Communist experiment by crushing the independence of the Baltic peoples with the same ruthlessness, as he put it, with which Lincoln crushed the South. Foner has been elected president of both of the two most important academic historians' organizations in the United States and is retained by the Disney Corporation as a consultant.

The sins of omission are even greater. The most important work of history published in this country in the second half of the 20th century was John Lukacs's *Historical Consciousness*. It has been through three or four editions. To the best of my knowledge, it has never been reviewed or even noticed by any of the leading academic historical journals in this country. Why? Because it lies outside of the blind alley where academic historians follow their road to perdition. By the same token, if Jesus were to return tomorrow, the news media would not report the story. As in the case of the historians, it would not fit into their prefabricated pseudo-reality. If the story became widespread enough, the reporters would go to work to discredit the motives and sanity of those who were testifying to it. That would be the only reaction to truth of which they are capable. The reporters' knees jerk the same way as the academics these days.

History can take many forms, but I am speaking chiefly here about its most familiar form—history as the story of the nation-state—and in its American version. This history is supposed to be objective and factual, but it implicitly also is charged with a social purpose—to sustain a community from the stories of common ancestors and their legacy. As Ernest Renan remarked: "Getting history wrong is part of being a nation." The conflating of the Alamo and the U.S. army is a product of the nationalist history that long dominated American thinking, but which has now been virtually supplanted by multiculturalism. The nationalist history was fake. It was really the history of New England Yankees, and it ignored, slandered, or co-opted the stories of other Americans. Early on, the "intellectuals" of Massachusetts set out very deliberately—and you can document this with great specificity—to make the American story their exclusive property. With victory in the War to Prevent Southern Independence, their mission was complete. The proud fox-hunting Virginia planter George Washington was turned into a prim New England saint, and the heroes of the Alamo were co-opted for Lincoln's war on the South. To explore how Bostonian "American" history became multicultural/gender history would also keep us till Christmas. I will only say that the two things are more closely related than many are willing to admit, just as debauchery and Puritanism are two sides of the same coin. But at least the old nationalist history had a limited fungibility. The new history has no redeemable value whatsoever.

It used to be academic historians were trained by immersion in primary sources. A historian might have a bias or a theory to prove, but his first duty was to absorb the primary sources and bring back an honest summary of what they had to tell. This was a pretty good rule, and I won't deny that there is still such good craftsmanship going on here and there. But academics as a group have abandoned the search for accuracy and proportion and weighed judgment. The primary sources are there to comb for illustrations of pre-established dogma, no matter how ripped from context the illustrations might be. And what is this dogma and where does it come from? It is an abstraction about the conflict of classes. The prevailing "mainstream" interpretations of American history today are interpretations that 50 years ago were current only in the Communist neighborhoods of the New York City boroughs. Except that now few practitioners are naïve enough to deal only in economic class conflict. Today it is the much more destructive weapons of race and "gender."

Back to my all too commonplace example of the historians who equates George Washington with the Taliban. It is a sadly true consequence, I think, of the dissolution of American peoplehood, that the great Virginians of the War of Independence really are not a part of this historian's story. They are really not a part of the story of most of the inhabitants of the American Homeland Insecurity today—for whom George Washington can signify little more than a cartoon character with wooden teeth. What this historian has done is superimpose on the Virginia story something familiar from his own story—the oppressors of the Old World, the Cossacks who harassed his ancestors. But that is not all, this historian has further confused the thing by a false theory that human life is forever and only a story of oppressors and oppressed. As a result, the Czar's Cossacks, the Taliban, and the great Virginians are best understood as equivalent oppressors. Such historianship constitutes neither a contribution to knowledge nor a useful teaching for society's young. But such is the educational regime which is being dispersed today with immense resources and the prestige of the supposedly learned. Such malicious word-games destroy the chance that we, or the rest of humanity, might gain wisdom from the stories of our forefathers.

Even when it is not badly distorted, academic history has become not the remembered story of human life but only a commentary on dogma. This falsifies the vast contingency and complexity of our existence and action in time and converts it into a tawdry, diminishing determinism. It poisons the community by denying its existence apart from conflicting elements. It converts great segments of humanity into oppressors who deserve only annihilation. The result is today's academic history—a weird combination of supposedly objective "social science" and romantic exaltation of favored minorities designated as the oppressed. This history fails both as accurate record and as material for social comity. As Christopher Lasch pointed out years ago, scholars have abandoned the search for reality in favor of the classification of trivia. But it is worse than that. It is in the nature of dogma that dissenters are quickly suppressed. Conformity of opinion about what is significant and true about the past has never been as rigorous among academic historians, and all who listen to them, as it is today.

What then are we to do about our stories? And about the historian's duty to tell stories that are true and useful?

Our only hope is where it has actually always been—in art, that is, imagination disciplined by honest evidence. It was observed long ago that the novel and history have a common ancestor, narrative. It has been more recently observed by John Lukacs that the two, where they are of the pure descent, may be moving together back to their origins. We already see much evidence that I could cite. It is not coincidence that the greatest history of the American war of 1861-65 was written by a novelist, Shelby Foote. Foote observed at the end of his twenty years labor in writing history that the novelist and historian were both engaged in the same work—a search for understanding—though operating by partially differing methods. The academics don't treat the works of Solzhenitsyn as history. But how could the history of the Russian people in the last century ever be told more truthfully than by this great artist and thinker?

American history here on out is likely to be only the story of the rise and fall of the imperial machinery and its masters. There is no people who can cherish an American story. However, there are some remnants of peoples with stories to tell left in this imperial heartland. For instance, traditional Catholics and Southerners. The real Californians described by Roger McGrath and the authentic Westerners that Chilton Williamson writes about. Let us hope that the future brings forth scholars of art and integrity to craft and preserve for these remnants their stories. For it has been truly said that we are what we remember.

[H.L. Mencken in the 1920s, reflecting on the readiness with which historians were mobilized to rewrite history at federal direction during World War I]:

> Nearly all our professional historians are poor men holding college posts, and they are more cruelly beset by the ruling politico-plutocratic-social oligarchy than ever the Prussian professors were by the Hohenzollerns. Let them diverge in the slightest from what is the current official doctrine, and they are turned out of their chairs with a ceremony suitable for the expulsion of a drunken valet.]

Chapter Two

The War—My Myth or Yours?

The Greatest Sacrifice

A review of *The Confederate War*, by Gary W. Gallagher, Cambridge, Massachusetts: Harvard University Press, 1997, 218 pages.

Imagine America invaded by a foreign power, one that has quadrupled the population and industrial base. Imagine that this enemy has free access to the world's goods as well as an inexhaustible supply of cannon fodder from the proletariat of other countries, while America itself is tightly blockaded from the outside world. New York and Cincinnati have been taken. For months, Boston and Chicago have been under constant siege, the civilian population driven from their homes. Enemy forces roam over large parts of the country burning the homes, tools, and food of the non-combatants in a campaign of deliberate terrorism. Nearly 85 percent of the nation's able-bodied men (up to 50 years of age) have been called to arms. Battlefield casualties have run to 39 percent and deaths amount to nearly half of that, far exceeding those from any other war. On the other hand, the enemy, though its acts and domestic propaganda indicate otherwise, is telling the American population that it wants only peace and the restoration of the status quo antebellum. Lay down your arms and all will be as before.

What would be our state of morale in such conditions? Americans have never suffered such misfortune, have they? Alas, they have. This was the experience of the Southern people from 1861 through 1865 in their lost War for Independence.

Gary Gallagher has established himself of late as one of the leading historians of the period, a somewhat surprising and consoling occurrence since he is an old-fashioned historian who relies on evidence and is not afraid to challenge fashionable interpretation by following where the evidence leads. *The Confederate War* examines with skill and careful research the forgotten Southern experience, which was marked by greater suffering and sacrifice than that ever endured or made by any other large group of Americans. Gallagher presents an important and ignored perspective for those who wish to grasp the sweep of American history in the cold light of reality rather than through the rose-colored glasses of democratic globalism.

War, in the experience of the American people, has typically brought suffering and death to only a small part of the inarticulate youthful population, mostly from the poorer classes; dislocation and discomfort to a larger segment; high wages and profits in general; and a great glow of patriotism and righteousness to the many. This was war as the North knew it (except that dissent was a great deal more widespread than has been admitted), setting the pattern for subsequent American conflicts. (We only have to think of the delight with which so many celebrated, from the comfort of their recliners, the incineration of Iraqi women and children.) It was not so, however, for the Southern people in that period. (Our author says nothing, of course, about Reconstruction.)

How hard the Southerners struggled for independence from the American Empire has been, and continues to be, suppressed by a nationalist culture that can only wonder: How could any group possibly have dissented from the greatest government on earth? But a very large number of Americans did not consent to that government (the regime, after all, was supposedly founded on the consent of the governed). They were willing to put their dissent on the line in a greater sacrifice than any large group of Americans has ever been called upon to make. Until finally, as a disappointed Union officer quoted by Gallagher remarked: "the rebellion [was] worn out rather than suppressed."

The burden of *The Confederate War* is that military defeat—not lack of faith in the cause, internal class struggle, want of sufficient nationalist theory, or any other such thing offered by recent historians as explanations—ended the War for Independence. Historiographically, Gallagher's work is juxtaposed, with evidence and close reasoning, with a raft of literature speculating upon the weaknesses of the South. One learns very early in academic historical training that a sure road to success lies in finding a new twist on South-hating, supported by quotations selected out of context and references to currently fashionable abstractions that pass for reasoning, such as that the South was not only evil but weak and stupid, its War for Independence having been waged ineffectively, inadequately, and incompetently. I can cite several cases where books along these lines have catapulted their authors into professional celebrity and endowed chairs. Writing history is easy if you only need theory and not evidence.

Gallagher, by contrast, has documented the obvious: the South was militarily defeated only after an extraordinary effort unmatched before or since by Americans. Given the sad state of American scholarship, to accomplish that much is cause for celebration. (1998)

The War—My Myth or Yours?

Your enemy is not a criminal just because he is your enemy.
—Saying credited to the founder of Israeli intelligence

How could we help falling on our knees, all of us together, and praying God to pity and forgive us all!
—Joshua Chamberlain, on the surrender at Appomattox

A review of *The Myth of the Lost Cause and Civil War History*, by Gary W. Gallagher and Alan T. Nolan, Bloomington: Indiana University Press, 2000, 231 pages.

The Progressive historian Howard K. Beale (mentor of C. Vann Woodward) published in 1946 an essay called "What Historians Have Said About the Causes of the Civil War."[2] He intended not so much to comment on the Civil War as to present an exhibit of the patterns made by successive changes in historical interpretations. Beale thought that historical scholarship did, with the passage of time and the accumulation of knowledge, make progress, though slowly and unevenly, in approaching the ultimately unreachable "truth" of history. However, the predominant pattern of historical interpretations, Beale found in reviewing the literature on the Civil War, is not progressive but cyclical. Every "new" interpretation has its precedent in explanations made at the time of the event by actual participants and commentators. Historians offer not new interpretations but only new versions of old ones.

The Myth of the Lost Cause and Civil War History offers stunning proof of Beale's prescience. The mainstream explanation of the War which flourished from 1861 to about 1900, Beale wrote, was the "devil theory": the war was caused by a "conspiracy of selfish or wicked men" against the Union. (Confederates had their own version of the devil theory but it had little influence prior to 1900.) Nolan's essay, "The Anatomy of the Myth," and a complementary one by co-editor Gallagher, contain nothing new except in the packaging. Their case is a militant re-assertion of the thesis that the war was caused by the wickedness

---

[2] "What Historians Have Said About the Causes of the Civil War," in *Theory and Practice in Historical Study: A Report of the Committee on Historiography*. Social Science Research Council Bulletin 54 (1946): 53-102.

of Southerners, a case made in such works as Joshua R. Giddings's *History of the Rebellion* (1864) and Henry Wilson's *History of the Rise and Fall of the Slave Power in America* (3 vols., 1872-1877). Not since the War generation have the good guys and bad guys been so starkly differentiated as by Nolan.

Nolan presents the world with what he considers to be an undisputedly accurate summation of the War. Eleven seceding Southern states, under the domination of a small group of slaveholders, attempted without justification to "destroy the United States" and initiated war by an unprovoked attack on Fort Sumter. The "United States" rose up in righteousness and put down the evil rebellion, in the process securing emancipation for African-Americans and generously refraining from the severe punishments the traitors deserved. "Having swept away the counter-factual Myth of the Lost Cause," Nolan believes he has established the true "historical image of the war" which is "undisputed as accurately describing the central aspects" of the Civil War era.

But unfortunately, alas, according to Nolan, "despite the undisputed essentials, the War is today surrounded by a vast mythology." On the one hand there is the true history of the war, and on the other hand there is the mythology of "the Lost Cause," which seems to persist despite the agreement of all good and informed persons that the "Lost Cause" is a "caricature of the truth" which "wholly misrepresents and distorts the facts of the matter." The "Lost Cause," presumably a belief that the Confederates had a few points on their side of the argument, was something, according to Nolan and Gallagher, invented after the War by Southerners to rationalize their evil, destructive, and failed actions. In support of this conclusion, they present a history of the development of this false and pernicious "Lost Cause Myth," beginning with the postwar writings of Edward A. Pollard and Jubal A. Early. These writings, the authors claim, foisted on an unsuspecting world false and deceptive notions such as the admirable character of Robert E. Lee, the skill and heroism of Confederate soldiers against heavy odds, and the honorableness of Southerners in their cause.

There are many things wrong with this treatment of so vast and complicated an event as the American Civil War. To begin with, and Gallagher is far too fine a historian for this, it confuses books with life. A few books cannot create a popular belief so widespread and enduring. The editors are clearly offended and alarmed by the power and persistence of the "myth" and long to destroy it completely. The timing of their attack surely relates, as "new" historical interpretations usually do, more to concerns of the present day than to the pursuit of historical "truth."

A fundamental problem is the authors' failure to define and stipulate what they mean by myth. They apparently mean myth in a petty sense as a group of untrue "facts" that influence people's beliefs and understanding. This is inadequate. Myth, in fact, is a fundamental human way of understanding human experience. It is found in all times and places. It is neither true nor false. It is art. A myth may be questionable (like the story of Magna Charta, say) in the view of literal-minded pedants and still be true and meaningful in an important sense. Southerners are not the only people to have "myths." To accept Nolan's "undisputed" interpretation one has to have the implicit belief that Northerners *always* deal in true "facts," that their motives are always good, and that the words of Southerners about their own motives and actions are *always* untrue. Apparently, only Southerners among all Americans suffer from self—flattering myths.

This implicit assumption in dealing with evidence is so fundamental to his attack on "the Lost Cause" that Nolan is not even aware of it. In a well-known essay, "History and Morality," the great English historian Sir Herbert Butterfield said that historians who are aware of and allow for their prejudices are more reliable than those who are convinced of their own objectivity.[3] He also warned that what historians present as moral judgments of acts and actors in the past are too often not really moral judgments at all but merely preferences. It all depends not on expert discovery of "fact" but on who you like and dislike. According to Butterfield, the historian will do well to keep his moral judgments aside until after his investigation of the evidence. Like any other person, historians are entitled to moral judgments after they fully investigate the situation, but being a historian does not per se qualify one as an unbiased judge of right and wrong in historical events and conditions. In other words, contra Nolan, the historian should have better things to do than exhibit his own likes and dislikes. (But I prefer the great classical scholar and poet A.B. Housman's description of a historian's work: a historian is not like a scientist looking through a microscope, but more like a dog searching for fleas. You can never be sure you have got them all.). The authors never really grasp the nature and importance and function of Myth.

A "myth" like the "Lost Cause" surely does not spread so widely and last so persistently without a basis in "fact." (One is reminded of the

---

3   In Butterfield's *History and Human Relations*. London, 1931, pp. 101-130.

The War—My Myth or Yours?

Yankee girl's exclamation on seeing Lee passing through Pennsylvania: "I wish he was ours!") To truly understand a myth, you must investigate the human purposes it serves. The "Lost Cause Myth" is international and enduring, which is why Confederate battle flags appeared all over occupied Europe during the fall of the Soviet Empire. It must serve some purposes beyond use as a rationalization by long dead Confederates for their sins and errors—even if one accepts that "the purpose of the legend was to hide the Southerners' tragic and self-destructive mistake." (A mind-reading insight which I reject since in a lifetime of research I am yet to find a single Confederate who thought he had been mistaken, as opposed to being regretful at having lost.)

Gallagher and Nolan mightily lament but seem to have no adequate explanation as to why the "Lost Cause" shows such vitality. A serious investigation might look into why the North (and the rest of the world) has had such a voracious appetite for "Lost Cause mythology." Is it possible that the myth owes much of its creation and force to Northern psychological needs instead of being just a Southern self-deception? (Ah, but we have already proved that all such delusions are traceable to the South alone.) But why did such mythologizing Southerners as Thomas Nelson Page, Margaret Mitchell, and D.W. Griffith have such impact on mostly Northern audiences? There is a question for fruitful research!

But, alas, in spite of Nolan's having established for all time the true and undisputed understanding of the War, the world finds itself enveloped and blinded in the smoke of the Lost Cause mythology. (Like those poor dupes of Southern apologetics, Churchill and Eisenhower, visiting with Douglas Southall Freeman to be misinformed and deceived?) But don't effective myths have to have some real if not exact relationship to fact? Gallagher in his essay laments that Lee, and even his horse, have received frequent and favorable attention from creative writers (not all of them Southern by any means), while "No successful novels [or movies] have been built primarily around Grant, his campaigns, or the armies he led."

Could there maybe be some reason for this besides Jubal Early's obscurely published pro-Lee writings of more than a century ago? Heaven forbid, but could it be that there is something to the idea of Lee as a Christian gentleman, that there is something intrinsically attractive in the man? To put it another way, could any writer plausibly imagine Lee using his men as cannon fodder as Grant did in the Wilderness, or Lee conducting the most corrupt presidential administration in American history? Or Grant kneeling to pray for guidance? If I had to pick a starting point of the mythology of celebrating Lee as a great American hero, I would not choose Early. I would select the speech made in 1907 by the great Lost Cause dupe and former Union officer from Massachusetts, Charles Francis Adams, Jr., "Lee's Centennial."[4]

Nolan presents little evidence, which is understandable since his piece, whether admitted or not, is not an historical article but a polemical essay (just like the one you are reading). However, it would be nice if he showed a trace of occasionally having weighed some evidence. Instead, he relies on argument from authority, supplemented occasionally by ad hominem. Abraham Lincoln said that secession was a conspiracy of lawbreakers and not the will of the people. Question settled. Discussion over. And since he is backed by the authority of "almost all [professional] historians" in the unquestioned starting-point that Confederates were always evilly motivated and dishonest, our author is justified, is even entitled to the name of a perceptive historian, in finding whatever hidden meaning he wishes behind their deceptive words.

In this Nolan is working safely within the commonplaces of a contemporary unexamined consensus that approaches the rigor of a party line. Perhaps he cannot be blamed too much. Some historians think the North was bad, too, but all historians are today required to "know" that the South is bad. That is his real "authority." But unlike most of his peers, Nolan has not learned the uses of subtlety and apparent balance. He admits Northern racism, as he can hardly avoid in the state of today's literature, but minimizes its importance in the same way that Confederate apologists minimize slavery. His essay literally reeks with assumptions of intellectual and moral superiority and dismissive contempt for those fellow citizens who disagree with his characterization of the most important period of American history. The ideal of judicious weighing of evidence and balance in presentation before passing sentence never makes its appearance.

Let us look into some of the points asserted in "The Anatomy of the Myth," as presented in the author's division of his subject matter. This is not easy to do since the argument is repetitive and not very well organized, though Nolan evidently believes that he has conclusively vanquished into oblivion every claim ever offered in opposition to the Unionist Southern-devil interpretation of the War.

---

4   Adams gave this talk a number of times in North and South, including Boston and Charleston.

The War—My Myth or Yours?

"*The Lost Cause as Advocacy.*" Southern writers before, during, and after the War had the effrontery to actually defend themselves against the accusations of their enemies and present their cause in a favorable light. Nolan seems to find something surprising and conspiratorial, even diabolical, about this. I wish Gallagher and Nolan would research a little into the extravagant glorification of the Union cause that dominated American discourse for decades after the War and involved, among other things, the virtual (and blasphemous) deification of Lincoln. That mythology persists powerfully to this day. It is arguably just as unfactual as "the Lost Cause" and the source of far more evil consequences. A little admiration for Lee and the boys in gray by their descendants and others is harmless in comparison with a self-righteous stamping-out-the-grapes-of-wrath mentality. Robert Penn Warren in a little book about the legacy of the Civil War at the time of the bicentennial chided the South for using its defeat as an excuse to do nothing about its problems. He also warned the rest of America about its own problematic legacy, a "Treasury of Virtue," which encouraged a thoughtless presumption of unblemished righteousness as the basis for our country's actions in the world.

Establishing his discussion to describe and refute "*The Claims of the Legend,*" Nolan presents various "false" ideas sustaining the "Lost Cause myth." It would be child's play to compile volumes and volumes of evidence qualifying and contradicting his sweeping and rather imperial assertions. I offer only a few examples here.

"*Slavery Was Not the Sectional Issue.*" According to Nolan, Confederates dishonestly presented issues other than slavery as the real cause of the War—putting forth such trivial and imaginary factors as economic and cultural conflict instead. A single-issue treatment of the causes of any other great war in history, like Nolan's of the Civil War, would be laughed out of school. One of the greatest of American historians, Charles A. Beard, thought economics played the major part. But in Nolan's universe Unionists are always governed by the highest motives—they are never moved like other human beings by self-interest, vanity, a lust for domination, opportunism, and just plain old misapprehension and fecklessness. Apparently the long-standing economic conflict of the sections was insignificant.

As long as one views the conflict entirely through Nolan's eyes, it is easy to dismiss all considerations except slavery. I wish Mr. Nolan would do a little research into the North. He might begin to notice the thirty years Cold War against the South that preceded secession. Powerful elements of the North had an aggressive and innovative economic and cultural agenda that had something to do with the accumulation of irritations among Southerners. Northerners were not all just pious patriots. He could start with the works of Ernest Lee Tuveson, Anne Norton, Richard F. Bensel, Harlow W. Sheidley, Joan Pope Melish, and Susan-Mary Grant on the antebellum North. Could there be some mitigating factor in Southern behavior that the devil-theory can explain only as a product of an intrinsically evil Southern character? Surely Nolan is the only historian who has failed to notice that one result of the War was the institutionalization of a cozy relationship between the federal government and Big Business/Big Banking that persists to this day?

Further, Nolan's argument fails to distinguish between the immediate cause of a war and the underlying causes; or between the causes of a war and the reason men fight and continue to fight a war. It is common to claim, with little evidence, that the white supremacist and agnostic Lincoln "evolved" during the War into an egalitarian and a Christian. Can't Southerners evolve, too, under conditions that were far more stressful for them per capita than for Northerners? If the North developed a mission for emancipation as it went, could not the War in its course come to mean something else to Confederates than the reasons for secession mentioned in the South Carolina justification? Is it even possible that most Confederates in the end came to put the objective of independence ahead of that of preserving slavery? (Many said so.)

The preservation of slavery, or more precisely the protection of slavery from outside interference that was considered irresponsible and self-interested, was the immediate cause of the first secession. However, in what sense was slavery the cause of the federal government's military suppression of the elected governments of the Southern states? That was what constituted the War. The War was formally declared not to be against slavery but to enforce the power of the "United States." If irritation over the slavery issue caused the secession of the first seven states, what caused that of those who followed after Fort Sumter and the enthusiastic enlistment of most opponents of secession into the cause of independence? Lincoln's intent to subdue states by military force, which to Southerners, and to a great many more Northerners than is usually admitted, involved a false and revolutionary interpretation of the Union. How can the War be only about slavery when the War consists of the federal government "preserving the Union," and there is voluminous evidence that Northerners who were making war did not consider emancipation as a primary goal or a goal at all.

Slavery under several headings forms a large part of Nolan's case. Slavery was wrong and the South would not give it up. True, but that was not the issue. The issue, as Jefferson (and Lincoln, too) realized, was how to go about getting rid of slavery. This everyone believed would be an immense and dangerous undertaking. Abolitionists did not contribute to this practical undertaking, but contented themselves with the most extreme perfervid abuse of Southerners. Lincoln had no proposal except colonization and blocking of slavery from the territories. The first was impractical and the second was driven more by economic, racist, and political power objectives than by a very hard to find Northern benevolence toward African Americans.

I tend to agree with Nolan in dismissing historians who came to the too-easy conclusion that slavery was moribund and would have easily and naturally ended. But we have the authority of no less a figure than Daniel Webster, who declared so in 1850, that it was the abolitionists who were responsible for retarding and halting the process of emancipation. However, since I am inclined to believe that Southerners of the Civil War era did not lie every time they opened their mouths or put pen to paper and that they were basically a Christian people of good will, much evidence suggests to me that the peculiar institution had evolved and was evolving in the South. It is even possible that such evolution could have had results more beneficial all around than what actually happened as a by-product of a war of conquest. And certainly, the Unionist devil theory fails to convince in its assumptions about "dying to set men free." The North's greatest thinker, Emerson, said he was less concerned about the welfare of a thousand black people than he was about one white man corrupted by slavery.

"*The Nationalist/Cultural Difference.*" Cultural differences as a cause of conflict Nolan dismisses as "fiction." Of course, "nationalism" and "culture" are both rather slippery and elastic terms, but the argument seems to be that cultural differences between the sections were imaginary or insignificant and Southern pretensions to cultural distinction phony. But, alas, from before the Revolution up to the present day, Americans North and South have been remarking upon cultural differences that were significant to them. There were many facets to this, but the predominant aspect was the insistence of New Englanders on cultural stereotypes that portrayed themselves as the true Americans and Southerners as different, evil, and bad Americans. This latter stereotype may have sometimes ascribed slavery to be the cause of the differentness, but in fact it preceded the slavery conflict, beginning in early colonial times, and covered every element of Southern life that differed from the Northern ideal (myth?). (There has always been a countercurrent of Northerners and foreigners who found that the South was different—and better.) Why does every respectable university in the world today offer Southern Studies courses if it is all a "fiction"? For that matter, why do even Confederacy-bashing historians seem mostly to want to live in the South?

Volumes of evidence could be collected about the reality of cultural conflict, but perhaps it is enough to point out that many Northerners considered the cultural differentness of the South to be the cause and justification of the War. Your Honor, may the defense submit as its Exhibit No. 1, Mr. Alan Nolan, a historian who asserts it to be an undisputed fact that the North was democratic and progressive and the South was possessed of a guilty, destructive, un-American culture. A number of foreign visitors declared before the War that the North and South were essentially two different countries. They are still doing so.

For Nolan, Southerners do not deserve any cultural identity of their own; they are only an inferior and defective version of himself. (Ideologies don't allow much notice for music, literature, attitudes, manners, and other aspects of culture that distinguish peoples.) Could there be something to this cultural conflict, after all? Our author, perhaps in this exemplary of a "Northern" way of thinking, views the War as the triumph of a righteous agenda that is a bit abstract and self-justifying. Southerners tend to take history more personally, to remember what great-granddaddy did and why he did it.

Could that be a cultural difference? If so, it might help explain the strange vitality of "the Lost Cause Myth." Could the same cultural variation be at work in the contrast between Sherman's "War is Hell," and Forrest's "War means fighting and fighting means killing"? Abstraction versus personalism? Sherman, it appears, was not responsible for the devastation of Georgia and Carolina. All that burning and looting was caused by a terrible impersonal force called "War." Likewise, according to Lincoln, "the war came." Apparently his actions had nothing to do with it. For Forrest, no folderol. If you are going to do war you have to own up to reality and face the personal responsibility of killing.

The United States always seems to have a need to rationalize acts of war in terms of a noble crusade like "saving the world for democracy," in the process demonizing the enemy. I bet my "Forget Hell" poster against Nolan's framed portrait of John Brown that an opinion survey of the many Southern-born fighting men in the forces today (and the Southern public) would find a lot less of that and more of a justification of war in terms of self-respect requiring response to a threatener. A high sounding motive is not required.[5]

"*The Idealized Homefront.*" Nolan has discovered that there were divisions and conflicts within the Confederacy, which he believes Lost Causers are guilty of covering up, and therefore the notion of the Southern people united in their cause is another one of those Lost Cause fictions. Well, yes, there are always divisions in a society subject to stress as extreme as that endured by the Southern people during the Civil War. But the obviously significant larger point is that there was so relatively little internal disaffection from the Confederate cause (as opposed to opposition to particular government measures). Despite the penchant of feminist historians to make every Confederate woman's private complaint about hardship into evidence of an underground rebellion. With their main cities taken, much of their country overrun and pillaged, sacrifice and hardship everywhere, Confederates still fought and remained hopeful until a fourth of their men were dead, a sacrifice never remotely approached by any other group of Americans. The only authority that really needs to be cited here is *The Confederate War*, a recent book by Professor Gary Gallagher, who has apparently since gone into rehab and become a recovering Lost Causer. And there is a false implicit assumption that every Southerner who did not like secession, slavery, or the War therefore must have liked Lincoln and the Union cause.

Nolan is able to make much of internal divisions in the Confederacy by wrongly assuming a kind of righteous unity among the people of "the United States," like that after Pearl Harbor. If the truth is known, and it is one of the great untold stories of American history, support for the Northern cause was not nearly as solid as claimed. (Just ask Governor Seymour of New York and the federal agents who were busy arresting dissenters.) Even though most of the population suffered little stress compared to the lot of the South. In retrospect it was easy to ignore the role played by Unionist military forces in the border states and military forces and vigilantes in the Northern states in putting down opposition to the government (like the New York City "draft riots," which were not

---

5 In Ridley Scott's recent powerful film *Black Hawk Down*, there is a conversation along these lines between a Northern and Southern soldier. The Southerner rather has the better of the argument.

riots but a mini-rebellion against the Lincoln administration. And, yes, Mr. Nolan, the Union side had vigilantes.) Lincoln and the Republicans themselves realized how uncertain their support was, which is why they suppressed dissent, managed elections with the army, made massive use of patronage, recruited abroad, and spent immense sums on enlistment bounties.

What would have been the morale of the North if it had suffered a comparable extent of occupation, devastation, and death as the South had by 1863, instead of enjoying a quiet and prosperous home front? Imagine New York (New Orleans) and Chicago (Memphis and Nashville) occupied, Pennsylvania and Ohio (Virginia and Tennessee) overrun and ravaged, the capital besieged, privation the order of the day everywhere, nearly the whole male citizenry under arms. Would the population still be determined to prosecute war to the last extremity?

"The Idealized Confederate Soldier." The Confederate Army had deserters our writer discovered. Therefore, the widespread image of the heroic Confederate soldier is all hogwash. All the foreign writers who have considered the Army of Northern Virginia one of the finest military forces in history are just another bunch of Lost Cause dupes. But consider: Northern armies were normally well-supplied (except for the massive corruption among Lincoln appointees and contractors) and got perhaps two hundred thousand recruits from abroad. Man per man, the average Confederate soldier made more hard marches, suffered more privations, risked his life more frequently, was wounded more times, and died more often than the average Union soldier. Out-numbered and out-supplied, Confederate leaders had to show more skill and audacity and take more risks. This is all the "myth" ever contended, and it is true. No brag, just fact, as Walter Brennan used to say. One could easily make up a whole volume of tributes to Confederate heroism made by combat-veteran Northern soldiers during and after the War! And witting and unwitting tributes by admiring or frustrated Northern commanders to the accomplishments of Confederates with inferior forces.

Repeating a claim that goes back at least to the romantic Union partisan Fletcher Pratt, Nolan makes much of the highly dubious notion that Confederates were not usually outnumbered in combat. Perhaps so, but the legend of Confederate valor rests largely upon the skill and effort required to achieve that equality at contact when there were usually two or more additional large federal armies in the same theatre to be out-maneuvered. Nolan also makes a lot of a conclusion that Confederates never lost a battle through lack of supply as disproving the Southern belief that Confederates were not outfought but overwhelmed. If Confederate armies did not suffer from lack of supply (which is questionable) why not acknowledge the tremendous skill and dedication in the "backward South" that went into making that so?

The fact is, there is such a thing as a dauntless spirit, admirable to most people at all times, though perhaps invisible to those who are busy stamping out the grapes of wrath. Somewhere in his works, that noted Southern apologist Bruce Catton has a moving tribute to the particular intangible but real spirit of the Confederate soldier. Admiration for a brave underdog is, or used to be, a great American quality. That is why a normal little boy, or a re-enactor will usually pick the gray cap over the blue when given a choice. I suspect, also, that Lost Cause dupes understand, unlike current historians, that the Confederate Army was not just another military machine, but a true manifestation of a people.

Nolan cannot understand why Bedford Forrest is considered a hero by many: "To a thoughtful and humane person, he seems an anomalous hero." To those who think of heroes in terms of politicians, athletes and movie stars, Forrest certainly won't qualify. But to those who think in terms of Western Civilization, the definition of a hero is one who fights with great skill and courage in defense of his people against long odds: the 300 Spartans at Thermopylae, Hector before Troy, Horatius at the bridge, Roland at Roncesvalles. In that light, it is hard to find a better qualified hero than Forrest.

"*The Lawfulness of Secession.*" The paragraph Nolan devotes to secession attempts to pre-empt the very question that was at issue. One could easily fill ten volumes with evidence supporting the lawfulness of secession, from the reservation of sovereignty made by the New York ratifying convention and the centralist Alexander Hamilton's assurance in *The Federalist* that the U.S. government could never have the right or ability to coerce a state; through the words of Jefferson, Madison, Tocqueville, Lord Acton, and countless others; right down to the statement in 1861 by the soon-to-be elected Governor of the largest Northern state that secession, though regrettable, was lawful (and understandable).[6] The Illinois state motto, adopted 1818, begins with "State Sovereignty," followed by "National Union.")

But the nub of the argument for coercion of the seceding states, then and now, was the need to preserve the territorial integrity of the

---

6   Speech of January 31, 1861, to the New York Democratic Convention, in Thomas S. Cook and Thomas S. Knox, eds., *Public Record of Horatio Seymour*. (New York, 1868).

United States and to preserve government of, by, and for the people. To make war to preserve the United States as one territory (and, incidentally, one market) is nationalism, a very powerful force in the modern world, which is supported by both practical interest and sentiment. The nation-state is a territorial monopoly of force and exploitation. It has no necessary connection with democratic government or constitutionalism, however. In what sense, really, did secession threaten to "destroy the United States" or democratic government. Nolan rather assumes that the federal government and the 39 percent of the people who voted for Lincoln are "the United States" and may decide who counts and who doesn't when it comes to "the consent of the governed." As H.L. Mencken wrote, the Gettysburg address is beautiful, but it is poetry, not truth, because it reverses the realities as to who was fighting for and who was fighting against self-government at Gettysburg.[7]

A questioning of the soundness of Lincoln's appeal to government of, by, and for the people can only be answered by the purely subjective conspiracy-theory claim that the Confederate government was not really the voice of its people, but only a "combination" of lawbreakers who made the Southern people deluded pawns. If so, the pawns put on a damn good performance of acting like men who believed they were fighting the invaders of their country and the enemies of their freedom. (Of course, all true historians, and all good people too, already know that you can't believe a thing those slave-owning traitors said. Those poor Southern dupes only imagined the invaders they were fighting and that their liberties suffered from their being Reconstructed.)

If Nolan would set aside Lincoln's prettier orations and take a look at evidence of what Northern prosecutors of the War were actually saying among themselves and in public, he will find a strong emphasis on enforcing obedience to government, i.e. to those who control the government, and much less emphasis on celebrating democracy and the consent of the governed. A desire for authority and order and sometimes a naked lust for domination is evident. Something that foreign observers noted and that perhaps a few contemporary historians are beginning to notice.

Secessionists had to win the support of their fellow citizens on the open hustings. Nolan seems to have completely forgotten what Progressive historians knew well—that there were special interests and powerful minorities in the North that had more than a democratic influence on the conduct of the Union's war. The difference being that the

---

7 "Abraham Lincoln," *The Vintage Mencken* (New York: Vintage Books, 1958), 77-80.

influence of the bankers and industrialists was somewhat clandestine and their interests more remote from those of the average Northern citizen than the interests of the slaveholding and non-slave-holding Southern farmers were from each other. There is heavy evidence, indeed, that Northerners at first widely viewed secession with a "let the erring sisters go in peace" attitude. The tone changed and hardened when influential men began to point out the loss of economic benefits that the North would suffer if an independent South was allowed to establish free trade. Is it possible that Northern people were misled by their leaders into sacrifices for hidden unworthy motives? ("A rich man's war and a poor man's fight"?) But, of course, we have already been assured by the author under consideration of the "undisputed" fact that economic interests had nothing to do with the Civil War, unlike every other war in history.

Nolan is entitled to his opinion like everybody else, but could we not expect from a historian just a little more nuance about the effects of the War on democratic government—say some notice of the expansion of Presidential power and the establishment of national mercantilism that accompanied the Union victory? Not to mention that today, along with the disintegration of the Soviet Union and the relentless absorption of power by the U.S. government, many thoughtful people around the world have begun to question the necessity, utility, and sacredness of the centralized state, even to reflect that a right of secession might be a better guardian of democracy than the presumed benevolence of a centralized government.

"*The Saints Go Marching In.*" Nolan is greatly offended that many people think of Lee and Jackson as Christians. (Note that he uses for his title a refrain that smears Confederates with a religious militance which is more in a Northern style. Marching secular saints are definitely not a Southern thing. Has he never heard "Dixie" and "The Battle Hymn of the Republic"?) Lee was "hateful and bitter" toward the North. I wonder why? In Nolan's book Stonewall Jackson was "like Oliver Cromwell among the Irish, killing people zestfully for the glory of God." This historian is really reaching anywhere for mud to sling. True, Jackson was a Presbyterian and true he advocated relentless warfare against the invading army. But surely the true analogy to Cromwell in Ireland, in both spirit and fact, is not Stonewall but Sherman in Carolina? Nobody on either side ever doubted that, like it or not, it was Northerners, not Southerners who were the Puritan side of that conflict. But I must tell Mr. Nolan that there are in the civilized world today thousands of people who have carefully and seriously studied these things and have found Lee and Jackson to be truly inspiring examples of Christian faith in trying conditions.

It was not the Confederacy that had a General Hooker! Mr. Nolan's eagerness to marshal every scrap of anti-South rhetoric he can find reminds me of the professor I recently stumbled across on the net. This thoughtful intellectual was complaining that the "Southern Gun Culture" is polluting America with violence. Timothy McVeigh? Ted Bundy? The Unabomber? Columbine shooters?

Yet our author is not entirely without balance—sort of: "It is not my intent in any way to disparage the common soldier of the Confederacy. In many ways he was the principal victim of the Lost Cause myth." How can the Confederate soldier be "victimized" by a flattering myth? As a descendant of common soldiers of the Confederacy on both sides, I am sure I speak for us all in affirming that we can do without this condescending sympathy. Southerners still know an insult when they see one.

"*The Yankee Soldier.*" Our author regrets that in *Gone With The Wind* and other expressions of popular culture we sometimes see portrayals of mean and predatory Union soldiers, "bad people who were gratuitously upsetting the genteel and benign Southern culture." (Actually, in recent years there have been pervasive and untruthful portrayals of Confederates as the bad guys, but never mind.) I don't think that upsetting genteel culture is exactly what the victims of burned houses and empty larders were complaining about. In fact, "the Lost Cause myth" never suggested that all Yankees were like that. Lost Cause writings are full of tributes to brave and honorable Union soldiers, a sentiment that was reciprocated by those Union soldiers who actually were brave and honorable.

For Nolan, and he is unfortunately very typical of today's writers in this, all that needs be said about atrocities in the Civil War is that there were atrocities on both sides, as in any war. Discussion closed. But wait a minute. Is there really a moral equivalence between Stonewall Jackson's advocacy of ruthless and relentless warfare against invading soldiers (which was never really implemented) and the Union's fully implemented and official policy of systematic terror and devastation against civilians to facilitate their conquest? I think not, and I am in the good company of a lot of disinterested observers of the time and later.

Making an amateur mathematical projection from my own acquaintances, there are still today in the South hundreds of thousands of people who remember what was done to their own families—houses burned, churches desecrated or torn down, crops and livestock gratuitously destroyed, 12 and 13 year old boys and black men shot and hanged, women (including African-American women) molested, such dangerous war materials as jewelry, silver, furniture, pianos, silks and satins, family Bibles, and paintings hauled away. As I said before, Southerners tend to take history somewhat personally. After all, it's our history we are talking about here.

I find it hard to believe that anyone can seriously assert the equivalence of atrocities on both sides. It is easy to overlook other peoples' suffering, but morally perilous. One is reminded of those U.S. leaders who speak with callous casualness about the incineration of innocent women and children as "collateral damage." Nolan's most salient proof of atrocity by Confederates is the claim that Lee's army captured black people (number unspecified) in Pennsylvania and returned them to slavery. Alas, real life and real people are a lot more messy and complicated than the "undisputed truth" of history. A forthcoming book by a respected authority will document the story of thousands of black men who willingly went with Lee's army to Pennsylvania *and back*. Colonel Fremantle saw one of them marching a Yankee prisoner along.

"Having swept away the counterfactual Myth of the Lost Cause," our author modestly proclaims, "a historian may briefly state the history of the Civil War as follows." How's that for careful scholarship? Many facets of Nolan's what follows—Reconstruction, Fort Sumter, and others I have not even touched upon. But I return to my earlier question. How did "the Myth of the Lost Cause" come to be and what purposes has it served in the life of the American people?

Nolan offers as an explanation of the Lost Cause mythology an analogy that is his lowest blow and least defensible assertion of all. Confederates who thought they were overwhelmed rather than fairly defeated, he thinks, were like the Germans who excused their loss of World War I because of being "stabbed in the back." Hinting at a Nazi connection is nearly always a sign of a weak case and a shifty argument, and we must count Nolan as among those historians who seem to think that it is a shocking manifestation of incipient fascism when the Museum of the Confederacy actually displays a Confederate flag. The two cases are not at all alike. Germans used the excuse to launch a war of conquest of other lands and peoples. The Southern idea served only what seemed then to be the good purpose of making Southerners feel more at home in and more loyal to the United States. If there is any Nazi analogy to be found in the Civil War, it is the vainglorious exultation in conquest displayed by many on the victorious side. Perhaps it is worth considering what role Northerners played in creating the "Lost Cause Myth" and what psychological function it served for them: reassurance that Southerners who had scared them badly were no longer a threat to their power and privilege and amour propre?

Mr. Nolan, I think, knows not enough about post-Reconstruction America. The "Lost Cause mythology" was but a part of an understanding reached by most Americans around the end of the 19th century. (I am aware this agreement excluded African-Americans, but that is another story. There was little North/South difference of opinion on that.) The understanding, which was deemed essential to the strength of the country, went something like this: The Civil War had been a terrible ordeal for Americans. But perhaps it had been the crucible necessary to create a new, strong nation out of the original Union. At any rate, most people on both sides were satisfied that in the end America was held together. Nearly all Southerners sincerely accepted this. They would ever after be staunch supporters of the United States, as they have proved many times over ever since in countless ways, including their persistent over-representation in the combat arms of the national forces. All they asked in return was an acknowledgment that, if they had been wrong in the pursuit of independence, they had not been dishonorable and that they had fought a good fight that could be appreciated as a part of the pride of all Americans. Until rather recently that little has been granted, but "America" is now in the process of reneging on its part of the bargain.

Ambrose Bierce, who saw as much combat as any Union soldier and was not noted as a sentimentalist or superficial observer, honored the bargain when he wrote that Confederates had been "honest and courageous foemen" who represented "the dignity and infinite pathos of the Lost Cause." Americans who were willing to fight when they believed their liberties were threatened should always be honored, said Bierce. Replying to a Bloody Shirt orator who wanted to suppress the decoration of Confederate graves, Bierce wrote:

> The brave respect the brave. The brave
> Respect the dead; but you—you draw
> That ancient blade, the ass's jaw,
> And shake it o'er a hero's grave.

And surely one of the finest statements in the history of the American people is Union hero Joshua Chamberlain on the surrender at Appomattox:

> [There stood] before us in proud humiliation...the embodiment of manhood, men whom neither toils and sufferings, nor the fact of death, nor disaster, nor hopelessness could bend from their resolve.... [They were] thin, worn, and famished, but erect, and with eyes looking level into ours....[Shared memories] bound us together as no other bond.[8]

"Fact" is, that mutual respect flourished quite well for a long time until it was destroyed by history being put to the uses of new political agendas. Any reader of Professor Gallagher's first book, on General Ramseur, CSA, who measured it by Nolan's yardstick, would have to judge it to be an example of Lost Cause Mythology. It is not; it is only a good piece of historical writing within the old consensus.

A further irony is the use of the well-known romantic painting of Lee and Jackson together on horseback for the dust jacket of this latest book. As a Confederate icon, it is an appropriate illustration, of course, of the theme of the book. (This picture, I am told, was selected by that Lost Cause dupe Harry Truman for the lobby of his Presidential Library.) I will wager that the Lost Cause icon on the cover will sell more books than the "Lost Cause" critique inside. It won't be the first time that bashers of Confederate heroes have piggybacked upon their still-living glory. (2002)

---

8   Chamberlain, *The Passing of the Armies...* (New York, 1915), 248ff.

General Richard Taylor

Foreword for a new edition of *Destruction and Reconstruction: Personal Experiences of the Late War*, by Richard Taylor, Nashville, Tennessee: J.S. Sanders, 1998, 279 pages.

The War Between the States occurred on a vast scale, and no other period of American history is so full of dramatic events, remarkable personalities, and revolutionary changes. The body of literature produced by participants in the War is immense. There are hundreds of memoirs by generals, lesser officers, privates, politicians, and civilians. Thousands of observers and participants, even if they did not write books, left published record of their experiences in pamphlets and newspaper and magazine articles—the stuff of memories and postwar controversy and raw material for historians.

Of all Confederate memoirs—I cannot speak for the Union—Richard Taylor's *Destruction and Reconstruction: Personal Experiences of the Late War* is the best, and for many reasons. The author held a command, at various times, in all three main theaters of the War—Virginia, the Tennessee Valley, and the Trans-Mississippi. This, with his social prominence—he was the son of President Zachary Taylor and the brother-in-law of Jefferson Davis—gave him an unexampled opportunity to serve in a number of the great battles and to know personally many of the most important players on both sides. As Taylor himself put it, he had followed the Confederacy from cradle to hearse.

Further, unlike many generals in their postwar memoirs, he had no personal axe to grind. His military career had been as successful as was possible under the circumstances—there were no big losses or mistakes to explain away. While he knew most of the major political actors on both sides and was on hand for many political events, he regarded himself always as a soldier serving his people, and he had no political ambitions to advance.

But all these advantages would have counted for little if Taylor had not been, as Douglas Southall Freeman wrote: "the one Confederate general who possessed literary art that approached the first rank." Taylor is a very good writer. The account of his experiences is vivid and unflagging. We always have sufficient detail to understand without ever losing the movement of the narrative. His asides are always relevant and entertaining. (See, for instance, the passage on the mint julep on page 78 or his call on the ladies to have correct notions of male character on page 68.) His characterizations of people he met are concise, telling, balanced. "No firmer, more accurate pictures are to be found in Confederate literature than those Taylor penned," wrote Freeman.

For instance, he describes the ill-starred Braxton Bragg thus:

> Possessing experience in and talent for war, he was the most laborious of commanders, devoting every moment to the discharge of his duties. As a disciplinarian he far surpassed any of the senior Confederate generals; but his method and manner were harsh, and he could have won the affections of his troops only by leading them to victory. He furnished a striking illustration of the necessity of a healthy body for a sound intellect.

It would be impossible to say more that was true, fair, and perceptive in so short a compass. His many vivid encounters with Stonewall Jackson are memorable, as when Taylor forgot himself and cursed his men into steadiness under fire. Jackson, who had already praised Taylor for his marching, laid his hand gently on his shoulder and said, "I am afraid you are a wicked fellow." Then rode away and left Taylor to his part of the battle.

So good and convincing are Taylor's portraits of the leaders of the Confederacy that they have become almost standards and truisms, even among those who do not know where they originated. But Taylor was more than just a good writer, able to describe character and retell his experiences in good form. Even more important, he had a far-ranging, Olympian mind, able to see the greater pattern of events, the deeper meaning of the revolutionary changes that overtook American society in his time. For that reason, his is one of the most important statements of the Southern understanding of the War, and truly a Southern classic.

Richard Taylor states several times in his memoir that Louisiana was his native state. That is substantially but not literally true. He was actually born on January 27, 1826, at an old family plantation near Louisville, Kentucky, but the family had already settled in Louisiana and soon returned there. He was named for a grandfather who had been an officer of Virginia Continentals in the Revolution. His father, then Colonel Zachary Taylor, one of the ranking officers of the small United States Army, was connected to a vast and prominent Virginia-Kentucky cousinage, and his mother was similarly connected in Maryland. When he was nine, his older sister married a young officer, Jefferson Davis, though she died tragically shortly after.

By the time of his graduation from Yale in 1845, Richard Taylor was widely traveled and acquainted. Shortly after, he spent some time with his father at army headquarters in Mexico, his nearest thing to actual military experience before the Civil War. His father's year as President broadened still further Taylor's acquaintance at the highest levels of American society, North and South.

The 1850s, Taylor spent as a prosperous sugar planter in St. Charles Parish, Louisiana. He married into a prominent Creole family, served in the state legislature, and attended several national political conventions as a delegate. But his greatest interest seems to have been his vast library, which he knew well. His memoir reveals a mind well-stocked with literature and history and able to apply its learning appositely. No one who met Taylor had any doubt of his cultivation, power, and distinction. The subtitle of a recent, fairly good, biography by T. Michael Parrish, *Richard Taylor: Soldier Prince of Dixie* (1992), is just.

Taylor's inheritance, like R.E. Lee's, was the Virginia Federalist-Whig tradition of Washington and Marshall. In Southern terms he was a conservative Unionist, without enthusiasm either for state rights or for radical action. All his instincts were conservative and aristocratic, in the best sense. This gave him a certain detachment from the disaster that overcame the United States under the direction of politicians claiming to serve the people. "Vox populi, vox diaboli," he remarks.

Throughout the 1850s his weight was on the side of moderation. He looked on the breakup of the Democratic party at Charleston in 1860, where he was a delegate, with regret. But like most men of his orientation, he never doubted that the cause of the South was right, and by 1861 was with the majority of his state for secession. Thereafter he regarded himself as a soldier bound to duty and swept up in events that might be understood but not controlled. These events "followed with bewildering rapidity," he writes, "and the human agencies concerned seemed as unconscious as scene-shifters in some awful tragedy."

Taylor's accomplishments as soldier are all the more remarkable when we consider that he did not expect success for his cause; he suffered several times from severe illness during the War; his plantation was gratuitously plundered, leaving many of his slaves to starve, and then confiscated; his wife was reduced to the status of refugee; and two of his four children died in his absence.

The War—My Myth or Yours?

Taylor made no claim to military genius: "Genius is God-given but men are responsible for their acts." We see how he shouldered that responsibility, putting to use all his prewar study, learning as he went, and exercising great care and industry, to make himself into a good commander. Always performing his immediate duty, he never lost sight of the big picture, even where he was not involved. He understood perfectly, for instance, the ill feeling between President Davis and General Joseph E. Johnston, how it arose, and what it cost the Confederacy. His judgment on all the larger military issues is simple and sound.

By the autumn of 1861 Taylor was a brigadier general. He commanded what became the notable Louisiana brigade of the Army of Northern Virginia. It took a conspicuous part in Jackson's Valley campaign. Taylor's account of these events, and of the leading personalities—Jackson, Ewell, Ashby, and many others—is superb. He also took a part, though a lesser one, in the Seven Days.

In July 1862 he was promoted to major general and assigned to command in Louisiana west of the Mississippi. He hoped, at the least, to restore morale and contain the federal invasion of the state, at best to relieve Vicksburg and recapture New Orleans. Chapters VII through XI recount two years' experiences in this lesser known quarter of the War.

It was here that Taylor showed his real worth. He restored morale among a depressed civilian population, created war production, armed and organized troops, and with always inferior forces began to inflict checks and losses on the enemy. The culminating achievement was his victory in the Red River campaign in the spring of 1864, aided by such sterling soldiers as the Creole aristocrat, General Alexander Mouton and the Texas frontiersman, General Tom Green.

The Federals sent a large and well-equipped expedition under the political general Banks up the Red River, the primary purposes being to steal cotton and terrorize civilians, as Ludwell H. Johnson has shown in his excellent history of the campaign. Taylor was outnumbered about seven to one, not even counting the large Federal fleet of armored and heavily armed gunboats. With a few thousand Creoles and Texans, he sent Banks running back to New Orleans.

This Yankee debacle was parodied in one of those rollicking high-spirited Confederate songs that have been collected by Bobby Horton ("Songs of the CSA," Vol. 2). A disappointed Yankee speculator sings to the tune of "When Johnny Comes Marching Home":

> We all went down to New Orleans for bales. For bales!
> To get a seat behind the scenes. For bales! For bales!

> We thought when we got in the ring. For bales! For bales!
> It would be a dead sure thing. For bales! For bales!
> The ring went up Red River with bagging and rope
> Hoping to make a pile of soap. For bales! For bales!
> But Taylor and Smith with ragged ranks
> Burned up the cotton and whipped ole Banks.
> Our ring came back and cursed and swore.
> We got no cotton at Grand Ecore.
> So let us all give thanks
> For the victory gained by General Banks.
> For bales! For bales!

Taylor always believed, and with grim sarcasm argues, that he was prevented from further gains for the Confederate cause by the obstinate caution and blindness of his superior, General Edmund Kirby Smith, commander of the Trans-Mississippi Department. Taylor often has scornful (though always pointed and persuasive) things to say about various leaders on the Northern side. But his greatest scorn is for those Confederates who proved obstructive or gave less than their best, like Kirby Smith and Vice-President Stephens.

Finding further service under Smith useless and intolerable, Taylor requested relief. He was promoted to lieutenant general in August 1864, and assigned to command in Alabama, Mississippi, and east Louisiana. Of the twenty-five highest officers of the Confederacy (full generals and lieutenant generals) Taylor was one of only three who had not been a professional soldier.

The others were Wade Hampton and Bedford Forrest. In his new command Taylor got to know Forrest, for whom he had the greatest respect and whom he describes memorably (pages 203-205). Forrest returned the respect and is reported to have said of Taylor: "He's the biggest man in the lot. If we'd had more like him, we would have licked the Yankees long ago."

Taylor briefly in early 1865 commanded what was left of the Army of Tennessee after Hood had wrecked it at Franklin and Nashville, and in the closing weeks of the War, again described vividly, operated with dwindling hopes and resources in Alabama. He surrendered the last Confederate force east of the Mississippi to the Federal General Canby, the civil authority of the Confederacy having ceased to exist. Or as he puts it: "On the 8th of May 1865, at Citronelle, forty miles north of Mobile, I delivered the epilogue of the great drama in which I had played a humble part."

The War—My Myth or Yours?

Taylor's account of the surrender negotiations reveals beautifully his style and viewpoint and much about the Southern motivation in the War. With one officer he went in a railroad hand-car to meet Canby. Negotiations done, he gratefully accepted an invitation to a bounteous luncheon spread by the Federals. Most of the Northern officers behaved with great courtesy and respect for their defeated enemy's feelings. But:

> There was, as ever, a skeleton at the feast, in the person of a general officer who had recently left Germany to become a citizen and soldier of the United States. This person, with the strong accent and idioms of the Fatherland, comforted me by assurances that we of the South would speedily recognize our ignorance and errors, especially about slavery and the rights of the States, and rejoice in the results of the war.... I apologized meekly for my ignorance, on the ground that my ancestors had come from England to Virginia in 1608, and in the short intervening period of two hundred and fifty-odd years, had found no time to transmit to me correct ideas of the duties of American citizenship. Moreover, my grandfather, commanding the 9th Virginia regiment in our Revolutionary army, had assisted in the defeat and capture of the Hessian mercenaries at Trenton, and I lamented that he had not, by association with these worthies, enlightened his understanding. My friend smiled blandly, and assured me of his willingness to instruct me.

Taylor's portraits of Confederate leaders are often quoted. His similar characterizations of Northern leaders, though quite as perceptive and balanced, are, of course, much less fashionable. He knew many of the Northern leaders before the War, and after the War was well-acquainted with Andrew Johnson, Grant, and others. His characterizations of Harriet Beecher Stowe, Edwin M. Stanton, Charles Sumner, Thaddeus Stevens, and others, are harsh but too just to be comforting to the victors' mythology.

Those Northerners he considered to be honorable soldiers, not making war upon women and children, Taylor often complimented. But he had, understandably, no tolerance of the vast depredations on civilians committed by the Union forces, something all too often and too conveniently forgotten. And his general assessments of the character and military performance of Grant, McClellan, Sherman, Pope, Butler, and other Union generals is instructive. His greatest contempt was reserved for self-serving politicians and all-knowing newspaper editors on both sides who never smelled powder.

Taylor passed away in 1879 at the age of only fifty-three, and not long after *Destruction and Reconstruction* had been completed. The title encompasses, it should be noted, not only the War but its grim aftermath. Taylor played an important, though largely behind-the-scenes, role in the affairs of the Reconstruction period. His observations and opinions are well worth considering. Though very much out of the fashion at this publication, it is not at all improbable that one day the pendulum of judgment will swing back, as it has done before.

His picture of the results of the War—the decimation of the South and the rampant corruption of official Washington and of the national morale—is as vivid and telling as any of his narratives of battles and campaigns. "Already shortened by the war," Taylor writes, "the standard of morality, honesty, and right was buried out of sight."

Taylor's view of postwar America somewhat resembles that of displaced Northern "aristocrats" like Henry Adams, whom he knew. But there is a morally qualitative difference. Taylor's is not the disdainful aloofness of the pampered rich, too fastidious to play the game, but rather the well-earned wisdom of one who had given all and lost. Adams, after all, was on the winning side and should have assumed some responsibility for the consequences.

Taylor reminds us, eloquently, that for one who remembered the standards of the Old Republic, the great triumph of democracy, nationalism, and material progress in the 19th century was not an advance at all, but a degeneration. He thus delivers a profound and final Southern judgment on the great cataclysm of destruction and reconstruction that remains the key to American history. And the clarity of mind, courage, and integrity that shine through this book remind us of much that was best about the Old South. (1998)

The War—My Myth or Yours?

Tar Heels' Revenge

An article by a Canadian historian in a recent issue of the North Carolina Historical Review lays to rest an old canard—the charge that during the War for Southern Independence North Carolina soldiers were notable for desertion. After an exhaustive study of all available records, Professor Richard Reid concluded that it simply is not so. North Carolina had more deserters for only one reason: because it had more men in the Confederate Army than any other State. But the percentage of deserters compares favorably with other States.

The research turned up by Reid sheds some interesting light on the War and the Confederate effort. Desertion was not always desertion. Confederate records did not make the modern distinction between desertion and AWOL, leading to over-estimation of the former. And being AWOL from the Confederate Army was not usually a product of "Unionism." Just as Southern folk tradition has it, soldiers tended to leave when they were exhausted or in order to care for families in areas ravaged by the enemy, and they often returned to the ranks when they had recuperated or finished their business at home. The "Unionism" of the western mountain region of North Carolina has also been greatly exaggerated. The troops from that area served as loyally and well as any others. The Tar Heels got a reputation for disloyalty from irresponsible Richmond newspapers, Reid surmises.

It is good to have old falsehoods put to rest. There are no better Southerners anywhere than the common folk of North Carolina. They have remained loyal to the inherited ways while many of their prosperous neighbors have sold out for a mess of pottage. It is Charlie Daniels, from Wilmington, who tours the Midwest with the Battle Flag flying, and Doc Watson, from Asheville, who finishes every concert with "Dixie." It is Andy Griffith from Mount Airy who succeeded in making the most durable favorable impression a Southerner has ever made on the mass media. And what about Richard Weaver? Sam Ervin? Jesse Helms?

The data on Confederate desertions provides an interesting comparison with modern American armies. The Confederate army had a much wider age distribution among the men in the ranks. Every age from 15 to 50 was substantially represented. This people's army is in stark contrast with recent American wars where the combat arms were disproportionately made up of men, many of them Southerners, who were either too young, too naïvely patriotic, or too lacking in influence to get safer assignments.

There are many honorable exceptions, of course, but it is broadly true that in American wars, the privileged and well-to-do, who ought to lead in war as well as peace, seldom do. In World War II a lot of "smart" conservatives stayed home and made big bucks in war industries and a lot of "smart" liberals had desk jobs in Washington where they wrote propaganda to establish what the war was "about" and drew up plans for the social engineering to be implemented after the war was over. The actual fighting and dying and the men who were doing it was the last thing that ever crossed the consciousness of the average Washington liberal.

The extent to which the fighting forces in World War II were made up of Southerners, referred to contemptuously in those days as "hillbillies," is indicated by the British slang name for the American flying arm: "The Royal Texas Air Force," and by the apocryphal story that Japanese suicide charges used to be prefaced by the shout: "To hell with Roosevelt! To hell with Babe Ruth! To hell with Roy Acuff!" I don't have figures to prove it, but I suspect the story was not a lot different in Vietnam. Southerners didn't do it alone, of course; but they did their share or more and, as usual, got no thanks for it. Needless to say, the war experienced by the "hillbillies" in the field was quite a different war from that experienced in the high-profit, high-wage economy and Hollywood mass consciousness at home.

There has been a tendency in recent years for historians to disparage the Confederate war effort—to emphasize defeatism, lack of will to win, etc. Of course, those elements were present in the War of Southern Independence, as in any human effort. However, any just and sensible view cannot escape the conclusion that by American standards the Confederate effort was the most heroic in our history.

Suppose that during World War II the Germans had taken New York and were advancing on Cincinnati; that the Japanese had taken L.A. and were moving east; that the enemy controlled all the transportation arteries and was making war on the civilian population; that the economy was staggering; that not just healthy young men were being sent into the trenches but the old, the sick, and the wounded as well. How would American morale have held up? But this was exactly the situation of the Confederacy by 1864, yet the fight was kept up. Defeatists? Not according to General Sherman, who was moaning in the late winter of 1865 that the damned Rebels had already been beat, had already lost everything, but wouldn't give up! Surrender came, not when the will to fight had disappeared, but when leaders like General Lee decided there was no longer means to carry on resistance without resort to all-out guerilla warfare. Being the kind of men they were, the Confederates chose what they considered a conditional surrender to a struggle that would have been most damaging to their own people.

The Confederate War was a people's war. Some 12,000 North Carolinians were killed in World War II. If the percentage had been the same as of the white male population who died in the Civil War, there would have been 300,000 deaths (one in four men). Liberals are always rummaging through history looking for "people's movements." Usually what they come up with looks a lot more like a cocktail party conspiracy or an obstinately unsystematic labor revolt than a people's movement. The Southern War of Independence, far and away, was the biggest and most authentic people's movement in American history. (1982)

Blue Grass Belligerents

A review of *The Civil War in Kentucky: Battle for the Bluegrass State*, edited by Kent Masterson Brown, Mason City, Iowa: Savas Publishing Company, 2000, 320 pages; and *The Atonement of John Brooks: The Story of the True Johnny "Reb" Who Did Not Come Marching Home*, by James Louis Head, Geneva, Florida: Heritage Press, 2001, 288 pages.

One of the most common putdowns of Southerners is that everything good they believe about their history is "myth." That is to say, we are suffering from self-flattering delusions that we ought to get rid of. True, there is always room in any matter for criticizing false beliefs and replacing them with facts. But, of course, what the enemies of Southerners are really saying is not that we should face facts but that we should throw away our history and accept their myths.

For that matter, myths are not necessarily bad things, but are natural human contrivances. A myth can be a poetic truth that is not counter-factual but supra-factual. The trouble with the Civil War myth of the righteous North, the accepted American "truth," is that it is counter-factual at every point (unlike the "myth" of Confederate heroism). Unionist mythology has to deny plain facts such as secession was a constitutional right and the federal attack on the South was actually against government of the people; Northerners did not fight in the interest of the slaves; Abraham Lincoln was not a saint but a ruthless politician; U.S. government war-making was unprecedented in its brutality and illegitimacy.

I have always thought that a subordinate Unionist myth is that the Border States—Delaware, Maryland, Kentucky, and Missouri—were Northern in sympathy. These two books on Kentucky substantiate my suspicions. True, the Border States furnished more Northern than Southern troops, but many of the Northern troops were conscripts who could only be used in safe tasks, and all of the Confederates were volunteers who underwent great sacrifices for the South. And even those Border State citizens who were not active Confederates did not usually support Abe Lincoln's war on the Southern people.

The fact is that "Unionist" areas were so because of military occupation: arrests and sometimes execution of citizens, newspaper editors, and elected state officials, and fraudulent elections held at bayonet point. This is even true of "Unionist" areas like East Tennessee and West Virginia, which were held by a pro-Northern *minority* with military force. Many of the counties in East Tennessee voted for secession and "Unionists" were never a real majority in West Virginia, as evidenced by the fact that West Virginia after the War regularly elected prominent Confederates to high office, as did all the Border States.

The Civil War in Kentucky contains a variety of essays by different writers, mostly about military campaigns, and emphasizes the pivotal strategic importance of Kentucky to both sides. Some of the writers accept without notice the Northern myths about Kentucky, though the thrust of the evidence they ably present is against it. There are a number of fine essays, the best being Kent Masterson Brown on the Munfordville campaign and on the Orphan Brigade, Wiley Sword on General Pat Cleburne's formative experiences in Kentucky early in the War, and James A. Ramage on John Hunt Morgan's raids.

The Atonement of John Brooks came about from the author's persistent investigation into his family history, which turned up the story of John Willet Brooks, his great-great-grandfather, one of Morgan's men executed by the Union Army in Kentucky.

What unfolds is the story of the ruthless occupation of the Bluegrass State, a story that has never been fully told, as far as I am aware. It is important to know this story today, because the enemies of Southern heritage are persistently asserting the mildness and benevolence of the federal army's treatment of Southern civilians.

The story centers on the federal prison at Louisville, commanded by the ruthless General Stephen Burbridge. Interestingly, Burbridge was a Kentuckian and a slave-holder. Apparently he delighted in the opportunity to punish his fellow Kentuckians for their refusal to give him political preferment before the War. So much for the War being only about slavery. The prison housed civilians, including African-Americans, who had aroused the hatred of the occupiers, sometimes for the most trivial "disloyal" offense, and sometimes simply because they had been seized as hostages.

The Louisville Military Prison was known as "the Killing Pen," because of the continual executions carried out there. John Brooks, a heroic and regularly enrolled Confederate soldier, captured while a part of Adam Johnson's small partisan force in western Kentucky, was one of those executed as "guerrillas" along with three of his comrades. That execution was only one of many. It is obvious that the U.S. Army resorted to extreme measures because it could not completely suppress the resistance of a hostile population that was used to freedom and self-government. The story resembles nothing so much as the Nazi occupation of European countries in World War II.

The Atonement of John Brooks brings to light these events in abundant detail. It is worth a look by anyone interested in demolishing the real myths about that part of American history. (2002)

The War—My Myth or Yours?

High Tech Hunley

As the slow process of excavating the marvel continues, more and more revelations are coming to light about the technical sophistication of the H.L. Hunley, the world's first successful submarine. This prompted a U.S. government historian to declare, according to the newspapers, that the discoveries are surprising and that "we" will have to revise our ideas about Confederate technical backwardness.

For anyone who has paid close attention to the War Between the States, the discoveries are not at all surprising. Unlike the government historian, we already knew that Southerners performed miracles of invention, engineering, and production during their fight for independence. But, alas, it is also not surprising that Yankees never seem to be able to overcome their prejudices about the South and continue to think they know everything without even taking a look.

The comments reported go back to the old prewar Yankee mythology that proclaimed to the world that Northerners were innovative and industrious, and Southerners were backward and lazy.

It is true, Southerners did not have a lot of factories before the War. For a simple reason—they had better ways of making a living. They did not need them. Northerners had to have factories and had to have them supported by government subsidies and protective tariffs, which could work only because of Southern productivity.

This does not mean that Southerners were backward. Before the War, the South had Matthew F. Maury, who quite literally revolutionized ocean navigation for the whole world, America's greatest naturalist, John J. Audubon, and many other scientists and inventors. Though he made his career in the North, Cyrus McCormick, who invented the reaper that contributed more than any other single development to the prosperity of the Midwest, was a native of Virginia. Likewise, Richard Gatling of Gatling gun fame was North Carolina born. The Colt revolver, the sidearm that conquered the West, was manufactured in New York—on a design made by Texas Rangers.

It is a fact that during the War, Southerners established factories that provided nearly everything that was needed for the armies, like the powder manufactory at Augusta, Georgia, under Col. George W. Rains. The two LeConte brothers in Columbia, South Carolina, went from Confederate service to found the sciences at the University of California. There was never any lack of materiel for the Confederate armies. Shortages arose when the railroads were torn up faster than they could be replaced, obstructing distribution. Besides the *Hunley*, Confederates pioneered in ironclad ships, torpedoes, fortifications, small arms improvement, and numerous other areas.

By the way, the most important Northern war invention, the *Monitor* ironclad, was designed and built not by a Yankee but by a Swedish immigrant, John Ericsson.

Here's hoping that Yankee observers will continue to "discover" the obvious about us. (2002)

THE WAR—MY MYTH OR YOURS?

The War Lover

The American Enterprise magazine, a slick-paper, coffee-table arm of the neocon publishing empire, has recognized the premiere of the Civil War film epic "Gods and Generals" by devoting its March issue to the Late Unpleasantness. TAE brings out some deep thinkers to examine American history 1861-1865 under the rubric "Just War." (Shouldn't there be a question mark in that title? Just for the sake of suspense, if nothing else.)

A proverbial put-down of historical works which presume to be original and important goes like this: The part that is original is not accurate and the part that is accurate is not original. The reverse is nearer true for *TAE*. What is new is the only accurate and interesting part: That is Bill Kauffman's review of the movie along with his informative interview with the film's creator, Ronald Maxwell. But then, Bill Kauffman is not a neocon, but a western New York populist stranded far from home.

Historian Jay Winik contributes a piece on the current Lincoln criticism which makes the standard, respectable case of historians who actually know something about the subject but are loath to disturb the Lincolnian nationalist mythology: Yes, some bad things happened under Abe, but they were unavoidable necessities, and after all the end justifies the means. Dinesh D'Souza contributes a sermon on Lincoln as "A True Philosophical Statesman" that is also standard fare. D'Souza actually knows less about the real history, the real lived human experience, of his adopted country than I do about Paraguay.

But in ignorance is strength, because by the Straussian cult ritual, which D'Souza here popularizes, you are not supposed to know any history. In fact, knowing history and giving it any weight is prima facie evidence of fascist tendencies. It demonstrates that you are incapable of seeing the universal principles by which proper interpretations are made. That is, the universal and eternal meaning of history is only to be obtained by Straussian exegesis of a few sentences which Straussians select, from a few documents which they select, written by a few men they select. This methodology is perfection when one wants to sacralize Lincoln and what he wrought. All one need do is quote a few pretty phrases that evoke nationalist and egalitarian sentimentality. Though the methodology does tend to break down when challenged by the well-informed, as when Professor Harry Jaffa, in his debate with

Professor Thomas DiLorenzo, was reduced to irritable denials of plain historical facts.

Most of the rest of *TAE*'s "Just War" contribution to understanding the central event of American history is fluff designed to catch Civil War hobbyists, including a pointless and less-than-coherent exposition of Mr. Robert Duvall's historical wisdom.

And now we come to *TAE*'s piéce de resistance, as they say, "A Class War," by the military historian Victor Davis Hanson, who has had quite a bit of attention lately among all the Usual Suspects. Hanson first came to notice by pointing out how Greek democracy was a product, not of theory, but of the importance to the state of the body of armed citizen-soldiers. There was not much really original about this—the point had already been made by German scholars, and it is the old story of the Anglo-American yeoman—but it was useful to point it out.

Since then, Professor Hanson has gone on to writings about modern history that appear to glorify war, at least war as carried out by the armed forces of what he regards as democratic societies. This celebration (not too strong a word, I think), of the allegedly wholesome benefits of war has obviously provided comfort to the "democratic" global imperialists with which America is cursed today—and has thus made Hanson something of a celebrity.

In "A Class War" Hanson glorifies the great democratic achievements of General Sherman's notorious March through Georgia and South Carolina in the winter of 1864-1865. Let us quote the blurb: "How 60,000 armed Midwestern men, in a 300-mile march taking less than 40 days, squashed aristocracy in America, and changed the entire psychological and material course of our national history."

One might ask where, exactly, General Sherman got the moral and constitutional authority to change the psychological and material course of American history, but such questions do not occur to those who are preaching crusades. This is not a new story. It is the same old stamping-out-the-grapes-of-wrath rationalization: Northerners rising in righteous might to put down the treason of Southerners who, corrupted by slavery, harbored an evil desire not to want to belong to The Greatest Nation on Earth. It's the same familiar story, but the old girl has had a make-over. She has a new hair-do and different cosmetics.

Here is a fair summary of Hanson's description of Sherman's March: a brave and democratic army of sturdy, idealistic Midwesterners performed a great military feat. In the process their democratic spirit was outraged by haughty Southern aristocracy and by the oppression of black people, whom they heartily embraced. As a result, they resolved to destroy Southern society once and for all, and thereby bestowed on the universe a new birth of freedom.

There are so many things wrong about this paean to Sherman's March that it amounts to a fantasy. Historians, before the era of PC, were expected to study primary sources, documents of the time, before they expounded on the meaning of historical events. Anyone who has spent some time with the primary sources knows what a dubious characterization Hanson has made. That war was an immense event, occupying a huge area and involving several million people, and one can snip quotations to provide examples of anything one wants to find. I am referring here to the bulk and weight of the evidence and only the evidence left by Northern soldiers.

You do not have to pay heed to a single Southern testimony to understand what happened on Sherman's March and why. It is all in the letters and diaries of the participants. I urge anyone who lives above the Ohio and Potomac to go to your local historical society or state library and read some of those letters and diaries for yourself. You will see how "A Class War" creates a fantasy of righteous virtue and intention that badly distorts the weight of the evidence.

Why would anyone who wanted to celebrate American military prowess pick out one of the U.S. military's most inglorious episodes, and one which involved brutality against other Americans? When there are a hundred more edifying examples?

To begin with, the march was not a military feat. What was left of the main Confederate army, after self-inflicted wounds at Atlanta, was in Tennessee trying to attack Sherman's supply lines and deal with two huge federal armies that were holding down the people of Tennessee and Kentucky. Sherman's advance from Chattanooga to Atlanta, opposed by a small but seasoned Confederate Army, had not been so easy. The March through Georgia and Carolina was contested only by a few thousand cavalry and old men and boys of the home guard. When Sherman got to North Carolina he was met by the remnants of a genuine Southern army and was defeated by a small force at Bentonville.

Three hundred miles in 40 days against slight opposition is no feat of arms. It is rather slow progress—unless you allow for the time consumed by looting and burning out civilians. There was never any doubt as to the purpose of the March. It was to bring as much destruction as possible to the civilian population of an area of the South not previously invaded and occupied. And there is no doubt that Sherman was not acting against "aristocracy" but against the entire population. And no doubt that his motive was not "democracy, democracy, democracy," but "authority, authority, authority," that is, enforced obedience to government.

Many of Sherman's men were veterans who had been occupying (and burning and looting) parts of the South for over three years. Yet we are supposed to believe that their experiences on the March suddenly opened their eyes to the evil of "Southern aristocracy" and drove them to relish its destruction. Charges of domination by "Southern aristocracy" were a part of Republican party propaganda before and during the War, but seldom a main theme. Lincoln himself never spoke of class conflict, tended to blame Northern and Southern Democratic politicians, and said: "The Southern people are exactly what we would be in their situation." The real complaint against the "Southern aristocracy" was not elitism but the fact that they kept a brake on surrendering the federal government completely to mercantilism.

In generalizing about Southern society and the Confederate Army, Hanson, alas, is in a numerous company of historians who feel free, on this subject if no other, to declaim grand interpretations on "knowledge" that consists mostly of the propaganda of one side of a conflict. (The righteous side, which is their side, of course.)

Into the heart of this allegedly class-ridden Southern society marched the great democratic army of Midwesterners, where officers and men were seen strolling arm in arm and pitching in to do the chores together. We are supposed to assume such never happened in the Confederate army, where units were all from the same neighborhood and officers were elected in the first part of the War? The clandestine insinuation is false, and egregiously so. During the War, many Union generals, even subordinate ones, went about with a squadron of cavalry for personal escort, lavish ceremonial uniforms, and elaborate staffs and headquarters. Robert E. Lee fought the War in a colonel's field jacket with a tent, two staff officers, and a few couriers. (Many of the Union generals were, after all, not soldiers but Lincoln's political patronage appointees.) A foreign military observer who dined with Joseph E. Johnston's Confederate Army headquarters staff found that there was a scarcity of tableware, so that its use had to be rotated among the officers, including the commanding general.

If one wants to declare that the Union fought against "aristocracy," then accept the obvious corollary: The Union fought not for democracy but for plutocracy. One wonders if those sturdy Midwesterners didn't feel a little class resentment of their draft-exempt factory owners who paid them large bonuses to enlist. Or of the Wall Streeters who dined every day at Delmonico's, lit their cigars with $50 greenbacks, and grew rich off government war contracts and loans, the tariff, and national bank charters. If Northern soldiers didn't notice this, they were a little naïve, and perhaps even deluded by propaganda.

There was, however, at least one significant difference between the top echelon of the North and the South. General Sherman complained explicitly that rich men who had sacrificed everything were fighting as private soldiers in the Confederate Army, while Northern men of property showed no such willingness.

Hanson is operating with the old propaganda claim that since only a quarter of the white population was involved in slave-owning, the South must have been dominated by a minority. Even worse, it was dominated by the five percent of large slave-owners. (A fourth is a bigger percentage than Northerners who owned industrial or national bank stock.) In fact, the richest planters were opponents of secession, nor did the greater part of Sherman's March pass through the areas where they were concentrated. The South had universal white male suffrage. If Hanson really believes that the men who carried out the feats of Confederate soldiers were bossed around by a few snobs, then I invite him to spend an evening discussing the question with their descendants in a blue-collar bar anywhere from Southern Maryland to West Texas.

Hanson would have us believe that the Union army was concentrating its destruction only on wealthy estates. This is not true, and to the extent that it happened, it was because the bigger farms had more valuable loot.

Letter from a Union soldier to the home folks in Indiana, one of hundreds of a similar import:

> It is a shocking sight to see how the soldiers sarve the farmers[.] Tha take everything before them[.] I saw them today go into a hous and take everything tha cood lay their hands on and then went for the chickens out adoors and the worst of all it was a poor widow woman with fore little children. I was mity sorry for her. She begged them not to take her things for her little children would starve.... I have saw a heepe such cases as that tell [sic] I am tired out of such doings.... if I was at home I cood tell you a heepe such things as I hav seen.

It is true that Sherman's force contained many good Midwestern Americans who were doing what they believed was right. It also had larger contingents of mercenaries, criminals, and foreigners than any American army before or since. Why would such good Americans want to destroy the statue of Washington at the South Carolina capitol and burn up William Gilmore Simms's library with its hundreds of irreplaceable manuscripts of Washington, Nathaniel Greene, Francis Marion, and other Revolutionary heroes?

Or destroy churches and schools and convents? Put pistols to the heads of women and black servants to frighten them into disclosing the whereabouts of the valuables? Open fresh graves (of which there were a great many in the South) as possible hiding places for silver and jewelry. Or, like the foreign-born, syphilitic Union general Kilpatrick, force women to dance to gay tunes with his men while their homes and their town were being forever wiped off the map by fire. Or tear up little girls' dolls and nail the family pet to a door? One Georgia lady was visited by several wives of Union officers who choosily selected and divided up her possessions. When she protested she was called a spy and sent without ceremony to a brutal prison in Tennessee.

The simple and ought-to-be-obvious truth is that the Confederate Army, an extended network of kinsmen, neighbors, and friends fighting the invaders of their country and the threateners of their freedom, much more resembled Hanson's ideal citizen soldiers than did the forces of the federal government.

Union soldiers fighting to destroy aristocracy? In letters by the hundreds, in the midst of campaigns and nearly to the end of the War, Northern soldiers blamed the War on abolitionists and Lincoln! I believe these men greatly outnumbered Hanson's starry-eyed idealists destroying "aristocracy."

General Sherman writes General Grant:

> [T]he amount of plundering, burning, and stealing done by our own army makes me ashamed of it. I would quit the service if I could for I fear we are drifting toward vandalism.... [T]hus, you and I and every commander must go through the war justly chargeable of crimes at which we blush.

Some crusade for democracy.

Professor Hanson is certain that after Sherman had passed on his way, "every child of the South knew that the will of the Confederate people, as well as their army had been crushed." This is not strictly true, but more to the point, we are assured, that "Sherman killed very few, and with genuine reluctance. Rapes during the march were almost unknown."

If Professor Hanson wished to tell us that Sherman's March was a mild affair compared to the Rape of Nanking or to the Nazis and Communists in Poland, and that not all Union soldiers were guilty of atrocities and many were shamed by what they did or saw, then he would have a point. But the statement, as it stands, is absurd. Prussian officers were shocked by the accounts of Union campaigns, and indeed, in the Franco-Prussian War which followed a few years later, there was no deliberate war on private persons and property. Thirty years after the War the American public was outraged by the newspaper accounts of the methods of the Spanish General "Butcher" Weyler in Cuba. But Weyler was merely applying what he had learned as an observer with the U.S. Army during the Civil War.

It never seems to occur to Sherman apologists, that when a plantation, or a whole agricultural area, is devastated, not only the white women and children but the much more numerous blacks are left without food and shelter. It is true the Union army fed some refugee slaves, but no one knows to this day how many more thousands of the uprooted died in the wake of the devastation. Just the masses of wantonly killed livestock left a disastrous ecological and public health situation. Nevertheless, for the next twenty years newspapers will be reporting that: "Distinguished military historian Victor Davis Hanson has proved that Union army atrocities were negligible and largely the creation of frantic Southern propaganda." Such is the reign of PC.

One can know for certain that our historian is working from his active imagination rather than from historical sources by his treatment of the subject of cotton:

> The pragmatic Sherman scoffed at these paternalistic rationalizations. [Huh?] He demonstrated how much he thought cotton was really worth to the United States when one head of local Confederate forces in South Carolina offered to cease burning cotton if Sherman's men would in turn stop torching estates. Sherman replied: "I hope you will burn all the cotton and save us the trouble. We don't want it; it has proven a curse to our country. All you don't burn, I will."

What Hanson wants us to learn from this quote is sheer unfounded silliness from beginning to end. The Confederate officer offered to stop burning cotton, which he knew the Northerners lusted after, if Sherman would stop burning houses, not "estates." Cotton was the most valuable commodity in North America and had made up the bulk of American exports for decades previously. Sherman's statement was merely one of his frequent attempts at dark-humor hyperbole. Northerners wanted cotton very much. This is why federal generals and officials stole literally millions of bales of it during and after the War. At that very moment, some of Lincoln's biggest industrial supporters were buying cotton illegally from the Confederates in exchange for materiel.

We come at last to the worst but also the hoariest part of the Hansonian fantasy history. We are told that the Union army on this expedition was characterized by "revulsion" against Southern aristocracy and that we are to rejoice in "the Union army's embrace of the slaves." False, on the overwhelming weight of evidence. Sherman's soldiers did not feel a lot of revulsion at Southern whites, except for some of the most backward and isolated people perhaps, though they often found them unfamiliar. Mostly they felt irritation at the continued stubborn recalcitrance of all classes of the population to being conquered and governed by Northerners.

To say that Sherman's army "embraced" the slaves is to propose a proposition that is laughable to anybody who will spend half a day with the primary sources. When Northern soldiers felt "revulsion" it was for the slaves. Amidst the flames of Columbia, federal soldiers were seen often driving away blacks with blows: "We are Western men, and we don't want your damned black faces among us." This is far more representative of what happened than a happy tale of friendly GIs in blue handing out candy bars to children.

One could easily compile a volume of Union soldiers' unfriendly and unflattering comments on the black people of the South that would rival the collected works of Joseph Goebbels for racist invective. This sentiment was stronger and more widespread than what genuine compassion there was. Blacks were robbed and killed as readily as whites, and could be beaten without reserve. Black women were more vulnerable to rape and rape-murder than white. The army, it is true, absorbed part of the black refugee population, while raising their status to that of camp laborers, and servants and concubines of Union officers. And, of course, each able-bodied black man enlisted in an all-black regiment saved one Massachusetts or Connecticut Republican from having to dirty his hands in the service.

Hanson's Sherman is just a crusty old Walter Brennan, tough on the outside but with a heart of gold within. He sometimes complained about the masses of refugee blacks interfering with army operations, but really he "embraced" them and fed them.

Not at all a fair characterization of Sherman's well-documented attitude, which was a desire to eliminate Africans out of the pure white man's country he was fighting for, and in the meanwhile to keep them hard at work.

But perhaps we should not blame *TAE* and its writers too much. They are giving the customers what they want, and they will find many takers. A more basic question is why do so many Americans, or at least American "spokespersons," feel compelled to force our history into a pattern of collective self-glorification? All peoples tend to mythologize their important experiences, but it would be hard to find one more self-righteous and uncritical and so much in need of cosmetology as triumphal American exceptionalism. History, after all, is the remembrance of the usually ambivalent and complicated struggles of us poor fallen creatures in a fallen world. As two of Faulkner's characters say to each other, in contemplating the human race: "the poor sons of bitches."

I think the sanitizing of evil comes from the deformed Christianity of Puritanism, which was planted in Boston in the 17th century and has been a cancerous growth in America ever since. (Though, of course, material interests always play a part as well.) I am of the elect, so it goes, and therefore my will is righteousness, and undoubted righteousness is my license to annihilate the un-elect. Or in the public form: America = Democracy = God. That's my hypothesis, though I'll gladly listen to yours.

Clearly, this kind of thing is stronger at some times than others, and sometimes it sweeps all before it. And clearly it is a rising curve in the United States today, which Professor Hanson has caught and is riding. An even more basic question is what does this kind of militant self-righteousness portend for us, both concretely and morally? (2003)

Thank Heaven for the "Amateurs"

Books reviewed: *Wade Hampton: Confederate Warrior, Conservative Statesman*, by Walter Brian Cisco, Washington, D.C.: Brassey's, Inc., 2004, 401 pages; and *Retreat from Gettysburg: Lee, Logistics, and the Pennsylvania Campaign*, by Kent Masterson Brown, Chapel Hill: University of North Carolina Press, 2005, 534 pages.

Since they first appeared in the late 19th century, professional academic historians in the United States have been pretty much Establishment men. Though in other days they did observe some canons of evidence and reasoned argument, and an occasional maverick appeared to remind that historical understanding should be an evolving debate and not a party line. Where we are now is signaled by the fact that academic historians a few years ago gave lavish praise and their highest award to a book purporting to prove that gun ownership was not widespread among early Americans—a proposition that was later shown to rest upon fabricated evidence.

Aside from Revelation, and perhaps biology, history provides our only clue to understanding the strange drama of the existence of our human race on this planet. Its usefulness lies in its attention to human experience. But, more and more, academic historians don't write about people, or even about groups of people. They write about categories of victims and oppressors—abstractions pre-defined by Cultural Marxism. Historianship is starting to resemble a bureaucratic exercise in spreading official ideology.

In the future we will place increasing reliance on amateur historians, as in these books. "Amateur" was once an honorable term—suggesting not lack of skill but gentlemanly excellence for its own sake rather than for money. Wade Hampton III had not had a biographer in half a century until Mr. Cisco, retired from business, undertook the task. The Hampton name is barely recognized today, but he was once the best known historical South Carolinian after Calhoun. Grandson of pioneers and Revolutionary soldiers, Hampton was a type that Americans today can hardly believe existed, much less understand.

One of the richest men in the South—more than a thousand slaves on plantations spread over three states, he was able to dispatch a bear single-handedly with a knife and write cultured letters and speeches.

The War—My Myth or Yours?

Not an eager secessionist, when the die was cast Hampton raised and equipped at his own expense a legion—horse, foot, and guns—for the defense of his people. Like his forebears he was never a professional soldier but a willing and gifted amateur in time of need. Hampton fought most of the War in the cavalry of the Army of Northern Virginia, assuming its command on the death of "Jeb" Stuart. Near the end he went south to see what could be done with Sherman's banditti. Wade Hampton III led from the front, was wounded several times, lost his son to a Yankee bullet, and performed great feats with dwindling resources against long odds. In February of 1865, Sherman's men went out of their way to destroy his home outside of Columbia. Sherman put out the lie that Hampton in retreating had started the fires that destroyed the city. He hoped to damage Hampton's standing with his people. It did not work.

Hampton's greatest service, however, was post-war. He organized and led the resistance that redeemed his state from ten years of military rule. His election as governor in 1876 was crowned by the departure of the U.S. Army, with the carpetbaggers and their loot in its train (although they left public debts that were not paid off until 1955). If you believe the prevailing Marxist notion that Reconstruction was a noble social revolution that simply did not go far enough (rather than an orgy of stealing and oppression as everyone used to believe) you will dwell on the electoral fraud and coercion by Hampton's men that brought it to an end. And you will never mention the fact that such action was simply a response to a regime that had never allowed an honest election during its decade of rule.

Retreat from Gettysburg is another "amateur" contribution, by a distinguished attorney, Kent Masterson Brown. Unlike most of the endless stream of books about the War, *Retreat from Gettysburg* tells us new things and gives us new ways of seeing familiar events. Lee's battered army moved from Gettysburg to the south bank of the Potomac—in intense heat, heavy rains, and deep mud, with a 50-mile long wagon train full of supplies and wounded, interspersed with vast herds of livestock and thousands of prisoners. Within ten days of the failure of "Pickett's charge" Lee had restored a balance of power and an army that would remain a deadly fighting force for almost two years more. It was a great military success, perhaps the greatest of the many brilliant exploits of Lee's army.

This understanding casts a new light on the great Union "victory" at Gettysburg. The Confederate army, though greatly out-numbered, moved freely in Northern territory until it met enemy forces by accident. For three days the smaller force attacked the nearly immobile larger one defending its own land, with large re-enforcements only a few days' march away. Barely failing of a decisive blow, the Army of Northern Virginia quit attacking and made the difficult journey home. The victorious army kept a safe distance and only feebly molested the retreat. Some victory.

America amour propre will never allow the admission, but man for man, the Confederate soldier did more than his opponent. People invading and laying waste your country to destroy the liberty won by your fathers and grandfathers is a great motivator. Much more so than enlistment bounties, the tariff, war contracts, and government loans, or even the "national greatness" to be established by a reconstructed "Union." Like earlier American armies, but unlike the U.S. Army then and later, the Confederate army was not a military machine but a large expedition of cousins and neighbors, which has advantages in morale, adaptability, and teamwork.

The Confederate move into Pennsylvania has usually been attributed to strategic considerations. Brown's careful study highlights the role of logistical needs. Lee needed re-supply, which could not be obtained in devastated Virginia nor in adequate quantity by the railroads to the further South. The Army of Northern Virginia went home from Pennsylvania with vast quantities of grains and vegetables, clothing and transport, equipment, and meat on the hoof. This vast haul was seized and receipted in accordance with the widely recognized rules of war. Unlike the Northern armies in the South from the first day of hostilities, the Confederates engaged in no systematic wanton destruction of private property and oppression of civilians. In this respect, the Prussians who invaded France a few years later compare favorably with the U.S. Army.

Another interesting discovery by Brown, which could only have been made by a historian who had not been socialized into the "profession": more than 5,000 and possibly as many as 10,000 black men, bond and free, accompanied the Southern army to Pennsylvania and back. (Ambrose Bierce wrote that in four years of hard fighting in the Union western army he never saw a black person except the conscripted servants and concubines of Northern officers.) Col. Fremantle of the Coldstream Guards observed in Pennsylvania one of the black Confederates marching a Yankee prisoner to the rear. He wondered what the London abolitionists would make of that. When the Confederate survivors turned back from the attack on the third day, they returned to lines occupied entirely by black men. Many of those men performed signal services during the battle and the difficult retreat including the protection and evacuation of wounded masters. This is really not hard to understand and accept if you remember that these men were people and not categories. (2005)

A Comment on Cold Mountain

Comment requested by national columnist Ilana Mercer:

Your negative reaction is basically sound. There were home guards in the mountains of western North Carolina during the War, and part of their activity was to find deserters. Since all able-bodied good citizens were in the army, without the home guards the criminal element, which partly coincided with deserters, could have a field day terrorizing isolated women and children. The home guard did not go around terrorizing and killing people. Home guard generally means under 16, over 55, or disabled. The leaders of the home guard were picked personally by Governor Vance, who was a native of the mountains and knew the people well, and were usually the most respected old men in the communities. They were definitely serious about finding deserters and persuading them to go back. The point was to get men back to the army, not kill them. The Southern people needed every man—they were after all, fighting a desperate struggle to prevent their freedom from being snuffed out by a much larger and ruthless invader, though desertion was not nearly as massive a problem as in the North where it reached to hundreds of thousands.

There was some small scale skirmishing between home guards and criminal gangs, which could be called guerilla war. It was easy for the gangs to declare themselves "Unionists." In fact, during Reconstruction, some of the most notorious leaders of criminal gangs, like George W. Kirk, were put in charge of the militia and continued their depredations under "lawful" authority.

The situation in the mountains was complicated by the isolation of some groups who would resist the state, Confederate or any other government invading their domain, and by standing family feuds. If one family joined one side in the War, the enemy family would choose the other. This was the basis of the longstanding and famous Hatfield-McCoy feud on the border of Kentucky and West Virginia. In general, the idea that the mountains of North Carolina, Tennessee, and even West Virginia were "Unionist" is misleading. There were more "Unionists" there than in other parts of the South, but the majority was Confederate.

I would say of the book, at least, that what was portrayed is not totally implausible. The War was so vast, and involved so many people, over so huge a region, and so many hundreds of encounters, that anything is possible. But it is not representative. The fundamental dishonesty is that it simply plays to the stereotype that Southerners were always evil; the unexamined assumption being that the other side was virtuous.

Cold Mountain is a well-written novel. But it is no better than many other stories by Southern writers at the same time. Its popularity is in its invoking the evil Southerner image. While the book has a slight plausibility, the same cannot be said of the film. The scenes of Confederate soldiers wantonly slaughtering women and whole families are absurd and disgusting lies. (2003)

Confederate Connections

A friend of mine, a scholar of international reputation and a Tar Heel by birth, was visiting professor at a very prestigious Northern university a few years ago. In idle conversation with some colleagues, he happened to mention that his mother was an active member of the Daughters of the American Revolution and the United Daughters of the Confederacy.

His colleagues were shocked with disbelief. Their families had come from remote parts of Europe long after the War for Southern Independence. Their understanding of American history went like this: America had been founded by noble, freedom and equality loving patriots, and then that noble founding had been saved by other great patriots against a wicked rebellion of traitors seeking only to preserve the un-American institution of slavery. How could one celebrate both the founding and the treason?

Of course, these distinguished professors' view of American history is absurd. But it illustrates the dilemma that Southerners face when they try to give correct accounts of their history. The wrong view has been taught as gospel truth for generations. It has been taught to generations of later immigrants who regard it as the true story of America. It promotes the self-esteem of Northerners. Many Northerners (not all) have no felt historical connection with America, which they regard in abstract terms as "a proposition nation." They literally do not know what Southerners are talking about when they defend their heritage, the real experience of their own families, because they do not know what a real heritage is.

The false view of history is a very powerful tool in its emotional appeal to centralized government, to unthinking nationalist fervor, and to the eternal mission for correcting the world that motivates leftists. It is also the same type of mentality that thinks bombing women and children in the Balkans is OK because it is done in the name of "human rights," "democracy," and American righteousness.

You know your Confederate ancestors were not fighting for slavery. But the people you are arguing with have no relevant ancestors. Their minds deal in abstractions, not lived human experience. They know what has been promulgated as the national mythology—that Lincoln saved the government of, by, and for the people and the ideal that "all men are created equal."

So, our Confederate forebears, who were in both blood and principle literally sons of the American Revolution, go down as traitors, while those who destroyed the work of the Founders and reconstructed America on a new centralized basis, are considered its saviors!

As a small contribution to correcting historical views, I have compiled, from ordinary reference sources, an account of the kinship relations of Confederates to the patriots of the Revolution (and to other important figures in the founding and early development of the U.S.). The connection of the Confederate effort for independence with the principles of self-government of peoples expounded by the American Revolution has been well-defended and is (or rather ought to be) obvious. I want to show the actual connection of families. It is true that descendants sometimes lose or mistake the principles of their sires, but that is not the case in the three score and eleven years from the founding of the U.S. to the founding of the C.S.A. Do we really believe that the leaders of the North, few of whom had a significant family connection to the founding patriots, better represent the American Revolution?

(After the discussion of how Confederates relate to the Revolutionary War, I have added sections describing the Confederate contributions to settling the West and to democratic, popular movements after the War, and a section on minority group Confederates.)

Confederate Connections to the American Revolution and the Early History of the U.S.

CSA President Jefferson Davis was the son of a soldier in the American Revolution.

Vice President Alexander H. Stephens was the grandson of a soldier in the Revolution.

Gen. R.E. Lee was the son of a cavalry general in the Revolution and the nephew of two signers of the Declaration of Independence. His wife was the great-granddaughter of Martha Washington.

Samuel Cooper, Jr., ranking general of the CSA, was the son of a Revolutionary officer from Massachusetts. He was born in New Jersey and appointed to West Point from New York. His wife was the granddaughter of the Virginia Revolutionary statesman George Mason. Her brother was the Confederate minister to Great Britain, James M. Mason.

William Henry Chase, who commanded the Florida state forces in the early days of the Confederacy, was a native of Maine and was the great-nephew of John Hancock, famous signer of the Declaration of Independence from Massachusetts.

Brig. General Hylan B. Lyon, CSA, was born in Kentucky, but his grandfather, Matthew Lyon, was a congressman from Vermont who was one of the few strong supporters of Jefferson in New England and was famous for having been prosecuted under the Sedition Act.

Brig. Gen. and Secretary of War George W. Randolph was the grandson of Thomas Jefferson.

Gen. James E. Slaughter was the grand-nephew of James Madison.

Maj. Gen. Daniel S. Donelson was the nephew of Andrew Jackson.

Brig. Gen. Lucius M. Walker was the nephew of President James K. Polk.

Lt. Gen. Richard Taylor, CSA, was the son of General and President Zachary Taylor and the grandson of a Revolutionary officer.

Lt. Gen. Leonidas Polk's father was a Revolutionary colonel as was his maternal grandfather.

Maj. Gen. Matthew C. Butler was the nephew, on his mother's side, of the great Connecticut naval heroes, Oliver Hazard Perry and Matthew Calbraith Perry. Butler's wife was the great-granddaughter of the Revolutionary Gen. Andrew Pickens.

A number of the early heroes of the U.S. Navy were Southerners like Stephen Decatur. Most of the rest of the outstanding Naval officers were from the Middle States and almost none from New England, though New England was supposedly the most seafaring part of the Union. The U.S. Marine Corps from its beginning to the War was mostly led and manned by Southerners. After his experience before the mast, Herman Melville, author of *Moby Dick*, contrasted Southern navy officers very favorably with others for their decency and fairness to lower ranks.

Maj. Gen. David E. Twiggs was the son of Gen. John Twiggs of the Revolution.

Brig. Gen. Hugh W. Mercer was the grandson of Revolutionary Gen. Hugh Mercer.

Brig. Gen. Joseph E. Johnston, CSA, was the son of a Revolutionary army colonel.

Maj. Gen. Benjamin Huger's grandfather was a Revolutionary officer and a friend of Lafayette.

Lt. Gen. John C. Pemberton was descended from one of the prominent first settlers of Pennsylvania.

Brig. Gen. William Nelson Pendleton's forebears included Thomas Nelson, Revolutionary governor of Virginia and signer of the Declaration of Independence, and Virginia patriot Edmund Pendleton.

At least two grandsons and many other relatives of Patrick Henry served in the Confederate Army.

President John Tyler was a member of the Confederate Congress, and his son Robert was Treasurer of the Confederate States.

Lt. Gen. Richard H. Anderson, CSA, was a grandson of a Revolutionary officer.

Lt. Gen. D.H. Hill was the grandson of a Revolutionary officer.

Lewis A. Washington, a grandnephew of George Washington, was one of the people slaughtered by John Brown on his raid on Harpers Ferry. (Brown stole a sword of George Washington's which he regarded as a talisman.)

The father of Gen. Edmund Kirby Smith, CSA, was a distinguished War of 1812 officer from Connecticut, and his brother, a colonel, was killed in action in the Mexican War.

Maj. Gen. Joseph B. Kershaw was the grandson of a Revolutionary officer.

Lt. Gen. Wade Hampton's grandfather was a Colonel in the Revolution and a general in the War of 1812.

Brig. Gen. Humphrey Marshall was grandson of the first U.S. Senator from Kentucky.

Maj. Gen. John C. Breckinridge, besides being Vice-President of the U.S., had a grandfather who was an early Senator from Kentucky and a member of Jefferson's cabinet.

Brig. Gen. Turner Ashby's grandfather was an officer in the Revolution.

The father of Brig. Gen. William Carroll, CSA, was a general in the War of 1812.

Brig. Gen. Henry A. Wise was the son-in-law of John Sergeant, distinguished Pennsylvania political leader and candidate for Vice-President of the U.S.

Brig. Gen. William Preston, CSA, was the grandson of two Revolutionary officers.

Brig. Gen. Bradley T. Johnson, CSA, was the grandson of a Revolutionary officer.

John P. Maclay, Gen. of Louisiana state forces in the Confederacy, came from a family who were the leading Jeffersonians in western Pennsylvania, including an important Senator.

Brig. Gen. Lewis A. Armistead had a father and four uncles who fought in the War of 1812.

Robert W. Johnson, member of the Confederate Congress from Arkansas, was the nephew of Richard M. Johnson, Vice-President of the U.S.

The father of Brig. Gen. Thomas F. Drayton was born in St. Augustine, where his family had been exiled because of Revolutionary activities.

The New York Revolutionary War Gen. William Henry's son, Gustavus, was a member of the Confederate Congress from Kentucky and his grandson a Confederate colonel.

William R. Caswell, Confederate officer from Tennessee, was the grandson of North Carolina Revolutionary War general and Governor Richard Caswell.

The great American painter James McNeill Whistler, though born in Massachusetts, was a Confederate sympathizer, which partly explains why he spent his life in Europe, according to a recent biography. His brother was a Confederate surgeon.

The words to the U.S. national anthem were written by Francis Scott Key, as is well known. Less well-known is that his grandson, Francis Key Howard, was one of the Marylanders imprisoned by Lincoln for Southern sympathies. Howard was also the grandson of Col. John Eager Howard, commander of the famous Maryland Line in the Revolutionary War. Another Francis Scott Key grandson was Richard Hammond Key, Confederate soldier who died in a Yankee prison camp.

This is just to scratch the surface. This list of Confederate family connections to the American Revolution and to the early development of America could be expanded for many pages. This is not even to touch on the political and military leaders of the Confederacy who were themselves or whose close relatives were leaders in the 19th century prior to the War. Senators, Congressmen, cabinet members, jurists, diplomats, soldiers, educators, clergy, and many others.

The South and the Frontier

Let's look at another area of Southern and Confederate contributions, the West, the frontier. According to the Northern mythology (which in this as in so much else is exactly opposite of the truth), Southerners were effete slave-owners and not sturdy pioneers like Northerners. In fact, most acquisition, exploration, and early settlement of the frontier before the War was by Southerners. Nobody from Boston, despite the movies, ever went west in a covered wagon. The Philadelphia gentleman Owen Wister had it right when he called his Wyoming novel *The Virginian*. Here are some connections, just a few of many that might be cited.

The War—My Myth or Yours?

Nearly all of the Mountain Men who opened up the Rocky Mountains and beyond, were Southerners—Kit Carson, Jim Bridger, Charles Bent.

Sons, grandsons, and nephews of the following great pioneer figures served in the Confederate Army: Daniel Boone, David Crockett, Sam Houston, William Clark of Lewis and Clark, Isaac Shelby.

William Clark's son, Meriwether Clark, was an acting general in the Confederate Army. More distant relatives of David Crockett and Daniel Boone: John W. Crockett, member of the Confederate Congress, and Andrew R. Boone, secession leader and Confederate Congressman from Kentucky. Confederate Gen. Joseph O. Shelby was Isaac Shelby's grandnephew. Sam Houston's initial "Unionism" is well-known; Sam, Jr. was severely wounded in the Confederate Army.

The national mythology treats Texas as "Western" when it is to be praised and "Southern" when it is not. The whole historical glory of Texas is Southern. It could not have existed as it was except as an extension of Southern culture. (Think about South Dakota.) Consider the heroic Texas frontiersmen who were Confederate soldiers: Tom Green, Ben McCullough, "Rip" Ford, Sul Ross (and many others).

The Southern badmen (the Jameses, the Youngers, John Wesley Hardin) were driven to their crimes by the oppressions of Reconstruction. The Yankee Western heroes (Earp, Cody, Hickock) were in real life criminals and frauds who got their fame by killing for the winning side in Reconstruction.

The cattle kingdom in the North was opened entirely by Texan ex-Confederates, although wealthy Yankee and English capitalists and eastern playboys like Teddy Roosevelt moved in after the real pioneering work had been done.

The Confederacy, Immigrants, Catholics, and Jews

As is well-known, or ought to be, the antebellum South was much more ethnically tolerant and open than the North, where the predominant elements can truly be described as bigoted. The South was electing Catholics and Jews to office when Bostonians were burning down convents.

The flourishing critics of the Old South like to paint it as a narrow society that could attract allegiance only from slave-owners and slavery defenders. One of the many falsehoods that are becoming accepted as fact among academic historians is that only slave-owners were for secession and Southern independence. Currently fashionable interpretations rely on unrepresentative snippets of information to declare that non-slaveholders and women did not support the Confederacy—patent misrepresentations of plain historical facts.

To the contrary, consider that nearly one-fourth of general officers in the Confederate Army were born in Europe or the North and many others had northern connections. In fact, almost every Northerner and foreigner who had lived in the South for any period of time was a loyal Confederate.

Furthermore, many Southerners came home from the North and West where they had successful careers in order to share the fate of the Southern people in war. Let me mention just a few: Simon B. Buckner of Kentucky gave up a fortune in Chicago real estate; George W. Rains of North Carolina left a prosperous iron foundry he had established in Newburgh, New York; Alexander C. Jones of Virginia resigned a judgeship in St. Paul, Minnesota, where he had lived twenty years; Joseph L. Brent of Louisiana gave up a lucrative law practice and leadership of the Democratic Party in Los Angeles.

The same solidity of support for the Confederacy among immigrants to the U.S. in the South can be shown. Some good recent books on immigrants to the South: Robert N. Rosen in *The Jewish Confederates* documents how nearly all Jewish Southerners were loyal Confederates who sacrificed and bled as readily as their neighbors and also shows the antisemitism rife among abolitionists and Republicans. Kelly J. O'Grady in *Clear the Confederate Way: The Irish in the Army of Northern Virginia* does the same for Irish Southerners. The book really covers a good deal more than just the ANV and among other things shows how Irish allegiance to the Northern cause has been exaggerated.

There is a large literature about Yankee prejudice against everybody who was not WASP (except they liked North Germans, i.e., proto-Nazis). Nancy Lusignan Schultz in *Fire and Roses: The Burning of the Charlestown Convent, 1834* tells the story of Massachusetts' anti-Catholic rioting, encouraged and protected by the Yankee authorities. I am displaying all these biographical details because hard facts about real people are useful to measure against the abstractions and the slanders against Southerners that are common currency in the usual retailing of United States history.

Confederates After the War

Let me introduce another category: Ex-Confederates who became postbellum leaders. Many, of course, held political offices, college and corporation presidencies, and the like. I want to first illustrate a particular type. Through the clever writings of the late C. Vann Woodward, it has been established as fact among academic historians that Southern leaders after the War were reactionary servants of Northern Big Business interests. This is convenient for left-wingers to believe, and some examples can be found, but as a generalization it is not true. (For establishment historians, of course, anything that Southerners do is evil: Southerners are more evil for collaborating with the evil system in power than are the Northern creators of it who had conquered them. That is, Northern sins are fobbed off on Southerners. This is the implicit assumption of academic historians.)

Southern Democrats after Reconstruction remained, by and large, much more Jeffersonian than Northerners, even Northern Democrats. It was Ben Tillman who wanted to take a pitchfork to Grover Cleveland for his monetary policy. The strongest anti-Big Business Populists came from the South. Tom Watson learned his politics from Alexander Stephens and Robert Toombs. Leonidas L. Polk, who died in 1892 shortly before being nominated by the Populist Party for President, had been sergeant-major of the 26th North Carolina Regiment, famous for its two charges at Gettysburg. "Alfalfa Bill" Murray, Populist governor of Oklahoma, was the son of a Confederate soldier.

Jim Hogg, noted populist governor of Texas, was the son of a Confederate general. Roger Mills, another Texan leader of the more "liberal" wing in Congress, had been a Confederate officer. Sam Jones, noted progressive mayor of Toledo, Ohio, came from a Southern family. Ewing Cockrell, noted as an anti-big-business judge in Missouri, was the son of a Confederate general.

Harry Truman's mother came from a staunchly Confederate Missouri family. When it became widely known that Truman's mother refused to sleep in the Lincoln bedroom, leftists put out the story that it was because Lincoln was a Republican, that is, not a New Dealer. The fact was that she despised the leader of the Yankee invaders. Truman himself picked a well-known picture of Lee and Jackson for the entrance lobby of his presidential library.

John H. Reagan, Postmaster General of the Confederacy, was a pioneer member of the Interstate Commerce Commission. J. Allen Smith, a leading Progressive scholar, though he made his career at the University of Washington (state), came from a Missouri Confederate family. Representative Henry D Clayton, Jr., of Alabama, author of the Clayton Antitrust Act, was the son of a CSA general. Even one of the "anarchists" judiciously murdered by Chicago Republicans after the

"Haymarket Riots" was a former Confederate soldier, Albert Parsons. A number of Southern progressive and populist leaders opposed U.S. entry into World War I on anti-imperialist grounds, notably Claude Kitchin of North Carolina, a stand which took considerable courage.

Many Southerners succeeded in the north and west after the War: a chief justice of Washington State; O.P. Fitzgerald, founder of Methodism in California; John A. Wyeth, who rode with Forrest, president of the American Medical Association. These are just a few that readily occur to me. And it is interesting that all the supposedly Unionist border states, Maryland, Kentucky, Missouri, and even West Virginia, readily elected ex-Confederates to high political office after the War, that is, as soon as the occupation forces were removed. H.L. Mencken wrote that his native Baltimore was less corrupt than other big cities because of the influence of honorable ex-Confederates.

Finally, let me mention a few more contributions of the Confederacy to American life. Sons of Confederate soldiers: D.W. Griffith, central figure in the creation of an American cinema; Will Rogers, beloved humorist; Archibald Gracie, Jr., who died heroically in the sinking of the *Titanic*; William C. Gorgas, credited with controlling yellow fever; William G. McAdoo, Senator from California and Woodrow Wilson's Secretary of the Treasury who almost received the Democratic presidential nomination in 1920; financier Bernard Baruch, who delighted in showing to guests at his New York townhouse his father's Confederate uniform and Klan regalia—it is said that the internationally famous Baruch would stand up and give a Rebel Yell whenever he heard "Dixie"; Generals Nathan Bedford Forrest, Jr., and Simon Bolivar Buckner, Jr., U.S. Army, killed in action in World War II. Gen. George S. Patton, the fighting general of World War II, was the grandson of a Confederate officer killed in action.

Herbert Lehman, noted New Deal Senator from New York, was the son of an Alabama merchant who was sent by President Davis on a relief mission to Confederate prisoners. He was repulsed by General Grant. Adolph S. Ochs, founder of the *New York Times*, came from Chattanooga. Although his father was a "unionist," his mother was an active Confederate sympathizer who smuggled medicine across Yankee lines and had a Confederate flag on her coffin. And not least Helen Keller, granddaughter of a general of Arkansas state troops in the Confederacy.

Conclusion

The thrust of the concerted anti-Southern campaign which dominates our time, even being officially enforced by Southern public authorities, is to segregate the Confederacy off from American life as an inhuman Nazi-like thing based only on slavery. (This gains impetus, among other reasons, because of a totally dishonest linking of the domestic slavery of the Old South with modern totalitarianism. It was the Union invading forces who most resembled modern totalitarians in every way.) What is presented here is, it is hoped, something of an antidote. The suppression of Confederate symbols has no justification in history, even when promoted by alleged academic experts. It is not motivated by historical understanding. It resembles, rather, propaganda labels used by Communist and Nazi zealots to intimidate and control. (See the Hate Sessions in Orwell's *1984*.)

We really cannot blame Americans too much for holding on to their myths, even though they can only achieve pride by putting us down. If Americans had to take a look at the real Constitution, the real Declaration of Independence, the real Abraham Lincoln, the real war for Union and emancipation, which was neither noble nor necessary, their whole national morale would start to fall apart. That is why the anti-South people have been talking less about slavery lately and starting to dismiss the Confederacy with nasty and summary charges of "treason," as if the right to secede was not what the War was all about. What else have Americans got to sustain their society which has pretensions to world domination while disintegrating from within. The Melting Pot?—only a half-truth at best. Global Democracy?—a pernicious abstraction.

Still, it is true that until a very few years ago, the Confederacy was an accepted and honored part of the American national heritage. The current jihad against our forebears indicates a radical forward step in the movement toward government suppression of free thought and expression. (2001)

American Iliad

A review of *The Civil War: A Narrative*, by Shelby Foote, New York: Random House, 1958, 1963 and 1974, 3 volumes.

In the long view, the most important aspect of any civilization, nation, or epoch is its literature. Great Britain will be known through Shakespeare, Chaucer, Milton, Spencer, Scott, and Kipling long after the Bank of England and Buckingham Palace have crumbled into dust and the last jaunty Union Jack has sunk beneath the waves. It may be true that the German tribes of Northern Europe had a more decisive influence on forming our own Western Civilization than the Greeks, the Romans, or the Hebrews. But that influence will never he fully appreciated because the literature in which it is embodied is—relatively speaking—insignificant.

By the same token, perception of the Old South has been clouded by the neglect of its literature. Although its essayists—Albert Taylor Bledsoe, Hugh Swinton Legaré, George Tucker, to mention just a few—were the equals of any in their time, they go unread. Many of its creative writers—like Augustus Baldwin Longstreet and George Washington Harris—have been dismissed with the condescending label "frontier humorists," when in fact they were pioneers of modern literature, especially by contrast with many once vaunted but now unreadable New England writers who have bored at least six suffering generations of schoolchildren into a distaste for literature.

The completion of Shelby Foote's *Civil War* in 1974 was the occasion for a considerable amount of recognition and praise. A major work on the central event in American history, to which a talented writer had devoted a quarter of a century, could not go unnoticed. Nonetheless, the full extent of Foote's achievement remains to be assessed. It is my contention that Shelby Foote's *Civil War* will be one of those enduring works that will be turned to in centuries hence, that it is a major event in world literature and in the Southern contribution to world literature.

Our Civil War contains more dramatic events, unforgettable personalities, and crucial issues than any part of the American experience. No other event in our history occurred with such vast scale and complexity and is so pregnant with import for our self-understanding as a nation. It is deserving of an epic treatment, as indeed, Walt Whitman

The War—My Myth or Yours?

predicted more than a century ago, it must inevitably produce. Foote's history is that epic. It qualifies in the grandeur of its conception, in the deceptive simplicity of its execution, and in the artistry which it has cast great events into the timeless form of great literature. Foote, in the note which closes his third volume, refers to his work revealingly as "this Iliad." His purpose, he remarks in looking back over his quarter century's labor, was "re-creating that war and making it live again in the world around us," which is certainly a fair analogy to Homer's purpose, and one in which Foote has succeeded.

The claim I am making for the work is a large one and one that I will not expect to be conceded in many quarters. Were Foote not a Southerner and were the Civil War still not intertwined in the self-image, indeed central to the amour propre of the American nation at large, several obstacles would be removed to the widespread appreciation of the stature of the work. But those obstacles are likely to be with us a while longer yet and I shall have to wait for the future to do my contention full justice. For the time being I shall be content to make the assertion and to add a few observations to build a case for Foote's greatness, without assuming that they will be conclusive.

Like most great works, *The Civil War: A Narrative*, is simple and straightforward in its business. It is a narrative of events. The success of this narrative is an achievement of both literary skill and historical scholarship. Foote's history is literature and not "social science." But it is nonetheless, or, to put it better, it is all the more great history for being great literature. Its extraordinary literary value, in fact, is what it shares with all great works of historical writing and what sets it apart from the historical writing of its own time. Some of the latter has literary value but little of it is great literature. Like all great historians, Foote is first of all a writer. He has, he tells us in the note to his first volume, accepted the historian's standards without the historian's paraphernalia; he has employed the novelist's methods without the novelist's license. He wishes the reader to relive an experience, not merely to read a book. He has, in short, set out to tell a story. His position is a valid one, but the skill with which he has done this primary task and the form which it has taken have aroused a certain amount of criticism, or at least suspicion. Quibbles have been raised, for instance, about Foote's "methodology."

By "historian's paraphernalia" is meant footnotes, of which Foote has not any. We are supposed to suspect the history without footnotes. But this is to confuse means with ends, a common modern error. The purpose of footnotes is to give the reader the means to verify the integrity of the writer or to pursue a point further. Foote's sources are self-evident in his pages, as is the certainty that he has immersed himself in those sources as a historian should and has dealt with those sources honestly. That is all that can be asked, and footnotes could have added nothing. In recent times footnotes have been used as often to deceive as to enlighten.

It has been contended that Foote is ignorant of "modern" scholarship, that his interpretations are "outmoded." This is true, perhaps, in a narrow sense. If he had understood a little more, for instance, about the industrialization of the South during the War as described recently by Raimondo Luraghi, he might have written a slightly different book. But what the critics mean is not this limited sense of failing to have kept abreast of the literature, indeed an impossible task. What they mean is that Foote has not adopted contemporarily fashionable (that is to say, neo-abolitionist and neo-Radical Republican) interpretations of the War, its issues, events, and personalities. Exactly. His vision is far too wide to be contained within or to be satisfied by such narrow axe-grinding. He is an artist, not an ideologue. (It is a curious phenomenon that, while historians know and acknowledge that interpretations of past epochs change every generation or so, many of them remain slavishly devoted to the interpretation that is currently most fashionable.) But, in fact, "modern scholarship," in points of interpretation, is no truer than old scholarship; sometimes it is less so. It is just a different perspective.

Foote's accomplishments as a narrator and his wariness of explicit interpretations should not be taken to indicate that he tells a story without any understanding of deeper meanings. In fact, he does understand (whether intuitively or by investigation and reason and portrays the meaning of these great events including their political implications in a higher frame of reference than they have ever been grasped before. Here again, art and scholarship are inseparable. The understanding is within the storytelling. Sound interpretation proceeds from the artist's eye, from taking in the canvas whole, not from analyzing the subject into pieces on the dissecting table. (Which is not to deny that a certain amount of scholarly analysis must go into the artist's preparation.)

Contained within the straightforward, satisfying narrative is a treasury of meaning. For instance, no finer and fuller sketches of the great personalities of the War exist than emerge from these pages. Foote has grasped them better than they have ever been grasped. All of them—Lincoln, Davis, Grant, Lee, Sherman, his favorite Forrest, and all the others—are revealed here clear, simple, whole, convincing, free equally

The War—My Myth or Yours?

of glorification and slander, as real as Hamlet, Don Quixote, or Lord Jim. If we do not know them true in Foote's pages we will never know them true.

Here, alas, we run into practical problems. Like all the other major characters, Foote's Lincoln is round and real. Lincoln is shown with all his warts—the politician whose left hand did not always know what his right hand was doing; the small town wheeler-dealer who was not above asking for a safe berth for his own son; the homely middle-aged man whose dealings with his emotionally disintegrating wife were more human than saintly. This is not to say that Foote muckrakes Lincoln. He says, and doubtless means it, that he much admires the creator of the modern American state. There are ample materials in the work out of which Lincoln may be made out a great man. But he is a real Lincoln, seen whole, one who has to be taken without cant and self-righteousness and convenient shading of facts. Probably only a Southerner could have written this Lincoln, and, as yet, only a Southerner can apprehend the truth of the picture. Lincoln is still too much at the center of national self-image to be apprehended truly by the mainstream American. The mainstream American can no more see Lincoln true than he can see himself as others see him. But Lincoln is merely treated here with the same artist's all-encompassing eye, the same admiring candor as all the other characters.

Foote's genuine admiration for both sides is a part of the strength of his battle narratives. Even-handedness, however, by no means exhausts their virtues. Analysis of military history often revolves around techniques. How does one reconstruct with truth so multi-faceted an event as a great battle? In Foote you are not even conscious of technique. You slide into a battle without realizing it—certain things happen, certain indicators begin to accumulate, and then before you know it, you are in the midst of the toils of war without having stopped to think, "Now I'm going to read about a battle." In other words, the battle comes on for the reader as a participant. He truly does make "that war" live again. One can have read everything ever written about Gettysburg Yet read Foote, and you will close the book with the realization that never before had you really understood, never had you seen it all whole and clear until now. "Yes," you will say to yourself, "That was the way it was." And you will enjoy one of those rare moments when you have participated in a completely satisfying performance, a satisfaction that can be renewed many times.

A little more accounting of Foote's successes and we will close the catalog. No work has ever given a juster proportion of the different phases of the War—the eastern, the western, and the trans-Mississippi, than this one. No work has ever done so much justice to the second-rank characters on both sides, for Foote has brought out many dozens of them as memorably as he has the major figures. Finally, it is one of the characteristics of a great piece of literature—the King James Bible or Shakespeare, for instance—that it may be picked up and read with profit at random moments. Pick up *The Civil War: A Narrative*, let it fall open where it will, and begin to read. If called away in a few minutes, you will take with you the sense of having spent a bit of time with profit and satisfaction. And you will have stored up matter that can be usefully contemplated at leisure.

The South has contributed several masterpieces to American historical writing in the 20th century—Douglas Southall Freeman's *R.E. Lee*, Walter Prescott Webb's *The Great Plains*, and others. Foote's *Civil War* will, in the long run, outreach and outlast these because its subject, its scale, and its art are greater. It is said that the American Civil War has generated more printed words than any event in the history of the globe except the life and works of Christ. We have now reached the summit of that literature. *The Civil War: A Narrative* is the best work that has ever been or ever will be written about the great War. It is the place to begin and the place to end any study of America's crucial experience. (1980)

Chapter Three

The Bloody Banner—Long May It Wave

The Flag in South Carolina:
An Unofficial History

The Confederate battle flag continues to be a source of conflict and controversy. One year ago, Michael Westerman of Elton, Kentucky, 19-year-old father of twins, was murdered by black teens who took offense to the Confederate flag hung in the back of Westerman's truck. When one of the black teens, Freddie Morrow, was sentenced to life in prison for the murder, he and his relatives blamed everything on the flag. As the Lexington Herald-Leader reported in January, though "last week's trial was conflicting over the symbolism of the flag, Morrow's grieving relatives have no doubts: the Rebel flag is a provocative symbol of hatred and oppression. [They] blame it for his life sentence in prison."

John Shelton Reed argued a few years ago that the country needed some other symbol for the South than the Confederate battle flag, which so many people, particularly black Southerners, found offensive. I replied that we had little choice in the matter. History gives you your symbols—you cannot make them up. The battle flag has entered into the folk consciousness of the country—indeed of the world—as the symbol of the South. Had I been quick enough I would have added: Because skinheads wear crosses, do we have to take down all the crosses from the churches? The American Nazis in the 1930s, (and American Communists, too) met under the Stars and Stripes and huge portraits of Abraham Lincoln. Does that mean we have to burn all five dollar bills? The Confederate battle flag is too large a symbol to be invalidated by its use or misuse in one particular period.

Sheldon Vanauken, author of the Christian classic *A Severe Mercy*, tells in his autobiography how he, a Virginian, went through a bohemian period in New York after the early untimely death of his wife. During this period, he took part in a number of civil rights demonstrations carrying a placard with the battle flag on one side. More than once, he was stopped by a friendly New York cop with: "Buddy, you're in the wrong demonstration." Vanauken then would turn his placard around to the other side, which said: "Confederates for civil rights."

A report in my local press recently told the story of a World War II incident, typical of many, because it is my impression that the battle flag was carried proudly in that war, in Korea, and even in Vietnam. The Fifth Marine Division, after desperate fighting, took Shuri Castle, the last point of resistance on Okinawa. The only flag available to the first men in was a Confederate battle flag carried in the helmet of Captain Julius Dusenberry, a South Carolinian, which was unfurled and hauled up. As far as I am aware, no one on the front lines objected to the display of that honorable American symbol. Certainly not the local commander, General Simon Bolivar Buckner, Jr., son of a Confederate general, and who was later killed in action.

During the televised events of the fall of Soviet occupation in the Baltic states, I remember a glimpse of one man in the jubilant crowd waving a Confederate battle flag in a sea of Estonian flags. I would like to know what that man was thinking. We ought to consider what the flag meant to him; I do not think it is explained merely by reference to neo-fascism. Did he view the flag as an expression of high spirits? As a symbol of heroic resistance by an outnumbered, conquered people? Was it sympathy expressed by someone whose own national symbols had been forbidden for half a century with another people whose symbols were threatened?

And where is the offense to be found in this honorable American symbol? A Harris poll in 1994, reported by Reuters, found that American adults, by a three-to-one margin, saw nothing offensive in the use of Confederate symbols in state flags. Some 71 percent of Southern whites wanted the symbols kept. Most interestingly, 68 percent of black Americans said they did not find the flag personally offensive, though 31 percent did. (Presumably, the young black men who chased down and murdered Mr. Westerman were among those offended.) These figures suggest that the issue today is an artificial one, agitated for the sake of agitation and to assist the otherwise flagging careers of certain politicians and "civil rights leaders."

Certainly, the efforts to suppress state flags have failed, as in Georgia, despite the entire weight of the civil rights establishment and the Atlanta plutocrats. And since the United States Senate offended the United Daughters of the Confederacy over the flag, the number of chapters of the Sons of Confederate Veterans founded or revived has doubled. I think a number of things happened besides resistance to forced integration to bring the flag into use as the chief symbol of Southern identity. I remember my own father and uncles returning from World War II with stories of how Southerners, particularly rural and working class ones, were denigrated and ridiculed by conscripted urbanites for their speech, manners, attitudes. There was a general cultural attack at the time on "hillbillies." This was the beginning of their sectional consciousness, which had hardly existed before. It was after this that we began to display the flag from the front porch. It was ten years before *Brown v. Board of Education*, and our actions had nothing to do with the Dixiecrat movement or with football, which current academic "experts" claim are the sources of modern use of the flag.

Nor have time and the success of the civil rights movement diminished the Confederate flag as a symbol of Southern identity. On the contrary, the fact that the United States is increasingly a multicultural empire rather than a federal republic will make ethnic identities, including the Southern, even sharper in the future, and their negotiation much more complex. Imagine, for instance, the struggles over symbols that are in the offing in a few years, when Hispanics will be a larger minority than blacks.

I have often spoken to meetings of the SCV, UDC, Civil War roundtables, various heritage groups, all places full of defenders and displayers of the battle flag, and my impression is that for most of these good Americans the flag is a symbol not of white supremacy but of identification with their own ancestors and heritage and an affirmation of their own identity. For those interested in extending the civil rights movement, I suggest that you find another and more constructive battle to fight, and one that you have some hope of winning, because you will not win this one.

The Chicago press reported last year that a Mr. Ernest A. Griffin, a black man of advanced age and a grandson of a member of the United States Colored Troops in the Civil War, owns part of the land which was once the Camp Douglas prison, where some 6,000 Confederate soldiers are buried who died of starvation, disease, exposure, and neglect. Mr. Griffin flies the battle flag in honor of these men, disdaining criticism.

Last May, the United States and Confederate flags were displayed and trooped together at a memorial service for the POWs who perished at Camp Douglas, jointly sponsored by the Confederate POW Society and the re-enactors of the 29th United States Colored Infantry. The program included an invocation by a black pastor, the Reverend Leon Perry, speeches about Camp Douglas, and a series of talks on Native

American Confederates, Hispanic Confederates, Jewish Confederates, and African-American Confederates, in most cases delivered by descendants of the same. Then there was the main address by Mr. Walter Kennedy, an energetic, color-blind defender of everything Southern: "Confederate Diversity: Our Common Ground." The program concluded with Mr. Kennedy's presentation of an award to Mr. Griffin and the singing of "Dixie" by another black American, Mr. Al Ingram.

Much of our present unease comes from a sense of threatened identities and the scars of past conflicts. But it seems to me that our future, if it is to be a happy one, will be in the direction of the reconciliation and mutual respect for all our identities offered by the example of Mr. Kennedy and Mr. Griffin, and not in useless confrontations from which no one can gain. (May 1996)

***

The flag of Quebec flies alone on the government buildings of Quebec province, not alongside or underneath the national flag of Canada. The latter flies only over national installations, like the post office. The flag of Quebec alone is over the parliament building (capitol). So, instead of talking about bringing the Confederate battle flag down from the South Carolina capitol dome, we ought to be talking about removing the spangled symbol of the American Empire, to be replaced at the top by the noble Palmetto banner of South Carolina. Why should the U.S. flag fly over the seat of state sovereignty? (January 1997)

***

The Confederate battle flag is in the news again—specifically the one that has flown from the state capitol dome in Columbia, South Carolina, by legislative resolution, every day since 1962. A combination of leaders of civil rights organizations, out-of-state-owned mass media, and big business powers has been trying to get the flag down for years. Every such effort has been voted down, even with Democratic majorities, and every poll shows quite overwhelming support for the status quo. (The flag flies below the Stars and Stripes of the Empire headquartered in Washington and the traditional Palmetto banner of South Carolina. Strangely, the federal district judges, who usually settle these matters, have kept out.)

Keeping the flag up was something of an issue in the last statewide elections, where every Republican candidate promised, repeatedly, to leave the banner of Southern identity and heritage exactly where it has been. (The party of Lincoln, by a strange twist of fate, is now more or less the conservative party in the South.) The Republicans won all the statewide offices and one house of the legislature—for the first time since the last bluecoats left in 1877.

Suddenly, the flag issue, which seemingly had been put to rest, has been revived by the new Republican governor, one David Beasley, who has proposed that "it is time to bring the flag down." By way of compromise, he suggests flying Confederate banners at the two Confederate monuments on the capitol grounds, though this "compromise" has already been rejected by black legislators.

In so doing, the governor, a former Democrat and self-described born-again Christian, has reversed the stand he took repeatedly in his campaign. According to his explanation, he was led to his new position by prayer (whether to the Almighty or to His earthly deputy Ralph Reed, whose Christian Coalition possibly gave Beasley his small margin of victory, is not clear). The less trusting suspect the advice of political consultants who think the young governor can position himself as a national figure, a foolish hope. But it is pressing for him to try to recapture some political momentum since there is widespread suspicion of administrative incompetence and chicanery. Moreover, this darling of the Christian Coalition is widely believed to have Clintonesque personal tendencies, and he has a father-in-law who operates an abortion mill.

In many ways, battles over symbols are the most important political battles of all. The continuing effort to denigrate and suppress the protean symbol of the bloody St. Andrew's cross of the Confederacy, known universally as the chief representative symbol of the American South, reveals much about the forces at conflict in present American society. Beasley has enlisted all the former governors of both parties and the two United States senators behind his proposals, indicating careful advance orchestration. (None of them had proposed bringing the flag down when they were in a position to!) Whenever all the top old pols of both parties gather round to push something, it is positive proof that a fast one is being put over on the people. (Remember all the senile ex-Presidents who were herded together to support the NAFTA swindle?)

Opponents of the flag claim it is a symbol of slavery, segregation, white supremacy, and defiance of the federal government. It might just as well be argued that its raising had to do with the Civil War bicentennial. In fact, a symbol as large as the Confederate flag has many meanings, the most important being simply an expression of traditional Southern pride and distinctiveness. That is what it primarily means to the large majority of working and middle class citizens of South Carolina who feel that their own values will be betrayed at the behest of special interests, once again, if the governor has his way. And they believe, rightly, that the anti-flag people will only use this as a base to carry on further attacks, since there is hardly a monument or even a street name in the state that is not imbued with Southern history.

The conflict in South Carolina, in fact, comes down to a conflict between the establishment and the people. As always and everywhere, the Republican Party ends up carrying water for its opponents and betraying its constituents. As always, the establishment seeks to put over whatever "respectable opinion" has decided, no matter what the voters think. That is the only real political confrontation in America today. But it seems entirely possible that the establishment, this time, will lose. The common term being applied to the governor's action is "betrayal." Nobody expects much of politicians these days, and the electorate will overlook much, but a "betrayal" is a serious thing that will be remembered and punished.

In this case, the establishment not only seeks to thwart the will of the people. It is also in a relentless pursuit of mediocrity and sameness. Columbia, South Carolina, must become indistinguishable from Columbus, Ohio, which is only a small and early step on the road to the New World Order. (March 1997)

***

The Confederate battle flag still flies every day over the capitol building of South Carolina. Readers may remember that I have several times reported in these pages on the attempts to remove this lonely anti-imperial symbol from public view. One discussion a few years ago even elicited a complaint from then Governor David Beasley. Mr. Beasley, alas, is no longer governor, having to console himself with a part-time position at a Harvard think tank. Having promised not to mess with our flag, he turned around and mobilized the entire Republican establishment to take it down in order to catapult himself into the national limelight, claiming to have received instructions from the Almighty. He thus did the only thing that a Republican could do to ensure that he would not be reelected. A fourth of the Republican voters defected and elected a lackluster Democrat who also promised not to mess with our flag. His sincerity, of course, is already in question. (I sadly must tell folks that they are mistaken if they believe that Republicans in South Carolina are rock-ribbed conservatives. The Republican establishment is merely a pork-barrel machine, though manned by folks who are instinctually more conservative than their compatriots in Connecticut or Illinois, which is why none of our federal judges has interfered in this matter. The legendary Strom Thurmond long ago traded the role of Dixiecrat for that of the World's Greatest Patronage Artist.)

The battle has been joined again, with the NAACP declaring a boycott of the state until the flag is removed. So far, this has had little effect. In some quarters, there have been expressions of satisfaction: "Does this mean Myrtle Beach won't get to host Freaknik?" But the social forces that have so far defeated an anti-flag campaign backed by Big Politics, Big Business, Big Civil Rights, Big Religion, and Big Media are worth some attention.

To begin with, members of the legislature, which has the deciding say in the matter, have to listen to real voters rather than to banks and newspapers—at least part of the time. And *pace* Samuel Francis, the Council of Conservative Citizens was not responsible for saving our flag. Its efforts, including rallies by tattooed motorcycle thugs and David Duke followers, have been resoundingly counterproductive—just what the media wanted.

Rather, the battle has been won because we are still a people, nearly unique among turn-of-the-millennium Americans, with a real historical memory. A lot of us know how great-grandfather died with the colors at Gettysburg or was starved and frozen to death by the Yankees at Elmira. Or how great-grandmother was burned out of house and home and had the jewelry ripped from her ears by liberators in blue.

We also know that we made a bargain at the end of Reconstruction: As long as we served the United States loyally, our history would be a respected part of the American story. We have done our share—or perhaps more—in every one of the wars since. The other side, as usual, has failed to keep its part of the bargain. There is now a concerted effort to expunge us. Several U.S. military directives have banned "the Confederate flag, the Nazi swastika, and curse words" from the empire's property. In neighboring North Carolina, civilian employees of the Coast Guard were threatened with security investigations for having Sons of Confederate Veterans stickers on their private vehicles. Isn't this the way ethnic cleansing starts?

Recently, a Catholic academy in Greenville fired its best teacher because he refused to remove a small Confederate flag that hung in his classroom along with a number of other historical American flags. The demand for removal resulted from a complaint by a *prospective* parent, a recent arrival from Jamaica, who also complained about the crosses.

And St. Michael's Episcopal Church, one of the two most historic churches in historic Charleston, has refused, because of the flag, to permit the Sons of Confederate Veterans to hold a memorial service for the heroic crew of the CSA submarine *Hunley*. (This is the second crew, not the one the movie was made about. They are still at the bottom of the bay.) Not only does St. Michael's yard contain the bones of numerous Southern heroes, but its steeple was used as a rangefinder by the Unionists during the brutal 1863-65 siege of the city. The Episcopal hierarchy continues its apparently irreversible slide into communism and sodomy. The Confederate battle flag, someone should tell the authorities at St. Michael's Church, is only one of two national flags in the Western Hemisphere that is based on a Christian, rather than a Jacobin, design. The other flies in Quebec.

We begin to see a pattern here, and one we don't like. We are not going down that slippery slope if we can help it. So our flag on the capitol has become an issue transcending a merely prudential matter. The main argument for removal has been that the flag offends black citizens. (Opponents also claim it is bad for business, which is patently untrue.) But it is not at all clear that black citizens, as distinct from their self-appointed spokespersons, feel this way. And interestingly, according to polls a good half of the thousands of Rust Belt refugees who have settled among us in recent times are pro-flag. Indeed, I would think even admirers of Old Abe and Billy Sherman would take alarm at the anti-Confederate hatred that is in full cry these days.

The real impulse behind the well-financed anti-flag campaign is imperialism. Columbia, South Carolina, is not to be permitted to differ from Columbus, Ohio, except in cutesy ways that will attract outsiders who will graciously employ our people to change their sheets and fix their toilets. Our newspapers, which used to be local, are now owned by chains and manned by lowbrow creatures from Detroit. The Columbia paper is Exhibit A. Founded by a family that included a Confederate cavalry general and a heroic Cuban revolutionary (pre-1898), it is now the property of Knight-Rider. The paper recently invited an articulate local citizen to write a pro-flag op-ed. They changed his language to mean the opposite of what he had said in order to make it sound "racist."

Yours Truly has been interviewed numerous times by journalists, several of whom have told me that everything reported on the issue is tightly controlled by management. Recently, the AP carried a long story with a few paragraphs of pro-flag comment by Yours Truly. The "local" newspaper cut my comments out. Normal journalistic practice would be to emphasize the local angle of a story. But pro-flag comments from a local semi-dignitary who has never belonged to the Ku Klux Klan could not be permitted to mar the official line.

The flag of our ancestors goes along with the Nazi swastika! That is the story now repeated everywhere. Nazi Germany was a totalitarian state. There was no barbed wire around the plantations. They were places where people were born and lived. Places that many of them, black and white, remembered as consoling, at least compared to what came later. The Southern Confederacy was so free that, even in the midst of ruthless invasion, the government never suppressed persons, newspapers, or local or state governments, something Mr. Lincoln found necessary repeatedly. And we never tried to conquer another country. We were the ones invaded and conquered by a stronger power. That our flag represents Nazism would be a surprise to the South Carolina captain who raised it over the castle on Okinawa as part of the first squad inside. And to his commander, Gen. Simon Bolivar Buckner. Jr., son of the CSA general of the same name. And to Gen. Nathan Bedford Forrest, Jr., who died in the skies over Germany in 1944. Will we now have to change the name of the "Memphis Belle" to the "Cleveland Playmate"? (January 2000)

***

The Confederate flag which has been in a place of honor (though not sovereignty) above the South Carolina capitol for almost forty years was removed on July 1. The removal is made possible because Republicans in the legislature, who had pledged themselves not to touch the flag, showed the white feather and accepted, as Republicans are wont to do, a "compromise." (It is not a com-promise.) Curiously, the GOP members had a remarkable change of heart right after the filing deadline for primary opposition had passed.

A Confederate flag (another version than the universally familiar one) will supposedly now be flown next to a monument on the capitol grounds, while the state will build an African-American monument and establish an MLK holiday. And, in a provision kept quiet by the legislators and media until the last moment, Confederate flags will also be removed from the legislative chambers where they have hung from time immemorial.

It is no compromise because the NAACP has not lifted its (totally ineffective) boycott. Though the customary payoffs (and more than the customary) were made to get the "compromise" through, the Black Caucus has already declared war against the flag that is to go on the monument. The bottom line is that the Republican leadership in the most conservative state had a chance to say No to political correctness in a way that would have garnered international attention, and they chickened and ran.

But perhaps the only surprise is that they held out as long as they did given the pressures brought to bear. The President of the United States visited us and told us that people who honor the Confederate flag are backward looking and should seek a better life. Given the source, we have some doubts about exactly what was meant by a "better life." But we were not in doubt when he likened those of us who honor the rebel banner to Serbs. We know what happened to them. Students rioted at the University of Washington State and burned our flag. Apparently they were aroused to passion after an Asian-American student wrote a defense of the flag in the campus rag. Southerners have always been at a tremendous disadvantage in these matters. It would never occur to us to tell people in Washington State what to do. Why, we can go for months without even thinking of them. But they sure are concerned about us.

Of course, the easy answer is that they are naturally righteous against our notorious racial oppression. We are known sinners who always need correction, and they are just the folks to do it. This excuse worked better forty years ago. Has anybody noticed lately that the most segregated states are Massachusetts, New York, and Illinois? That there is a net migration of black Americans back to the South?

A Southerner can maybe be forgiven for suspecting that there is something going on here that does not have much to do with objective conditions. We might even suspect there may be a little something psychologically wrong with people whose life seems to revolve around correcting other people who live at a distance. It is not a part of *our* national character, but it definitely is of theirs.

Surfing the net during our controversy, I came across a diatribe against our flag by a certified academic. According to this learned gentleman (and he is rather typical) the South is a demonic culture responsible for all the evils of the known world. He is alarmed that "The Southern gun culture" is in danger of taking over the whole country.

Now let's see, a weirdo from New York, trained as a killer by the U.S. government, comes to the South and blows up several hundred people. Ah, the evil "Southern gun culture" at work again. Doubtless, the Unabomber from Harvard and Berkeley is just one more example. Not to mention the Columbine shooters. After all, Walter Cronkite told us that it was evil Texas right-wingers who were responsible for Oswald (New York) and Ruby (Chicago). It's an old story. The abolitionists proclaimed the depravity of Southerners and their own whiteness while they were financing looting and killing on a mass scale. Do you think the Branch Davidians would have been massacred if their headquarters had been in Ohio? In films, the dangerous killer is Southern-accented, of course. The facts are that most of the notorious serial killers of recent years have been Yankees who roamed the South for their victims. Like the nice Mormon boy, Ted Bundy. (The Mormons seem to have a genetic psychotic streak, like Apaches and Albanians.) Yes, what an ideal place America could be if we could just finish wiping out those Rebs!

No doubt the 150,000 Yankees who move to South Carolina every year are braving the perils out of unselfish dedication to missionary work.

We Southerners are in many ways a simple people. We like to think of ourselves as Americans and don't even notice the hate we get. Many of the turncoats in the legislature blathered at length about their dedication to the USA. That misguided sentiment and a vague (and false) hope that removal of the flag would enhance racial conciliation were the only decent motives involved in their betrayal. Being Republicans, the turncoats spent less time talking about the meaning of their capitulation than they did debating whether they could still collect the money from selling the popular Confederate flags that have flown over the capitol, when the flag moved to the monument. It is difficult to see what the Republican leadership hoped to gain (except that doubtless visions of federal judgeships and assistant secretary of this and that in the Bush administration danced in many heads). But it is easy to see what the NAACP got out of the controversy. Formerly wracked by debt and leadership scandals, they are now riding with full coffers and great momentum. Of course, they don't see the "compromise" touted by Republican leaders but merely another victory.

I will bet that the campaign against Confederate symbols is building toward a demand for reparations for slavery. A gentleman I know was browsing the Walmart with his family in a Confederate T-shirt and was hustled out by two security men. Parents with flags on their vehicles have been refused entrance to school grounds to pick up their children.

And this is in South Carolina! You heard it here first: After the elections, expect a Democratic bill for $10 billion a year for ten years. The Republicans will compromise with $9 billion and federal gun confiscation.

The public obsession with the domestic servitude that existed in this country (and others) up until a century and a half ago, has reached the dimensions of Bolshevic indoctrination. We are very close to having an official version of history for which punishment will be made for dissent. The National Park Service is now de-emphasizing battles at its battlefield parks and emphasizing slavery. That slavery was the most important thing in American history or the most important thing even in the War of Southern Independence would astonish Lincoln, Grant, and Sherman. The bureaucratic historians of my state have declared it to be unquestionable historical *truth* that the War was over slavery and only slavery. *Truth*, not an interpretation.

Yet the victory in the banishing of the rebel banner from honor in South Carolina does not go to African-Americans or even to their official leaders. It goes to the state Chamber of Commerce, which spent hundreds of thousands of dollars and carried out a lobbying campaign of vicious intensity over a period of years.

The state Chamber of Commerce's wholly owned subsidiary, the state Republican party, doubtless hopes to make the best of the situation, expecting that the NAACP will get the blame and that the voters will forget after a while. They are politicians and politicians always look at the short-range personal benefits, the next poll, the next brown bag of cash, etc. That is how you tell the difference between a politician and a statesman. They may be surprised.

Remember that a Republican governor has already been kicked out for betraying us flag people and that over 70 percent of the Republican voters in a non-binding referendum voted not to move the flag. The most popular bumper sticker in Carolina now is "No Votes for Turncoats." followed by "Take it Down" next to the Stars and Stripes.

Our flag was not only international news, but a major issue in the Presidential campaign comedy. Of course, Gore is against us, though he comes from a state (nominally) that is replete with Confederate observances and symbols. The real issue was with the Republicans. The statesmanlike Mr. Bush opined that the flag was a matter for South Carolinians alone to decide, which allowed him easy victory in the primary. The traditionalists and pro-flag people don't trust Bushes and were poised to vote for Alan Keyes. Two or three days before the election, in a move obviously orchestrated to benefit Bush, Keyes attacked the flag and Bob Jones University, leaving the field to the Governor from Connecticut (er, Texas).

In regard to the sincerity of Mr. Bush's neutral position on the flag, let me mention merely that Bush's Number One campaign man in the state is the same fellow who has been heading up the massively funded business anti-flag campaign for the past several years.

But the real comic relief was provided by McCain, who, indeed, like many more prominent Americans than are willing to admit it, has Confederate ancestors. His position was that he understood why people honor the flag, implying that it is OK with him. After the election he made a special trip back to tell us that he had lied to help his chances in the primary. The flag of the Confederacy is evil and must be banished. As if anybody cares what he thinks. The comedy is heightened when you realize, which he apparently had not figured out, that his lie did not help him at all because the Bush people made sure his real opinion was widely circulated.

So, our legislators have agreed with those who say that our flag is a symbol of hate. They caved in to pressure. But this is what Republicans do. Remember how Nixon campaigned against the Democrats and then adopted all their programs and their unpopular war. You can no doubt recall your own favorite treason against conservative voters.

We made a mistake in allowing the politicians to treat the issue as merely one of "heritage." Heritage can be acknowledged in one place as well as another. Those of us who wanted to keep our flag where we could see it every day did so because we realize that the bloody St. Andrew's Cross has not so much to do with history, the Civil War, or slavery. It is rather the most potent symbol in the world today of a spirit of resistance to all that is summed up by the label New World Order—and universally recognized as such.

The showboating mayor of Charleston organized a march from the sea to the capitol to protest the flag, with various sports and other celebrities. The march was a media event, only three people actually doing it, though crowds were brought out for media occasions. The "marchers" reached the capitol and held their rally, with about 400 people, reported in the media as 2,000. On the other side of the capitol we pro-flag people gathered, about 400, reported by the media as 200. (We were at a disadvantage because it was a workday.) The press missed, of course, what was the real news—the real history being made. (One of the characteristics of the imperial mind is rigid repetition of formula in place of actual thought.) On the pro-flag side two dynamic articulate black men, J.J. Johnson and H.K. Edgerton, spoke out *for* the flag! On the anti-flag side a bunch of pasty old politicians and academics mumbled their leftist incantations. Those incantations are vile and false, but they speak in the voice of Power. (August 2000)

***

Well, the flag came off the capitol dome, but let's look at the positive side. We really got their attention. Our battle flag became the focus of international discussion as well as an issue in the presidential comedy, er, campaign.

The politicians succumbed, as they usually do, because pressure groups are nearly always more powerful than plain folk. What the politicians thought they had to do signifies a lot about them but absolutely nothing about our flag. The conservative party in the most conservative State in the Union had a chance to say *no* to political correctness in a way that would have garnered international attention and applause. Instead, they got lost in details.

They chose to make it simply a "heritage" issue. In retrospect it was a mistake for us flag supporters to let the politicians deal with the flag as a "heritage" issue. Heritage can be acknowledged in one place as well as another. As usual, the leftists grasped the real issue while the conservatives dithered. The flag does not represent only or even primarily the Confederate soldier. It represents Dixie and its four centuries of unique and admirable culture.

But why it really gets so much attention (and will continue to do so) is this: It is the most potent symbol in the world today of brave resistance to authoritarian government. That is why it was unfurled by the Eastern Europeans a few years ago when they were liberated. That is why it is hated by every New World Order flunky in the universe. That is why it is now banned from the public space of the world, though it appeared with honor as an American symbol until very recently.

Our representatives have succumbed to the campaign to brand our flag as no more than a symbol of hate. Very well. The bloody and beautiful St. Andrew's cross won't fly over politicians anymore. That's for the best. It is not a government banner—it is the people's banner, and I predict we are going to be seeing it in the future more often and in more places than ever before because they will never be able to suppress the universal symbol of the spirit of liberty. (September 2000)

***

The Bloody Banner—Long May It Wave

He's back. No, not Jason, not Freddie. It's David Beasley. You remember him. He was turned out of the South Carolina governor's office in 1998 after betraying a campaign promise not to disturb the Southern flag on the state capitol dome. He turned a certain reelection victory for a Republican incumbent into a loss to a lackluster Democratic nobody. (The Democratic Nobody, of course, then betrayed *his* promise not to disturb our flag.)

Beasley is now a candidate for the Republican nomination for the U.S. Senate. If you believe the newspapers and the announced polls, he is the front-running candidate, likely nominee, and future Senator.

Those readers with long memories may recall that Governor Beasley reversed himself and tried to get rid of the flag because the Lord told him it was the right thing to do. There was speculation that he had also been tempted, by whom was not stated, with the prospect of a Vice-Presidential nomination with George W. Bush. (Not the first "progressive Republican Southern" governor to fall for that old trick.)

Where has Beasley been since he went down to defeat, enquiring minds may want to know? Well, after his election loss he was rewarded by Harvard with the John F. Kennedy Profiles in Courage Award. This almost never goes to Republicans, but an exception was made for a Southern governor who had heroically tried to bring his backward, bigoted constituents into line with Massachusetts enlightenment and virtue. After that (according to a two-page puff piece in the Columbia *Snake*. March 14, 2004) Beasley moved his courageous profile over to Merrill Lynch as "senior bond expert" at $1 million per annum. The newspaper is sympathetic about the pay cut their hero will have to take when he goes to the Senate.

We all should be sympathetic to the heavy price that has to be paid by heroic liberal statesmen who take a stand against ignorant and depraved Southerners. After all his suffering the Profile is back. It just proves, I suppose, that you can't keep a good man with a million dollars down.[9] (March 2004)

---

9   Beasley lost the Senate primary badly.

Scholars' Statement in Support of the Confederate Flag

Statement of College and University Professors in Support of the Confederate Battle Flag Atop the South Carolina Statehouse, drafted just before the legislative "compromise."

To the General Assembly and People of South Carolina:
Certain academics have issued a statement on the cause of the Civil War as it relates to the controversy over the Confederate battle flag. They held a press conference on March 31 for the purpose of avowing on their authority as professional historians that the flag represents only the evil waging of war against the United States in defense of slavery and not an honorable heritage as most South Carolinians believe.

We consider that statement misleading in its content and an inappropriate intrusion of supposed academic expertise into a political controversy. Their statement reduced to essentials declares that the people of South Carolina are suffering from ignorance and delusions about their history and must be corrected by the superior wisdom of these professors.

This is presumptuous under any circumstances, but especially so when it attempts to settle a public question by declaring as gospel truth what is in fact a highly debatable historical interpretation.

There are no immutable truths in secular history. History is human experience and may be viewed always from many different perspectives. Indeed, it is a truism that historical interpretations are always changing. This is especially so in regard to an event as huge and complex as the War for Southern Independence of 1861-1865, a war in which an estimated one quarter of the white men of South Carolina lost their lives and in which we suffered invasion and devastation, aimed with malice forethought at civilians, unprecedented in American history. Devastation which brought suffering and death to black as well as white South Carolinians.

It should be an elementary lesson in historical scholarship that so immense and revolutionary an event as the War has no one single and simple explanation or cause. The primary social value of the study of history is developing the ability to see different sides of a question, an ability needed for wise and temperate citizenship, and which is available to all, not just to "experts." This balance is conspicuously absent in the statement we contradict.

The anti-flag historians appear to be unaccustomed to having their ex-cathedra declarations of truth challenged. This in itself shows an inappropriate attitude towards historical knowledge, which is, properly understood, the product of evolving debate. And if their interpretation is to be accepted as official public truth, as they wish, then it will require not only the suppression of the Confederate flag but of almost every tradition, memorial, and monument celebrating the history of South Carolina. In effect it requires the people of South Carolina to accept the judgment that their heritage is shameful and should be erased. And who can doubt that the removal of the flag would be followed by further demands to conform public displays to the official historical "truth."

The scholars we contradict violate another elementary rule of scholarship by asserting that sweeping historical judgments may be established by cutting and pasting snippets of quotations. To the contrary, such judgments are justified only by deep knowledge of the context. They quote some Confederate statements that secession was undertaken solely for the defense of slavery. Yes, Confederate leaders said some of the words attributed to them. They also said a great many other things during the course of the War and the years of political strife that preceded it. We have attached to our statement, to show how the game is played, our own collection of snipped quotations on the causes of the War.

It is quite true that anticipation of federal interference in local affairs after the unprecedentedly one-sided administration took office in 1861 was one of the reasons the Southern States sought to regain the independence their fathers and grandfathers had won in the American Revolution. Indeed, their fathers had declared that governments rest on the consent of the governed, who may alter or abolish them. To say that differing opinions in regard to the longstanding institution of domestic slavery were involved in the conflict is not the same thing as proving that the War was caused solely by slavery.

A historical generalization that we can make confidently from the evidence is that opposition to slavery before and during the War did not rest upon benevolence toward African-Americans, nor did it provide any sincere or realistic program for their freedom and integration into American life as citizens. We know that racism was pervasive in the North, even among that minority who sincerely opposed slavery.

Indeed, the great French observer, Tocqueville, found racism stronger in the North than in the South.

Our seceding forebears knew perfectly well that the agitation over slavery was hypocritical and self-interested and that its chief motivating factor was resentment that Southern society provided skilled and determined opposition to the desire to turn the United States into a centralized pro-business state. When the South seceded the Northern majority immediately enacted high tariffs, a national bank system, land giveaways and business subsidies as national policy, long before emancipation was adopted (as a war measure).

More importantly, though the desire to defend a longstanding way of life from outside interference was a partial cause of secession, slavery did not cause the War, the invasion and conquest of Southern States and the destruction of their legal and democratically-elected governments was justified by the desire to preserve the Union, as was stated repeatedly by Lincoln. There is evidence that many of the soldiers fighting for the Union felt angered and betrayed by the emancipation proclamation (which did not, however, free any slave).

Had Southerners been motivated solely by the desire to preserve slavery they would hardly have chosen secession since slavery was securely protected under the Constitution. Lincoln avowed repeatedly that he had no intention to interfere with slavery in the States and was willing to accept what could have become the Thirteenth Amendment—a permanent guarantee of slavery. It is also clear that Lincoln and most of his supporters did not believe in racial equality and that his preferred solution to the racial problem was to ship the African-Americans away, and short of that to leave them to "root hog or die."

A reasonable interpretation of secession is that Southerners left the Union because they saw an inveterate hostility toward their society, culture, political heritage, and economic interests, which promised endless irritation and strife in a Union which their fathers had founded in a spirit of harmony. In no way did secession threaten democratic government. Rather the contrary is true, as detached foreign observers nearly unanimously observed at the time.

It is relevant that the Confederate government late in the War made an offer of emancipation to European governments in exchange for help in winning Southern independence and was enlisting black Southern volunteers. At the time of secession, James H. Thornwell, probably the most influential clergyman in South Carolina and a strong believer in Southern independence, outlined a program for an evolutionary emancipation.

It is clear to those who have studied the record and not relied on recent Hollywood for their understanding of the War, that the War was fought by the Southern people honorably against overwhelming odds and ruthless tactics with skill, courage, and proportionate suffering not equaled by any other group in American history. (Except for Native Americans whose extermination was underway by the same federal government that invaded the South.) Those of us who are descended from these people are justifiably proud of a great heritage.

In fact, respect for the Confederate heritage, until very recent political agitation, was a near universal American sentiment. The Confederate battle flag was carried by fighting men in World War II, Korea, and Vietnam. The display of our flag has been officially supported by the organized descendants of Union veterans. Shelby Foote, the greatest historian of the War, has publicly endorsed leaving our flag alone, a weight of authority greater than many ordinary historians put together.

We deny that the statement we criticize contains unquestionable historical "truth" and undisputed consensus of experts. Along with the natives there are many signers who come from the Northern part of the country, where the brutal invasion and conquest of the Southern States has long been justified by the myth that it was motivated by righteous idealism in behalf of the oppressed. This myth is what the great Southern writer Robert Penn Warren called a pernicious "Treasury of Virtue." The adoption of this myth by so many of our professors indicates a sad conquest of our minds.

The anti-flag professors discount the "Lost Cause," which means they believe that everything said by Southerners after the War about the conflict was a deceitful rationalization and everything said by Northerners was a pure truth. Those scholars' statement does not represent historical "truth." It represents the currently fashionable interpretation in prestigious northern institutions and their imitators (institutions which are dubious guides for the people of South Carolina on this as on other public matters). If there is any lesson to be drawn it is not that our flag is shameful but that our institutions are in a sadly colonial condition. This is all the more true when we reflect that several professors, some very distinguished, who agreed with our statement, declined to sign in fear of future professional reprisals. With that reality in mind, we have declined to use the names of a number of young, untenured professors who support our statement.

Indeed, the conformity of opinion that was expressed in a pseudo-official press conference (held in the South Caroliniana Library amongst the portraits, busts, and written records of South Carolina heroes) is a far cry from the lively debate and dispute that should characterize institutions of higher learning. The putting forth of unquestionable historical interpretations is quite obviously a dangerous tendency in a democracy.

The signers below were gathered in a short time. They are not all historians but represent a variety of humane fields, which may allow them a broader perspective than that of historians obsessed with the history of racial strife. (Most of the signers of the anti-flag statement are not specialists in Civil War history.) All of the signers below hold doctoral degrees and most are professors in institutions of higher learning. While many of the signers from other States are South Carolina natives and/or holders of degrees from our institutions, a number of them are northern born.

Even if the anti-flag professors' interpretation of the cause of the War for Southern Independence were entirely correct it would be irrelevant to the present controversy. To argue, as they do, that the present form of the flag was never flown over the capitol during the War is to make only a trivial point. Many forms of banners were used at that time. The battle flag in its now familiar form is understood all over the world, form Helsinki to Timbuktu, as the symbol not only of the Confederacy but also of the American South.

As such, it represents not only the Civil War, but all three and a half centuries of a unique and admirable Southern culture. It also represents around the world a symbol of gallant defiance of authoritarian governments. In that use it has been often displayed in recent years in European countries escaping from communist captivity.

The controversy is no longer a mere housekeeping matter for South Carolina. The fact is that the nationalization of the issue has made our flag the symbol to millions of Americans of a last stand against Political Correctness and increasingly uniform and dictated views of our history. And, finally, racial reconciliation is best sought by the mutual understanding of black and white South Carolinians, not by the distortion or suppression of Southern heritage.

The Bloody Banner—Long May It Wave

Quotations

"The North, it seems, have no more objections to slavery than the South have."—*John Stuart Mill, 1861*

"The Northern onslaught upon slavery was no more than a piece of specious humbug designed to conceal its desire for economic control of the Southern states." —*Charles Dickens, 1862*

"Resolved, that the several States composing the United States of America, are not united on the principle of unlimited submission to their General Government." —*Thomas Jefferson, 1798*

"Our present condition, achieved in a manner unprecedented in the history of nations, illustrates the American idea that governments rest upon the consent of the governed, and that it is the right of the people to alter or abolish governments whenever they become destructive of the ends for which they were established." —*Jefferson Davis, inaugural address as President of the Confederate States, 1861*

"I deemed that you were fighting the battles of our liberty, our progress, and our civilization; and I mourn for the stake which was lost at Richmond more deeply than I rejoice over that which was saved at Waterloo." —*British historian of liberty Lord Acton to Gen. R. E. Lee, 1866*

"Although the South would have preferred any honourable compromise to the fratricidal war which has taken place, she now accepts in good faith its constitutional results, and receives without reserve the amendment which has already been made to the constitution for the extinction of slavery. This is an event that has long been sought, though in a different way, and by none has it been more earnestly desired than by citizens of Virginia." —*Gen. R.E Lee, 1866*

"Any people anywhere, being inclined and having the power, have the right to rise up and shake off the existing government, and form a new one that suits them better. This is a most valuable, a most sacred right—a right which we hope and believe is to liberate the world. Nor is this right confined to cases in which the whole people of an existing government may choose to exercise it. Any portion of such people, that can, may revolutionize, and make their own so much of the territory as they inhabit." —*Abraham Lincoln, 1848*

"What then will become of my tariff?"—*Abraham Lincoln to Virginia peace delegation, March 1861*

"Slavery is likely to be abolished by the war power and this I and my friends are in favor of, for slavery is but the owning of labor and carries with it will see to it is made out of the war must be used as a means to control the volume of money."—*Private circular of Northern banker, late 1861*

"If I could save the Union without freeing any slave I would do it, and if l could save it by freeing all the slaves I would do it; and if I could save it by freeing some and leaving others alone I would do that. What I do about slavery, and the colored race, I do because I believe it helps to save the Union, and what I forbear, I forbear because I do not believe it would help to save the Union."—*Abraham Lincoln to Horace Greeley, August 22, 1862*

"It must be admitted, truth compels me to admit ... Abraham Lincoln was not, in the fullest sense of the word, either our man or our model. In his interests, in his associations, in his habits of thought, and in his prejudices, he was a white man. He was preeminently the white man's president, entirely devoted to the welfare of white men. He was ready and willing at any time during the last years of his administration to deny, postpone, and sacrifice the rights of humanity in the colored people, to promote the welfare of the white people of his country." —*Frederick Douglass, noted African-American leader, 1876* (2000)

Maurice Bessinger's Stand

Foreword for *Defending My Heritage: The Maurice Bessinger Story*, by Maurice Bessinger, West Columbia, South Carolina: Lmbone-Lehone Publishing Company, 2001, 221 pages.

A historian of the future who wants to know about our present times in South Carolina will learn nothing—or rather less than nothing—from perusing the "local" newspapers. They are being written and edited by lackeys of distant press lords. Their mission, like Orwell's press in 1984, is to present an official view of reality. The corporate media are vicious to those who don't accept their version of truth. Worse, their paid hacks are so unbelievably ignorant that they think parroting labels is equal to historical knowledge and political judgment. If that future scholar wants to know about the real experiences and feelings and thoughts of real South Carolinians, and about the real causes of important events, he will look into Maurice Bessinger's spirited memoirs.

Recent experiences and friends' urgings have prompted Mr. Bessinger to set down the recollections of his first seventy years. In May 2000, the South Carolina General Assembly removed the Confederate battle flag, the starry St. Andrew's cross, from a place of honor (though not sovereignty) on the capitol dome, where it had been for almost 40 years, and from the legislative chambers where it had been from time immemorial.

This victory came after a long anti-flag campaign largely sustained by the aforesaid newspaper culprits and by big business interests represented in the Chamber of Commerce. The action was against the opinion of the democratic majority, was obviously the product of backroom deals, and required a number of Republican legislators to break their explicit and repeated promises to their constituents. Had there been a popular referendum, as in Mississippi in April 2001, the flag would still be up.

The reasoning apparently was that what is good for the Chamber of Commerce is good for the people. What it proved was that the Chamber of Commerce does not even know what is good for itself, much less for the people. The NAACP boycott was a failure. Though the media never let the public know, tourism was up. The state's economy had been booming during the entire time the flag had been over the dome.

The Chamber of Commerce wished to flex its muscles, a (small) segment of society wanted to kowtow to Political Correctness, and Republican legislators wanted to remove an embarrassing issue from George Bush Junior's election campaign (in return for which they might hope for federal favors). So much for majority rule.

A lot of us, and not only in South Carolina, were committed to keeping the flag up. It is one of the last symbols in the world of a spirit of defiance to centralized power. It also is universally recognized as a symbol of the South, of our unique people, culture, and history. The General Assembly in effect had validated the claims that our history is shameful, that everything we believe about it is a lie, and that all the attacks on us as a people by vindictive and self-interested outsiders were justified. The flag haters were not just attacking our history, which they ignorantly and consistently misrepresented, they were attacking *us*.

Mr. Bessinger was one of us. A true American patriot, he had for years flown over-sized U.S. government flags at his chain of highly successful barbecue restaurants. In response to the General Assembly's slight to the St. Andrew's cross, Mr. Bessinger raised the noble palmetto banner of South Carolina, with the battle flag below it, at all of his locations around the capital city metropolitan area.

In a press conference he announced that he was taking this action to focus public attention on the lost constitutional heritage of states' rights. Why should not the palmetto banner fly over the sovereign state's institutions rather than the flag of the federal government, which can appropriately be flown over federal institutions? (This is actually the case in the Canadian province of Quebec.) Mr. Bessinger was hoping to open a public discussion and debate on Constitutional principles.

The press lords and the money lords do not even know what you mean when you call for discussion and debate. That idea comes from the old days of democratic government in the U.S. All they know about is handing down commandments. The media barely mentioned the constitutional point. Instead, they got in an uproar about *slavery*, which ended a century and a half ago and no one has proposed to re-institute. So much for the people's right to know.

But that was just the beginning.

Mr. Bessinger is a well-known public figure, a Korean War combat veteran, and a hugely successful entrepreneur in the true Horatio Alger fashion. He produces unique products that have received national attention and sales, and his entrepreneurship has been awarded a number of prizes. He is also well known as a good employer, rare in his industry, a devout Christian, and a community philanthropist.

As he tells herein, within a short time after his raising of the state flag, most chain stores (many of them Southern-based) had pulled his frozen products and world-famous barbecue sauce from their shelves, and in some cases had shipped them back to him at his expense. Now, of course, free enterprise means that a company can do business with whomever it wishes, or not. But what do we have here? Gigantic corporations colluding simultaneously to break contracts and *destroy* an independent businessman, not for business reasons but to punish him for his opinions on history and current events!

It should be obvious that the freedom of discussion necessary for democracy cannot exist in such an atmosphere, where money conspires to stifle political dissent. Especially when the corporate media are making sure only one side of a debate reaches the people and slandering dissenters with labels rather than considering their ideas.

Is this a "conspiracy theory"? Conspiracies don't have to consist of men in black raincoats meeting furtively in alleys. History is full of real conspiracies. In fact, conspiracy is the natural way of proceeding for people who want to control events without revealing their true agenda, or who want to achieve power and wealth by manipulation rather than work and achievement. Anyone who has ever seen office politics in action knows that. The various confused and phony excuses given by spokespersons to the thousands who complained about the suppressed food products indicated a striking lack of corporate candor.

In effect, big government, big business, and big media are acting in con-cert, deliberately or not, to suppress public expression of opinions that do not conform to official interpretations of history! Given recent instances of use of deadly federal force against non-conformists and FBI intimidation of people who have done nothing except conduct public activities in support of Confederate symbols, one should think that anybody concerned with true freedom would be alarmed. Remember, it has only been a very few years since the Confederate flag was a universally honored American symbol. The interpretation we are under pressure to accept is a recent invention, like the news broadcasts in *1984*.

In a matter of days, a business built by decades of hard work and customer service had lost a large chunk of its value. Mr. Bessinger might have surrendered and kowtowed to the official line. Those who expected that did not know Maurice Bessinger. Or he could have done what most companies have done in the same situation, pay extortion money to civil rights groups to have the sanctions against his business lifted, and pass the costs on to his customers.

Mr. Bessinger has chosen to fight, unequal as the contest may be. Anybody who knows him would expect nothing else.

I should make clear that Mr. Bessinger's memoirs are concerned with more than current events. We are also privileged to see his experiences as a soldier, a Christian, and a businessman. He gives us an insider's history of forty years of politics. His observations about faith, work, education, and many other matters are evidence of that rare breed, a man who thinks for himself, and thinks well.

My favorite parts of this autobiography are the accounts of his early years in the rural poverty that was the common experience of white as well as black South Carolinians. Mr. Bessinger observes that poverty was the most controlling experience of life for South Carolinians during the century just passed, even more than the color bar.

No truer words were ever written. The South was far from perfect, but neither did it fit the picture held by critical outsiders. My recollections, growing up ten years later, and in another state, are similar to Mr. Bessinger's in regard to the daily relations of the races. My grandfather raised five children on the meager proceeds of a country store. I often saw him give groceries gratis to fatherless black families, I also observed his friendship with better-off black people, some of whose children were doing well even before 1954.

Someday, these real experiences will have to be taken into account if true understanding is to be achieved of the minds and hearts of Southerners, black and white, during the tumultuous decades just passed. Meanwhile, we seem to have made a pretty good peace. It is not the South that today enjoys riots and hatred. Nor is the South, whatever its past misdeeds, responsible for the catastrophic social pathologies of Northern cities. If that were so, why do the conditions get worse the further away from the South in time and space they are?

Mr. Bessinger leaves us with an enlightening experience for anyone who really cares about the life of our people during the historical times just past. He also leaves us with the advice to stick to God, the Constitution, and free enterprise. Who can rightly argue with that? (2001)

The Bloody Banner—Long May It Wave

Confederate Memorial Day Address

At Orangeburg, South Carolina, May 18, 2003

We are here today both to remember and to honor our Confederate forefathers. We remember and honor them, first of all, because they are *ours*. They made us what we are. To honor one's forebears is a deep and universal human inclination.

General Lee, in his farewell address to his men, told them that their four-year struggle for freedom had been marked by "unsurpassed courage and fortitude" and that their "valor and devotion" had endeared them to their countrymen.

Our Confederate forefathers' "valor and devotion" did more than make for themselves a place in the hearts of future generations of Southerners. They also won the lasting admiration of everyone in the world who values skill, sacrifice, and indomitable spirit in defense of freedom.

This is why our bloody St. Andrew's cross appeared spontaneously among many peoples of Europe during their celebrations of liberation from foreign tyranny. Our fathers are admired by the world to a degree seldom granted to lost causes. Their battle flag is a universal symbol of man's striving for freedom.

Gen. James Johnston Pettigrew wrote home on his way to Gettysburg, a few days before he was mortally wounded, "Our reputation, next to the Greeks, will be the most heroic of nations."

What the learned Confederate meant was that, from the long perspective of history, the human action most exemplary of heroism was the stand of the small Greek city-states against the mighty Persian empire in the 5th century B.C. Next to that, most worthy of lasting admiration from the same long perspective, were the outnumbered soldiers of the Confederacy in their resistance to a ruthless conqueror.

Let us remember and never underestimate their sacrifice. One fourth of the white men dead from "our gallant little State of South Carolina," as John C. Calhoun called it. Imagine if WWII had taken the lives of one-fourth of our men as did the War to Prevent Southern Independence!

And the survivors' sacrifices, too, must be remembered by us. General W.R. Cox of North Carolina had been wounded six times previously, but still what was left of his brigade drove back a larger enemy force the day before the surrender at Appomattox. Wade Hampton's restored government of South Carolina in 1876 was almost literally a government of one-legged men because so many of its members had lost limbs in the War, though that had not stopped them from fighting to the last, often strapped in the saddle. These are merely a few examples, out of tens of thousands, of Confederate "courage and fortitude."

And what deeds they had done! I will read from the memoir of the Union General Don Carlos Buell, one of the more generous and decent of the enemy commanders. Here is what he told Northern readers to keep in mind should they be tempted to grow boastful about their victory:

> It required a naval fleet and 15,000 troops to advance against a weak fort, manned by less than 100 men, at Fort Henry; 35,000 with naval cooperation, to overcome 12,000 at Fort Donelson; 60,000 to secure victory over 40,000 at Shiloh; 120,000 to enforce the retreat of 65,000 after a month's fighting and maneuvering at Corinth; 100,000 were repelled by 60,000 in the first campaign against Richmond; 70,000 with a powerful naval force, to inspire the campaign which lasted nine months against 40,000 at Vicksburg; 90,000 to barely withstand the assault of 60,000 at Gettysburg; 115,000 sustaining a frightful repulse from 60,000 at Fredericksburg; 100,000 attacked and defeated by 50,000 Chancellorsville; 85,000 held in check for two days by 40,000 at Antietam; 70,000 defeated at Chattanooga, and beleaguered by 40,000 at Chattanooga to Atlanta; ... and finally 120,000 to overcome 60,000 with exhaustion after a struggle of a year in Virginia.

I cite this testimony from an honest Union commander because there is a prevailing tendency among historians these days to slight and ridicule the efforts of our forefathers to keep their freedom.

Very different from today's historians was the comment about our Confederate forebears made by Union hero Joshua Chamberlain Appomattox; and Chamberlain was typical of real fighting Union soldiers: "[There stood] before us ... the embodiment of manhood, men whom neither toils and sufferings, nor the fact of death, nor hopelessness could bend from their resolve."

Another hard-fighting Union soldier, Ambrose Bierce, was enraged by a Republican bloody shirt orator who wanted to prevent decoration of the graves of Confederate soldiers. Bierce wrote some verses addressed to the Unionist politician:

> The brave respect the brave. The brave
> Respect the dead; but you-you draw
> That ancient blade, the ass's jaw,
> And shake it o'er a hero's grave.

Compatriots here today, no generation of Southerners has ever faced a greater challenge in defending the honor of our forefathers. If we don't do it, it will not be done. We need observances like this. We need to record knowledge about the War that is still carried in family lore and not written down. We need re-enactments. But most of all, we need to realize the nature of the struggle that has been thrust upon us by unscrupulous aggressors against our heritage.

The current President of the United States, while governor of a Southern state, sent flunkies sneaking in the middle of the night to remove two harmless Confederate plaques from a state building. He feared any shred of Confederate remembrance might embarrass his campaign for President.

The current Vice-President of the United States refused to be seen at a funeral in our state if the Confederate flag was displayed or "Dixie" played. These are the acts of "conservative" Republicans, not of Politically Correct leftists.

These are the acts of men who would not be in power without the votes of descendants of Confederates. These are men who carry out their acts in secret, who do not even have the courage to wield the weapon of the ass's jaw.

These actions are vile, insulting, and unforgivable. They must have appropriate response. These people are repulsed or embarrassed by that flag which is to us a beautiful and hallowed object.

Franklin D. Roosevelt was not afraid to be seen in the same place as our battle flag. Neither was Harry Truman, nor Jimmy Carter, nor Ronald Reagan. If you will look at the magazines and newsreels from World War II (and later wars) you will see the Confederate battle flag flying over the tents of American fighting men in the Pacific and painted on American fighting planes, and even appearing in Hollywood versions of the War.

The people who want to suppress our symbols are not friendly folks who will cease and desist if we politely tell them the War was not all about slavery and that we are today good and loyal Americans who only want to honor our heritage. These people don't know what you are talking about when you mention heritage, the recognition of your own forebears. They are not interested in a balanced weighing of the evidence of history. For them history is an abstraction and a weapon of power over others.

In my opinion, it is not really the flag they hate—it is us. They hate Southerners and are determined to defame and eradicate everything Southern. They are repeating a pattern evident before in American history and the very thing our fathers fought so valiantly against. We are not in a fight over historical interpretation; we are in a war against our culture. Until we realize that, until we are prepared to fight the enemy on a broad front, we will not make much progress in truly preserving the honor of those we remember today.

I am certain we can restore our heritage to its rightful place. We need determination. We need the tactical skill that our forefathers used against overwhelming odds. And we need a firm and clear understanding that we Southerners are in a war for our survival as a people-that the relentless barrage of lies against our heritage is more than a series of petty skirmishes about historical interpretation. Despite the enemy's efforts, we have a tremendous well-proven advantage on our side. The heritage we remember and honor today validates itself. It is intrinsically powerful and beautiful and good.

Southern Heritage Then and Now

Order of the Southern Cross Banquet, Sons of Confederate Veterans National Reunion, Asheville, North Carolina, August 1, 2003

As the direct descendant of a private in the 42nd North Carolina and a sergeant in the 20th North Carolina, I am honoured to talk to a group descended from notable officers in our War of Independence-or the War to Prevent Southern Independence, as I like to name it.

Nobody gave me any orders as to what to talk about, which is a happy situation. I am going to talk about "Southern Heritage Then and Now," about the place of Southern heritage in American life.

We all know that before and during the War, and during Reconstruction and for years afterward, our ancestors were officially the demons of American history. We were the evil people who tried to "destroy the greatest nation on earth" because of our lust for slavery. This is easy to believe if you start out with the assumption that everything Yankees do is always righteous and that, obviously, any people who don't want the inestimable blessing of being governed by Yankees are by definition bad people.

There were always decent Northerners who decried this bloody-shirt mentality. It was, interestingly, the Northerners who had actually fought in the War who wanted to treat defeated Southerners with respect and to do what they had fought for-restore the American Union-rather than continue to oppress, exploit, and slander the South.

Joshua Chamberlain at Appomattox saluted the defeated. He later wrote of the Confederates: "There stood before us ... the embodiment of manhood, men whom neither toils and sufferings, nor the fact of death, nor hopelessness could bend from their resolve." And he remembered his feeling was not of triumph but rather that *all* Americans should fall down on their knees and beg forgiveness.

Another hard fighting Union soldier, Ambrose Bierce, was enraged by a Republican orator who wanted to prevent the decoration of Confederate graves. He wrote these verses:

> The brave respect the brave. The brave
> Respect the dead; but you-you draw
> That ancient blade, the ass's jaw,
> And shake it o'er a hero's grave.

But such generous foes then were a minority.

In the 1890s, things began to change. A truce was called to which most Northerners and Southerners subscribed in good faith. It was symbolized by Charles Francis Adams, Jr., who in 1907 made a speech on the centennial of R.E. Lee's birth called "Lee, the American." This speech was delivered in Boston and Charleston and other places. (Charles, Jr. was the only one of the Adamses who actually fought in the War, by the way.)

The *truce* was also symbolized by Fitz Lee and Joe Wheeler and many Southern volunteers joining up for the war with Spain and by joint reunions of Union and Confederate veterans. And by D.W. Griffith, the genius of early American cinema and son of a Confederate soldier, who produced *The Birth of a Nation*, which combined a sympathetic account of Southern experience with an admiring portrait of Lincoln.

The terms of the Truce went something like this. Northerners agreed to stop demonizing Southerners and to recognize that we had been brave and sincere and honourable in the War, although misguided in trying to break up the Union. Northerners agreed also that Reconstruction was a great wrong that would not have happened if Lincoln had lived. And they willingly accepted Confederate heroes like Lee and Jackson as *American* heroes.

For our part, Southerners agreed, in exchange for a little respect, that we were glad that the Union had not been broken up and that we would be loyal Americans ever after, something which we have proved a thousand-fold since.

And both agreed that the War had been a great tragedy with good and bad on both sides, a great suffering out of which had emerged a better and stronger United States.

The Truce held pretty well for a long time, 'til past the middle of the 20th century. I have seen a photograph of Franklin D. Roosevelt making a speech before a huge Confederate battle flag. Harry Truman picked the romantic equestrian painting of Lee and Jackson for the lobby of his Presidential Library. Churchill wrote admiringly of Confederates in his *History of the English Speaking Peoples*. *Gone with the Wind*, book and movie, was loved by audiences worldwide.

If you look at the Hollywood movies and also the real pictures from World War II, you will see battle flags painted on U.S. fighter planes and flying over Marine tents in New Guinea.

Well, my friends, that truce is over.

Let me tell a few stories from recent history. George W. Bush, while governor of a Southern state and running for president, sent his henchmen in the middle of the night to remove two harmless UDC plaques from a state office building. Governor Pataki of New York banned the true Georgia flag from the display at the state capitol.

More recently, Vice-President Cheney refused to come to the funeral of a longtime respected Congressman if that Congressman's wishes to have a Confederate flag and "Dixie" at his funeral were followed. The Secret Service was on hand to make sure that the V.P. as not embarrassed by any display of evil symbols of the Confederacy, (Nevertheless, a few months later, he came back and South Carolinians gave him a dinner at which they contributed $300,000 to his campaign chest.)

These are not leftwing multiculturalists. These are so-called "conservative" Republicans These are people who could not have been elected without the votes of Confederate descendants.

I could spend the rest of the month talking about the total unconditional surrender of Southern institutions to organized hatred of the South. Right now, there is a carpetbagger who holds an endowed chair in history at a major Southern state university who teaches that America would be a better place if Southerners had been exterminated at the end of the War. Another carpetbagger in another endowed chair in history in the South teaches that so-called Southern honour was nothing but crude, violent suppression of dissent. Another teaches that Southern women did not really support the War and their menfolk, but were in secret rebellion against the white male ruling elite. Another teaches that every favourable thing we believe about our ancestors' courage, skill, and honour is a "Lost Cause Myth," a pack of lies made up after the War to cover up our evil and failure.

When the Confederate flag controversy was raging in my state, some 90 historians in the state signed a statement which said that the Confederate flag represents slavery and nothing but slavery, and that this is not an opinion but is a "fact" established by their expert knowledge. The unstated premise was that South Carolinians are deluded about our own history and need to be corrected by wiser people. What they are really saying is that we should discard our history and accept their myths.

Of course, many of these historians were in other fields and knew nothing about the War. Some were recent imports from strange places like Burma or California. Their position did not rest on study and knowledge. It is a party line that you must agree to, to be a member of the club of so-called "experts," an officially proclaimed "truth" not too different from what used to pass for history in the late Soviet Union.

But my main point is: The Truce is over. Those times are gone, gone, gone. Yet many of those who are charged with the defense of our heritage are living in a dream world, pretending that it is still 1950. The breaking of the truce has nothing to do with us. We did nothing to cause it. We kept our part of the bar-gain. It has happened because *they* have changed and *they* are in a mode which requires them to scapegoat *us*—and not for the first time in history.

We have been for several years now fighting brush fires instead of realizing that we are in a war—a cultural cold war with an enemy who wants us dead. Our Confederate heritage is being banished to a dark little forbidden corner of American life labeled "Slavery and Treason." And incidentally, all the vast admirable contributions of Southerners to American history over four centuries are redefined as "American" and not really "Southern."

The people who are after our heritage are not folks we can win over by presenting historical evidence and assuring them that we are good, loyal Americans free of hate. They could not care less about truth or heritage. In fact, they don't even know what we are talking about when we speak of honouring heritage, that is, respecting our forebears. We are not in an argument over the interpretation of the past. Our very identity as Southerners—today and tomorrow, as well as yesterday—is at stake.

If I am right, what should we do? First, I think, we need to embrace and claim all of Southern history, from Captain John Smith and Pocahontas right up to this moment. The four years of war, as important as that is, is only a part of the long and continuing history of Southern people. The SCV summer camps are a great idea. So is the "Lincoln Reconsidered" conference recently sponsored by the Virginia SCV and other groups, and the League of the South and the Abbeville Institute summer schools. We need many more such events where respectable scholars can be mobilized to challenge *their* mythology. We ought to commission a thorough, comprehensive documentation of Union army atrocities, which are now being played down as insignificant, and perhaps mount a campaign for reparations - for after all, Southerners are a people who have been, and still are being, economically exploited through the whole existence of the United States.

But most of all, we need to reorient our thinking and fight this war rather than the last one. And I must say that many of those Southerners who have the most power and influence have betrayed the Southern people and left the real fight to be carried on by blue collar Southern white males, who have less public power than any group in the United States today. We need action from Southerners who have influence, who make campaign contributions, who can call up governors and state legislators and newspaper editors and put on some real pressure.

In one of the greatest of all war films, the 1964 *Zulu*, there is a scene just before a few hundred British soldiers are attacked by thousands of war eager natives. An anxious young soldier asks: "Why us?" The veteran unflappable old sergeant-major replies: "Because we're here, boy, that's why." We are here. If we are going to save our heritage as a part of American life, it will have to be done by us. After us, it will be too late.

The Pledge of Allegiance

By the time this issue of your favorite journal reaches you, the Northern California federal circuit judges' banning of the Pledge of Allegiance will probably have been reversed and the public furor will have faded away. (Two judges decreed that the Pledge violates separation of church and state because of its "under God" interpolation.) In the end all that will have happened is that the politicians had an opportunity to exhibit their courageous support for God and the flag.

In the last half century the federal courts have rearranged race relations in the country in a way that has affected private as well as public life; they have overturned most state constitutions, adopted by the people, in the interest of "one man, one vote"; they have overturned laws of most of the states in order to make possible massive baby killing; they have taken over numerous local governments and school districts and levied taxes on citizens, though the right of the people not to be taxed without their consent has always been the core principle of freedom; they have made criminal law into a contest of technicalities rather than of proof and justice. This very same circuit court is the one, I believe, that interdicted the California democratically adopted proposition barring state benefits to illegal aliens, thereby endowing foreign lawbreakers with all the rights and privileges, indeed with more rights and privileges, than citizens.

In short, whether you like these "policy decisions" or not), a judicial oligarchy has seized massive amounts of power from the people and their elected representatives, has subverted the Constitution and government by the consent of the governed. In response, there has been little more than scattered murmurs from the victims.

But let the courts meddle with something really important, like the Pledge of Allegiance, and outrage knows no bounds. Of course, the Pledge is not a right or a privilege or a duty; it is just a custom and a rather pointless and intrusive one at that. As my friend the Rev. Tim Manning points out, the virtuous do not need a Pledge and the rest will not honor it anyway.

A look at the history of the pledge to the national flag, which is actually a pledge of allegiance not to the country or people but to the federal government, reveals the great irony of the recent controversy.

Such pledges did not mark the early years of the United States. They were unknown until they were employed as coercive devices in the South during the War Between the States and Reconstruction. Note that the Constitution of the United States does not require pledges to the flag or the government. What the Founding Fathers called for is an oath to uphold the Constitution and laws.

The present Pledge was written in 1892 by Francis Bellamy, a defrocked Boston minister and Marxist, for the 400th anniversary of Columbus's first voyage to the New World. It was taken up and promoted by the National Education Association as a way to enforce conformity to "Americanism" among its captive students, especially the first and second generation immigrants.

It really became pervasive during the public frenzy of World War I, when dissenters or suspected dissenters from "100 percent Americanism" were subject to harassment and worse from petty officialdom nearly everywhere. It was recited with great verve at Ku Klux Klan rallies in the 1920s under batteries of United States (not Confederate) flags.

It was not until 1954 that the offensive phrase "under God" was inserted into the Pledge, largely the result of a lobbying campaign by the Knights of Columbus. It was a well-meaning but useless effort. It is not possible to transform what was clearly meant as a technique of mass government-worship into something pious. Meanwhile, I will gladly take oath at any time to uphold the Constitution, but free people should not be asked to give allegiance to a government's flag. (2000)

What is Patriotism?

Southerners are the most loyal to their region of all Americans. Paradoxically-or perhaps not-they are also the most loyal to the United States, quick to repel insult or injury to the country, without the need of folderol about "saving the world for democracy." There is really no paradox at all. Southerners have the old-fashioned virtue of loyalty, and virtues are not divisible.

To put it another way, Southerners are patriots. True patriotism is always built from the ground up-love of family, community, state, and country go together. Thus, it has always been in healthy societies. Patriotism, one of the noblest sentiments of mankind, must be distinguished from nationalism. Patriotism is the love of one's people and land. Nationalism is the worship of one's government, usually accompanied by an aggressive impulse toward other countries.

To the prevailing political and cultural powers of the U.S., America is not a people at all. It is a "proposition." Any human being who manages to reach the shores and affirms the "proposition" can be an American. The "proposition" can change its definition as suits the ruling powers, but it seems to mean something like: prosperity and equality and the divine mission of the United States to transform the world in its own image.

The believers in that kind of America live entirely in the present. That is why they do not even know what Southerners are talking about when they call on their heritage, the real experience of their own families. If one has no heritage to honor and no people to love, then one can only worship government, which presumably will enforce the "proposition." Men will willingly die for their faith and their people. For their propositions they will only send others to die. The stock market, Disneyland, and sports teams do not inspire the kinds of actions that require sacrifice.

Southerners have the least reason of any group of Americans to be loyal to the collective enterprise known as the United States of America.

They have been the victims of ruthless war and occupation. They have ever since been held up by the prevailing powers of the United States as The Other, the evil to be exorcized or the defective to be abolished. Yet, having naturally the virtue of loyalty, Southerners are hardly aware that the power of the "United States" is hostile to them. Take notice of row upon row of crosses at Verdun and Normandy that say

Georgia, and North Carolina, and Texas, and Tennessee. Doubtless a majority of the reservists to be called up in the future, as in the Gulf War, will come from a despised minority of the people—Southerners.

There are perilous times ahead for the United States. Only two things can be known with certainty. Southerners will continue to be loyal, and the ruling powers will never reciprocate. Our role is to pay the taxes, fight the wars, keep our mouths shut and take whatever abuse is heaped upon us.

If they wanted to reciprocate they could give our battle flag, the best American symbol there is of valor and devotion, a place of honor rather than treat it as an object of hatred. And how about a monument to Southerners who died fighting U.S. wars in the 20th century, with a size proportionate to the sacrifice?

Don't hold your breath. (2002)

Chapter Four

State Rights Revisited

War, Reconstruction, and the End of the Union

There is not a more perilous or immoral habit of mind than the sanctifying of success. —Lord Acton

A distinguished American historian of two generations ago once remarked that the historical knowledge of a great many people consists of an enthusiastic belief in a few things that are not so; he had in mind such stories as George Washington and the cherry tree. This is certainly the case today in regard to the War Between the States - still the most important event in American history in the scale of mobilization, casualties, and revolutionary change, and the most definitive event in terms of long-range consequences. A great deal of what passes for common knowledge about this great war in public discourse and government subsidized television propaganda is simply not true.

I have in mind the image of the victorious side marching into battle singing hymns with noble hearts intent on freeing the poor suffering black man from his chains. Or a little less fantastic—to preserve the sacred Union (though why the Union is so sacred remains a little vague). The triumph in 1861-65 of the Republican Party over the will of the American people and the invasion, destruction, and conquest of the Southern States like a foreign territory has somehow, strangely, gotten mixed up with the idea of government of, by, and for the people.

Lest this appear just the ruminations of a nostalgic Confederate, I intend to use mostly Northern and European authorities in my discussion of the War Between the States and its costs. In 1920, H.L. Mencken wrote a little essay on the Gettysburg Address. He praised its "gemlike perfection" and commented that there is nothing else like it in literature:

> It is genuinely stupendous. But let us not forget that it is poetry, not logic; beauty, not sense. Think of the argument in it. Put it into the cold words of everyday. The doctrine is simply this: that the

Union soldiers who died at Gettysburg sacrificed their lives to the cause of self-determination-"that government of the people, by the people, for the people," should not perish from the earth. It is difficult to imagine anything more untrue. The Union soldiers in that battle actually fought against self-determination; it was the Confederates who fought for the right of their people to govern themselves. What was the practical effect of the battle of Gettysburg? What else than the destruction of the old sovereignty of the States, i.e., of the people of the States. [10]

Edgar Lee Masters, the distinguished Illinois poet, wrote in 1931:

Lincoln carefully avoided one half of the American story.... The Gettysburg oration, therefore, remains a prose poem, but in the inferior sense that one must not inquire into its truth. One must read it apart from the facts.... Lincoln dared not face the facts at Gettysburg.... He was unable to deal realistically with the history of his country, even if the occasion had been one when the truth was acceptable to the audience. Thus we have in the Gettysburg Address that refusal of the truth which is written all over the American character and its expressions. The war then being waged was not glorious, it was brutal and hateful and mean minded. It had been initiated by radicals and fanatics. [11]

A different-from-the-official view of what was at stake at Gettysburg is given by the great Alexis de Tocqueville, writing in the antebellum period:

The Union was formed by the voluntary agreement of the states; and these, in uniting together, have not forfeited their sovereignty, nor have they been reduced to the condition of one and the same people. If one of the states chose to withdraw its name from the contract, it would be difficult to disprove its right of doing so, and the Federal government would have no means of maintaining its claims directly, either by force or by right. [12]

To spell it out a little further: the Union was transformed, in the Gettysburg Address and in the actions which it celebrated, from the

---

10 H.L. Mencken, *The Vintage Mencken*, Alistair Cooke, ed. (New York: Vintage Books, 1958), pp. 79-80.
11 Edgar Lee Masters, *Lincoln, The Man* (New York: Dodd, Mead, 1931), pp. 478-479. Reprinted: Columbia, South Carolina: The Foundation for American Education, 1997.
12 Alexis de Tocqueville, *Democracy in America* (New York: Vintage Books, 1990), vol. 1, pp. 387-388.

rational device of self-government and social comity established by the founders into a mystical, self-justifying goal. The use of Biblical language, as M.E. Bradford showed so skillfully, transfers us from political tradition and reason to pseudo-religious faith-refounding the American polity by sacred mythology. [13] In his first message to Congress Lincoln used the traditional term "Union," implying a confederacy of States, 32 times and "nation" three times. In the Gettysburg Address the word "Union" is not used. There and in the second inaugural we are told that the War is fought to preserve the "nation" - though how that reconciles with destroying a good part of the "nation" is not made clear.

The historian John Lukacs, among others, has written about the important distinction between patriotism and nationalism. Patriotism is the wholesome, constructive love of one's land and people. Nationalism is the unhealthy love of one's government, accompanied by the aggressive desire to put down others—which becomes in deracinated modern men a substitute for religious faith. Patriotism is an appropriate, indeed necessary, sentiment for people who wish to preserve their freedom; nationalism is not, as the history of this century demonstrates fully. What we have with the Gettysburg Address is the creation of a nationalist mythology—one under which we still live. What it celebrates is not the American republican Union established by our forefathers, which was—unlike the authoritarian governments of the Old World- based on the consent of the people.

The "Union" was preserved, but it was not the Union established by the founders. The real union was described by John C. Calhoun, with his usual prophetic power, in his last speech in 1850:

> But, surely, that can, with no propriety of language, be called a union, when the only means by which the weaker is held connected with the stronger portion *is force*. It may, indeed, keep them connected; but the connection will partake much more of the character of subjugation, on the part of the weaker to the stronger, than the union of free, independent, and sovereign States.... The cry of "Union, Union, the glorious Union!" can no more prevent disunion than the cry of "health, health, glorious health!" on the part of the physician, can save a patient lying dangerously ill.... Besides, this cry of Union comes commonly

---

13   13 M.E. Bradford, *A Better Guide Than Reason: Studies in the American Revolution* (LaSalle, Illinois: Sherwood Sugden, 1979), pp. 29-57, 185-203; and idem, *Remembering Who We Are: Observations of a Southern Conservative* (Athens: University of Georgia Press, 1985), pp. 143-156.

from those whom we cannot believe to be sincere.... For, if they loved the Union, they would necessarily be devoted to the Constitution. It made the Union, and to destroy the Constitution would be to destroy the Union. [14]

James Madison, the "Father of the Constitution," tells us that the meaning of the Constitution is to be sought only in the opinions and intentions of the "State conventions where it received all .... authority which it possesses."[15] That is, the sovereignty of the people means purely and simply, and can mean nothing else in the American system, the people of each State acting in sovereign constitution-making capacity—as they did in the American Revolution and in forming their own and the federal constitutions, and as the Southern States did in 1861 in rescinding participation in the federal Constitution. The sovereignty of the people was ended by the outcome of the War Between the States so that the real sovereign is now not the people but the nine berobed deities in Washington who at will decree what our Constitution means.

The greatest cost of the War, then, was the end of the old Union and the substitution of one of force - the end of the American idea of consent of the people and the substitution of the Old World idea of obedience to those in power by whatever means.

Let us recall that Lincoln in 1860 received the suffrages of only 39.9 percent of the American electorate, that his public statements were deliberately ambiguous, that he was by a large measure the most unknown and undistinguished man who had ever entered the White House, and the first entirely sectional candidate. And that the vote against him in the North increased by 10 percent in 1864. Lincoln only carried that election by engaging in the arbitrary warrantless arrests of political opponents, suppression of hundreds of newspapers, conducting the count at bayonet point in the border states, New York City and other places, and the hasty admission of several new States. We need to examine closely what Lincoln meant by government of, by, and for the people.

The Republican Party, even after having won the War, maintained its power only by force and fraud, known as Reconstruction. The War had been fought on the basis that the States could not leave the Union, but were only temporarily under the control of a conspiracy of rebels. But, when the "rebel-lion" was ended, rather than restoring the States,

---

14 John C. Calhoun, *The Works of John C. Calhoun*, Richard K. Crallé, ed. (Columbia, South Carolina: A.S. Johnson, and New York: D. Appleton, 1851-1857), vol. 4, pp. 558-559.
15 James Madison to Thomas Ritchie, September 15, 1821, in *Writings of James Madison*, Gaillard Hunt, ed. (New York: G.P. Putnam, 1900-1910), vol. 9, p. 372.

the Republicans declared that the States had committed suicide and were now "conquered provinces." Reconstruction was built on an utterly dishonest reversal of ground. The Constitution has never recovered from these lies.

It would have been far better to allow the American Union to dissolve at the will of the people into two or more confederacies. There is nothing whatever in the legacy of the founders or in the theory of self-government to prevent this, or that argues against it. In fact, Jefferson rather expected it. The point for him was to preserve the principle of the consent of the governed, not the Union as an end in itself, which might or might not be conducive to the consent of the governed.

But it might not have been necessary to destroy the Union had there been in 1861 an honest government in Washington—one really interested in preserving the real Union and Constitution rather than carrying through a revolutionary party platform. Given Lincoln's minority status, he would have been sustained by much Northern and all border-state and upper-South opinion had he sought compromise. Instead, he kept silent except for disingenuous statements that did not meet the occasion. That is, he put himself and party above country and exhibited the most conspicuous failure of statesmanship that any American President has ever shown.

Though it is not widely known, the Confederacy had commissioners in Washington ready to make honorable arrangements—to pay for the federal property in the South, assume their share of the national debt, and negotiate all other questions. Lincoln would not deal with these delegates directly. Instead, he deceived them into thinking that Fort Sumter would not be reinforced - thus precipitating reaction when reinforcement was attempted. Even so, the bombardment of Sumter was largely symbolic. There were no casualties, and, remember, almost all the other forts in the South had already peacefully been handed over. Sumter in itself did not necessarily justify all-out civil war; it was simply the occasion Lincoln was waiting for.

Even after the War had progressed it would have been possible, with a Northern government on traditional principles, to have made a peace short of the destruction that ensued. Or it would have been possible, as millions of Northerners wanted, to have sustained a war for the Union, a gentleman's disagreement over the matter of secession, that was far less destructive and revolutionary than the War turned out to be. Many, many Northerners favored this and supported the War reluctantly and only on such grounds—a suppressed part of American history. A great deal of death and destruction, as well as the maiming of the Constitution, might have been avoided by this approach.

This did not happen. Why? Because, in fact, for Lincoln and his followers it was the revolution that was the point. Throughout the War and Reconstruction, the Republican Party behaved as a revolutionary party-though sometimes using conservative rhetoric—a Jacobin party, bent on ruling no matter what, on maintaining its own power at any cost. At times they even hampered the Northern war effort for party advantage. It is very hard to doubt this for anyone who has actually closely studied the behavior of the Republicans during this period rather than simply picking out a few of Lincoln's prettier speeches to quote.

Lord Acton, the great English historian of liberty, wrote: "The calamity ...was brought on...by the rise of the republican party—a party in its aims and principles quite revolutionary." And when it was all over, Acton remarked that Appomattox had been a greater setback for the cause of constitutional liberty than Waterloo had been a victory.[16] James McPherson, the leading contemporary historian of the Civil War, though he approves rather than deplores the revolution that was carried out, agrees that it was a revolution.

War is inseparable from the growth of the leviathan state and the shrinking of liberty—the greatest problem of our time. By liberty I mean self-government of the individual and of the community; what our founders understood as liberty -freedom from rule by exploitive minorities against the sense of the people. The growth of total war is inseparable from the growth of the leviathan state. They rise or fall together.

It has been said that the only thing worse than fighting a war is losing a war. But winning a war has its costs also. I would like to address the costs of winning the war for the Union—costs moral and economic. The subject is worthy of a book and my treatment will necessarily be summary. Everything that I have to say is well known, long known, and well documented by historians. There is nothing new or surprising or very controversial about any of these observations. They are usually ignored, explained away, or simply not put together logically. Historians who are well aware of the corruption that followed the War, for instance, seem to imply that it mysteriously appeared after Lincoln's death, and somehow miss the obvious conclusion that it was implicit in the goals of the Lincoln war party. This is to abandon fact and reason

---

16   Lord Acton, *Selected Writings of Lord Acton*, J. Rufus Fears, ed. (Indianapolis, Indiana: Liberty Press, 1985), vol. 1, pp. 256 and 363.

for the mysticism of Union and emancipation, a pseudo-religious appeal inappropriate to the discourse of free men.

In our day, it is easy to overlook the extent and unprecedented nature of Lincoln's actions - organizing armies and spending money, suspending the writ of *habeas corpus*, declaring blockades, confiscating property without legislative Sanction until after the fact and often in the teeth of court rulings. The precedent for the "Imperial Presidency" is obvious.

James G. Randall, who was a great Lincoln scholar and a great excuser of Lincoln's conduct, which he portrays as reluctant, unavoidable, and moderate (compared to the Radicals), yet writes:

> When the government of Lincoln is set over against this standard (of the rule of law), its irregular and extra-legal characteristics become conspicuous.... Lincoln, who stands forth in the popular conception as a great democrat, was driven by circumstances to the use of more arbitrary power than perhaps any other President has seized..... While greatly enlarging his executive powers he also seized legislative and judicial functions as well."[17]

If Lincoln did these things from "necessity," the evidence is abundant that many of his supporters did them with glee. They deliberately smashed economic liberty and abandoned the republican virtue the fathers had considered essential because they considered that these stood in the way of their profit and power. [18]

Indeed, it is in the economic program that we find the real reason for the War, and not in the sacred bonds of Union nor the welfare of the suffering blacks. The exit of the South from Congress led to the immediate enactment of a host of economic measures which the South had previously been able to block or ameliorate.

Foremost among these, of course, was the tariff. The movement of influential segments of Northern opinion toward a policy of coercion, from an original stance of "let them go in peace," as is well documented, was based on a realization within big business that if the South was independent there would be, to them, an intolerably immense free-trade zone along the Atlantic and Gulf.[19] Though Republicans liked to allege

---

17 James G. Randall, *Constitutional Problems Under Lincoln*, revised ed. (Gloucester, Massachusetts, Peter Smith, 1963), Pp. 513-514.
18 See T. Harry Williams, *Lincoln and the Radicals* Madison: University of Wisconsin Press, 1965).
19 This point was recently made by Charles Adams, *For Good and Evil: The Impact of Taxes Upon the Course of Civilization* (New York: Madison Books, 1992). See also Kenneth M. Stampp, *And the War Came: The North and the Secession Crisis, 1860-1861* (Baton Rouge: Loui-

that Southerners were lazy and unproductive (a lie), they knew perfectly well that their economy was dependent upon Southern productivity both for its markets and its government revenue.

More than half the export of the country was made up of cotton and other Southern staple crops, of which the North got the benefit of the finance and transport. This cotton made possible much of the domestic trade and nearly all the foreign trade, which in turn made possible the tariff which protected Northern manufactures and provided most of the revenue for the Northern political class, revenue which had been consistently spent on building up the Northern infrastructure.

The high tariff became permanent policy after 1861-at great cost to the American consumer, to agriculture, and to American development. It was accompanied by contract laws by which millions in immigrant labor gangs were brought to Republican sweat shops, thus depressing the wages of native American labor—a system implemented at the same time as emancipation of the blacks. And to the record of Republican "progressive" economic measures we must add a national banking system that was so partisan and corrupt that the Federal Reserve was actually an improvement, the first income tax, and the first federally induced inflation.

Then there is the vaunted Homestead Act—the giving away of the public domain, which was the country's greatest resource. The policy had been to sell off the lands gradually at moderate prices to encourage legitimate settlement. This also provided revenue for the government, which obviated the need for other taxes, like the tariff. This was the wise policy designed by the Southern statesmen who had acquired most of these lands.

Of course, the public lands should have gotten into private hands for settlement and development. But that is not what the Homestead Act was really about. In fact, less than 20 percent of the lands given away went to *bona fide* settlers, and many of them were foreigners lured here for that purpose. The rest went to railroad and mining corporations amidst vast corruption and at the expense of the taxpayer.[20] Here we have the origins of the widespread American folk prejudice against business corporations, of which demagogues have made such good use.

Then we have the arbitrary arrest by military authorities, in the North where there was no "rebellion," of some 30,000 persons, as well

---

siana State University Press, 1950).
20   Ludwell H. Johnson, *Division and Reunion: America 1848-1877* (New York: John Wiley and Sons, 1978), pp. 110-112. Reprinted as *North Against South: The American Iliad, 1848-1877* (Columbia, South Carolina: The Foundation for American Education, 2003).

as the suppression of 300 newspapers. In most cases this was not for overt acts but for merely criticizing the Lincoln government and no judicial charges were ever brought. (The 30,000 refers only to federal arrests, and does not include those by Republican state and local authorities and vigilantes.)[21] Let's put a human face on these acts of destruction of the old Republic. They included the arrest of the son of Francis Scott Key, author of the "Star Spangled Banner," the seizure of the Washington family property at Arlington, and the herding of women into concentration camps in Missouri.

Secretary of State William Henry Seward is said to have bragged to the British ambassador: "I can touch a bell on my right hand and order the arrest of a citizen of Ohio. I can touch the bell again and order the arrest of a citizen of New York. Can Queen Victoria do as much?" She could not, nor could the Emperor of France or the King of Prussia. And Seward was one of the mildest of the Republicans, an easy-going Hermann Goering compared to Secretary of War Edwin M. Stanton's Heinrich Himmler.

Then there was the immense corruption involved in the financing of the War and the vast favoritism and fraud in the letting of war contracts. The wise Orestes Brownson wrote some years after the War:

> Nothing was more striking during the late civil war than the very general absence of loyalty or feeling of duty, on the part of the adherents of the Union, to support the government because it was the legal government of the country, and every citizen owed it the sacrifice of his life, if needed. The administration never dared confide in the loyalty of the federal people. The appeals were made to interest, to the democracy of the North against the aristocracy of the South; to anti-slavery fanaticism, or to the value and utility of the Union, rarely to the obligation in conscience to support the legitimate or legal authority; prominent civilians were bribed by high military commissions; others, by advantageous contracts for themselves or their friends for supplies to the army; and the rank and file, by large bounties and high wages. There were exceptions, but such was the rule.[22]

---

21 Dean Sprague, *Freedom Under Lincoln* (Boston: Houghton Mifflin, 1965). See also Harold Frederic's classic novel, *The Copperhead* (1893), arising out of the real experiences of a family of Democratic farmers in New York who were persecuted for declining to join the war frenzy of their Republican neighbors.
22 Orestes Brownson, "The Democratic Principle," in *Orestes Brownson: Selected Political Essays*, Russell Kirk, ed. (New Brunswick, New Jersey: Transaction, 1989), pp. 204-205.

All of which involved a fall of ethical standards and ideas of liberty from which we have never recovered. Indeed, Brownson was describing the way politicians ever since have led Americans to war. It was then that we began to take such abuses for granted; we have become used to them. We fail to recognize how revolutionary this was for Americans who had prided themselves on their individual liberty, rule of law, and republican virtue and patriotism compared to the corrupt and arbitrary regimes of the Old World.

Another great moral cost of the War, as Richard Weaver pointed out, was inauguration by the Republicans of the "total war" concept, reversing several centuries of Western progress in restraining warfare to rules. General Sherman himself estimated that in his march across Georgia and the Carolinas, only 20 percent of the destruction had any military value. The rest was sheer wanton terrorism against civilians—theft and destruction of their food, housing, and tools.[23] One egregious example was the burning and sack of Columbia—a city which had already surrendered and was full of women and children and wounded soldiers - a looting which marked the emancipation of black women by their wholesale rape.

The assessed value of wealth in the South in 1870 was 59 percent of what it had been in 1860, not including slave property. If we count the loss of slave property, the wealth of the South in 1870 was 37 percent of its pre-War value. In the same period the wealth of the North increased by 150 percent - though this wealth was much more unevenly distributed than before the War.[24] The War was carried out on the backs of Northern farmers and workingmen. Read Herman Melville's poem on the New York City draft riots in his *Battle-Pieces*.

Along with destruction went immense confiscation and theft, much of it under cover of a Confiscation Act which was enforced without ever being legally passed. The Republican Speaker of the House of Representatives simply declared the bill passed and adjourned. This high-handed legislative practice continued throughout the War and Reconstruction. The Republican Governor of Indiana suspended the legislature and acted as dictator for two years. Republicans continually agitated for an open dictatorship under Fremont or some other trustworthy Radical; all of this is known but seldom acknowledged. [25]

---

23 Johnson, *Division and Reunion*, p. 187.
24 *Ibid.*, pp. 189-190.
25 Williams, *Lincoln and the Radicals*.

In addition to the Confiscation Act for rebel property, there was a mechanism for the government to collect taxes in the occupied regions of the South to finance the War. At least $100,000,000 in cotton (the most valuable commodity in North America) was seized—$30,000,000 more or less legally under the confiscation and tax acts, the rest sheer theft. Of the $30,000,000 only about 10 percent ever reached the Treasury. The rest was stolen by Republican appointees. A Secretary of the Treasury commented that he was sure a few of the tax agents he sent South were honest, but none remained so very long. We know, for instance, of that great hero Admiral Porter, who with General Banks was badly beaten by vastly inferior Confederate forces in the Red River campaign, yet emerged from that campaign with $60,000 worth of stolen cotton for his personal profit. The confiscation and theft continued in full force until at least 1868; they did not end with the hostilities.[26]

But, you say, did we not free the slaves? I have had the argument a hundred times, and this is what the defenders of Lincoln always come back to when cornered. Set aside that emancipation was not the declared purpose for which the War was initiated against the South. It became a war aim 18 months into hostilities. As the letters of Northern soldiers reveal, a great many of them were opposed to emancipation as a war aim and felt betrayed. Set aside that in the British and French Empires and elsewhere slavery was ended gradually, peace-fully, and with compensation, while in the United States it cost the life of every fourth Southern and every tenth Northern white man. The implied premise is that the freeing of the slaves was justified at any cost.

And of what did freeing the slaves consist? At the Hampton Roads conference, Alexander Stephens asked Lincoln what the freedmen would do, without education or property. Lincoln's answer: "Root, hog, or die."[27] Not the slightest recognition of the immense social crisis presented to American society by millions of freedmen. The staple agriculture of the South, the livelihood of the blacks as well as the whites, was destroyed. While the federal government had millions of acres of land in the West to give away to corporations and foreigners, there was none for the ex-slaves. That would have brought the blacks into Northern

---

26 Johnson, *Division and Reunion*, pp. 115-118 and 188-189.
27 Alexander H. Stephens, *A Constitutional View of the Late War between the States* (Philadelphia, Pennsylvania: National Publishing, 1870), vol. 2, p. 615. "Root, hog, or die" was the refrain of a popular minstrel tune. On April 16, 1863, Lincoln wrote on a War Department document, in regard to the blacks, "They had better be set to digging their subsistence out of the ground." Cited in *Freedom: A Documentary History of Emancipation*, Ira Berlin, et al., eds., (Cambridge, England: Cambridge University Press, 1987), vol. 1, p. 306.

territory. Let them stay in the South, give them the vote to sustain the Republican party, and organize them to keep down Southern whites. This was the sum total of the Republican freeing of the slaves.

In fact, social statistics indicate that the black people were in many respects worse off in 1900 than they had been under slavery—in work skills, family stability, health and mortality, crime.[28] Our brilliant pundits have, curiously, blamed the Southern antebellum regime for all the current problems of Northern cities. But in fact, the further away from the plantation we get in both time and space, the worse the problems become. Not slavery, but the way it was ended is to blame.

We have only scratched the surface of the damage done to the Old Republic in the winning of the War. It saw our first government propagandizing of the citizens. Then there were the soldiers' pensions. Pensions under the old Union had been regarded as a reward for the disabled and the extremely meritorious. After the War this was turned into a vast entitlement for anyone who had ever worn the blue uniform for five minutes—the first of the great entitlement programs. And, of course, there was the 14th Amendment - illegally adopted and a source of endless mischief.

Our greatest constitutional historian, Forrest McDonald, has recently called our attention once again to the fraud and coercion in the adoption of the 14th Amendment. But the problem was not conferring basic citizenship rights on the freedman, which was necessary and inevitable, but the debasement of the concept of citizenship that ensued. Citizenship had been a state matter, subject only to the federal power of uniform rules of naturalization. Immigrants became citizens by being accepted into existing communities as members in good standing. The wholesale granting of citizenship by the federal government, not only to the freedmen but to the vast numbers of Irish and Germans who filled up the ranks of the Union armies, rendered citizenship a federal entitlement rather than an earned privilege and led us to the present situation where the government forces vast numbers of immigrants on American communities whether they want them or need them.

Did the War leave America a full-fledged Empire? No, but not from lack of trying. Reconstruction was ended, finally, by Northern exhaustion and Southern resistance.[29] The courts, not then completely

---

28   C. Vann Woodward, *Origins of the New South, 1877-1913* (Baton Rouge: Louisiana State University Press, 1951), pp. 205-221 and 360-368.
29   A great deal of historiographical effort has been devoted in the last three decades to ree deeming the besmirched reputation of Reconstruction, a hopeless task for any but the blindest ideologues. There is no question that the carpetbagger regimes were made up of criminals and

corrupted, invalidated many of the acts of the Lincoln government. It was after the fact, but at least kept them from being repeated for a time. The fabric of self-government was too strong in the American people to be destroyed all at once in normal times.

But all the precedents were set—the precedents that the Progressives were able to adopt in the following decades, culminating in our intervention into World War I in Europe, a purely Lincolnian exercise.

One of our greatest artists summed up the costs of the War for the Union. The thoughtful Northerner Herman Melville, in the midst of the conflict, wrote:

> Power unannointed may come
> Dominion unsought by the free
> ...
> The Founders' dream shall flee. [30]

The Republican Party victory was a Jacobin Revolution. What are the signs of Jacobinism? A power grab by a minority leading to a centralized state, an egalitarian ideology masking the will to power of one-party rule, a great transfer of wealth, a ruthless disregard for tradition and law, an overturning of organic social relations, a tendency toward a totalitarian state. The revolution was not perfected because 19th century America did not have the instruments for totalitarianism, but it was not from lack of trying.

So, I suggest that we are living with a tainted inheritance. If our desire is to restore the principle of liberty as it was originally understood by Americans, if that is possible, we need to rid ourselves, intellectually and morally, of the superstitions of unionism and emancipation, which are the fountain of all the other statist superstitions and all the other statist usurpations from which we have suffered and by which we have been cursed in this century. It seems a very unlikely thing to happen, I admit, although recently the French people celebrated their Revolution and a great many of them rethought the heritage of Jacobinism, which they had been taught was a great tradition. There was a real revulsion of opinion about that, rejection of what had been regarded as a great

---

opportunists who did not have even the respect of decent Northerners, who looted, and who betrayed the black people they had supposedly come to help. Reconstruction certainly involved corruption, lawlessness, tyranny, and a deceitful violation of the terms under which Lee and Johnston had laid down their arms.
30 30 Herman Melville, "The House-top: A Night Piece (July 1863)," in *Battle-Pieces and Aspects of the War* (Amherst: University of Massachusetts Press, 1972).

accomplishment. Americans will have to do no less if they wish to recover genuine self-government.

This essay was delivered as a paper at the Ludwig von Mises Institute conference on "The Costs of War" in May 1994, and was published in *The Costs of War: America's Pyrrhic Victories,* edited by John V. Denson *(Transaction, 1997).*

Our First President

A review of *The Papers of Jefferson Davis*, Volume 7:1861, edited by Linda Lasswell Crist and Mary Seaton Dix, Baton Rouge: Louisiana State University Press, 1991, 557 pages.

Our Founding Fathers understood that they had inaugurated a republican federal union unique in its balance and distribution of powers. Unlike their descendants, who self-indulgently congratulate themselves on their democracy, the Fathers also understood that the preservation of such a regime was a daunting and demanding task, requiring virtue (in the masculine Roman sense) on the part of the citizenry as well as national good fortune. How to prevent rulers from usurping the rights of the people in the long run—as rulers inevitably tend to do-and, on the other hand, prevent majority rule (in its proper role as the deliberate sense of the people) from devolving into tyranny?

From the beginning, the founding generation identified dangers to the republican federal union under two antagonistic rubrics worked out in the quarrels between the friends of Mr. Jefferson and the friends of General Hamilton. The latter believed the greatest danger to be "disunion," that without a vigorous central power, self-government would perish from its own anarchic tendencies. The Jeffersonian party felt that liberty could be destroyed just as surely by another danger, "consolidation": the absorption of the sovereignty of the inhabitants of the various states by any or all branches of a "general government" intent on grasping powers beyond its legitimate and limited few.

Jefferson clearly regarded disunion as the lesser evil. Disunion would disperse but not necessarily subvert government of the people, especially since no one generation could irrevocably bind posterity. It mattered little if the Union broke into independent states or into two or more confederacies: self-government would survive and thrive. But to invest the central government with the powers and divinity that had once been attributed to monarchs (i.e., "consolidation" would certainly destroy self-government.

No people has ever forgotten, misunderstood, and misrepresented their history as have Americans, who recently celebrated the bicentennial of their Constitution without even mentioning the ideas of republicanism and federal-ism, though these were once considered to be the essential and unique features of the American regime. This is, to make a long story short, because in the middle of the 19th century the ideal of - and the instinct for—republican liberty was replaced by the doctrine of the state as a divine instrument of progress, both economic and moral. Each succeeding generation has enhanced the progress of consolidation through the pursuit of bestowed and managed prosperity and of the most socially destructive goal, egalitarianism. Impatient of constitutional principles that present obstacles to this pursuit, the American regime calls itself a "democracy" because it reflects "majority rule." Very seldom, though, does majority rule express the deliberate sense of the people. More often than not it is a fluctuating coalition of self-interest groups ("factions" to the Founders) or an accidental "majority" like the 43 percent of the half of eligible citizens who voted that elected Clinton and the 39 percent that elected Lincoln.

One of the few certain laws one learns from the study of history is this: the pendulum always swings back, in some fashion or other. Throughout the civilized world people are, after more than a century of the seemingly inevitable progress of "consolidation," seeking once more to constitute their own self-governing communities and to take back their fate from the swollen, greedy, incompetent, and irresponsible bureaucracies that govern them. So, it may be time for a fresh look at the great conflict that lies at the center of our history, the last great anti-consolidationist rising that is still, in terms of the quantities of bloodshed and the revolutionary objectives consummated, the largest event in our life as a people. To crush self-government in the Southern states required the life of every tenth northern, and every fourth Southern, white man.

For the current generation it is difficult, in fact nearly impossible, to imagine a conflict over principle. The Civil War, it assumes, could not have been about *principle*; it must have been about *conditions*: i.e., the status of the African-American (a misreading re-enforced by the tendency to equate victory and virtue, even retrospectively). Yet while the War certainly crushed disunion, the status of the African-American remains even today a largely unsolved problem in the north as well as in the South. It is a neat historical serendipity that the fine documentary edition of the papers of President Jefferson Davis has just reached the secessionary year of 1861. The very skilled and knowledgeable editors have included Davis's most important state papers, a judicious selection out of an overwhelming corpus of documents that illuminate the creation of the Confederate government in the midst of life-and-death struggle.

The glamour of the Confederate military leaders is fixed in the understanding of the world; as long as men continue to admire courage, chivalry, dash, and honor, only the hopelessly churlish can fail to be moved. The civil leaders of the South have fared much less well. Yet Davis is one of the most interesting men in American history, a tragic hero of epic dimensions. If the moguls of Hollywood docudrama had any taste and any sense of history they could find in Davis a story worthy of the pen of Shakespeare. Jefferson Davis and Varina, his wife, had one of the truly great romances of American history. I exaggerate not in the least: she was beautiful, passionate, highly intelligent, courageous, and loyal almost beyond crediting—truly one of the handful of the most remarkable and admirable women in all of American history.

Lincoln was lucky to leave the scene when he did, a martyr without the stain that Reconstruction would inevitably have brought to his reputation. Davis, by comparison, was traduced by a government that kept him shackled in prison for two years, while denying him the trial he craved. He could not be brought to trial because, of course, any open and fair judicial proceeding would have established beyond any doubt that secession by state governments from the Union is not treason. Who knows but that we might have here a rediscovered hero of the future, when the impatience of the people with the ever-encroaching state has reached its limit. In the meantime, if you wish to begin to understand the story of our country, I recommend that you read the letter Jeff Davis wrote on January 20, 1861, to his northern friend Franklin Pierce, as well as his farewell speech to the Senate the following day as he withdrew to join his seceding state: "We recur to the principles upon which our government was founded. We but tread in the path of our fathers when we proclaim our independence." Or his inaugural address on February 18 of the same critical year: "Our present condition... illustrates the American idea that governments rest upon the consent of the governed.... We have changed the constituent parts, but not the system of our government. The Constitution formed by our fathers is that of these Confederate States." (1994)

Our Second Constitution

A review of *The Confederate Constitution of 1861: An Inquiry into American Constitutionalism*, by Marshall L. DeRosa, Columbia: University of Missouri Press, 1991, 182 pages.

A few months after the close of the American Civil War there was a brief but intense and interesting correspondence between Lord Acton, the European historian of liberty, and General R.E. Lee, hero of the defeated Confederacy, on the issues of the War. In the course of this correspondence Acton commented that Appomattox had been a greater defeat for the cause of constitutional liberty over despotism than Waterloo had been a victory. It is an arresting statement that ought to have received more attention from lovers of liberty and students of constitutionalism than it has.

DeRosa's study of the Confederate Constitution provides one way to approach the unexamined question raised by Acton. The book is a good deal more than its title suggests; its subtitle should be taken seriously. The author has, correctly, viewed the Confederate Constitution neither as anomalous nor insignificant, but rather as an illuminating part of American constitutional his-tory. This is in itself a feat of intellectual courage, because nothing is harder than to discuss the issues of the American War rationally and fairly. Invariably there is the attempt to close off debate and understanding by the shout of "Slavery!" Nothing is easier for a scholar than to succumb to this pressure. Yet nothing is a surer sign of either ignorance or dishonesty. Such was the flaw of the public television series on the War. Professor DeRosa has avoided this common fallacy and treated the constitutional issues of the War—and in its most essential aspect it was a constitutional dispute—seriously.

The Confederate framers took the high ground. They intended to found a lasting federal republic, and their deliberations were carried out on a serious intellectual plane. This is in itself remarkable when we consider that they were at the time under the greatest military threat that any large group of Americans has ever suffered—that is, under prospect of intense invasion by superior military forces from every direction—and that their more rabid opponents have managed to hand down as a historical "fact" the partisan charge that the Confederacy represented nothing but the attempt to found a slavocracy.

At stake was possession of the Fathers. Southerners always said and believed -throughout the antebellum conflicts, the War, and after—that their only goal was to preserve the American Constitution as it had been handed down, that theirs was an eminently conservative effort. Yet victors write the history, and the North was able to co-opt the Founders, portraying the Confederacy as a wicked rebellion against American principles. So the Northern cause got the credit for conserving, but also, very curiously, the credit and élan for being revolutionary, of having proclaimed new and wonderful principles. It perhaps explains the magical power of Lincoln to say that he managed by rhetoric and victory to combine the prestige both of preservation and revolution.

The Confederate Constitution, as has been often observed, embodied the Constitution of the United States, with minor adjustments. It is these adjustments that form the subject of Professor DeRosa's analysis and that are useful in understanding the U.S. Constitution. For the changes represented a heritage of very seriously considered reactions to the experience of practice with the Constitution of 1787. Therefore, they are of interest in American constitutional history and, as the author suggests, of pertinence to some of the dilemmas of today. Put another way, the few but significant innovations in the Confederate Constitution represent corrections of portions of the U.S. Constitution that had not worked to intent. In terms of political philosophy, the innovations embody the amendments made by Calhoun, the greatest American political thinker of the 19th century, to the commentary of "Publius" in *The Federalist*, which, after all, had been written before the Constitution was ratified, much less put into effect.

The Constitution of the Confederacy did not establish slavery. It left the matter to the states, just as did the Constitution of the United States, and it contained a stronger prohibition against the African slave trade than did the old Constitution. Its innovations related to other matters. Broadly speaking, they were of two types: those that spelled out the federal nature of the system to be established; and those that made adjustments to the functioning of the federal government, particularly the Presidency, in certain respects. In the first instance, the Confederate Constitution merely made explicit what had been intended by the Tenth Amendment, so explicit that agenda-oriented centralists could not evade it. It also put certain small but significant limits on the power of taxation and expenditure; that is, it expressed a real bias in favor of the free market and limited government, to correct the sectional and class favoritism that had been carried out by congressional majorities under the old government. This should be of interest to all real friends of free markets and limited government.

Most interesting were the changes in the federal executive and judiciary. The Confederate Constitution clearly intended to make the President the high and honorable Chief Magistrate that had been intended by the U.S. Constitution, rather than the party leader that he had devolved into. The President was to serve one six-year term, at one stroke abolishing the re-election question and the second-term impasse. He had a line-item veto in appropriations, meaning a check against irrelevant riders in congressional bills, which under the American system had already developed into a tremendous abuse. There were limits on the degree to which the Congress could exceed the President's spending recommendations, and Cabinet Secretaries had seats on the floors of Congress, to enhance the process of deliberation beyond the exchange of formal messages, with the intent of increasing economy and accountability in the public business.

So far as the judiciary was concerned, the Confederate Constitution reflected the pure Jeffersonian principles of the early Republic. The right of judicial review was concurrent-shared by the state and federal courts. For the most basic principle was that the people ruled - that government rested upon the consent of the governed, the people, and that this did not mean simply whatever temporary majority happened to get control of the Supreme Court or Congress or presidency. It meant rather the consent of the people acting through all branches of their state and federal governments. At bottom were, as Jefferson had said, two different ideas of government: a national authority with power to coerce obedience to the governing elite (Hamilton), or a system of dispersed power that trusted the rule of the people through diverse institutions of power and consent (Jefferson). The Confederate Constitution represented the second alternative, and therefore, the author writes, "there is much to be learned from the theories that gave life and death to this American constitution."

De Rosa does not focus simply upon the Civil War, but provides deep back-ground. In every question he gives us an original and illuminating discussion of basic ideas with the agreements, disagreements, and ambiguities at the time of the Founding; follows these ideas through the antebellum conflicts; and shows how the conflicts issued in particular features of the Confederate Constitution. This is a work of interest to all serious students of American constitutional history and political philosophy.

More impressive even than the content of DeRosa's book is the intellectual tone and approach-the spirit. He works in the same spirit as did the Founding Fathers and the Confederate framers. He regards the Constitution as an object of rationality. This is the true Jeffersonian spirit, which animated Calhoun, who once observed: "Constitutions are human contrivances, and what man does and his reasons for it, surely ought not to be beyond his capacity fully to comprehend." This is the proper spirit to approach the Constitution, as an instrument of self-government to be rationally preserved and employed by free men. (1992)

The Consent of the Governed Revisited

A review of *A Constitutional History of Secession*, by John Remington Graham, Gretna, Louisiana: Pelican Publishing Company, 2002, 460 pages.

    Americans have lost the habit of constitutional government. Judges hand down commands derived from their own personal revelation, in the teeth of law and majority rule, and are tamely obeyed by millions. A President, recently sworn to uphold the Constitution of the United States, announces his intention to commit the blood and treasure of the citizens in war against a distant state that has provoked his personal ire or the suspicions of his unelected entourage.

    To have lost constitutional government is to have lost self-government. Self-government has apparently come to mean no more than counting up punch-card holes to determine which of two interchangeable celebrities will preside over the immense, unreachable, and unlimited machinery on the Potomac that can take our property and even our lives in a fit of pique or even of absent-mindedness. But note: The Founding Fathers spoke not of throwing the rascals out to make way for another bunch of rascals; they spoke of changing the "form of government."

    Much of the problem results from the inclination of too many Americans to conflate the state apparatus and the people, to fail to distinguish government from society. Thus, people say "New York City is broke," though the statement does not apply to the place and the people, in all their multifarious life, but only to the passel of politicians who locally monopolize the powers of taxation and legal deadly force. Thus, many Americans seem to regard the President-any president—as a benevolent uncle (the way many Russians viewed Uncle Joe), as a fountain of good will and competence who can do no real wrong and make no serious mistake. After all, we are one big, happy family that plays together.

    For the Founding Fathers-or, at least, for the better part of them— the entire point of constitutional government was to provide means for the people to restrain the office-holders. These office-holders were not coterminous with the existing human society but delegates who needed to be kept from overreaching the authority the people had given them.

Politicians were, unfortunately, a necessary evil. Like all the rest of us sons and daughters of Adam, they were vessels of vanity, greed, and lust with a perpetual temptation to take advantage of their position. A constitution set limits to help ensure that rulers enhanced society rather than preyed on it.

John Remington Graham has gone back to the origins of our self-government and has found them in the same place the American statesman of independence found them—in England's Glorious Revolution of 1688-89, with a nod further back to Magna Carta. The society of England changed the form of its government by casting off the legitimate Stuart monarch and establishing a new royal house with the consent, and on the terms, of the society. In Graham's words, "the occasion was revolutionary, and it was also lawful, peaceable, bloodless, orderly, necessary, beneficial, and glorious."

On the same principle, the 13 North American colonies changed their form of government by an act of constitution-making by the sovereign people: dissolving their allegiance to the British Crown, creating 13 constitutional republics, and later giving their consent to a mutual agreement in the Constitution of the United States.

Another name for this is *secession*; the withdrawal of consent from the existing form of government. As Graham puts it:

> The right is universal, rooted in natural law and legal tradition—a right of peaceable and lawful revolution.... it is a right necessary in extraordinary circumstances for every free and civilized people, whatever their race or culture, wherever their location in the world, whenever they have entered into federal relations with neighboring peoples for mutual advantage. Without it, federal relations are too dangerous to consider. With this right, federal relations can be a great blessing to mankind, and can assure peace and friendship among nations.

Graham brings to the question his considerable knowledge of law and history, a great power of synthesis, and—perhaps most importantly—the experience of his participation in the *amicus curiae* brief for the judicial proceedings in the Canadian high court on the rights of Quebec. The case of Quebec serves as a model of a society claiming and receiving the right to protect its own peculiar qualities from a central power in control of a potentially hostile majority. Would that Americans had as much allegiance to their own Constitution and tradition.

Unfortunately, we seem more intent on constructing a police state manned by bully-boy *federales* who regard criticism of "our President" as treason and who are far more adept at murdering dissident citizens than at protecting us from foreign enemies. Nevertheless, there are signs, as in Graham's work, that some of us are beginning to emulate the Founding Fathers and to think about the legitimacy of forms of government. (2003)

Albert Taylor Bledsoe

Introduction to *Is Davis a Traitor?* by Albert Taylor Bledsoe, 1866. Reprinted: Charleston, South Carolina: Fletcher and Fletcher, 1995, 263 pages.

The polymath, one of vast encyclopedic learning and of genius in many fields, was a familiar character in the lore of the 18th and 19th centuries, though now seldom seen. If there were ever a Southern version of this phenomenon, Albert Taylor Bledsoe was it. Soldier, lawyer, mathematician, astronomer, philosopher, theologian, educator, clergyman, and journalist were all roles that he played with extraordinary ability, according to the testimony of his contemporaries.

But Bledsoe's most lasting achievement was undoubtedly this little book, *Is Davis a Traitor; or Was Secession a Constitutional Right Previous to the War of 1861?* Its importance is evident from the story Bledsoe often related of his encountering General Lee shortly after the War Between the States. Lee remarked to him: "Take care of yourself, Doctor; you have a great task; we look to you for our vindication."

And vindicate the Confederacy Bledsoe did—as ably as it has ever been done; as ably as it ever can be done in an indifferent world where might is often mistaken for right. A number of Southerners wrote books on the constitutional understandings and political and moral motives that governed the Southern people in their great lost struggle for independence. None did it better than Bledsoe. His argument for the right of secession is absolutely irrefutable to any honest mind. No single Northern apologist-and he takes them all on-is left with a leg to stand on. As a great 20th century Southern scholar, Richard M. Weaver, put it, Bledsoe's book is "a model of conciseness and cogent argument" which presents a case "formidable in law and equity."

What Alexander H. Stephens did in two brilliant but prolix volumes of *A Constitutional View of the Late War Between the States*, Bledsoe did better in 263 pages. Other Southern defenses all have their virtues and bear the stamp of truth and honor—Jefferson Davis's *Rise and Fall of the Confederate Government,* Robert L. Dabney's *A Defence of Virginia* and *Through Her of the South,* Basil L. Gildersleeve's *The Creed of the Old South,* Jabez L.M. Curry's *The Southern States of the American Union Considered in their Relations to the Constitution of the United States and the Resulting Union*, Edward A. Pollard's *The Lost Cause*, and others. But Bledsoe did it first and best.

There has been for many years a historical canard afoot that says that the States Rights philosophers of the Old South were pettifoggers, lost in tedious abstract arguments that had no relevance to real life and were merely rationalizations for an indefensible society of limited intellect and imagination. Nothing could be further from the truth. In the last twenty years or so the intellectual life of the Old South has received for the first time serious attention from competent and honest scholars. What has been revealed is what was evident all along—that the Old South had a rich and high culture with many outstanding intellectual figures, men, and women, of whom Bledsoe was one.

But more importantly in this context, when we look at Bledsoe's book we find not a pettifogging lawyer's treatise but a closely argued work of philosophy and history. This is indeed true of all of the Southern defenses. Stephens in his work is Socratic, not legalistic. Dabney was a theologian, Gildersleeve the greatest American classical scholar, Pollard a fiery editor, Curry a distinguished educator. The Southern view of the Constitution was always philosophical and historical, as anyone can see by reading Jefferson or Calhoun. It was the Northerners who were pettifogging legalists, resorting to semantics and often outright deception to prove a bad case. The Northern spokesmen Bledsoe so effectively skewers herein are not philosophers, but lawyers accustomed to arguing for pay, whatever the merits of the case, or paid publicists. Their goal was not truth but plausibility, not justice but victory.

Albert Taylor Bledsoe was born in the Kentucky bluegrass at Frankfort in 1809. On his father's side he was descended from a good Virginian family which had fled to the wilderness of Kentucky that they might exercise their Baptist faith away from the establishment Episcopal Church. His mother was also of Virginia stock and was related to Zachary Taylor. Like many young men of the time, Bledsoe was educated at West Point, then one of the best colleges and certainly the best scientific college in the land. His time as a cadet overlapped with that of Jefferson Davis, Robert E. Lee, Albert Sydney Johnston, and Leonidas Polk. At West Point he developed his lifelong interest in both mathematics and theology. The latter interest was promoted by Charles P. Mellvaine, the chaplain, a Northerner and noted Episcopal minister who was later the Bishop of Ohio. Bledsoe subsequently married Harriet Coxe who was Mrs. Mellvaine's sister and the daughter of William Coxe of Philadelphia, one of the best-known American botanists of the day.

Graduating from the Academy in 1830, Bledsoe spent two years as a junior officer on the frontier. Then he resigned from the service, studied theology at Kenyon College in Ohio, and took orders in the Episcopal Church. Bledsoe remained theologically questing all his life. In a few years he left the church, which he described, unflatteringly, as an English institution with a Catholic ritual, an Armenian clergy, and Calvinist articles of faith. Later he joined the Methodists, thus reversing the usual pattern of moving from a lower to a higher church.

There followed an interesting period from 1839 to 1848 when Bledsoe practiced law at Springfield, Illinois, a state capital with a distinguished bar that included Abraham Lincoln and Stephen A. Douglas. It is said that Bledsoe won six out of eleven cases tried against Lincoln, and that he once gave Lincoln lessons in the use of the broadsword when Lincoln was challenged to a duel. (Lincoln had published an anonymous, scurrilous attack on a political opponent. The duel never came off.)

Bledsoe knew Lincoln well and did not have a high opinion of him either as a man or a statesman. In postwar years Bledsoe described Lincoln as the most obscene man he had ever known, a fact to which there is abundant (though suppressed) other testimony. He also believed that Lincoln was without any religious or moral beliefs whatsoever, though he hypocritically pandered to the sentiments of the masses. Once during the War, Lincoln gave Mrs. Bledsoe a pass to cross the military lines to secure necessities for her family. Whether this was because her brother-in-law was a preacher for the Union is not clear. In 1848 Bledsoe became professor of mathematics and astronomy at the University of Mississippi on the opening of that institution. Bledsoe's mathematical genius was already legendary. The president of Ole Miss at the time was Augustus Baldwin Longstreet, noted Methodist minister, author, and editor. Bledsoe's assistant was Lucius Q.C. Lamar, later the Confederate minister to Russia and a Justice of the United States Supreme Court. From 1854 until the War, Bledsoe held the post in mathematics at the University of Virginia. The university was one of the outstanding institutions of the time, and Bledsoe was particularly friends with another professor, William H. McGuffey, creator of the famous readers that are still in use among the children of English-speaking Americans.

While still practicing law, Bledsoe had published a work of theology, *Examination of President [Jonathan] Edwards' "Inquiry into the Freedom of the Will,"* in which he took on the problem of free will and predestination, one of the most difficult in theology. During the period of his professorship he wrote prolifically: *A Theodicy: or Vindication of the Divine Glory*; a number of works on mathematics, astronomy, and physics; and an *Essay on Liberty and Slavery*. When the War began, Bledsoe, who was in his early fifties, became briefly colonel of a Virginia infantry regiment. But President Davis thought his brains would be of better use in the War Department, where he was assigned to head a bureau. In the fall of 1863 Bledsoe ran the blockade from Wilmington to Europe. He was, apparently, assigned, with others, to work on influencing British public opinion on the justness of the Confederate cause. The statements that survive about the reason for his voyage are so vague that one suspects an element of secret service work. After all, who better than a brilliant mathematician to work with codes?

While in England Bledsoe began gathering materials and preparing a defense of the South's position. He worked in the British Museum, perhaps at the time that Karl Marx was there preparing his destructive screeds. The end results of Bledsoe's work was *Is Davis a Traitor?* His materials and perhaps the manuscript or some part of it he brought back with him to the South in early 1865. The Confederacy was too near collapse for books of vindication to be of much use, no matter how able.

In 1866, while President Davis languished in irons in Fortress Monroe, Bledsoe completed and published the book as a part of the campaign of Davis's defense. In these darkest days of Reconstruction, it was to be employed by the fallen President's counsel if he were brought to trial for treason. Contrary to what is often implied, the Northern government did Davis no favor by releasing him, after two years, without trial. Davis wanted his day in court, perfectly confident that no charge of treason could stand against the right of secession as a legitimate option available to an American state at the time it was exercised.

Bledsoe's statement of the case is unanswerable. The South was correct in its constitutional position. The right of secession was implicit in the nature of the Union, in the ratification of the Constitution by the consent of the people of the states, and in the American ideas of the consent of the governed and the limitation of power. No honest student of the subject can doubt that Bledsoe has vanquished all his Northern opponents—Webster, Story, Curtis, Lincoln, Motley.

From the end of the War until his death in 1877, Bledsoe's life was one of brilliant, heroic intransigence. He edited, in Baltimore, the *Southern Review*, in which he eloquently continued to argue the justice of the Southern cause and the truth about the War. Richard Weaver has described this phase of Bledsoe's life and thought in his *The Southern

Tradition at Bay, in which Bledsoe is one of the central figures. Bledsoe also fought hard to rally the South to hold on to its republican virtue and Christian orthodoxy against the atheism and utilitarianism of the age.

The Southern Review was a totally unremunerative enterprise. He wrote much of the magazine himself and was aided by his daughter, Sophia Bledsoe Herrick, who subsequently became a distinguished editor of *Scribner's Magazine*, the most important journal of the later 19th century. In 1871 Bledsoe was ordained in the Methodist Episcopal Church South, though he was too intellectual to be a great success in the pulpit.

Is Davis a Traitor; or Was Secession a Constitutional Right Previous to the War of 1861?, the ablest of all defenses of the Confederacy, was first published in 1866 by Innes & Company of Baltimore. It has been printed twice since: by Hermitage Press of Richmond in 1907, and by J.P. Bell of Lynchburg, Virginia, in 1915 under a different title, *The War Between the States; or Was Secession a Constitutional Right Previous to the War of 1861?* Both of these later reprintings were done at the personal expense of Southerners who wished to make Bledsoe's message more widely available.

So, this edition, which ought to be at the hand of every loyal Southerner, makes the book available for the first time in eighty years. Bledsoe's passion, brilliance, and eloquence in a "lost cause" reminds us that Southerners have always believed in the sanctity of the word. For them, the Constitution was an agreement that meant what it meant, that belonged to those who ratified it. For Northerners it was merely an instrument to be made use of and manipulated for whatever ends were determined by the predominant powers, and a plaything for legal and political sophists. It was this and not slavery that was the irrepressible conflict of the sections.

Military victory may settle questions of power, but it cannot settle questions of right. Our Southern forebears knew that they were right. This they never doubted for a moment. No one was more eloquent and indefatigable in maintaining that truth than Albert Taylor Bledsoe, who wrote in the introduction of his book: "The calm and impartial reader will, it is believed, discover therein the grounds on which the South may be vindicated, and the final verdict of History determined in favor of a gallant, but down-trodden and oppressed, *people*." (1995)

Devolution

Preface to *Confederates in the Boardroom: The New Science of Organisations*, by Micheal C. Tuggle, College Station, Texas: Traveller Press, 2003, 185 pages.

Equipped with an abundant knowledge of history, Michael Tuggle has cast a discerning eye on the trends of the present. Not the "trendy" trends but the real ones, those which can guide our steps into the future (as far as the future can be known to us mortals). The trends suggest to him something very hopeful—the probability and suitability of a change in the principle by which human affairs are governed. We have been living for a long time by the organizing principle of command from the top down-something the American Founding Fathers decried as "consolidation"—and the opposite of liberty.

Throughout most of the course of Western Civilization, until a little over two centuries ago, centralized government was regarded as something bad and alien, characteristic of "Oriental despotism." The Greeks, for example, were divided into self-governing city-states. They were never united under one authority during the time when their excellence in knowledge, art, and government reached levels that still astonish the world. Herodotus, the first historian, ascribed the Greeks' defeat of the Persian Empire to the resilience flowing from their freedom from arbitrary control. In typical fashion, government-worship-ping historians of the 19th century forward preached the contrary: that the decline of the ancient Greeks resulted from their lack of unity.

However, a more reasonable interpretation is that, although they were damaged by fighting among themselves, the Greeks met with irredeemable disaster only after Athens had centralized a dangerous power to dictate to the other city-states. Thus, the Greeks' liberties and creativity ended precisely when they were united under the Macedonian monarchy.

John C. Calhoun, one of the great anti-consolidationist thinkers of the 19th century, pointed out that the Romans achieved their greatest freedom and strength as a people when there existed two centers of power—the Senate and the Tribunes - each with an absolute veto over the other's actions.

The workings of the state required co-ordination and agreement among the elements of society rather than dictation from above. Contrary to government-worshippers who complained that the lack of a commanding central authority made society helpless, Calhoun observed that an independent consensus of the parts led to actions that were highly effective and more satisfactory to the whole. No central authority could match the strength of free men who co-operated willingly. Mr. Tuggle enlightens us as to the current appropriateness of Calhoun's insight.

Even under the Roman Empire (while it was healthy), although policies were sent out from the center, vast areas of initiative remained in the provinces and cities—in military affairs, taxation, local government, and religion.

The Middle Ages were par excellence the age of decentralization; there was scarcely any real power that was not local. Kings and lesser lords essentially depended upon the voluntary cooperation of their vassals. The Church, at least in appearance, was centralized in its own affairs, but it preached the rightness of subsidiarity in government. Our modern thinkers who extol the necessity and glory of the nation-state consolidated under one supreme authority tell us that decentralization was the cause of the "darkness" of those times. Looked at another way, perhaps it was the creative force of many different points of light that illuminated the way of the West out of the darkness—a darkness brought on by the inevitable collapse of the muscle-bound inflexibility of the imperial government. Certainly, the lights came on earliest in the free and self-governing cities, while the Renaissance blazed most brightly in the free and independent cities of northern Italy—not in some centrally-managed society.

In the 17th century it was thought that the "Sun King" of France, Louis XIV, had brought centralized government to the height of its possibilities. Louis could oppress individuals; however, he could not—except through the traditional hodgepodge of taxes—oppress entire classes. He could declare wars, but he could no more command all the manpower and resources of the kingdom for his wars than he could the rotation of the planets. It was his nationalist successors of the Revolution and the Empire who marshaled the ability of a centralized government to command a whole society. Their handiwork was copied all over the Western world. The consolidated nation-state became the material and psychological focus of entire peoples while the ensuing conflicts among such states became the prevailing pattern of history. The American

Revolution -and the Articles of Confederation and Constitution which followed—preceded the triumph of the nation-state. During the long colonial peri-od, Americans enjoyed the benign neglect of the British Crown. The thirteen colonies barely felt the hand of central government (their citizens scarcely feeling the controlling hand of any government). It was the British government's attempt to end this happy condition that brought them to declare that the thirteen "are and of right ought to be free and independent states."

The American Founders intended to create a Union which would institutionalize bonds of co-operation among those states and among the new commonwealths that their descendants would create out of wilderness in the future. They did not intend to establish a central authority, such as the one they had just thrown off, from which there was no escape or appeal except by the sword They dreaded the specter of "consolidation" which, if allowed, would bring an end to their individual freedom and the self-government of their natural communities. Human associations in community were distinct from and took precedence over governments. Good governments were the servants of society, not its master.

The forces that reshaped the States United into the United State in the middle of the 19th century did so only as the result of the destruction of the essential elements of self-government and a holocaust of American lives.

The supposed deep thinkers of the 19th century (especially in Germany and the United States) celebrated the brutality employed against their fellow countrymen that was necessary in order to establish the nation-states they desired. Each sang the praises of his own country's new ability to mobilize the property and allegiances of the masses to the ends of the central state. Nationalist mania stipulated that the centralized state was a prerequisite for the liberation and progress of humanity.

Lord Acton, an immensely learned historian of liberty, was, like Calhoun, a nay-sayer of the 19th century, bringing into common reference the phrase "Power corrupts." The progress of man depended upon ordered liberty; and liberty depended upon the restraint and dispersal of power. Acton demonstrated that freedom in the Western world was a product of restrictions on power that had been painfully accumulated bit by bit over the course of centuries. Taking the long view, Acton wrote, the crushing of the principle of states' rights in the American war of 1861-1865 was not a victory for liberty, but a defeat.

One wonders why in the 21st century anyone should continue to give devotion to the principle of consolidation. The postulate of the all-commanding central government has resulted, for the first time, in mankind's long and painful existence, in what were literally World Wars. The central state has given rulers the power to murder the innocents of their own and other countries by the millions. Even at its least destructive, the central state inevitably, as Calhoun also observed, preys upon the people, or a part of them, for the benefit of those who hold power and their clients.

Surely the premier empirical truth that emerged from human affairs in the 20th century is that free markets are better than central planning. At least better for society as a whole, aside from those who profit from the Plan. As Tuggle makes clear, confidence in the necessity of centralized power in industrial management, education, and the organization of many other human affairs has proved to be a delusion over the past two centuries. The wisdom of experience and of insight into the real trends of the present which the author has brought to bear tells us that centralization has not fulfilled the promises of its apologists. Command from the top down has proven itself to be not only arbitrary and inimical to freedom, but also inefficient and unable to adapt to changing circumstances.

The wave of the future, the cutting edge, the hope of efficiency, abundance, and freedom for societies is just what the Western tradition has always told us- devolution of power to competing and co-operating authorities. There is no lesson that it is more important to take to heart at this moment in time. It seems that John C. Calhoun was right after all. (2003)

DiLorenzo and His Critics

Professor Thomas DiLorenzo's *The Real Lincoln* has provoked the utterly predictable torrent of abuse from state worshippers and self-appointed prophets of The True American Way. All DiLorenzo has done (and this does not in the least detract from his courage, eloquence, and insight) is to analyze Honest Abe as a historical figure just like any other, rather than treat him as a saint.

Professor DiLorenzo does not need any defense. He, along with Professor Joseph Stromberg and others, has exposed the ignorance and fanaticism of the critics to the satisfaction of any reasoning human. However, something more can be said about the Lincolnites, especially their egregious abuse and distortion of the nature and purposes of historical understanding.

One devotee of Lincoln hagiography, Professor Mackubin Thomas Owens, dismisses *The Real Lincoln* with the announcement that we need pay it no mind—its ideas were refuted fifty years ago by Professor Harry Jaffa. How comforting to know that the proper interpretation of the largest and most portentous event in American history, the War Between the States, has already been settled! We don't have to tire ourselves out any more examining evidence and thinking about the meaning of events!

However, I must demur at giving Jaffa the honors of discovering this forever valid truth. This wisdom was first given to us 125 years ago (1876) by Hermann E. von Holst in his eight volume history of the United States. Holst was an imported Prussian, ensconced, appropriately enough, in Rockefeller's University of Chicago. His view of the American founding and its alleged salvation by Lincoln anticipated Jaffa on almost every point.

Of course, like the Jaffaites, Holst knew absolutely nothing about American history before Lincoln, to which he devoted only a small portion of one volume. He knew nothing about English and American constitutional evolution, about the historical experience and ideas of the American people. What he did know was that the unitary state was righteous and inevitable. It was easy for him to proclaim that the great war of 1861-1865, the most violent and complex experience of the United States, was the necessary cleansing from the American state of slavery and its defenders. Not because slavery violated equality but because it was a contradiction in the way of the perfection of the central state. Any resistance to the state could only be motivated by an evil like slavery, which he treated not as an analyzable human institution or a political issue but as a reified Hegelian antithesis. And his convenient ignorance of actual American history allowed him to dismiss states' rights as a fiction, a made-up rationalization in defense of evil.

Professor Jaffa has been free in throwing out hints that opponents of his view are tainted with Nazism. In fact, it is more reasonable to argue that his views have their remote origins in the same state worship as Nazism. Except that the Straussians, who pose as defenders of democracy while appointing themselves as the "wise men" who are empowered to tell the rest of us rubes what everything really means, are guilty of an elitism that is more cynical than that of 20th century totalitarian movements, which at least claimed to believe in the people.

What is revealed by DiLorenzo's attackers is their pathetically impoverished idea of the nature and uses of historical knowledge. It is, in fact, a rejection of the historical consciousness that John Lukacs has defined, rightly, as the hallmark of Western civilization.

What Professor Owens calls for is the end of the search for historical understanding. The eternal true understanding has already been achieved by his saint! It is fixed forever.

Thus, one does not have to search among the records of human acts and experience to find understanding. Professor Jaffa's mystical contemplation of a few of Lincoln's prettier speeches establishes all we need to know! We are to terminate our search for understanding of the immense and complex past of our species on this planet and defer to our betters. This is not only anti-intellectual. It is also a rejection of democracy, which is supposed to be exercised by free thought and deliberation. It is also, of course, atheist, since it rejects the essential mystery of human existence and limitations of human knowledge.

To any serious historian of any breed, Professor Owens's position is laughable. Historians are by definition aware that historical knowledge is never complete and conclusive, that there is always more to be found out and always more than one way to look at things. I have always thought that the most important aspect of history was that it can teach us to see that there is usually more than one side of a question, that sweeping claims to final truth are deceptive, that moral judgments should be made after, not before, examining the evidence. Thus, we are made better, more savvy and less credulous citizens.

No serious historian of the War Between the States pays much attention to Jaffa or his works. The prevailing interpretation now, which has changed before and will change again (unless the neocons are able to suppress all unofficial thought) is that Lincoln carried out a revolution, not a salvation; a refounding, not a preservation. One may like or dislike the revolution (most historians today like it), but there it is.

The Straussians, for whom the Jaffaites are the commandos, are tireless networkers and noisy disputants. They do most of their work on the "conservative" side of American discourse, which itself constitutes a tiny minority. They are loud frogs in a small pond, and those of us on the "conservative" side tend to over-estimate their importance. Most historians know Jaffa only from *Crisis of the House Divided*, which they vaguely remember from a graduate school reading list decades ago. Political philosophers are perhaps more aware of them, but it is my impression that most are either indifferent or hostile to the Straussian message and resentful of their ruthless networking and authoritarian style of argument.

Texts such as speeches of leading men and constitutional documents, are important but they don't constitute all of history. History consists of all human actions, to which texts are only one guide. By reference to a few lines of a select few of Lincoln's speeches, Professor DiLorenzo's critics want to settle forever understanding of the War Between the States, which is the largest event in American experience in scale, casualties, and revolutionary impact.

How convenient when one can select the few documents out of thousands that contain the truth to be discerned by the elect! So, Jaffa has been fond of comparing Lincoln's paean to equality with a speech of Alexander Stephens, who became Vice-President of the Confederacy, as the defining text of the struggle of the Southern people for independence. Stephens is said to have declared that inequality, i.e., white supremacy, was the "cornerstone" of the Confederacy.

Set aside that this speech was an unofficial oration on the hustings and that the accuracy of the text is disputed and that Stephens was in several respects an eccentric figure. At face value this tells us that Stephens was a white supremacist. So, what? Though Lincoln never made white supremacy a "cornerstone" he, like 98 percent of his voters (including most of the sincere anti-slavery people) and most Americans of several succeeding generations, was also a white supremacist. In fact, in one of the two forthrightly truthful statements in his public career, Lincoln remarked that "the Southern people are exactly what we would be in their situation."

And why does this particular document sum up the whole of the case for the Confederacy. Why can't I, who actually know a fair amount about the context, make another selection. Something much more central and comparable to Lincoln's speeches on critical occasions. How about Jefferson Davis's first inaugural, in which he declared to the world:

> Our present condition, achieved in a manner unprecedented in the history of nations, illustrates the American idea that governments rest upon the consent of the governed, and that it is the right of the people to alter or abolish governments whenever they become destructive of the ends for which they were established.

Or given my unfortunate limitations as a mere historian and not a seer, I might point to a sermon preached by the Reverend James Henley Thornwell of South Carolina, one of the most respected churchmen in the South and a strong secessionist, upon the founding of the Confederate States. The Rev. Thornwell outlined and recommended as a necessary task a course of action that would lead to the eventual peaceful end of slavery.

It is a lot easier to win an argument when you are able to state your opponent's case for him, which is the stock-in-trade of Straussian discourse.

An entirely different kind of criticism comes from Professor Tibor Machan in his "Lincoln, Secession, and Slavery," a criticism that deserves respectful consideration. As I understand it, Machan is interested in laying down a rationale for the right of secession. This is a worthy endeavor which needs much more work. I would recommend to him the writings of Professor Donald Livingston on this subject in various Mises Institute publications and elsewhere, and in a forthcoming book.

His position is that the right of secession is generally valid, but does not hold when the secessionists take with them "hostages," in which category Professor Machan places the slaves of the Southern states. Therefore, the secession of the Southern states was not morally valid, and Lincoln was justified in refusing to allow it.

At the time when Lincoln inaugurated coercion against the seven seceding Southern states, there were (rounding off 1860 census figures) 1,387,000 slaves in the seceded states and 1,817,000 (or over 56 percent of the total American slave population) still in the Union, including nearly 3,700 in the District of Columbia and 18 in New Jersey. It is hard to draw much of a moral to support military conquest of seceding states from that, especially as Lincoln had already declared that he had neither the right nor the desire to interfere with slavery in the states.

And what about the 488,000 free black people in the United States, more than half of whom were in the slave states. How can they be Southern "hostages" when they were discouraged and often forbidden from entering Northern states where the black population was, according to much testimony, extremely depressed and oppressed!

Professor Machan is not alone in working to clarify the condition upon which secession of a portion of a people from a larger state is justified. The subject has received a good deal of attention in recent years. Let me state what I perceive to be a fatal flaw in Professor Machan's position and those of some other libertarian thinkers.

For them secession must meet certain pre-established moral criteria to be justified. But who, in fact, judges the criteria? If I have a right to secede only when you have determined that my motives are morally valid, *then I have no right at all*. I must be the judge of my claim to self-government. Otherwise, of course, the central power will always conclude that my motives are not sufficiently moral. And the fact that there are "hostages" in my territory, if allowed to impede secession, would invalidate almost every independence movement in history, including the American Revolution, since almost every territory has anti-secessionists or a minority ethnic group.

The right of secession is a technical form of the right to self-government, which is its own justification. Nobody put it better than Lincoln in his other true statement (1848): "Any people anywhere, being inclined and having the power, have the right to rise up and shake off the existing government and form a new one that suits them better. This is a most valuable, a most sacred right-a right which we hope and believe is to liberate the world." (2002)

Inventing the New Nation

For the Italian publication *Il Domenicale*

Few actors in history have been hallowed in as many points of the political compass as Abraham Lincoln. During the 1930s, portraits of Lincoln appeared at New York City rallies of American fascists and in the publications of American Communists. He was also the favorite of the most reactionary industrialists and the most advanced liberals of the time. "Getting Right with Lincoln," as the historian David Donald has described it, has been requisite for all political elements in the United States. [31]

Lincoln's Gettysburg Address is widely regarded as the definitive description and rationale of American nationhood and is the cornerstone of his fame. It has been memorized and declaimed by generations of schoolchildren. Its cadenced phrases are part of the American vernacular and have moved millions around the world.

One might wonder why this short and rather abstract composition, hardly remarked upon at the time it was given at Gettysburg a few months after the great battle there, has achieved such importance. Part of the answer is surely Lincoln's great rhetorical skill. In the Gettysburg Address (and other orations) he performs successfully the difficult feat of having it both ways. He appears in the famous brief oration as both the conservator of the sacred old Union and the herald of "a new birth of freedom." Rhetorically, he encompasses right and left, the revered past and the longed-for ideal future.

Sanctification of the Address has not gone entirely unchallenged in America, however. The iconoclastic Henry Louis Mencken, writing in 1920, described Lincoln as "the American solar myth, the chief butt of American credulity and sentimentality." Of the Gettysburg Address, Mencken wrote:

> It is genuinely stupendous. But let us not forget that it is poetry, not logic; beauty, not sense. Think of the argument in it. Put it into the cold words of everyday. The doctrine is simply this: that the Union soldiers who died at Gettysburg sacrificed their lives to the cause of self-determination-"that government of the people, by the people, for the people," should not perish from the earth. It is

---

31 David H. Donald, *Lincoln Reconsidered*, New York: Knopf, 1956.

difficult to imagine anything more untrue. The Union soldiers in that battle actually fought against self-determination; it was the Confederates Who fought for the right of their people to govern themselves.[32]

Edgar Lee Masters, a poet who immortalized his and Lincoln's home region of Illinois in *Spoon River Anthology*, was so troubled by the Lincoln legacy that he devoted an entire book to it (1931). Of the Address, Masters wrote:

> Lincoln carefully avoided one half of the American story.... The Gettysburg oration, therefore, remains a prose poem, but in the inferior sense that one must not inquire into its truth.... One must read it apart from the facts.... Lincoln dared not face the facts at Gettysburg.... He was unable to deal realistically with the history of his country, even if the occasion had been one where the truth was acceptable to the audience. Thus we have in the Gettysburg Address that refusal of the truth which is written all over the American character and its expressions. The war then being waged was not glorious, it was brutal and hateful and mean minded.[33]

Mencken and Masters were reflecting, in part, revulsion at the American entry into World War I, which had been blessed by Lincolnian rhetoric as a crusade "to save the world for democracy."[34] "Difficult to imagine anything more untrue," "Refusal of the truth"; these are strong charges. Coming from a poet and a cultural critic, rather than from patriotic orators, political advocates, or nationalist historians, they deserve consideration.

One would think that the Address should be considered less important and less definitive than the Declaration of Independence or the Constitution. These were, after all, not just the words of one man, but solemn acts of the whole American people, indeed important events in world history. But, in fact, the Declaration has come to be perceived and valued in American public discourse wholly through the interpretation that Lincoln put upon it at Gettysburg. The Declaration has been absorbed into the Address. The Declaration itself is seldom read beyond the first sentences, and Americans are often surprised to see

---

32 H.L. Mencken, *The Vintage Mencken*, New York: Vintage Books, 1958, pp. 79-80.
33 33 Edgar Lee Masters, *Lincoln, The Man*, New York: Dodd, Mead, 1931, pp. 478-479. Reprinted: Columbia, South Carolina: The Foundation for American Education, 1997.
34 See Richard M. Gamble, *The War for Righteousness: Progressive Christianity, the Great War, and the Rise of the Messianic Nation*, Wilmington, Delaware: ISI Books, 2003.

what it actually says and to have pointed out what it actually signaled in historical events.

"Four score and seven years ago," a "new nation" was "brought forth" (note Lincoln's biblical and almost mystical language). This new nation, "conceived in liberty," had been dedicated to a "proposition" of equality. By this formulation, since the new nation was "brought forth" in 1776, the Constitution adopted in 1787-1789 is merely an unfolding of the "proposition" in the Declaration. The Declaration and the Constitution are now conflated. The Constitution is merely the implementation of the Declaration - subservient to the proposition to which the new nation had already been dedicated.[35]

The two documents actually do not depend on or convey any dedication of a people to equality, either in text or context. They reflect, for the most part, the language and spirit of Anglo-American legal and parliamentary traditions. The Declaration created no new nation. It was an agreed-upon statement of why the thirteen united colonies "are and of right ought to be, free and independent states."

Its operative premise is not the equality of all men but that governments should rest upon "the consent of the governed." It was a Declaration of Independence, not a Declaration of the Rights of Man, having more in common with Magna Carta than with Jean-Jacques Rousseau. What the Constitution established might in some sense be called a nation, but it was customarily referred to before Lincoln (and even in Lincoln's earlier public documents) as a "union."

Something had happened to the Declaration between the American founding and Lincoln at Gettysburg—the French Revolution. The transition was perfectly illustrated by Karl Marx, who in January 1865 wrote an address in praise of Lincoln for an "International Conference of Workers." Marx described the American war as a contest between "the labor of the emigrant" and the aggression of "the slave driver," and lamented that an evil rebellion had sprung up in the "one great democratic republic whence the first Declaration of the Rights of Man was issued."[36]

---

35 35 I am drawing here on the brilliant analyses of Lincoln's rhetoric by the late Professor M.E. Bradford. Bradford's half-dozen ground-breaking Lincoln essays are scattered through almost as many of his books. See especially Melvin E. Bradford, *A Better Guide Than Reason*, Lasalle, Illinois: Sherwood Sugden, 1979, pp. 29-57 and 85-203; and M.E. Bradford, *Remembering Who We Are*, Athens: University of Georgia Press, 1985, pp. 143-156. On the dissolvable nature of the Union see Alexis de Tocqueville, *Democracy in America*, vol. 1, New York: Vintage Books, pp. 143-156.
36 The manifesto is printed in Philip S. Foner, ed., *Abraham Lincoln: Selections from His Writings*, New York: International Press, 1944, pp. 93-94. International Press was an organ of the U.S. Communist Party.

(A different European reaction to the American war occurred in the same month that Lincoln gave his Address. Father John B. Bannon, chaplain in the Confederate Army, had a series of audiences with Pius IX. Father Bannon emphasized the justice and conservatism of the Southern cause, the religious devotion of the Southern people, and their friendly reception of Catholics in contrast to the bitterly hostile Protestant North. His efforts resulted in a kindly papal letter to President Jefferson Davis and a mission to Ireland to preach against Northern recruiting of cannon fodder there, something which is glimpsed in the recent film *Gangs of New York*.)[37]

Lincoln begins the Address with language that is directly patterned on the King James Bible so familiar to his audience. "Four score and seven years" rather than "eighty-seven"; "brought forth" rather than "established." Thus, he invokes the ancient and sacred: the American Union as a special manifestation of God's plan for the improvement of humanity. The first Puritan settlers of Massachusetts had named themselves "a City upon a Hill" and "a beacon to all mankind."

As historians have shown abundantly in recent decades, this theme, projected rhetorically to an ideal America, was already well-developed in the post-Puritan culture of the North, especially in New England and New Englander settled areas of the West.[38] It is amply displayed in such highbrow places as the writings of Emerson and in such lowbrow places as "The Battle Hymn of the Republic." The notion of the special role of the United States in history has become a powerful and lasting motivation and rationalization. It has appeared in countless sermons down to the present day and in the rhetoric of President George W. Bush in the 21st century.

Lincoln thus, in practical terms, rhetorically nailed down one of the two most important and dedicated of his constituencies and one of the two most forceful ideological elements of the North. The second, like

---

37 Philip Thomas Tucker, *The Confederacy's Fighting Chaplain: Father John B. Bannon*, Tuscaloosa: University of Alabama Press, pp. 157-178.
38 In general, American historians have paid relatively little attention to the antebellum North, implicitly postulating it as the American norm, and the South as an un-American anomaly to be explained. However, recently attention has been paid to Northern society, showing an aggressive economic and cultural agenda that was something new. Among other things, these works have demonstrated the power of Northern forces desperate to prevent a free trade South, and, by emphasizing the racism of the politicians and soldiers of the Union, have cast new light on the supposed benevolence of the campaign against slavery. See Anne Norton, *Alternative Americas*; Ernest L. Tuveson, *Redeemer Nation*; Harlow Sheidley, *Massachusetts Conservative Leaders and the Transformation of America*; Richard F. Bensel, *Yankee Leviathan*; Susan-Mary Grant, *North Over South*; Joan P. Melish, *Disowning Slavery*; Charles Adams, *When in the Course of Human Events*; Thomas DiLorenzo, *The Real Lincoln*.

the first, disdained the Jeffersonian limited government ideals of the Confederacy and of Lincoln's Northern opponents. The second group, which Lincoln must capture and merge with the first to make a success of the Address, is made up of Marx's "emigrants."

Historians have long noted the influence of German refugees from the revolutions of 1848 in the founding of the Republican Party and in Lincoln's election, but usually without allowing its true weight. Between 1840 and 1860, the total free American population increased by one-third from immigrants alone—including at least a million and a half Germans. These settled mainly in Lincoln's Midwest and in 1860 made up from eight percent to 17 percent of the population of the Midwestern states.[39]

Lincoln recognized this constituency early on by secretly purchasing a German language newspaper and subsidizing others. German delegates were prominent in the convention that nominated Lincoln and in the campaign as orators who stimulated the grassroots on his behalf. It appears that these immigrants tipped the balance, swinging the traditionally Democratic Midwest into the Republican column and making Lincoln's election possible.

The German revolutionaries brought with them an aggressive drive to realize in America the goals that had been defeated in their homeland. Their drive was toward "revolution and national unification" in the words of the Party of the Left at the Frankfurt Convention. The most prominent among them, Carl Schurz, expressed disappointment at the non-ideological nature of American politics and vowed to change that.[40]

The Germans brought into the American regional conflict and into Republican rhetoric a diagnosis of class conflict (crusade to overthrow the "slave drivers") and a revolutionary élan. They also contributed out of proportion to the Northern military effort. Friedrich Engels remarked: "Had it not been for the experienced soldiers who had entered America after the European revolution, especially from Germany, the organization of the Union army would have taken still longer than it did."[41]

Thus, Lincoln consolidated his base, justified and sanctified the Northern cause and victory both as preservation of the hallowed old and a birth of the new. He created an image of the United States that

---

39   Charlotte L. Brancaforte, ed., *The German Forty-Eighters in the United States*, New York: Peter Lang, 1989; A.E. Zucker, ed., *The Forty-Eighters: Political Refugees of the German Revolution of 1848*, New York: Columbia University Press, 1950; *American Historical Review*, 16:774ff and 47:51ff; *Journal of American History*, 19:192ff and 29:55ff.
40   Hans L. Trefousse, *Carl Schurz: A Biography*, (Knoxville: University of Tennessee Press, 1982.)
41   Engels, quoted in the Lincoln pamphlet cited in footnote 36.

has had and continues to have incalculable effects on American public life and, indeed, on the world.

That Lincoln's accomplishment was a revolution and not a "preservation of the Union" (whether one finds the revolution pleasing or troubling) is beautifully illustrated by an incident in *Destruction and Reconstruction: Personal Experiences of the Late War*, the Civil War memoir of Confederate General Richard Taylor. Taylor was a learned man acquainted in the highest circles, an able though not a professional soldier. He also possessed an active sense of humor.

In May 1865, after the surrender of the main Confederate armies and the capture of his brother-in-law Jefferson Davis, Taylor found himself in command of a small army in Alabama. He opened surrender negotiations with the nearest Union commander, General Canby. With one staff officer Taylor went to meet Canby in a hand-driven railroad sled under a flag of truce. The formalities of capitulation completed, courteous federal officers invited the hungry Confederates to join them at dinner. Taylor relates what happened next:

> There was, as ever, a skeleton at the feast, in the person of a general officer who had recently left Germany to become a citizen and soldier of the United States. This person, with the strong accent and idioms of the Fatherland, comforted me by assurances that we of the South would speedily recognize our ignorance and errors ... and rejoice in the results of the war.... I apologized meekly for my ignorance, on the ground that my ancestors had come from England to Virginia in 1608, and, in the short intervening period of two hundred and fifty-odd years, had found no time to transmit to me correct ideas of the duties of American citizenship. Moreover, my grandfather, commanding the 9th Virginia regiment in our Revolutionary army, had assisted in the defeat and capture of the Hessian mercenaries at Trenton, and I lamented that he had not, by association with these worthies, enlightened his understanding. My friend smiled blandly, and assured me of his willingness to instruct me.[42]

Modestly, Taylor did not mention that his father had been President of the United States. (2004)

---

[42] Richard Taylor, *Destruction and Reconstruction: Personal Reminiscences of the Late War*, Nashville, Tennessee: J.S. Sanders, 1998, originally published 1879.

Chapter Five

The Other Southerners

The Redeemable South

A review of *Time on the Cross: The Economics of American Negro Slavery*, by Robert W. Fogel and Stanley L. Engerman, Boston: Little, Brown and Company, 1974, 286 pages.

Time on the Cross presents us with a favorable view of the *ancient régime* of the Southern United States, a view arising from an unexpected quarter—economic historians of unimpeachable egalitarian credentials—and resting upon the most massive and systematic accumulation of evidence ever made. In sum, *Time on the Cross* refutes every point in that elaborately constructed negative stereotype of the Old South which brought on the Civil War, motivated conquest and reconstruction, and has more recently supported the glib ascription of current racial problems to "the heritage of slavery." As a result, we must recast certain accounts of good and evil in American history which we had been told were forever closed.

Our recapitulation of the authors' conclusions must be brief and general, dangerously simplifying the qualifications, sophistication, and specificity of the original, and ignoring temporarily the particular nature of their evidence: According to *Time on the Cross*, the typical standard of living of the 19th century Southern slave, measured by life expectancy, birth rate, diet, clothing, housing, and medical care, was not only broadly speaking adequate, but, more important, was superior to what was enjoyed by the black population after slavery and by much of the laboring white populations of Europe and America then and later. By these measures the Southern United States was the most favorable environment in the New World and perhaps in the world for black people.

Further, the patriarchal "Victorian" family was the inculcated norm of plantation society: "breeding" was nonexistent, miscegenation was statistically insignificant, and "selling down the river" was a real but infrequent event which may have disrupted no more black families than the westward expansion of the frontier did white families. Plantation labor was not directed chiefly by physical coercion nor was it grudging, unskilled, or inadaptable. Slaves generally were neither rebels, saboteurs, nor skulkers but took an intelligent interest in the economic success of the plantation. Moreover, a greater percentage of slaves was engaged in skilled crafts and managerial functions than was true of blacks long after slavery.

The black people of antebellum America were, then, a laboring class not much different from what might be found in many other places and climes. The "slave" system, though erecting obvious barriers at many points, allowed a not insignificant degree of physical and psychological freedom that was often found preferable to the limited alternatives available to blacks elsewhere, and its evils appear less damning when measured against the real conditions (rather than the theoretical virtues) of other contemporary societies. Indeed, it appears that there was a measurable deterioration after slavery in the living standards, life expectancy, real compensation, work skills, and family stability of the black population. In other words, in the destruction of the old regime ground was lost that has only been recovered in this century, for those who destroyed it were better at rending than mending.

Nor was the Old South the backward, poverty-stricken, oligarchical society of hostile polemics, in which not only the slaves but the mass of whites were beyond the pale of civilization. To the contrary, Southern society was dynamic and prosperous. Its agriculture, on both slave plantation and yeoman farm, was more productive and efficient than the Northern. Far from stagnating, the Southern economy expanded at a rate in the late antebellum period that has few equals in history. Southern per capita income was equal to Northern, just as evenly distributed among whites, and higher than that of most of Europe in even recent times. Moreover, the slave received back in a lifetime ninety percent of the income he produced, "well within modern limits of exploitation," according to the authors. Any excess profits of the labor of slaves accrued not to their Southern owners but to worldwide consumers of cotton. In sum, the Old South's day-to-day view of itself as a settled, ethical, paternalistic order, so often derided as an absurd or pathological mythology, had an undeniable basis in reality.

As to the nature of the evidence which supports these findings, *Time on the Cross* is the most conspicuous example to date of "cliometrics"—the describing of the past by generalizations drawn from concrete data, expressed in quantitative terms, and tested for validity according to the formal laws of statistics. Clearly statistics cannot answer questions of value nor satisfy moral absolutists. But, allowing always for an unavoidable ambiguity in defining categories (what is a "skilled" worker?), certain kinds of descriptive and comparative facts can indeed be established more reliably by statistics than by less self-correcting and systematic researches. To put it another way, there is nothing "scientifically" conclusive about "cliometric" assertions, but competently arrived at and understood as aver-ages, they are entitled to credence in establishing the groundwork of given facts from which value judgments ought to proceed.

The work in hand has already received extensive methodological scrutiny and will receive more. The net of this scrutiny is to modify minor points, to require further data on some major points, and to change very little the broad thrust of the conclusions. In fact, the book's significant defects are two: the generalizations about the slave family rest upon insufficient data; and, after they overcame their own skepticism, the authors presented their findings in a way they knew to be deliberately provocative to various academic celebrities. In response, the official purveyors of "black history," who enjoy a large but sensitive vested interest, have reacted typically with abuse, sometimes perfunctorily disguised as argument. (One review concluded that if the South was not inhumanly backward, then it must have been inhumanly efficient: if Southerners were not lazier than Northerners then they must have been more ruthlessly utilitarian. Exactly what facts describe the South is moot, but that, whatever they were, they were evil, is axiomatic. No sensible middling explanation can arise because historic images of the South are merely stage props for moral self-preening) On the other hand, some scholars, including the authors, have found comfort and constructive hope in the realization that black Americans can recognize in their forbears more sympathetic and successful human beings than the bloodthirsty rebels or dehumanized chattels which their erstwhile advocates have alternatively pictured them to be.

Methodology aside, there are other reasons for accepting the *Time on the Cross* view as essentially correct or at least as more nearly correct than its opposite. It comports with common sense and with the instinctive feelings of those who are familiar with the best cultural survivals of the Old South in its human personalities, white and black. Moreover, it only tells us in different from what our best historians have told us already. Avery Craven understood (1942) that "slavery" amounted practically to a labor system not too different from contemporary "free" labor.

Lewis C. Gray in a classic work on Southern agriculture (1933) clearly portrayed the viability of the plantation economy. Frank Owsley, whose researches (1949) have never been successfully refuted, demonstrated that the Old South was not oligarchical. Howard Floan explained how urban, puritan observers perceived in the South's dispersed and informal society a backwardness that was more apparent than real. (In fact, almost all Northerners and Europeans who were intimately acquainted with the old regime defended it.) C. Vann Woodward has often made the point that the black population was in several respects more depressed in 1900 than in 1860.

Our best reason for accepting this picture of the Old South as essentially true, however, is our instinctive suspicion of its enemies—those who labored not to ameliorate its real evils but to destroy it for exaggerated sins of their own imagining. The Old South, imperfect, archaic even in its own time perhaps, did not deserve the hatred, slander, fire, and sword which it received. One might in fact reasonably request a refocusing of attention from the peculiar South to its peculiar critics.

Such a refocusing will tell us much about the intermittent aggressions against the social fabric which have convulsed our larger society, for the irresponsible consciences which eradicated the Old Regime without heeding the consequences in blood, in disaster to the constitutional settlement, or even in the up-rooting of the supposed beneficiaries of their zeal, are with us still. Further, in redeeming the South we redeem the nation's past, lately held hostage to guilt by the heirs of those same self-beatified saints. For, after all, that half or more of the founders and early guardians of the republic who arose from the plantation gentry were not really criminals against humanity, and, given the long view of the crimes and follies of mankind, our ancient sin was not nearly so irredeemable as permanently to damn our national enterprise. (1975)

Black Confederates

A review of *Black Confederates and Afro-Yankees in Civil War Virginia*, by Ervin L. Jordan, Jr., Charlottesville: University Press of Virginia, 1995, 447 pages; and *Black Slaveowners: Free Black Slavemasters in South Carolina*, 1790-1860, by Larry Koger, Columbia: University of South Carolina Press, 1994, 286 pages.

Black Confederates! Remember, you heard it here first. You will be hearing more if you have any interest at all in the Great Unpleasantness of the last century that is the focal point of American history. There are more things in heaven and earth, dear Horatio, than are dreamed of by Ken Burns.

In the film *Gettysburg* appears the English Colonel Arthur Fremantle, played as a somewhat silly character. Fremantle was a real person who accompanied the Confederate Army on the Gettysburg campaign and published a book, *Three Months in the Southern States*. One incident noted by Fremantle in his book did not, of course, make it into the movie—the spectacle of a black Confederate marching Yankee prisoners to the rear.

Real life is always a lot more complicated than ideological history. The image that most Americans carry around in their heads of the Old South and the black slavery that flourished over much of this continent for two and a half centuries is cartoonish and largely misleading. (Just think of *Uncle Tom's Cabin* and *Roots*.) It is also, of course, extremely comforting to the mainstream American consciousness to think of the heroic soldiers in blue marching forth to strike the chains from the suffering black people-setting aside the fact that emancipation did not become a war goal until well after hostilities had begun, and that in many cases it resulted only in destructive uprooting or a change of masters.

The material brought forth in these two recently published works has not been unknown; it has always been self-evident to serious historians who have worked with primary sources. Large numbers of black people identified the South and the Confederacy as their homeland and homefolks, and did not rush into the arms of the emancipators. This really is not surprising to anyone who knows anything about history or human nature, which, of course, does not include Ken Burns. The Confederate Army was vastly sustained by black men who drove teams, cooked, foraged, dug fortifications, cared for the wounded, and occasionally took up arms. George Washington Cable, the author, when a mere youth of 15 or so, served as General Bedford Forrest's headquarters clerk. At the beginning of the War, Forrest took 50 of his slaves with him, promising freedom if they served faithfully. Cable records how he was told by Forrest to make out emancipation papers for all but one of these. A number of units of free blacks volunteered for Confederate service, and near the end of the War the Confederacy had decided to enlist black units. There was much opposition to this invasion of private property, but there was also solid support. Unlike the Union Army, they were to receive the same pay as white soldiers. It is a fact that black men who had been with the army were welcomed at Confederate reunions and received Confederate pensions from Southern states.

Dr. Jordan's book presents a tremendous amount of documentation about the activities of black Virginians for and against the Confederacy. He is far from a Confederate sympathizer, which makes the data all the more telling. When one considers that over large areas of the South, the black population was 70 to 90 percent and most able-bodied white men were off fighting the War, and that nevertheless no uprisings or significant outrages occurred on the home front, one has to take a rather more complicated view of the Civil War than is usually passed around. It is true that many slaves left when they had the chance, when federal forces came near, but sometimes they had to be taken away by force. (Often they found themselves pressed into harsher service with the Union Army than with the Southern.) This attitude of the blacks was not due to ignorance or lack of understanding. When Sherman burned over 100 blocks of Columbia, the "winds" that were said to have been responsible did not spare the homes of black people, though they did, mysteriously, jump over that of the French consul. The mayor of Columbia observed three Union soldiers shoot to death a black man they considered insolent. When he reported this to Sherman he was told, "We don't have time for court martials and such." During Sherman's progress blacks, like white civilians, were left without food and shelter, and black women were much more vulnerable than white women were to rape and murder. Jordan's book is not the only one in this field of revisionism. *The Journal of Confederate History* a few years ago published as an entire issue a symposium on "Black Southerners in Gray"; while Professor Edward C. Smith of American University, an African-American, has produced two video tape lectures on the same subject.

Prior to the War there were almost a half-million free blacks in the United States, more than half of whom lived in the South. Historians have long noted that many of these were prosperous, and some were slaveowners. The situation has usually been explained as one of a few blacks having nominal ownership of relatives. There was some of that, but also abundant evidence, as marshaled by Koger for South Carolina (and for Louisiana by Gary Mills, *Forgotten People: Cane River's Creoles of Color*, 1977) that many participated in the Southern economy as masters of slave labor in exactly the same way as their white neighbors. (At the time of the averted Denmark Vesey insurrection in Charleston in the 1820s, 72 percent of free black households in the city held slaves.) All of this is not to provide a defense of slavery, but it does provide the grounds for a less simplistic and moralistic rendering of our ambivalent history.

In the 1970s, it was fashionable to attribute American racial problems to "the legacy of slavery." Is it not curious that, the further away we have moved in time and location from the regime of the Old South, the worse these problems have become? How simple it was, in the days before the Watts riots, to attribute all problems to the benighted South. If only the South were corrected with an iron hand, then all would be well. That was a false and destructive rationale, as should be evident to all. It is said that there is now a net in-migration of black Americans back to the South, reversing the pattern of most of this century. There is also evidence that the South (except for a few international metropolises like Atlanta, New Orleans, and Dallas enjoys more racial peace and progress than elsewhere in the Union.

It appears that Americans are in the process of rethinking some of the fundamentals of race relations that have been held sacrosanct for the past half century. These historical works are both a product of and a contribution to that rethinking, which yet has far to go. (1996)

Black Confederates Reconsidered

First-hand evidence abundantly demonstrates that black men were present in great numbers with Confederate armies at all times. A great deal of the cooking, wagon driving, tending wounded, and camp work was done by these men. Many Southerners remarked with gratitude after the War of the support of such people. Of course, some took off, but many others did not, despite many opportunities to do so. President Davis when in the army camps greeted and shook hands with the black men as well as the white. Despite the efforts of some historians to trump up stories of fierce resistance by and fierce put-downs of slaves, it is obvious that there was never any hint of slave insurrection, or the South could not have fought so long and so effectively. The women and children were perfectly safe at home from that possibility.

Kent Masterson Brown, a distinguished lawyer from Kentucky who is also well known as a Civil War historian, has recently completed a book on the Confederate retreat from Gettysburg. He found that when the survivors came back from the Pickett-Pettigrew charge, they returned to Confederate lines that were lined with black faces. Some 6,000 to 10,000 black men went with the army to Pennsylvania—and back. The English observer Col. Fremantle saw a black Confederate marching a Yankee prisoner to the rear. He wondered at their reaction if the abolitionists in London could see that. Brown has found that many of those black men after Gettysburg took their wounded and dead masters home, sometimes to distant places in the far South.

It is hard for current folks to accept, but relations between blacks and whites in the South were sometimes familial. In soldiers' letters (and this is also true of ante-bellum Southerners in general) it is sometimes difficult to determine whether people mentioned are family members or servants. When you think about it, this is not at all unusual. History is full of examples of faithful retainers and servants fighting for their masters and against their masters' enemies. It is a quite common human phenomenon. Faulkner, the great American artist of the 20th century, portrayed this situation often, along with its ambiguity and contradictions.

The interesting question, of course, is why acknowledgment of these facts is so fiercely resisted and misrepresented. There is a natural reluctance among many black people to accept that many "accepted" slavery, that all of their forebears were not in constant resistance and rebellion. But the choice for most of their people most of the time was not between slavery and freedom, but rather just making the best of the situation which life gave them. (Like most of us, most of the time.) Black and white Southerners have different histories, of course, but I very much believe that we should emphasize the good parts of the common history that we have shared. From my outsider's viewpoint, it seems to me a plus for African-Americans to recognize that their history is much more complex, multi-dimensional, and interesting than a simple (and false) story of repression and rebellion.

To really understand the position of the slaves of the South in the Civil War and to explain the resistance to ideas that contradict the official story, you have to understand that for mainstream America the Civil War is a morality play in which Yankees righteously liberate the grateful oppressed. That story has tremendous emotional commitment, but it is not true. Before, during, and after the Civil War, the Yankees never did anything from the primary motive of helping the black people. This is what Frederick Douglass meant when he called Lincoln "the white man's president." The denial of the existence of black Confederates has less to do with African-Americans than with American self-righteousness.

The American myth would have you think that the righteous soldiers in blue and the liberated slaves rushed into each other's arms. Nothing could be further from the truth. We can understand the black Confederate better if we understand that liberation by the Yankees was not always a positive experience. Southerners owned slaves and believed in white supremacy. But as many foreign observers pointed out, they were not as militantly racist as Northerners. In general, Yankees were more interested in getting rid of black people than in freeing them. Letters of Northern soldiers who were encountering black people for the first time make the biggest collection of racist literature before Goebbels.

Remember, Lincoln's Illinois had laws, of which Lincoln approved, forbidding black people to even settle in the state; and those who lived there had no civil rights. The Union was fighting for power, not freedom and equality. When black soldiers were enlisted, it was because they freed that number of white men from risking their lives.

When farms-houses, food, livestock, crops—are deliberately destroyed by an invading army whose policy is to demoralize civilians, black people as well as white are left starving. Black people are just as subject to murder, robbery and rape by invading troops as are white, probably more so. Historians have recently trumped up a good many stories of atrocities by Confederates against slaves. But that is minor and exaggerated compared to the Union armies' well-documented atrocities against and disdain for the black people of the South. We know that many black people left the plantations and farms in the wake of Union armies. Of course, people in a devastated area naturally take to the road and go where they think they can find food. And some were fed by the Union armies at times, though Yankee generals constantly complained of the freed slaves as a nuisance. Actually, it is not clear to what degree slaves went with the Union army willingly or they were actually kidnapped and forced. And what is their fate if they do follow the liberator? To become a forced laborer of the army or a servant or concubine of a Union officer. It is not too far a stretch to recognize that many people might choose to remain with the home and people they knew, even if they were slaves. (2004)

Spielberg's *Amistad*

A review of *Amistad* (1997), directed by Steven Spielberg, 152 minutes.

If *Amistad* is not yet a household word like *ET* or *Jurassic Park*, it soon will be with the power of Steven Spielberg behind it. (When I started this writing awhile back, that was my first sentence, but I may have been wrong. Late reports indicate the box office is lagging.) *Amistad* is really two movies. One, about the 19th century slave commerce between West Africa and Latin America, is a powerful piece of film-making. The other, about American politics and law, is completely hokey and misleading.

Nobody knows for sure, but from the mid-1500s to the mid-1800s between 11 and 15 million black Africans were transported to the New World, a vast undeveloped region with a voracious appetite for unskilled labor. Every maritime nation in Europe participated in this trade. Only about six percent of the Africans ended up in North America, the vast majority going to South America and the Caribbean. By the time of the *Amistad* incident, 1839, the market was largely limited to Cuba, a Spanish colony, and Brazil, a Portuguese dependency. And the shippers involved were limited to Spanish, Portuguese, and American New Englanders.

In case you haven't heard, the *Amistad* was a Spanish ship bound from West Africa with captured slaves to be sold in Cuba. The captives revolted and killed most of the crew. After drifting for a long time, the ship was intercepted by a U.S. coast guard vessel and taken into a Connecticut port. (How it got that far north is not made clear in the movie.)

Thus, the *Amistad* case relates largely to the history of West Africa and Latin America. Only by an accident of navigation did it become an American issue, and then only as a case in admiralty and diplomacy. In the long run it was a minor case that set no precedents. Spielberg wants to make this incident bear the whole weight of the American slavery that lasted two and a half centuries and the Great Unpleasantness that ended it. Thousands of *Amistad* study kits have been sent out to schools with this goal. The trouble is, as an account of American history, the thing will not bear the weight. The *Amistad* had exactly nil influence on (eve of Civil War figures) the nearly four million American slaves (most of whom had been here for some generations); on the 385,000 slaveholding families; on the 488,000 free blacks (most of whom, contrary to usual assumption, were in the South); nor on the issues and events which led to the bloodiest war in American history. Of course, if there had been no slavery and no slave trade, there would today be no such thing as an African-American. The people would not exist.

One of Spielberg's assistants called me early on, wanting advice on the characterization of John C. Calhoun, whom I am supposed to know something about. For a moment, visions of fat Hollywood fees danced before my eyes. Then, I remembered what Grandmother said: Stand up straight, look 'em in the eye, and always tell the truth. I had to say, well Calhoun had nothing to do with the *Amistad* case and nothing to say about it. (The assistant, by the way, identified himself as a South Carolinian. By his speech and the fact that he had had a scholarship to Harvard, I assumed he is an African-American. He was very good, almost as slick as a young Strom Thurmond. I would advise him to come home and go into politics.)

Calhoun is shown in the movie (and the actor who plays him is very good, by the way) as declaiming about slavery and impending civil war in relation to the case. This did not happen and could not have.

I have since learned where they got it. Like Ken Burns, Spielberg's people have been taken in by the great Boston-o-centric stream of American myth and "history." They got the idea of using Calhoun from Samuel F. Bemis's romanticized biography, *John Quincy Adams and the Union*, as well as the idea that the case was some kind of major event and triumph for Adams. The idea of having Adams, one of the nastiest major figures in American history, portrayed by Anthony Hopkins as a shrewd, cuddly old teddy bear, I assume they thought up in Hollywood itself. Get his picture and look at that cold hateful face sometime. I guarantee the next time you have indigestion you will see it in your nightmare as one of the devils tormenting you in Hell. Randolph of Roanoke called him Blifel after the puritan hypocrite in *Tom Jones*.

Bemis claimed that Calhoun introduced resolutions in the Senate on the *Amistad* case to thwart Adams. He even quoted two of the resolutions, conveniently leaving out the third, which was specific. In fact, Calhoun's concern at this time was a different question. British officials in the Bahamas were undertaking to free the slaves on American coastal vessels that came by accident into their waters. (It was common for plantation families to move with their slaves from the South Atlantic to the Gulf Coast states by ship.) The British freed any who came into their hands, as a matter of policy. They also executed those guilty of killing, like the *Amistad* Africans, and later paid indemnity to the U.S., an admission of illegality.

Adams was at this time a marginalized figure, a failed President who could not even get elected Governor of Massachusetts. Calhoun was much more influential. By falsely setting up Adams as an antagonist to Calhoun at this time, Bemis, and the movie, lend more importance to Adams than is deserved. There is also the question of motivation. It is all a love of liberty on Adams's part, according to this rendering. (Part of the larger myth that the later brutal conquest of the Southern people by the government to preserve a political and economic empire, something Adams longed for but did not live to see, was entirely explained as a righteous crusade to free the suffering black man.) Adams had become President in an election that was brokered in the House of Representatives under cries of "corrupt bargain." He had proceeded to propose grandiose plans of centralization and mercantilism, repudiating everything that had been taught by Jefferson, Madison and Monroe. He was immediately shot down and destroyed by Southern strict constructionists. He hated what one of his descendants called "the sable genius of the South" and devoted his last years to attacking it at its weakest point, slavery. It had nothing to do with freedom or with the welfare of people of African origin.

Foreign importation of slaves was illegal and negligible after 1808. Participation in the slave trade to other countries was also illegal for Americans. But in fact, New Englanders, who had plenty of shipping and entrepreneurial energy, continued to invest and participate in the traffic from Africa to Latin America on a considerable scale. Including the Brown family who endowed Brown University, and Thomas H. Perkins, the Boston merchant prince who bankrolled Daniel Webster's career, as well as many lesser fry. The last known New England slave ship, sailing out of Maine, was captured in 1862, a year in which oceans of blood were being shed for the alleged purpose of freeing the slaves.

By the 1830s the British, who had not long before been the largest slave traffickers in the world, had declared emancipation (of a sort) in their colonies and undertaken to suppress the transatlantic trade by naval power. Many nations, including the U.S., approved the object, but they were not too happy about the Brits claiming rights of search and seizure of other countries' ships on the high seas, something which indeed Americans had declared war against in 1812. In 1842, Americans agreed to participate in the suppression of the trade as long as the Brits followed strictly laid out rules. Southern naval officers, diplomats, and other officeholders carried out their duties in this regard conscientiously and generally favored the policy. For instance, Henry A. Wise, later governor of Virginia and a Confederate general, while he was U.S. Minister to Brazil in the 1840s made serious efforts to intercept the New Englanders trading Africans to that country.

The fact was, except for a few hotheads seeking to provoke the Yankees, there was no interest in the South in slave importations after the early 19th century, even though the demand was high. The natural increase was abundant, fertility and longevity being almost equal to the white. (There is still a difference today.) No one wanted to disrupt the settled and peaceful system that existed. The Confederate States Constitution, unlike that of the U.S., absolutely forbade foreign slave importations. The determination of Southerners to prevent malicious outsiders from interfering in their society is, of course, an entirely different question. *Amistad* diverts attention away from the real issues of American history.

Some other things about the movie that I find distorted. Adams makes a pretty speech about liberty to the Supreme Court. I do not find in research so far evidence that this speech was actually delivered. What appears in the printed court record is legalistic, though it is possible the speech could have been made in unrecorded oral argument. In the film, Cinque, the leader of the *Amistad* captives, is present in the Supreme Court, which did not happen. And there is a totally fictional character, played by Morgan Freeman, an affluent free black man. Contra the film, no black man, no matter how affluent, would have been permitted to sit in a courtroom or ride in a carriage with white people in the North in 1839. Especially in Connecticut.

This is mentioned in the film but not dwelt on: The Northern judges ruled against the freedom of the *Amistad* captives. The Supreme Court, with a majority of slaveholding Southerners, rendered the proper decision. The Africans had been illegally seized and were freed. Then, according to American law, they had to be sent back to Africa. In addition, a law professor friend tells me the movie badly distorts the legal issues and proceedings of the case, though these take up most of the film.

Here is the real clincher, which you can bet is not in the movie. Samuel Eliot Morison, one of the leading American historians of all time, wrote in his *Oxford History of the American People* that Cinque, the leader of the *Amistad* captives, went back to West Africa and became a slave trader himself! (1965 edition, p. 520.) Being from Boston, Morison did not have to give any source for this statement and does not. Some writers have affirmed, others have denied this story, none of them having cited any source. In fact, except for the court record, everything that has been printed about the *Amistad* case is in the realm of romance rather than historical scholarship. The court record is full of lawyers' and diplomats' lies, but at least it's a document.

Morison's story is inherently likely. He was well connected in New England maritime circles. New England ships frequently went to the coast of West Africa to sell rum and buy slaves and could have easily heard news of Cinque. Morison could have had the story word of mouth from an old man who had been there, or his descendants. Also, that Cinque became a slave trader is highly plausible. What else could the man do? His native village had been dispersed. West Africa had little else to trade for European goods except its people. It would have been the best entrepreneurial opportunity open to him. The region's economy and politics consisted largely of competition between chiefs for market share.

To further develop the hokeyness of *Amistad*'s portrayal of American life and politics, let me review the unknown history of another slave ship case. In 1858, a U.S. navy vessel intercepted a suspicious looking ship near the Cuban coast. It turned out to be the *Echo* out of Providence, Rhode Island, with over 400 Africans on board, many of them in very miserable condition. The officer who captured the slaver was John N. Maffitt, who a few years later would be famous as commander of the Confederate raider *Florida*. The captain and owner of the slaver was Edward Townsend, a well-educated man from what passed for a good family in Rhode Island. He alleged that the Africans were all war captives or families of executed criminals, and he had saved them from certain death. He also said that had he completed his voyage, he and his silent investors could have cleared $130,000, a staggering sum in those days.

Maffitt took Townsend to Key West to be prosecuted. The Northern born federal judge, later a Unionist, refused to take jurisdiction. Maffitt then had him sent to Boston, where the court had jurisdiction on the presumed point of origin of the *Echo*. There the federal judge also refused to proceed, and Townsend walked free, though guilty of a crime equivalent to piracy in U.S. and international law.

The *Echo*, its crew and captives were taken to Charleston. The people of Charleston provided them with food, clothing and other necessities and treated them with sympathy. The U.S. District Attorney in Charleston was James Conner, who a few years later would lose a leg fighting in the Confederate army. Unable to get hold of Townsend, he vigorously prosecuted the crew. The juries felt, however, probably correctly, that the miserable polyglot lot were as much victims as criminals, having been shanghaied or tricked into the voyage. The mortality rate of the *Echo* captives was over 30 percent. The survivors were returned to Africa, though it was reported that many of them did not want to go. (The story of the *Echo* case comes from the research of my former student, Dr. John C. Roberson.)

I recount this case to provide some contrast to the cartoon version of American history given in the movie. The movie gives a distorted picture and very possibly will arouse hatred at a time when it is the last thing needed. The rehearsal of ancient guilt and outrage is not a healthy activity for Americans, African or otherwise. It requires selecting out a few scapegoats to blame for all the long record of the crimes, misfortunes, and follies of mankind. The psychologists call this projection. Its purpose is to save us the trouble of examining our own problems and sins. (1998)

Race and Community

Written, on request, for the *Boston Review*

As one of the traditionalist conservatives mentioned by Eugene Genovese, it would be presumptuous indeed for me to comment on Eugene Rivers's "Responsibility of Intellectuals in the Age of Crack and Genovese's response had I not been invited to do so. Whatever rights and qualifications I may have rest on the facts that I too live in the age of crack, have some small claim to belonging to the intellectual class, and have spent most of a lifetime trying to understand the history of the South which is a point of origin if no longer a place of residence for almost all African-Americans.

The collapse of community among a great many African-Americans, so ghastly that Rivers has rightly likened it to social death, is, it seems to me, only a severe instance of the general collapse of community that has been taking place among us all. And the disengagement of African-American intellectuals from the real sufferings of many of their brethren is merely a specific case of the general phenomenon of the *trahison de clercs* that has characterized this century.

I do not know the answer to the problems that Rivers has addressed so courageously and insightfully. But it does seem to me that the answer must necessarily lie in the region of what Genovese (and no one has studied this more deeply) calls the unique African-American historical culture. That was a culture that worked—that filled the human need for community and spirituality under the most trying circumstances. That under those trying circumstances never permitted the degree of dispossession and dependency that characterizes the current situation. It is a culture that is a heritage, nearer or farther, to most African-Americans. Man is a culture-bearing animal-which is an attenuated modern way of saying he is made in the image of God. Cultures are grown, not made, we conservatives are wont to say—and where the grown culture is not carried on there is no culture—and no community.

I do not know if African-Americans can or want to rebuild community in the manner suggested. That is up to them. I do know that in other American communities patience grows shorter and shorter with the symptoms of "social death," as those communities face more problems of their own. Such is the moral authority and the goodwill that the civil rights movement owns that very few will say this publicly and many will not admit it even to themselves. Yet this dwindling patience is likely to lead to harsh confrontation in the future. Whereas a rebuilding of responsible Christian community along the lines suggested by Rivers and Genovese would appeal to the best instincts of all Americans and would be a shining example to other American communities. (1993)

Returning Home

Blacks are moving back to the South by the thousands. This is not supposed to happen, not if you trust the mythology of the mainstream media. How can this be? Affluent black families leaving Chicago to go back home to Mississippi, back to the land of church burnings and redneck sheriffs?

But according to a study by the Population Reference Bureau, this is exactly what is happening. In the first half of the 90s, the Northeast lost 233,600 black residents, the Midwest lost 106,500, and the West lost 28,700. This reverses a trend that has prevailed since World War I. And the migration back to the South includes professionals and the affluent—a fifth of returning blacks are college graduates.

It would seem the times have changed. The day is long gone when all racial problems could be confined to the South, and a righteous nation could make a pretense of solving them by offering correction and coercion to backward Southerners. It should be obvious to anyone who travels the country today that there is much less racial tension and much more good will between the races throughout most of the South than there is in any big liberal Northern city. And it should not be surprising that blacks feel inclined to return to where nearly all have their roots.

My Southern hometown was the scene of major protests and riots during the civil rights era. Today, things seem peaceful and prosperous. Except in one respect, where things have changed for the worse in a way that hurts white and black Southerners both. Thanks to the criminal irresponsibility of our ruling elite, we now have a huge and growing Hispanic underclass as well as Vietnamese and Iranian gangs. I can remember when the biggest conflict was between the Baptists and the Methodists. (1998)

On Reparations

There is a rising trajectory of demands for reparations for slavery. I hope, but am doubtful, that there is potential of this gambit for exposing the root absurdity of liberal social policy. But there is more to be said about the subject, especially in regard to the idea of social debts created by history.

When I think of reparations, I always remember a conversation I had some years ago with a rather aggressive Germanic economist-let's call him Professor Z. This scholar declared that *he* did not owe any reparations for slavery because *his* family came from Europe after slavery was abolished.

Well, it occurred to me there was more to be said about his debt to American society. My forebears came from Europe in the late 17th century. They played a part, albeit a modest one, in the founding of one of the original 13 states and in fighting the Revolutionary War. Some of their kin helped settle the frontier. None of them owned any Africans, but like everyone else, they would have if they had not been too poor.[43] They have taken part in every U.S. war; an uncle of mine was killed in the Battle of the Bulge, leaving a widow and orphan, and a great uncle was gassed in World War I.

If we are balancing the accounts of history, doesn't Professor Z owe a debt to those of us Americans whose ancestors made a perilous sea journey to create a free and prosperous country to receive the millions who came later? Why should he freely enjoy all the benefits of American history, but not bear any of the burdens, such as reparations for slavery? By his refusal of responsibility for slavery, Professor Z is the churlishly ungrateful beneficiary not only of my ancestors but of the labor of many generations of African-Americans who long preceded him on this continent.

Of course, the question of the involuntary bondage of Africans in British North America over the course of about two-and-a-half centuries is not likely to receive much light in the debate anticipated, especially considering the politically corrected condition of the historical profession today. But let's look into forbidden territory.

Begin with a paradox: If there had been no slavery, then there would now be no African-Americans to make claims. Could the institution in

---

43 Since writing this, I have learned that one of my ancestors did indeed free his slaves as a matter of conscience.

that sense be regarded as a benefit? To what extent did the servitude of Africans in the United States exceed in severity the servitude of countless millions of mankind in every land and age, including the serf ancestors of many of us? Most certainly, without the forced journey of their ancestors to America, many present-day African-Americans would not exist, because their ancestors would have perished. And how do we weigh the debts for the relative advantage of the Africans who came to the English colonies and proliferated with those sent to Latin America, who were used up before they could leave offspring?

All sensible economic historians are aware that, although servitude is not an enviable condition, the slaves of antebellum America received some return on their labor. In fact, if honesty and reason played any part in our national dialogue, it would be easy to demonstrate from data and from European travelers that the slaves in general fared better in food, housing, health, and working hours than the urban poor of the Northern United States and Europe. In calculating reparations, how do we account for the portion of their labor that they were able to enjoy, or for their relative advantage over the miserable unenslaved poor of past centuries? And can we not subtract the billions spent on the war against poverty since the 1960s against what is owed for past sins? (Of course, most of that went to upper-middle-class liberals to administer welfare, which was its purpose all along.) I know the Constitution is as dead as reason and honesty in public life, but reparations to the living descendants of slaves would qualify as the creation of an order of nobility—that is, special benefits conferred by blood—which is strictly forbidden.

What the American government certainly does owe African-Americans for is the chaos, suffering, and reactive oppression created by their unplanned and violent emancipation in the wrong way (the greatest seizure of property, by far, in American history) and for the wrong reasons (vengeance on recalcitrant Southerners). But in order to assess that debt, Americans would have to reassess the myth that makes a ruthless imperialist-Darwinian war for national consolidation in the last century into a holy crusade. And that would be too painful. (2001)

Chapter Six

The Upper Right Corner

Yankee Slavers

Slavery they can have anywhere.
It is a weed that grows in every soil. —Edmund Burke

A review of *Proslavery: A History of the Defense of Slavery in America, 1701-1840,* by Larry E. Tise, Athens: University of Georgia Press, 1987, 501 pages.

The better part of a century ago, the great scholar A.E. Housman observed whatever "except to interrupt our studies." This is certainly the case today with the vast literature in American history. And, generally speaking, the more prestigious the publisher and the institution of higher education after the author's name, the more useless the book is.

That is not true, however, in regard to the work in review, which exhibits truly what many dust jackets proclaim falsely: original research and insight and real "relevance" in pursuit of the historian's duty to make the past comprehensible and usable. That is, *Proslavery* cuts through existing conventions and old propaganda and uncovers fresh and truthful aspects of that great middle era of American history which preceded the Civil War. What Tise has discovered will disappoint and demoralize many, I suspect, but a society which engages in convenient forgetfulness and comforting distortion about critical aspects of its past is at least as deluded and in need of therapy as an individual who does so.

It is not too much to say that what Tise brings to light suggests the need for major revisions in American intellectual and religious history, as they have been commonly recounted. And, though unintended, the book also creates a new and interesting perspective on the genealogy of the American right and left, whatever they may be. Nor does it detract from the credit of the author that the evidence he adduces has always been obvious in the historical record for anyone who has eyes to see, and that it really should not be surprising. Because American historians, in general, are incapable of thinking except along the lines of conventions that have been prefabricated for them, and often look without seeing, it is always an achievement to break through their orthodoxies. For the evidence presented here has not been so much unknown as it has been deliberately thrust from conscious recognition.

To place this book among the many books on slavery, we need to look closely at its time period, its intellectual terrain, and its geographical focus. The time period is what Tise calls the "neglected period" of proslavery thinking before the political intensification of the issue in the mid-decades of the 19th century (though he overlaps both ways when useful). It is an era covered from the other, antislavery, side by David Brion Davis in his *Slavery in the Age of Revolution*. This leads us to what many will find an unexpected intellectual terrain and geographical focus. To put an elaborately developed description succinctly, Tise finds every phase of the intellectual defense of black slavery fully developed in the North among the most respectable thinkers at a period before the South had even been prodded into any militant consciousness on the issue.

He finds this among conservative Northerners, if we define conservatives as persons who were alarmed by the French Revolution into developing a defense for traditional society. (And we must remember, unpalatable as the truth may be, that the subordination of the black people into a laboring caste was a long-established and pervasive tradition in the United States, and indeed throughout the New World, by the end of the 17th century.)

But the most shocking part of the findings for moderns will be the prominent role played by the Northern clergy in the full development of the articulated defense of Negro slavery in the United States as a part of the accepted order of things. For moderns, the un-Christian nature of slavery seems self-evident. But, alas, this is not much more than provincialism in time. Antislavery is not biblical; it is a quite recent notion, which draws its impetus from "modernization."

It is true that the abolition movement rested in considerable part upon religious impulses as they developed from the intellectual and social ferment of the Northern form of evangelicalism during the 19th century, when a new and very American synthesis was made between democracy and Christianity. But it is also true that the greater part of the orthodox clergy in the North, at least at the beginning, opposed abolitionism strenuously. (Sympathetic historians of anti-slavery have always known that the abolitionists' hardest battles were their early ones, in the North.) The opponents of abolition among the Northern clergy were not simply the musty standpatters—they were often among the ablest, most articulate, and most creative leaders of their denominations. And they were found in all of the major Protestant denominations, as well as among Catholics and Jews (to the extent that they were present in those days).

By influence and by migration to the South these clergymen provided the South with a ready-made defense when the time came. As Tise sees it—if I read him rightly—the South emerged from the Revolution basically Jeffersonian in its political ideals, despite its social structure. It accepted slavery as a kind of disagreeable necessity that had grown up, but did not undertake a philosophical defense, in part because it would have been in obvious conflict with its Jeffersonianism, in part because it had not been until the 1830s prodded into the need for any articulate defense.

In other words, for Tise the history of early 19th century America is marked by a reactionary anti-egalitarianism which rises in the North and spreads to the South. There cannot be any legitimate quarrel with the evidence that he has accumulated, though, of course, historians can and doubtless will quarrel about the import and the perspective. Indeed, I must part company with the perspective. For Tise, the development of an articulated conservatism at this period constitutes a repudiation of the egalitarianism of the American Revolution, and is therefore reactionary. But he greatly overestimates the egalitarian and especially the antislavery implications of both the Revolution and Jeffersonianism. That is, he makes assumptions about the egalitarianism of the Revolution that may not be defensible and may never have been accepted by the persons he thinks repudiated them. One can repudiate the tendencies of the French Revolution without in any way betraying the American.

By overestimating the antislavery element in the American Revolution, he portrays abolitionism as less of an innovation than it was, and the defense of slavery (which by his own and much other evidence was traditional) as more innovative than it was. Nor was there any real incompatibility between Jeffersonianism and the defense of slavery. The defense of slavery appeared in the South earliest and strongest precisely among the strictest Jeffersonians, and was not unknown among Northern Jeffersonians. If there had never been any French Revolution, the defense of slavery in America would have still taken the same course of reasoning from biblical and traditional authorities, bolstered by states' rights, since these were the native intellectual matter of Americans.

For Tise, then, the Northern thinkers who defended slavery constituted a kind of counterrevolutionary conspiracy which defended the existing system of black bondage because it deplored all egalitarian and revolutionary tendencies. But this is to set up the situation the wrong way and to shift the burden of innovation from the abolitionists to the preservers of the status quo, which tends to interfere with a proper understanding of both groups.

He sees proslavery sentiment in the North as closely linked to the sternest forms of conservative New England Federalism, which, alarmed by the French Revolution, repudiated the American Revolution and moved toward the consolidation and defense of hierarchical, traditional, religious society. There is a good deal of truth there, but I think I could very easily, by looking at other evidence, find a genealogy within New England Federalism for abolitionism as well. Certainly, the Southern defenders of slavery usually saw this as the case.

To put it another way, while correctly identifying the existence of vigorous proslavery sentiment in the North, he mis-locates its center and considerably underestimates its overall weight. By using some of his own evidence and other sources, I could create a convincing argument that while certain Northern Federalists did indeed defend slavery on conservative grounds, the defense of slavery was even stronger among the Jeffersonians of the North than it was among the Federalists.

The Jeffersonians, after all, were dedicated to states' rights and strict construction of the Constitution as it stood and to an economic philosophy that coincided with the South's. John C. Calhoun at the height of his career of sectional defense of the South had a considerable number of admirers in the North.

These were not among the "conservatives" (in Northern terms) but among the most zealous "liberals"—for instance, the young radical, Orestes Brownson, and Fitzwilliam Byrdsall, historian of the New York "Locofocos" (Of course we must realize that a "liberal" in those days was not the same thing as a "progressive" in Whiggish and modern terminology.)

Thus, Tise tends to suggest that Northerners who sympathized with the South before and during the Civil War were conspiratorial Federalist millionaires who believed in the Bavarian Illuminati. There were some people of that type who favored the Confederacy, but in fact, by my reading of history, people of that type were far, far more likely to be abolitionists and Republicans. Southern sympathizers like Franklin Pierce, Clement Vallandigham, and others came overwhelmingly out of a Jeffersonian background. This is clear even in much of Tise's own evidence. Such slavery defenders as Charles J. Ingersoll of Pennsylvania, James K. Paulding of New York, and John Mitchel, the Irish revolutionary, were Democrats and do not fit the stereotype of reactionary New England clerics. A considerable portion of both the "liberals" and the "conservatives" of the North defended the South's regime, right up to and, in some cases, even after the rumble of guns in Charleston harbor.

To take this analysis a bit further, we have to accept the truth that a 19th century "liberal" was not a progressive in the modern sense. The liberal elements in American society, those most strongly in favor of democracy and equality for white men, were also, generally speaking, the strongest supporters of white supremacy, of limited government, and of traditional (anti-egalitarian) social arrangements, and looked to the South as their political mainstay. On the other hand, the "conservative" elements—those in favor of social hierarchy and economic privilege—in the North were also the "progressives" who wanted forward movement in society, by government action if necessary, and found the South a political and social impediment.

It would be tremendously comforting for the modern liberal if majority rule, racial egalitarianism, and social progressivism always went together, and indeed much of accepted American history is written as if they did. But, in fact, such has seldom been the case in the reality of living, breathing America—whether in the pre-Civil War era, in the Progressive era, or, dare we say, in the present. Historically it is quite clear that enthusiasm for the common man has often gone hand-in-glove with white supremacy, and racial egalitarianism has often been accompanied by indifference or contempt for the common man.

I am sure that most will find this even more discouraging than Tise's perspective and that many will not and cannot accept it. It does not particularly discourage me, because I do not expect history to be convenient and pleasing.

The lessons it teaches are usually a good deal sterner than the inevitable triumph of democracy and progress. As I sometimes tell students who really want to know: History is like life—it is a good deal tougher, more complicated, and more ambivalent than television.

It was really not part of the author's purpose to provide a theory of the origins of the American right and left, except insofar as he adopts certain assumptions about the nature of the American Revolution. It would thus be unfair of me to quarrel with him in this regard. Indeed, he has given us, even if unintentionally, much food for thought in regard to the historical development of the right and left in America, a highly problematic intellectual puzzle which happens to interest me, and for which I believe no adequate theory has ever been provided.

Of course, a great deal depends on how you define such terms as liberal and conservative, and when dealing with them historically one is always shooting at a moving target. Such questions cannot be easily settled, and it may even be that it is impossible. But it does seem to me that the evidence of Proslavery has to be taken into account by anyone who takes an honest interest in constructing a genealogy of American conservatism.

How should American conservatives relate to the Civil War, for instance? I do not believe this question has ever been answered to any honest man's satisfaction. Was it conservative to defend the South and its inherited ways, its counterrevolution against modernization? Or was it conservative to preserve the Union, as did Mr. Lincoln, even at the expense of the most revolutionary acts and program in American history and with the enthusiastic approval of Karl Marx?

Personally, I have never been able to comprehend how any conservative who had any intelligent appreciation of the real texture (rather than just the theory) of American experience could fail to feel a surge of sympathy with the boys in gray. I can well understand how one could admire William Lloyd Garrison, Thaddeus Stevens, and Charles Sumner. But I cannot understand how or why one could admire them and still call himself a conservative. It takes nothing less than the sophistry of the Straussian political scientists to answer this paradox adequately. I know, however, that decent folks disagree with me, and I remain open to argument. As I said, history is not easy, and it may not be possible ever to settle such questions.

Perhaps the most significant thing about this book is that it is part of an as-yet-unrecognized and unlabeled shift of focus in American history—writing from the South to the North. Most of the historical literature, and of the common understanding in regard to our Civil War (still the largest and most critical episode in American history) has proceeded on the working assumption that the South constituted a peculiar minority, standing athwart the pre-ordained mainstream of American development. Thus, when one had explained satisfactorily the origin and nature of the peculiarity, one had explained how the immense and bloody civil conflict at the center of our history came about.

Though such an approach has long been axiomatic and unexamined, there are several things wrong with it. To begin with, it makes little sense to treat the South, at any time prior to the Civil War, as a minority. In territory, population, and political and cultural influence the South was an equal and often a preponderant part of American development during all this period.

But the main flaw with the approach is that it undertook to explain the peculiar while leaving the standard of normalcy undefined and undescribed. It was simply assumed that the North was a kind of universal and unquestionable norm against which all else was to be measured. (This is the same attitude with which Americans approach relations with foreign nations.) But the norm itself was never postulated, which gave a strange context 10 examinations of the South, which was deemed to be un-American but was always measured with an elastic ruler. Proslavery, along with another fine recent book, Anne Norton's *Alternative Americas: A Reading of Antebellum Political Culture*, at last shifts the attention to where it should have been all along—to describing the nature and development of the North. While they do not provide all answers, these books ask the right questions, and open new ground for more realistic ways of looking at a vitally important period in American history.

This historical revisionism is important not because it revises old sectional controversy, and not because it makes it no longer possible to comfortably assign all evil to the region below the Potomac, segregated from a shining and uncontaminated American—though that is pleasing enough. Rather, it is important because the study of the antebellum North will eventually allow us to know for the first time the true lineaments of development of what became the American mainstream. If there is any young historian out there who wants to know where the cutting edge is in American historical understanding, it is there—the new and coming field of Northern history. (1988)

The Yankee Problem in American History

It is true that we are completely under the saddle of Massachusetts and Connecticut, and that they ride us very hard, cruelly insulting our feelings, as well as exhausting our strength and substance. —
Thomas Jefferson, 1798

There is at work in this land a Yankee spirit and an American spirit. —James H. Thornwell, 1859

Books reviewed: *North Over South: Northern Nationalism and American Identity in the Antebellum Era,* by Susan-Mary Grant, Lawrence: University Press of Kansas, 2000, 250 pages; *Sectional Nationalism: Massachusetts Conservative Leaders and the Transformation of America, 1815-1834,* by Harlow W. Sheidley, Boston, Massachusetts: Northeastern University Press, 1998, 283 pages; *Yankee Leviathan: The Origins of Central State Authority in America,* by Richard F. Bensel, New York, New York: Cambridge University Press, 1990, 452 pages; *Alternative Americas: A Reading of Antebellum Political Culture,* by Anne Norton, Chicago, Illinois: University of Chicago Press, 1986, 363 pages; *Redeemer Nation: The Idea of America's Millennial Role,* by Ernest L. Tuveson, Chicago, Illinois: University of Chicago Press, 1968, 238 pages.

Since the 2000 presidential election, much attention has been paid to a map showing the sharp geographical division between the two candidates' support. Gore prevailed in the power and plunder seeking Deep North (Northeast, Upper Midwest, Pacific Coast) and Bush in the regions inhabited by productive and decent Americans. There is nothing new about this. Historically speaking, it is just one more manifestation of the Yankee problem.

As indicated by these books (listed above), scholars are at last starting to pay some attention to one of the most important and most neglected subjects in United States history—the Yankee problem.

By Yankee I do not mean everybody from north of the Potomac and Ohio. Lots of them have always been good folks. The firemen who died in the World Trade Center on September 11 were Americans. The politicians and TV personalities who stood around telling us what we are to think about it are Yankees. I am using the term historically to designate that peculiar ethnic group descended from New Englanders, who can be easily recognized by their arrogance, hypocrisy, greed, lack of congeniality, and penchant for ordering other people around. Puritans, who long ago abandoned anything that might be good in their religion but have never given up the notion that they are the chosen saints whose mission is to make America, and the world, into the perfection of their own image.

Hillary Rodham Clinton, raised a Northern Methodist in Chicago, is a museum-quality specimen of the Yankee-self-righteous, ruthless, and self-aggrandizing. Northern Methodism and Chicago were both, in their formative periods, hotbeds of abolitionist, high tariff Black Republicanism. The Yankee temperament. it should be noted, makes a neat fit with the Marxism that was brought into the Deep North by later immigrants.

The ethnic division between Yankees and other Americans goes back to earliest colonial times. Up until the War for Southern Independence, Southerners were considered to be the American mainstream, and Yankees were considered to be the "peculiar" people. Because of a long campaign of cultural imperialism and the successful military imperialism engineered by the Yankees, the South, since the War, has been considered the problem, the deviation from the true American norm. Historians have made an industry of explaining why the South is different (and evil, for that which defies the "American" as now established, is by definition evil). Is the South different because of slavery? white supremacy? the climate? pellagra? illiteracy? poverty? guilt? defeat? Celtic wildness rather than Anglo-Saxon sobriety?

Unnoticed in all this literature was a hidden assumption: The North is normal, the standard of all things American and good. Anything that does not conform is a problem to be explained and a condition to be annihilated. What about that hidden assumption? Should not historians be interested in understanding how the North got to be the way it is? Indeed, is there any question in American history more important?

According to standard accounts of American history (i.e., Northern mythology), New Englanders fought the Revolution and founded glorious American freedom as had been planned by the "Puritan Fathers." Southerners, who had always been of questionable character, because of their fanatic devotion to slavery wickedly rebelled against government of, by, and for the people, were put down by the armies of the Lord, and should be ever grateful for not having been exterminated.

(This is clearly the view of the anonymous Union Leaguer from Portland, Maine, who recently sent me a chamber pot labeled "Robert E. Lee's soup tureen.") And out of their benevolence and devotion to the ideal of freedom, the North struck the chains from the suffering black people. (They should be forever grateful, also. Take a look at the Boston statue with happy blacks adoring the feet of Col. Robert Gould Shaw.)

Aside from the fact that every generalization in this standard history is false, an obvious defect in it is that, for anyone familiar with American history before the War, it is clear that "Southern" was American and Yankees were the problem. America was Washington and Jefferson, the Louisiana Purchase and the Battle of New Orleans, John Randolph and Henry Clay, Daniel Morgan, Daniel Boone, and Francis Marion. Southerners had made the Constitution, saved it under Jefferson from the Yankees, fought the wars, acquired the territory, and settled the West, including the Northwest. To most Americans, in Pennsylvania and Indiana as well as Virginia and Georgia, this was a basic view up until about 1850. New England had been a threat, a nuisance, and a negative force in the progress of America. Northerners, including some patriotic New Englanders, believed this as much as Southerners.

When Washington Irving, whose family were among the early Anglo-Dutch settlers of New York, wrote the story about the "Headless Horseman," he was ridiculing Yankees. The prig Ichabod Crane had come over from Connecticut and made himself a nuisance. So, a young man (New York young men were then normal young men rather than Yankees) played a trick on him and sent him fleeing back to Yankeeland where he belonged. James Fenimore Cooper, of another early New York family, felt the same way about New Englanders who appear unfavorably in his writings. Yet another New York writer, James Kirke Paulding (among many others), wrote a book defending the South and attacking abolitionists. It is not unreasonable to conclude that in Moby Dick, the New York Democrat Herman Melville modeled the fanatical Captain Ahab on the Yankee abolitionist. In fact, the term "Yankee" appears to originate in some mingling of Dutch and Indian words to designate New Englanders. Obviously, both the Dutch New Yorkers and the Native Americans recognized them as "different."

Young Abe Lincoln amused his neighbors in southern Indiana and Illinois, nearly all of whom, like his own family, had come from the South, with "Yankee jokes," stories making fun of dishonest peddlers from New England. They were the most popular stories in his repertoire, except for the dirty ones.

The Upper Right Corner

Right into the War, Northerners opposed to the conquest of the South blamed the conflict on fanatical New Englanders out for power and plunder, not on the good Americans in the South who had been provoked beyond bearing.

Many people, and not only in the South, thought that Southerners, according to their nature, had been loyal to the Union, had served it, fought and sacrificed for it as long as they could. New Englanders, according to their nature, had always been grasping for themselves while proclaiming their righteousness and superiority.

The Yankees succeeded so well, by the long cultural war described in these volumes, and by the North's military victory, that there was no longer a Yankee problem. Now the Yankee was America, and the South was the problem. America, the Yankee version, was all that was normal and right and good. Southerners understood who had won the war (not Northerners, though they had shed a lot of blood, but the accursed Yankees). With some justification they began to regard all Northerners as Yankees, even the hordes of foreigners who had been hired to wear the blue.

Here is something closer to a real history of the United States: American freedom was not a legacy of the "Puritan Fathers," but of Virginians who proclaimed and spread constitutional rights. New England gets some credit for beginning the War of Independence. After the first few years, however, Yankees played little part. The war was fought and won in the South. Besides, New Englanders had good reasons for independence—they did not fit into the British Empire economically, since one of their main industries was smuggling, and the influential Puritan clergy hated the Church of England. Southerners, in fighting for independence, were actually going against their economic interests for the sake of principle.

Once Southerners had gone into the Union (which a number of wise statesmen like Patrick Henry and George Mason warned them against), the Yankees began to show how they regarded the new federal government: as an instrument to be used for their own purposes. Southerners long continued to view the Union as a vehicle for mutual cooperation, as they often naively still do.

In the first Congress, Yankees demanded that the federal government continue the British subsidies to their fishing fleets. While Virginia and the other Southern states gave up their vast western lands for future new states, New Englanders demanded a special preserve for themselves (the "Western Reserve" in Ohio).

Under John Adams, the New England quest for power grew into a frenzy. They passed the Sedition Law to punish anti-government words (as long as they controlled the government) in clear violation of the Constitution. During the election of 1800, the preachers in New England told their congregations that Thomas Jefferson was a French Jacobin who would set up the guillotine in their town squares and declare women common property. (What else could be expected from a dissolute slaveholder?) In fact, Jefferson's well-known distaste for mixing of church and state rested largely on his dislike of the power of the New England self-appointed saints.

When Jeffersonians took power, the New Englanders fought them with all their diminishing strength. Their poet William Cullen Bryant regarded the Louisiana Purchase as nothing but a large swamp for Jefferson to pursue his atheistic penchant for science.

The War of 1812, the Second War of Independence, was decisive for the seemingly permanent discrediting of New England. The Yankee ruling class opposed the war even though it was begun by Southerners on behalf of oppressed American seamen, most of whom were New Englanders. Yankees did not care about their oppressed poorer citizens because they were making big bucks smuggling into wartime Europe. One New England congressman attacked young patriot John C. Calhoun as a backwoodsman who had never seen a sail and who was unqualified to deal with foreign policy.

During the war, Yankees traded with the enemy and talked openly of secession. (Southerners never spoke of secession in time of war.) Massachusetts refused to have its militia called into constitutional federal service even after invasion, and then, notoriously for years after, demanded that the federal government pay its militia expenses.

Historians have endlessly repeated that the "Era of Good Feelings" under President Monroe refers to the absence of party strife. Actually, the term was first used to describe the state of affairs in which New England traitorousness had declined to the point that a Virginia president could visit Boston without being mobbed.

Yankee political arrogance was soulmate to Yankee cultural arrogance. Throughout the antebellum period, New England literature was characterized and promoted as the American literature, and non-Yankee writers, in most cases much more talented and original, were ignored or slandered. Edgar Allan Poe had great fun ridiculing the literary pretensions of New Englanders, but they largely succeeded in dominating the idea of American literature into the 20th century. Generations of

Americans have been cured of reading forever by being forced to digest dreary third-string New England poets as "American literature."

In 1789, a Connecticut Puritan preacher named Jedidiah Morse published the first book of American Geography. The trouble was, it was not an American geography but a Yankee geography. Most of the book was taken up with describing the virtues of New England. Once you got west of the Hudson River, as Morse saw it and conveyed to the world's reading public, the U.S. was a benighted land inhabited by lazy, dirty Scotch-Irish and Germans in the Middle States and lazy, morally depraved Southerners, corrupted and enervated by slavery. New Englanders were pure Anglo-Saxons with all virtues. The rest of the Americans were questionable people of lower or mongrel ancestry. The theme of New Englanders as pure Anglo-Saxons continued right down through the 20th century. The alleged saints of American equality operated on a theory of their racial superiority. While Catholics and Jews were, in the South, accepted and loyal Southerners, Yankees burned down convents and banished Jews from the Union Army lines.

A few years after Morse, Noah Webster, also from Connecticut, published his *American Dictionary* and American spelling book. The trouble was, it was not an American dictionary but a New England dictionary. As Webster declared in his preface, New Englanders spoke and spelled the purest and best form of English of any people in the world. Southerners and others ignored Webster and spelled and pronounced real English until after the War of Southern Independence.

As the books show, Yankees after the War of 1812 were acutely aware of their minority status. And here is the important point: they launched a deliberate campaign to take over control of the idea of "America."

The campaign was multi-faceted. Politically, they gained profits from the protective tariff and federal expenditures, both of which drained money from the South for the benefit of the North, and New England especially. Seeking economic advantage from legislation is nothing new in human history. But the New England greed was marked by its peculiar assumptions of moral superiority. New Englanders, who were selling their products in a market from which competition had been excluded by the tariff, proclaimed that the low price of cotton was due to the fact that Southerners lacked the drive and enterprise of virtuous Yankees! (When the South was actually the productive part of the U.S. economy.)

This transfer of wealth built the strength of the North. It was even more profitable than the slave trade (which New England shippers carried on from Africa to Brazil and Cuba right up to the War Between the States) and the Chinese opium trade (which they were also to break into).

Another phase of the Yankee campaign for what they considered their rightful dominance was the capture of the history of the American Revolution. At a time when decent Americans celebrated the Revolution as the common glory of all, New Englanders were publishing a literature claiming the whole credit for themselves. A scribbler from Maine named Lorenzo Sabine, for one example among many, published a book in which he claimed that the Revolution in the South had been won by New England soldiers because Southerners were traitorous and enervated by slavery. As William Gilmore Simms pointed out, it was all lies. When Daniel Webster was received hospitably in Charleston, he made a speech in which he commemorated the graves of the many heroic Revolutionary soldiers from New England which were to be found in the South. The trouble was, those graves did not exist. Many Southern volunteers had fought in the North, but no soldier from north of Pennsylvania (except a few generals) had ever fought in the South!

George Washington was a bit of a problem here, so the honor-driven, fox-hunting Virginia gentleman was transformed by phony folklore into a prim New Englander in character, a false image that has misled and repulsed countless Americans since.

It should be clear; this was not merely misplaced pride. It was a deliberate, systematic effort by the Massachusetts elite to take control of American symbols and disparage all competing claims. Do not be put off by Professor Sheidley's use of "Conservative Leaders" in her title. She means merely the Yankee ruling elite who were never conservatives then or now. Conservatives do not work for "the transformation of America."

Another successful effort was a New England claim on the West. When New Englanders referred to "the West" in antebellum times, they meant the parts of Ohio and adjacent states settled by New Englanders. The rest of the great American West did not count. In fact, the great drama of danger and adventure and achievement that was the American West, from the Appalachians to the Pacific, was predominantly the work of Southerners and not of New Englanders at all. In the Midwest, the New Englanders came after Southerners had tamed the wilderness, and they looked down upon the early settlers. But in Western movies we still have the inevitable family from Boston moving west by covered wagon. Such a thing never existed! The people moving west in covered wagons were from the upper South and were despised by Boston.

So, our West is reduced, in literature, to The Oregon Trail, a silly book written by a Boston tourist, and the phony cavortings of the Eastern sissy Teddy Roosevelt in the cattle country opened by Southerners. And the great American outdoors is now symbolized by Henry David Thoreau and a little frog pond at Walden, in sight of the Boston smokestacks, The Pennsylvanian Owen Wister knew better when he entitled his Wyoming novel, The Virginian.

To fully understand what the Yankee is today—builder of the all-powerful "multicultural" therapeutic state (with himself giving the orders and collecting the rewards) which is the perfection of history, and which is to be exported to all peoples, by guided missiles on women and children if necessary—we need a bit more real history.

That history is philosophical, or rather theological, and demographic. New Englanders lived in a barren land. Some of their surplus sons went to sea. Many others moved west when it was safe to do so. By 1830, half the people in the state of New York were New England-born. By 1850, New Englanders had tipped the political balance in the Midwest, with the help of German revolutionaries and authoritarians who had flooded in after the 1848 revolutions.

The leading editors in New York City, Horace Greeley and William Cullen Bryant, and the big money men, were New England-born. Thaddeus Stevens, the Pennsylvania steel tycoon and Radical Republican, was from Vermont. (Thanks to the tariff, he made $6,000 extra profit on every mile of railroad rails he sold.)

The North had been Yankeeized, for the most part quietly, by control of churches, schools, and other cultural institutions, and by whipping up a frenzy of paranoia about the alleged plot of the South to spread slavery to the North, which was as imaginary as Jefferson's guillotine.

The people that Cooper and Irving had despised as interlopers now controlled New York! The Yankees could now carry a majority in the North and in 1860 elect the first sectional president in U.S. history—a threat to the South to knuckle under or else. In time, even the despised Irish Catholics began to think like Yankees.

We must also take note of the intellectual revolution amongst the Yankees which created the modern version of self-righteous authoritarian "Liberalism" so well exemplified by Mrs. Clinton. In the 1830s, Ralph Waldo Emerson went to Germany to study. There he learned from philosophers that the world was advancing by dialectical process to an ever-higher state. He returned to Boston, and after marrying the dying daughter of a banker, resigned from the clergy, declared the sacraments to be a remnant of barbarism, and proclaimed the American as the "New Man" who was leaving behind the garbage of the past and blazing the way into the future state of perfection for humanity. Emerson has ever since in many quarters been regarded as the American philosopher, the true interpreter of the meaning of America.

From the point of view of Christianity, this "American" doctrine is heresy. From the point of view of history, it is nonsense. But it is powerful enough for Ronald Reagan, who should have known better, to proclaim America as the shining City upon a Hill that was to redeem mankind. And powerful enough that the United States has long pursued a bipartisan foreign policy, one of the guiding assumptions of which is that America is the model of perfection to which all the world should want to conform.

There is no reason for readers of *Southern Partisan* to rush out and buy these books, which are expensive and dense academic treatises. If you are really interested, get your library to acquire them. They are well-documented studies, responsibly restrained in their drawing of larger conclusions. But they indicate what is hopefully a trend of exploration of the neglected field of Yankee history.

The high-flying Yankee rhetoric of Emerson and Hillary Rodham Clinton has a neither side, which has its historical origins in the "Burnt Over District." The "Burnt Over District" was well known to antebellum Americans. Emersonian notions bore strange fruit in the central regions of New York State settled by the overflow of poorer Yankees from New England. It was "Burnt Over" because it (along with a similar area in northern Ohio) was swept over time and again by post-millennial revivalism. Here preachers like Charles G. Finney began to confuse Emerson's future state of perfection with Christianity, and God's plan for humanity with American choseness.

If this were true, then anything that stood in the way of American perfection must be eradicated. The threatening evil at various times was liquor, tobacco, the Catholic Church, the Masonic order, meat-eating, marriage. Within the small area of the Burnt Over District and within the space of a few decades was generated what historians have misnamed the "Jacksonian reform movement": Joseph Smith received the Book of Mormon from the Angel Moroni; William Miller began the Seventh-Day Adventists by predicting, inaccurately, the end of the world; the free love colony of John Humphrey Noyes flourished at Oneida: the first feminist convention was held at Seneca Falls; and John Brown, who was born in Connecticut, collected accomplices and financial backers for his mass murder expeditions.

It was in this milieu that abolitionism, as opposed to the antislavery sentiment shared by many Americans, including Southerners, had its origins. Abolitionism, despite what has been said later, was not based on sympathy for the black people nor on an ideal of natural rights. It was based on the hysterical conviction that Southern slaveholders were evil sinners who stood in the way of fulfillment of America's divine mission to establish Heaven on Earth. It was not the Union that our Southern forefathers seceded from, but the deadly combination of Yankee greed and righteousness.

Most abolitionists had little knowledge of or interest in black people or knowledge of life in the South. Slavery promoted sin and thus must end. No thought was given to what would happen to the African-Americans. In fact, many abolitionists expected that evil Southern whites and blacks would disappear, and the land be repopulated by virtuous Yankees.

The darker side of the Yankee mind has had its expression in American history as well as the side of high ideals. Timothy McVeigh from New York and the Unabomber from Harvard are, like John Brown, examples of this side of the Yankee problem. (Even though distinguished Yankee intellectuals have declared that their violence was a product of the evil "Southern gun culture.")

Since the Confederate surrender, the Yankee has always been a strong and often dominant force in American society, though occasionally tempered by Southerners and other representatives of Western civilization in America. In the 1960s the Yankee had one of his periodic eruptions of mania such as he had in the 1850s. Since then, he has managed to destroy a good part of the liberty and morals of the American peoples. It remains to be seen whether his conquest is permanent or whether in the future we may be, at least to some degree, emancipated from it. (2002)

The Yankee Problem, Again

Since the November election, the media have been full of observations about the United States being two countries with different ideas and values—the blue (Kerry) and red (Bush) states. Some of the Blues (Northeast, upper Midwest, and their colonies on the Pacific) have even been talking about secession from us ignorant bigots who inhabit the Heartland and South. (See "The Election, the Solid South, and Yankee Secession," in *Southern Partisan*, Vol. 24, No. 1.)

If the people who run and staff the media knew any American history, which they don't, they would know that there is nothing new about all of this. The Blue regions are simply the domain of the Yankees. Astute readers will remember that I explained it all previously in *Southern Partisan* in "The Yankee Problem in America."

In that article I pointed out that Yankees are a type produced by the Deep North who have been marked throughout American history by their greed, hypocrisy, fanaticism, and desire to lord it over the rest of us Americans—politically, economically, and culturally.

Thomas Jefferson pointed to the phenomenon of the Yankee just before his election as president when he wrote: "It is true that we are completely under the saddle of Massachusetts and Connecticut, and that they ride us very hard, insulting our feelings, as well as exhausting our strength and substance." At about the same time he remarked of New England, the original breeding ground of Yankees, that they were "marked with such a perversity of character" that the natural political division of the United States would always be between Americans (non-Yankees) and Yankees.

There is nothing new about Yankees threatening secession either. Twice during the administrations of Jefferson and Madison, and several times later, they threatened to break up the Union in fits of pique when they failed to get their way. The current Blue commentators are using extreme language to characterize the non-Kerry states. To hear them tell it, the red states are dominated by religious maniacs and militarists—i.e., people who actually believe the Bible and love their country. There is nothing new about this invective either. This kind of hateful demonization of those who resist domination by Yankees has been commonplace for about three hundred years or more.

And, of course, the South, being the biggest obstacle to Yankee domination, has always been the major recipient of Yankee slander and hate. This hateful rhetoric was used in the past and is now used to abuse Dixie for giving the essential winning margin to the Republicans (something which, in the light of Southern history, is in itself a bizarre development).

I can't see that the Blues really have anything to complain about. They already own the store—lock, stock, and barrel. Nobody with the least sense could detect any meaningful difference between Bush and Kerry. Bush is as likely to do something about "moral values" as his father was to follow through on "no new taxes." It takes a pretty short memory not to have figured out by now that the Bushes are Yankees through and through and that what they say to get elected and what they do are two unrelated things.

Southerners were given a choice between a weird rich boy from Connecticut and an even weirder rich boy from Massachusetts, and we picked the former, who at least did not come flat out for sodomy and treason. (Besides, the Massachusetts boy is descended from Yankee slave traders, the Forbes family, people who have never been popular in the South.)

Throughout the 20th century Yankees browbeat Southerners into becoming just ordinary mainstream Americans. I suppose they didn't realize that it would make us Republicans. But, in fact, the South is Bush country just to the extent it has been de-Southernized. The great M.E. Bradford pointed out in these pages long ago that a "conservative" (i.e., Republican) in the South is not the same thing as a Southern Conservative.

Some of the Blue fury against the Red states arises from the claim that the Blues pay more to the federals than they get back, that is, they are subsidizing us red staters. I have always been skeptical of the claim that the South was a net economic gainer from the federal government. Are we to believe that Blues are so generous and benevolent that they are supporting us? To believe that is to deny three centuries of Yankee behavior to the contrary and the evident nature of the liberal ruling class today. Raw state data about taxes paid and federal disbursements received tell us very little about who gets the profits. For instance, every time a Southern state institutes a new federally mandated program, Blue staters are imported to take all the high-paying jobs, and Blue state consultants and suppliers get a lot of the cash.

Of course, the Blues are not really serious about secession. Yankees have no civilization—only money, gadgets, and ideology. Without us to abuse and claim to feel superior to, they would not exist. Nevertheless, it is wonderful that the idea of secession—that is, self-government and devolution of power—has been given some public exposure. After all, our Founding Fathers affirmed that governments rest on the consent of the governed, who may alter or abolish them. If the United States was a normal country, the idea of breaking down a federal government that has grown much too big would be a normal part of political discourse. But, alas, the United States is not a normal country; it is the cannon fodder for a ruling class driven so mad by wealth and power that it seeks to dominate the Earth.

Reading the left wing anti-war commentary (as opposed to the conservative, *i.e.*, patriotic, anti-war commentary), one gets the impression that Bush's belligerent foreign policy can be blamed on his being a Texan and a Christian. Of course, a Skull and Bones carpetbagger does not make a Texan. As for the carnival tent religion Bush professes, it is sadly true that it is pretty widespread in the South today. But it is not the Southern tradition.

The identification of God with America and the United States with infallible righteousness is Yankee stuff through and through. It is exactly the type of "religion" that was used to deify Lincoln and justify the conquest of the South in 1861-1865. In Yankee history it is the stage they went through between the hyper-Calvinism of their early days and their present atheism. It did not arrive in Dixie until the early 20th century when various evangelists began imitating the style and content of the Yankee Billy Sunday. (See "The Real Old Time Religion" by the late theologian A.J, Conyers in Vol. 23, No. 3, one of the most important articles ever published in *Southern Partisan*.) Traditional Southern clergymen would have made short shrift of heretical mountebanks like Pat Robertson.

The flourishing of Bushian religion, like the flourishing of the Republican party, is a product of too many Southerners heeding the endless lectures about the need to forget the past, "join the 20th century," etc. The religion and the politics are the same thing, the adoption of Yankee ideology that equates America with God.

Some Southerners are starting to show less of our traditional patriotic loyalty and more of the idiot nationalism that thinks the U.S. government and the President can do no wrong and are entitled to bomb anybody who disagrees. In both religion and politics, the dilution of Southern tradition has been a loss to Dixie—and to the whole country. For Southerners, and our sympathizers over the border, have always been the only true conservatives in the United States.

The country has continued its leftward roll for almost a half century now, despite repeated Republican election victories. Northern "conservatives," as the Rev. Robert Lewis Dabney pointed out 150 years ago, have never, in the entire course of American history, conserved anything. The leftward lurch corresponds exactly in time with the loss of power of the old-time Southern Democrats in Congress.

There have been grave mistakes in the course of Southern history, apart from the original one of going naïvely into a Union with bad people. There was Bragg commanding the Army of Tennessee and Ewell and Longstreet fumbling at Gettysburg. In the same class is the decision of Southern leaders, when they were kicked out of the Democratic Party, to join the Republicans rather than form our own party. As a result, we are powerless. It was probably inevitable but nevertheless a great loss. Today there are no Southerners in Congress or in governors' chairs—only Republicans and Democrats.

But we still have something the Yankees don't have and have never had. There are still people writing books and poems and songs about Dixie. There is, despite all, a real Southern culture left. If you want to put secession on the table, let's consider the only part of the United States that really could be its own country. A true culture is the best basis for a viable country. Compared to that, all the Blue state talk of secession amounts to nothing but an adolescent tantrum at not having everything exactly their own way. (2004)

The Enemy Up Close

A review of *The Beechers: An American Family in the 19th century,* by Milton Rugoff, New York: Harper and Row, 1981, 653 pages.

American Protestantism divides into two distinct cultural traditions dating back to colonial times. One tradition derives from New England and is Calvinist in origin; the other is Southern and Anglican. Anglican must be understood here as referring to a spirit rather than a structure, the structure having been largely dissolved by the American frontier.

This dichotomy has gone largely unnoticed for several reasons. For one thing, it does not follow denominational lines. Also, though the latter tradition may include more adherents, the former has had better publicity, greater prestige, more get-up-and-go. Many Americans scarcely know that the second tradition exists and think that the first *is* American Protestantism. The New England tradition is Puritan, that is, disciplined, communal and concerned with the "purification" of the community. It is parent to the American civil religion, a fact easily demonstrated by the allusions in Presidential inaugural addresses to America as "a city upon a hill."

The Southern tradition is largely folkish and focuses upon the individual and the state of his soul. It goes quietly about its work and is forbearing toward the mote in its neighbor's eye. Its evidences, being largely manifested in private life and often among people beneath the notice of intellectuals, are seldom recorded by either contemporary observers or historians. Because of the ignorance of the intellectuals, its presence and significance have been greatly underestimated in American history.

One can grasp the distinction between these two varieties of Protestantism by imagining two different churches on the same Sunday morning. One church is in Massachusetts, say, or Michigan. The preacher sermonizes on "World Peace" and the congregation sings "The Battle Hymn of the Republic." The other church is in rural North Carolina, or perhaps Oklahoma, or a blue-collar section of Los Angeles. The sermon is on "Salvation" and the hymn is "In the Sweet Bye and Bye."

There is no question that the first church represents far more worldly power and prestige than the other, so much so that even late-comers to these shores often imitate it, unconsciously recognizing that assimilation to the New England model is the most respectable form of Americanization. One can find American nuns whose rhetoric and political activism resemble New England Unitarianism more closely than anything in European Catholicism. Martin Luther King, a man raised in the second tradition, became, almost instantaneously, a power in the land when he shrewdly resorted to New England-style rhetoric.

To distinguish these two traditions further, one need only consider two manifestations of the divergent traditions in human behavior. As a demonstration of the Anglican tradition let's take General Lee, who reconciled the duties of a soldier with unostentatious faith and piety as successfully as is possible in an imperfect world, so successfully that he provided a model for millions of what used to be known as "Christian gentlemen." General Lee understood Christianity as an imperative struggle for personal virtue, its social relevance being that a virtuous man is always valuable to his fellows. For the contrasting example, one can find no better than Henry Ward Beecher, General Lee's contemporary and the most famous reforming preacher of his generation. Beecher understood the imperative of Christianity as one of social improvement, and personal virtue as consisting largely of being on the right political side.

Milton Rugoff's thorough and intimate history of three generations of Beechers is an admiring but candid account of a brilliant, energetic and forceful family. His treatment of the Beechers shows the transformation of American society in the 19th century from Puritanism to Victorianism. Rugoff's book also offers a close-up view of the first of the two Protestant traditions and of how it was transformed, by virtue of the Civil War, from a peculiarity of New England into the American tradition. The intellectual, spiritual, and public careers of the Beechers exemplify that merging of democracy and purification ritual that has provided the predominant tone of American politics right down to the present. First there was Lyman Beecher, the leading Calvinist theologian of his day, who was instrumental in spreading the gospel to the West. (The "West" in New England parlance referred to areas north of the Ohio River settled by New Englanders. Nothing else counted.) Among Lyman's numerous children were Catherine Beecher, a pioneer feminist; Harriet Beecher Stowe, "the little woman who made the big war," in Lincoln's phrase; Henry Ward Beecher, the most admired and highest-paid preacher of his day; and a raft of other sons, all of them reformist clergymen.

This intimate review of the Beechers not only helps one understand the 19th century, but it has a more urgent pertinence as well. Let us assume that in the future some scholar will wish to write an objective history of the 1960s and 1970s in America. (It is optimistic, I know, to hope that anyone will survive our educational debacle and declining opportunities for free speech with sufficient intellectual curiosity and ability.) The most difficult problem such a historian will face in understanding these two decades will be this: How did it happen that during that epoch such a large number of people with low ethical and moral standards and transparently self-interested and destructive motives managed to pass themselves off as the moral leaders and benefactors of society?

This question can be answered only by looking back to the reformist movements of the 19th century and to the precedents and parallels they provided for our more recent ravagings of order and decency in the name of moral vision. The 1960s and 1970s resemble no period in American history so much as the 1850s. The keynote of both eras is irresponsible destruction and aggression in the name of democratic fulfillment. The earlier crusade, though now long hallowed by success, can be seen, when viewed through the medium of the Beechers, to have been as ambiguous in motivation and results as the later one.

The closest resemblance of the two periods is in the presence of that now-familiar intolerance and the extravagance of rhetoric and action that kicks over the traces of normal political life and postulates goals so self-evidently righteous that disagreement is sin, explicable only as the work of the devil. This style of politics demonizes the opposition and deifies itself. Anyone who has observed politics in this country in the last fifteen years or so understands the extent to which such violent and antirational posing has held sway in public discourse. The 1850s supply the model. From the imposing authority of his pulpit, Henry Ward Beecher exhorted young men to depart for Kansas and kill Southern settlers. This rhetoric represented more than the momentary and overwrought emotions of one man: it reflected the behavior of a large number of people and spilled over into private, apolitical matters.

When Harriet visited the South for the first time—after the War— she was quite astounded to encounter families who were kindly, cultivated, Christian, and militant rebels. Rugoff comments: "She had seen the barbarous enemy—the face of evil—and found that his sins had left no mark on him." But the Puritan ritual of demonization had already done its work. It is not the Beechers' desire for social improvement that should trouble us, but the self-aggrandizement and disregard for consequences with which it was pursued. From the phenomenon of busing, as with other social issues, we, too, have grown familiar with absentee moralism. Henry did all he could to hasten the onset of the conflict, but during the War which he had helped to produce and in which over 600,000 men died, the famous clergyman lived in luxury in Newport and Europe.

Recall also the 1970s, when philosophical and psychological weirdness sprouted constantly from the same soil as liberal politics. Again, the parallels and precedents are evident. The Beechers were almost all involved in spiritualism. Professor Stowe, Harriet's husband, had frequent "visions." Harriet, in response to the remark that the creator of Uncle Tom had never been to the South, said: "No, but it all came to me in visions, one after another, and I put them down in words." "There is no arguing with pictures," she explained on another occasion, a sentiment that would doubtless please our electronic journalists. One does not have to be a latter-day defender of slavery to recognize the disastrous consequences that ensued when people like the Beechers took slavery out of the arena of political realities in which the Founding Fathers had dealt with it and placed it in the realm of fiction, propaganda, sentimentality, and emotional self-indulgence.

By now we are all familiar with the extent to which the Great Society and its various attendant crusades for justice provided a cover for private pocket-lining. One recalls various political figures who were simultaneously great civil rights advocates and outright crooks. There seems an inescapable affinity between a certain kind of politically mobilized morality and dishonesty. Both Henry and Harriet became wealthy because of their antislavery positions. Harriet, for example, purchased a confiscated Florida plantation for a pittance. Henry's favorite money-maker was a mock slave auction that he staged over and over again. On every occasion the "slave" was young, attractive, female and almost white; there is no recorded instance of an "auction" of a male, child or ugly female "slave."

To draw a close to our catalog of precedents, there is a high correlation in both the 1850s and our own era between reformist politics of the Puritan stripe and sexual promiscuity and opportunism. We all know now that the New Frontier—Great Society epoch was marked by a cynical jettisoning of traditional sexual morality by the occupants of the seats of power, and that much of the Elan that fueled the New Left in the streets, and its fellow travelers in positions of power, resulted from the euphoria of the early stages of sexual license. The rhetoric, however, was mostly about peace and justice.

Henry Ward Beecher, the most popular preacher in America, famous for his spellbinding crusades against slavery, liquor, the secret vice and every other evil, committed adultery with at least one woman of his congregation, a woman who happened also to be a Sunday School teacher and the wife of an admiring protégé of Beecher's. The offense itself is not so revealing as the spirit of callous exploitation with which it was carried out and the deceit and hypocrisy with which it was covered up. Beecher was warmly defended by the establishment of his day. Most of the press declared his innocence and his parishioners raised $100,000 for his legal expenses, while those who brought the charges that we now know to be true were hounded. The powers that be, then as now, rush to the rescue when their most valuable asset, their pretense of superior moral vision, is threatened. Henry's deceit in this episode was not merely a weakness displayed on one painful occasion. It was a way of life to a man whose fame and riches were built upon a conveniently abstract, unscrupulously aggressive, politically irresponsible moralizing. In his memoirs, for example, Henry lied about so simple a thing as a college debate. He recounted an occasion in which he had carried the house against a proposal for the colonization of blacks outside the United States. In fact, he had not participated in the debate in question and the pro-colonization side had won. Characteristically, he had falsely glorified his own role and distorted the historical record to make his antislavery stand date to a much earlier and more dangerous period than it actually did.

The story of the Beechers is that of people who proclaimed themselves the champions of freedom and morality and demonized those who disagreed, while all the time keeping their hand in the till and their eye on the main chance. The chief lesson we can learn is that there is something in the American fabric that guarantees that now and then such people will succeed outrageously, Today's secular liberals will, of course, dismiss Henry Ward Beecher as simply a typical hypocritical Protestant moralist. Yet he was one of them. He was a leading liberal of his day, a crusader not for souls but for political and social reform. He was an establishment figure, not a small-town vigilante. He spoke from a position of power and respectability from which he safely and irresponsibly rode to the outer limits every fad of his day. Beecher is not the father of the Moral Majority; he is the father of the smug establishment figures who juggle morality and sybaritic life-styles in an everlasting shell game. Today's morality movement comes out of that other, quieter, Protestant tradition. Its adherents are the attacked, not the attackers. They are not dogmatists seeking to impose their narrow standards on more enlightened fellow citizens. They are rather provoked into defending their communities and standards from impositions by the arrogant purveyors of a false and imperialistic ethos.

That strange combination of Puritanism and democracy that wreaked so much havoc in the 19th century, having done its work and reached the natural limits of its expansion, began a retreat into narrower and less dangerous limits after the debacle of Reconstruction. Something very similar is perhaps happening now. If so, we can hope once again for leaders for whom public life, as for Lee, is an arena for the exercise of private virtue rather than, as for the Beechers, a vehicle for the social mobilization of private greed and discontent. (1982)

The Flight of the Kiwis

A review of *Descent from Glory: Four Generations of the John Adams Family,* by Paul C. Nagel, New York: Oxford University Press, 1983, 400 pgs.

John Adams was descended from a long line of Puritan yeomanry who were among the earliest settlers of Massachusetts. Though his father never achieved anything more than a modest local distinction, John Adams became a key figure in the revolution in New England, leading member of the First and Second Continental Congresses, political philosopher, diplomat, Vice-President, and President. But his greatest accomplishment was his marriage to Abigail Smith, one of the most remarkable women in American history, who added Anglican gentry, including the distinguished Quincy line, to the family stock. Of the four children of this remarkable couple who reached maturity, only one achieved distinction. John Quincy Adams recapitulated his father's success as a scholar, legislator, diplomat, Secretary of State, and President. But John Quincy's two brothers, Charles and Thomas Boylston, died young from alcoholism. His sister, Abigail, married William Stephens Smith, one of the most irresponsible and unscrupulous promoters of the day. Smith had all of Aaron Burr's profligacy and ambition, without Burr's charm and courage. He died owing vast sums and left his family destitute.

John Quincy Adams repeated the family pattern in more than his successes. His marriage was the luckiest aspect of his career. His wife was Louisa Johnson, daughter of a Southern family and the most attractive of all the Adamses. Louisa shrunk under the puritanical conceit and censoriousness of her husband—which was directed at himself, his family, and the world—but she never completely withered away. Though she wasn't to achieve the exemplary republican matronliness of Abigail, her kindness and liveliness were responsible for whatever was attractive in the later generations of Adamses. As is usually the case, the women made up the better part of the family.

Of the three sons of John Quincy and Louisa, John, Jr. died young after failing miserably in business and George Washington was a suicide before age 30, after what was referred to in the 19th century as a career of debauchery. Again, one son redeemed the line. Charles

Francis vindicated the high opinion the Adamses held of themselves by his achievements as a congressman and scholar and as the chief architect of Northern diplomatic success in Europe during the Civil War. Of his seven children, four sons are noteworthy: the historians Henry and Brooks; John Quincy, a gentleman farmer who felt only weakly and intermittently the impulse to thrust himself before the public; and Charles Francis, Jr., the only one of the family who saw military service in the Civil War or who took any active part in the postwar building of the American economy.

Paul C. Nagel, in *Descent from Glory*, presents the sad story of the Adams family as a family, from the inside. He narrates with clarity and shows a deft mastery of the immense Adams documentation, certainly the largest of any American family (though, despite the vastness of the record, there are strategic lacunae in regard to each of the black sheep). He approaches the subject in a spirit of sympathetic candor rather than of muckraking, and he significantly adds to our awareness of the 19th century America that lay beneath political rhetoric.

What strikes us most deeply in this sad account is the old, old lesson of the vanity of human ambition and the inevitable doom of all dreams of dynasty-building in a republic. What a price the Adamses paid for the ambition that flowed only too naturally from their talents and for those secularized remnants of their Calvinist conscience which left them, in the final analysis, unable to love themselves and even unable to love Creation except on their own unattainable terms! How much happier they would have been had they been able to confine themselves to the family circle and devote their talents to practical, local beneficence or to the vindication of American intellect!

In this admirable study, Nagel does not seek to draw sweeping lessons. He is content to show how the warring devils of ambition and conscience wreaked havoc time and again on those members of the family who were unable or unwilling to adapt to so relentless a view of life. A Puritan conscience can only avoid disaster if it is chastened by practical application or when it is balanced, as it was in the Founders and in the best of English statesmen, by a Cavalier magnanimity and sense of proportion.

Taking the Adamses as exemplary of the New England "aristocracy," history affords few examples of so swift and uncontested a decline. For the first half of the 19th century the heirs of New England and Southern Founders engaged in mortal combat to control the destiny of America. New Englanders devoted themselves with Puritan zeal to the destruction of the Cavalier side of the English inheritance, the Southern gentry, the annihilation of whom was to them the sine qua non of national progress. When the contest was over, New England had an immense share of the political and economic power of America and a near-total monopoly of the cultural power. Yet the fourth generation of Adamses, despite all their advantages and responsibilities, fastidiously picked up their skirts and retired to carp that things had not turned out as they expected. Henry and Brooks spent their talents blaming their own and their country's degradation on Southerners, Jews, the predetermined forces of history, uncouth new men like Grant (who were but the natural outcome of their own vision)—on everything except themselves. By contrast, the Southerners staked all on their vision, lost, and retired from the field chastened but with their honor intact.

The self-emasculation of the Adamses in the fourth generation was the real descent from glory. New England fell swiftly from overwhelming predominance into genteel irrelevance or arrogant nullity. To the extent that the Puritan ideal of America was preserved, it was preserved by simple, clearheaded Midwesterners, sprung of common or immigrant stock, who went to work to redeem the American dream and to preserve the American sense of decency. To the extent that that decency was preserved, it was largely extra-political. Politics was accepted as a degraded sphere, tolerable only because it was unimportant. The great dream of republican ethics and virtue that had inspired the Founders was dead, never to be resurrected. This descent from glory was more than the tragedy of one family. It was an American tragedy, the echoes of which still reverberate down the long hall of history. (1984)

Royal Teddy

A review of *Theodore Rex*, by Edmund Morris, New York: Random House, 2001, 772 pages; and *The Selected Letters of Theodore Roosevelt*, edited by H.W. Brands, New York: Cooper Square Press, 2001, 656 pages.

Theodore Roosevelt, Jr., was the first of our Northeastern rich boy Presidents, blazing a trail for his kinsman Franklin, John F. Kennedy, and the two Bushes. Even Nelson Rockefeller, who had no abilities and no popularity that was not bought and paid for, ended up a heartbeat from the Executive Mansion.

TR was also the first President to market himself as a Personality. A colorful and energetic man, head of the government at the dawn of the 20th century and at the high tide of the "Progressive" era, he played a decisive role in the creation of the America that we all live in today.

If you are one of those who suffer from that strange, widespread American folk delusion that Presidents are intrinsically interesting and their daily thoughts and actions are subject for retelling, then *Theodore Rex* is the book for you. His administrations (1901-1909) are given a thoroughly researched account at the level of good popular history or good journalism. Many readers will appreciate the close look not only at Roosevelt but at many other public characters of the period, and this is an offering not to be sneered at.

The author, to my taste, is a bit too eager to prove TR right on every occasion. He wants us to accept TR as an early racial liberal, which he supports by giving a few incidents greater importance than they had at the time. Roosevelt was, after all, a believer in The White Man's Burden. And if he behaved more generously toward black people than many at the time were willing to do, it was not a terribly unusual thing.

I thought I knew a good deal about TR, but only truly began to understand him by perusing the volume of selected letters. Though I would like to have seen a little more information than is provided about editorial practices, the editor has chosen an interesting and seemingly representative sample of private letters written by TR from the age of ten until his death, chafing on the sidelines of the Great War.

By "private" the editor does not mean merely personal, but letters expressing private thoughts, often about public matters, and even philosophical waxings. One sees his mind at work, and aside from certain individualities, the mind reveals its times very well. Though somewhat hampered by wealth and a Harvard education, TR really tried to understand and act constructively in the world that existed. His motives were consistent—constructive reform to adjust to new conditions without destructive radicalism. Whether his actions were appropriate to his goals is doubtful. His "trust-busting," for instance, was certainly made in ignorance of economics. (Though come to think of it, ignorance of economics might be an advantage in economic policy decisions.)

Perhaps inevitably for a man of intense action, he did not grow very much intellectually, but he kept learning. A letter to his friend Owen Wister, about Wister's novel *Lady Baltimore*, in 1906, shows a man reading and thinking with some range if not much depth. Neither FDR nor JFK could have written such a letter. Teddy Kennedy and George W. Bush would not even understand it. The great flaw of monarchy is that dynasties run down, and our American royals are no exception.

The Progressive Era was the seedbed for the century that followed and beyond. It is an endlessly fascinating and multifarious bit of history that could well occupy a lifetime of study. Nearly every controlling assumption and policy of today was formulated or anticipated in Progressive thinking or in its natural culmination, American intervention in the Great War. I suspect that TR would be pleased with the American empire of today, except for its multicultural aspect. (Multiculturalism was invented in the 1930s by European totalitarians.)

For me, the most important question that a historian can bring to the period is why the United States abandoned all its traditions and vigorously entered into the imperial competition for the regulation of the globe. The drive of the imperial impulse led TR qua historian to write silly books which portrayed the southwestern frontiersmen of the pioneer period as forerunners of the imperialists who wanted to dominate China. (His books were not nearly as silly as Woodrow Wilson's non-books, however: Wilson had a PhD and was a professional educator.)

One can explain American entrance, frequently enthusiastic entrance, into the hideous world power scramble and the insane mayhem of the European war in many ways. Big banking interests and the dishonesty and shallowness of politicians no doubt played a part as they do in every significant public question, but do not provide, I think, a sufficient explanation.

As far as I can tell, the American people never registered a wish for their government to become the world policeman. One has to look at the minds of the ruling class. And all the ruling class was involved, whether they were, according to Joseph Stromberg's apt classification, cooperative imperialists like Wilson or unilateral imperialists like Henry Cabot Lodge. Something—an aggressive sense of nationalism (that replaced patriotism), reasonable or unreasonable fear of the other armed powers of the world, a perverted Calvinist impulse to correct the unrighteous nations—made the American ruling class leap enthusiastically into the fiery doom of worldwide war.

Reading the letters of Theodore Roosevelt gives some insight into the mindset of the folks who made that critical choice, of which we are now perhaps seeing the ultimate expression in the imperial "New World Order." It gives some insight but does not really explain. Perhaps it is simply that power corrupts, and what corruption can be more tempting than the dream of benevolent global command. (2002)

Ambrose Bierce's War

A review of *Shadows of Blue and Gray: The Civil War Writings of Ambrose Bierce*, edited by Brian M. Thomsen, New York: Tom Doherty Associates, 2003, 282 pages.

There are several reasons why Ambrose Bierce, one of the finest American short story writers of the 19th century and one of the best war writers of all time, is not much in favor today—and perhaps even more reasons why he should be.

Though I suspect Bierce continues to have admirers among the dwindling ranks of general readers, especially for his delightfully cynical *The Devil's Dictionary* (1906), critics tend these days to dismiss his writings as "neurotic" and "grotesque." The editor of *Shadows of Blue and Gray*, a new volume of his Civil War stories, fictional and factual both, evidently had trouble tracking down a set of Bierce's twelve-volume collected works. These were published in 1909-12, after he had passed his heyday of popularity. The publisher went bankrupt shortly thereafter, which some attributed to an unwise investment in Bierce's writings.

His career as a journalist and occasional writer stretched back to the end of the Civil War and had been carried out in San Francisco, New York, London, and many more exotic places, usually when there was a war going on. Much of his writing was scattered and uncollected. In 1914, when he was over seventy, Bierce disappeared into Mexico, where revolution was raging, and was never heard from again. It is thought that Carlos Fuentes's novel *The Old Gringo*, which was made into a passable movie with Gregory Peck, is modeled on Bierce.

The real reason the critics don't care for Bierce, one suspects, is that his view of the world goes against the optimistic American grain—very much so. You do not go to Bierce to be encouraged by happy, progressive thoughts. Whether you can find in his writings true thoughts is another matter. He is supposed to have said to a lady who asked for advice on child rearing: "Study Herod, Madam, study Herod." W.C. Fields was a little in the same bleak vein, and so was Mark Twain. But Bierce's despair (which did not prevent his uproarious enjoyment of pleasures of the flesh) was much more profound and honestly earned.

The Upper Right Corner

It was earned in the Civil War as a frontline junior officer in the Western theater from beginning to end. Born in Indiana and raised in that state and Ohio in obscure and unaffluent circumstances, Bierce was apparently self-educated, but he possessed a natural writer's gift for language and for close observation and original reflections.

He enlisted on April 19, 1861, at the age of eighteen. According to some, he was the second man to volunteer for the Union army. He spent most of the War as a lieutenant on the staff of a brigade commander, which meant that he was often right in the firing line but was mobile enough to have a somewhat bigger picture of what was going on than was available to the private soldier. He was wounded several times, captured once, and saw nearly all of his fellow staff members killed.

The pieces in this collection can be divided into three types: (1) lucid, leanly written accounts of battles and other events of which he had personal knowledge; (2) obviously surreal and gripping ghost stories with a war setting, the most famous of which is "An Occurrence at Owl Creek Bridge"; and (3) accounts of bizarre events, which the reader does not know whether to take as fact or fiction.

Bierce's Civil War pieces were not published in book form until 1891 and were apparently written long after the War, for he assumes that his audience is made up of readers who grew up in a gentler time without firsthand experience of what was, by many multiples, the bloodiest conflict in American history. "Children, how little you know," the narrator says in one story. In another, he remarks that men now look much younger than men the same age did during the War, although the soldiers were much younger in spirit than the succeeding generation.

Despite being written up later, the battles and other events, so far as they came within his personal observation, are told with remarkable immediacy and with a cold fatalism that doubtless has put off many readers. "For countless ages," Bierce writes, "events had been so matching themselves together in that wonderful mosaic to some parts of which, dimly discernible, we give the name of history."

The reader always has an acute sense of sharing the experiences of the characters and, indeed, of being a member of that living thing, an army in action. For, says Bierce, armies have personalities and variable moods. This was certainly true during that war, which was much more personal than was to be the case later, where men of the same lineage stood by the thousands within rifle range or closer with the purpose of killing each other.

Bierce never takes credit for his own courage and skills and is not afraid to describe his real feelings in critical situations. He conveys the hope that infantrymen feel when the artillery arrives for their assistance, followed by hatred on the realization that the guns are drawing responding artillery fire in their direction. He reveals that he much preferred the company of the kindly Confederate home guards who captured him to that of a fellow prisoner from his own army, "a most offensive brute, a foreigner of some mongrel sort."

One of his specialties is the cruel ironies of war and the relentless but haphazard visitations of death, sometimes involving moral paradoxes. A sharpshooter must choose between picking off his own father, who is scouting for the other side, or exposing his sleeping comrades to attack. A junior officer carries out peremptory orders that he knows to be wrong, aware that he is damned whether he obeys or disobeys. Another soldier recovers from near-fatal wounds and then is killed in an accident with a rope swing.

Even crueler dilemmas, if that is possible, are presented by man's organization of himself into armies. Bierce describes the torment of a man who must decide whether to heed a hopelessly mangled comrade's plea for a quick end to his suffering. One story details the case of a soldier executed for striking his lieutenant. In fact, the two were childhood friends who had often fought. But by virtue of his friend holding a commission, what would have been a playful act a few weeks before has become a mortal offense.

Another reason for his unpopularity in some quarters: Bierce thought the cause for which he fought was right—but he never thought it was glorious. He had a fighting soldier's respect, typical of many on both sides, for a brave enemy and contempt for armchair (or today push-button) fighters and politicians. Neither cause was glorious. For Bierce, the only thing worthy of awe was the brave men on both sides whose lives were foreshortened.

His unflinching look at war might contain some useful wisdom for contemporary Americans, who, at least before September 11, 2001, tended to view war as something remote that happened to other people. I read recently an advertisement for a video about an American unit in World War I: German troops surrounded the Americans, "depriving their captives of sustenance, cutting off their lines of communication, and brutally assaulting them." Just what does this writer, who I suspect reflects the mind-set of many Americans, think war is supposed to be?

Should the Germans have played nice and refrained from making their attack so brutal?

Bierce scorned such attitudes toward the American bloodletting of his own time. His stories show us the cost, the price that was paid by some, with all the ugly details:

> Hidden in hollows and behind clumps of rank brambles were large tents, dimly lighted with candles, but looking comfortable. The kind of comfort they supplied was indicated by pairs of men entering and reappearing, bearing litters; by low moans from within and by long rows of dead with covered faces outside. These tents were constantly receiving the wounded, yet were never full; they were continually ejecting the dead, yet were never empty. It was as if the helpless had been carried in and murdered, that they might not hamper those whose business it was to fall tomorrow.

Bierce's flashes of humor, usually bitter, are wonderful, as when he reports himself to be in his "anecdotage," or describes "two patriots in blue carrying a stolen pig hung upon a pole." Or, in relating a postwar arrest for a killing: """ had never been hanged in all my life and was not enamored of the prospect." On a postwar visit to the Shiloh battlefield: "Here in 1862 were some fields and a house or two; now there are a national cemetery and other improvements."

Only one story, though, is in the vein of humor: "Jupiter Doke, Brigadier General," An incompetent political appointee mainly interested in political advancement and government patronage receives promotion and the thanks of Congress for a battle won by the sheer accident of a mule stampede dispersing the opposing force.

Bierce was fearlessly blunt in his contempt for soldiers with political ambitions. Of President James A. Garfield he writes, in regard to the battle of Nashville: "A good deal of nonsense used to be talked about the heroism of General Garfield, who, caught in the rout of the right, nevertheless went back and joined the undefeated left under General Thomas; there was no heroism in it; it was what every man should have done.... I did so myself, and have never felt that it ought to make me President."

Bierce did not share in creating or basking in the aura of Union glory that for decades after the War was a mainstay of American public discourse. He was glad the country was held together; it would have been a misfortune if it had been reduced in power and resources, but the effort, if necessary, was far more ambiguous than his fellows on the winning side were inclined to admit. African Americans play no role in his War, except occasional slighting mentions of them as servants of Union officers. His War had nothing to do with slavery.

Nor did he tolerate the political and clerical demonization of Southerners, the "bloody shirt" that was a mainstay of Republican politics for many years.

Instead, he reminded Northerners that resisting what one perceives to be oppression is necessary and admirable. To Bierce, "they were honest and courageous foemen" who represented the "dignity and infinite pathos of the Lost Cause."

Bierce's hero, if he had one, was Brig. Gen. William Babcock Hazen, a hard-fighting soldier on whose staff he served for much of the War and surely a man after his own heart. Hazen was a fearless critic of his superiors during and after the War. (He was later single-handedly responsible for exposing the corruption of President Grant's crony, Secretary of War Belknap.) Hazen was "the best hated man that I ever knew, and his very memory is a terror to every unworthy soul in the service.... He convicted Sheridan of falsehood, Sherman of barbarism, and Grant of inefficiency."

Hazen, of course, was not popular with his superiors, which was a cause of suffering to his men. In "The Crime of Pickett's Mill," Bierce relates how the brigade was sent on a sacrifice attack by Generals Sherman and O.O. Howard as a punishment for their commander's insubordination. At great cost, the brigade fought so well that the Confederates thought they were being assaulted by a whole corps and made much of the action in their reports, while Sherman and Howard did not even mention the battle in their memoirs.

In describing Reconstruction, Bierce plunges into the pit of the politically incorrect. At the end of the War, he was briefly employed to secure "captured and abandoned property" for the U.S. Treasury, namely, immensely valuable stores of cotton. His experiences and reactions support the old view of Reconstruction as corruption and oppression rather than the current view of Reconstruction as a good but unfinished revolution. There is no doubt, and Bierce was a firsthand witness, that the government agents stole most of the proceeds of cotton confiscation and engaged in many other fraudulent and oppressive actions.

Bierce did not blame the Southerners he encountered around Selma, Alabama, for resisting being looted. Rather than joining the propaganda chorus about unrepentant rebels in need of further chastisement after the War, he considered it remarkable that there was so little crime and disorder on the part of the occupied people.

Apparently, despite his bitter humor, Bierce was a good and convivial companion who made friends wherever he went. His experience in Alabama left him with disgust for carpetbaggers and sympathy for the defeated people, making friends in Alabama he described as convivial, well-educated, brave, generous, and sensitive to points of honor. This was a not uncommon attitude among fighting Union soldiers (Joshua Chamberlain followed a similar path) if not among politicians and journalists. During a postwar battlefield visit (not in this book), Bierce wrote to a close friend: "They found a Confederate soldier the other day with his rifle alongside. I'm going over to beg his pardon."

While the collection contains all, presumably, of Bierce's prose pieces on the War, fictional and factual, it does not contain all his writings on the subject. He also wrote poetry on the War, and his letters give additional insight into the formation and trajectory of his iconoclastic views. These other writings would make a tasty morsel for those with an insatiable appetite for Civil War books.

This is a good collection that ought to bring back to attention an important writer and give thoughtful people something to chew on. Bierce's view of war and of the Civil War in many ways contradicts conventional wisdom, which is exactly why he deserves to be read. (2002)

Scorcese's *Gangs of New York*

A review of the movie *Gangs of New York* (2002), directed by Martin Scorcese, color, 168 minutes.

Martin Scorcese, in an interview, candidly described his new film, *Gangs of New York*, as an "opera." He had been asked whether the events portrayed were true to history. I took his reply to mean that the events of the movie were selected and organized for dramatic emphasis and were not to be taken as literal factual record.

And, indeed, as a historical record of 19th century New York, the film has many failings. Nevertheless, it has provoked some useful discussion of the historical context—specifically for the light it sheds on the Lincolnite mythology of the Civil War era. It seems that the accepted idea of the gloriously united North trampling out the wrathful grapes of slavery and treason is not so sound a picture of the real thing after all.

For one thing, the film gives a glimpse of the rather nasty nativism among Northerners, a great many of whom hated Catholics and immigrants as much or more than they hated Southerners. None of the above fit into the Yankee ideal of true Americanism. Nativist gangs burned down convents in Philadelphia and Boston when such things were never dreamed of in the South. This window into the real history of the antebellum North becomes even more significant for three reasons.

1) Nativists of the American Party went en masse into Lincoln's Republican Party and made up a strong element of his support. Though, of course, Lincoln cared nothing about religion and he and other leading Republicans were too savvy politicians to embrace overt nativism. Republicans did not generally like immigrants, but they loved the militaristic German centralizers who flooded into the Midwest after the failed revolutions of 1848. Confederate General Richard Taylor recorded in his memoirs that when he surrendered at the end of the War, a German Union general lectured him on how Southerners were now to be taught true Americanism. Taylor was the grandson of a Revolutionary officer and the son of a President. (Does this maybe give you a little hint of where Straussians and Neocons are coming from?) These Germans made the most solid core of Lincoln's support, with the possible exception of tariff-protected manufacturers and New England "intellectuals."

2) The film can open the door on another dirty little secret. We have heard a lot about immigrant criminal gangs. The fact that vigilante law prevailed over much of the North during the War has been conveniently forgotten. Besides the thousands of his critics Lincoln jailed without due process, thousands more were killed, injured, intimidated, and run out of town by proto—fascist gangs of Republican bully boys called "Wide Awakes." They played a major role in making sure Northern elections turned out right, i.e., Republicans won. And you thought ugly mob violence was something that only happened in the South!

3) Although the film does not give a satisfactory view of the New York City draft riots, it lets us in on at least part of the secret when the draft rioters point out the $300 men who had bought exemption from conscription. The fact is that no affluent Northerner fought in the War if he didn't want to—certainly not Rockefeller, Morgan, Gould, Swift, Armour, Goodyear, and the others who were making fortunes out of government contracts. Nor most of the patricians—only one of five military age Adamses served, and Teddy Roosevelt's father bought an exemption. Lincoln's worthless son Robert spent most of the War at Harvard. Sherman once complained that men of wealth were found in the ranks of the Southern army and lamented that Northerners were not like that.

But that is not all the story. The "riots" did not start out as race pogroms, though they degenerated into that. They started out as organized civic resistance to the draft, encouraged by the Democratic state government. Everyone knew very well that the Lincolnites enforced the draft at a much higher rate in areas that opposed them than they did in friendly areas—according to forthcoming studies by the New York playwright and historian John Chodes, the draft was imposed in New York City at four times the rate for Massachusetts. And the conscripts were well aware that they stood a good chance of being used up as cannon fodder by Republicans who knew if they lost four men for every Southerner killed they would still end up on top, as long as the immigrant flow kept up. About a fourth of the total enrollment of Lincoln's armies were immigrants, many of whom were brought over and paid bounties for enlisting. The situation was so bad that the Pope sent one of his most persuasive priestly orators to Ireland to warn the people about being used up for Union cannon fodder.

Perhaps we can begin to recognize the historical fact that millions of Northern citizens did not willingly go along with Lincoln's War. And the opponents were not limited to the New York City draft rioters. A forthcoming book by H.A. Scott Trask will enlighten us about who opposed the War: freetraders who were on to the Republican tariff game; traditional Jeffersonians and descendants of Revolutionary families (outside of New England) who understood that killing Southerners and overthrowing legitimate state governments, as well as suppressing freedom of speech and press, were not exactly what the Founding Fathers had in mind; Irish and German Catholics, though that history has been suppressed as one of the fruits of Lincoln's victory.

The truth is that Lincoln's party did not save the Union and the Constitution. It was a Jacobin party that seized power and revolutionized the North as well as conquering the South. *Gangs of New York* can perhaps open a window that will encourage further historical discovery along these lines.

Alas, the wrong lesson is drawn by one of the usually fine writers at vdare.com, Steve Sailer, who sees the movie as Scorcese making points for the immigrants against the natives. According to Sailer: "When the Civil War came, many Irish and other immigrants in New York City refused to fight for the Union that had given them refuge."

Wait a minute. That was a civil war going on here. Can a newcomer really be faulted for not wanting to take sides in a civil war? I think rather it shows real patriotism and good sense. And how about that "refuge." Here is a Dublin paper commenting in 1861: "We cannot but recollect that in the South our countrymen were safe from insult and persecution, while 'Nativeism" and "Know-Nothingism' assailed them in the North."

How about John Mitchel, the Irish patriot who had been exiled to Van Diemen's land, from whence he escaped to the land of freedom, where he joined the Confederate cause of liberty, to which he gave the lives of two sons? It is not true, by the way, that the Union General Burnsides's sacrifice of the Irish Brigade at Fredericksburg was a great exhibit of Irish devotion to the Union cause. The so-called enthusiasm was political propaganda drummed up by Republican promotion of Gen. Meagher as an Irish leader, which he wasn't. Irish recruiting fell off sharply after Fredericksburg.

Let me recommend to those who want to use conditions in the War of Southern Independence as a tool for the otherwise worthy cause of immigration restriction a recent work: *Clear the Confederate Way!: The Irish in the Army of Northern Virginia* by Kelly J. O'Grady. The book covers much more than the title suggests. And while you are at it, take a look also at *The Jewish Confederates* by Robert N. Rosen. (2003)

Will They Never Learn?

The American Conservative, in its March 14 issue, carried an excellent article on "The Living Room War." The author, Professor Andrew Bacevich of Boston University, pointed out that the American home front seems to be disengaged from the actual current war. This, he writes, is a moral failure and is unlike the situation in previous wars.

Bacevish spoils it all when he starts out by likening Ft. Sumter to Pearl Harbor and 9/11. The last two were massive sneak attacks by foreign enemies. The firing on Ft. Sumter was preceded by a gentlemanly warning and was completely bloodless. It would not have happened at all if Lincoln had not dissimulated about re-enforcements and had a hostile fleet just outside. Nor does Lincoln's call for 75,000 troops after the fall of Ft. Sumter at all resemble American unity and determination after Pearl Harbor.

To begin with, the call for troops was illegal, and the 75,000 was either mistaken or deceptive, since the conquest of the Southern people and destruction of their self-government eventually required over a million men. Furthermore, its immediate effect was to drive four more states out of the Union and require military occupation to forestall the secession of three others. And despite a temporary upsurge of militancy after Sumter, Lincoln's government never had the degree of support in the North for its actions that characterized the public in the two more recent events.

Several hundred thousand men evaded the draft by various means, many others were enlisted only by cash bonuses, public speakers and newspapers had to be suppressed, and a fourth of the army had to be recruited abroad. When this kind of folklore is invoked, putting Southerners in the basket with Tojo and Bin Laden, we despair of Yankees ever learning anything and ever appreciating our contributions to the U.S.A. (2005)

Yankee Wars

Why should anyone be surprised at the prisoner tortures carried on by the U.S. armed forces in Iraq? Given the low quality of our national leaders and the amoral atmosphere of the forces, only an imperviously smug belief in American exemption from human evil could blind anyone to the likelihood of such. In October 2001, early in the Afghan War and before the Iraq debacle had begun, I used the generous freedom provided by LewRockwell.com in a piece called "Whom the Gods Would Destroy." I pointed out that we were in the power of a bully of a Defense Secretary and a mentally and morally dysfunctional President, and that too many Americans were in an irresponsibly bellicose mood more indicative of thoughtless aggression than of the sober determination with which people ought to go about avenging a great wrong.

I quoted the warnings of Richard Weaver and Alesandr Solzhenitsyn on the descent into brutality that beckoned. The points made then seem to me a little prophetic and still valid. I would add that the American military has always swung back and forth between two modes or spirits. The Washington/Lee mode and the Grant/Sherman mode. The first emphasizes skill, enterprise, and courage in achieving objectives with an economy of force and strives to keep warfare as honorable as possible. The second relies on marshaling overwhelming materiel to crush a weak opponent, heedless of the cost in life and taxes, and rewards its commanders appropriately.

The Grant/Sherman mode is self-righteous and recognizes no ends except boastful triumph. Our bureaucratized, politicized, technocratic armed forces have been in the amoral Grant/Sherman mode for a long time now. What kind of a regime sends women into harm's way and makes them into prison guards? Surely one not worth the allegiance of a civilized person.

"Whom the Gods Would Destroy" *was also printed in* From Union to Empire, *the predecessor to this book.*

Chapter Seven

A Mirror for Artists

New England Against America

The Fiction of Mr. Simms gave indication, we repeat, of genius, and that of no common order. Had he been even a Yankee, this genius would have been rendered immediately manifest to his countrymen, but unhappily (perhaps) he was a Southerner His book, therefore, depended entirely upon its own intrinsic value and resources, but with these it made its way in the end. —Edgar Allan Poe

A review of *Long Years of Neglect: The Work and Reputation of William Gilmore Simms*, edited by John Caldwell Guilds, Fayetteville: University of Arkansas Press, 1988, 248 pages.

In the heroic effort to establish an American literature, intellect, and culture before the Civil War, the main line of tension was not between cosmopolitans and provincials, nor between classicists and romanticists. It was regional. But the primary regional dividing line was not drawn, as you may think, along the Appalachians (East vs. West), nor along the Potomac (North vs. South). Rather, it was at the Hudson River (New England vs. America).

This descriptive historical truth is now obscured by the fact that the New Englanders were successful in convincing much of posterity that they were American culture, a process that was assisted by their colonization of Manhattan during the antebellum period through such figures as Horace Greeley and William Cullen Bryant. Yet the lines of tension were clearly drawn and obvious to everybody at the time: on the one hand, moralistic, reformist, sentimental, pushy, genteel, devolved Puritan, transcendental New Englanders, eager to impose the supremely virtuous model of the closed communities of Massachusetts as the pattern not only for America but for all mankind; on the other hand, a more leisurely and tolerant, open-handed, rural, frontier, traditional, Anglican, gentlemanly (not genteel) spirit that visualized the true American culture as arising from the open spaces South and West of the Hudson (or in the case of Melville, the seas). New York and Philadelphia were in many cultural respects closer to the South than to Boston, at least before the 1850s.

In the literary politics that characterized the antebellum period, a host of well-organized, industrious, mutually admiring New England scribblers pursued a totally ungenerous policy of self-aggrandizement, presenting themselves to the world as America and ignoring or slandering the rest of the country whenever it suited their purposes. After the Civil War, lacking any formal opposition, they had the field pretty much to themselves except for sporadic populist rumblings from the Midwest.

Anyone who will look at what passed for mainstream literary history and criticism in the late 19th and early 20th centuries, for instance, will find a host of second and third-rate New England writers (Longfellow, Lowell, Whittier, Bancroft, Motley, and many others now justly forgotten) shamelessly celebrated as the perihelion of American letters, with only an occasional slighting reference to Poe or Melville. When Hawthorne appears, it is in an interpretation sanitized to please New England schoolmarms of both sexes. It is little known but true, that the present stature of Poe and Melville and understanding of Hawthorne (all of whom were outside the New England canon) rests upon the heroic efforts of a few scholars and critics in this century to correct, in part, the incredibly mean-spirited and petty Bostonian warp that was imposed on the evaluation of American literature after the Civil War.

It is also a fact that the success of the Bostonians in literary reputation was not matched by the quality of their contributions as measured in the perspective of the ages. American creative literature of the first rank was made almost entirely outside of the Boston-Cambridge ethos. Poe was a self-declared Southerner in perpetual combat all of his short career with the New England spirit; Melville a New York Democrat who could write verse in celebration of the ancient honor of Virginia in the midst of the Civil War and whose obsessed Captain Ahab was possibly (possibly) a metaphorical abolitionist. Hawthorne was a friend of Franklin Pierce, the most Southern of all Northeastern politicians, and the main thrust of his work is a subversion of the self-congratulatory millennialism of his New England brethren. (I do not count Emerson and Thoreau in the first rank. Even those who admire them must admit that they are would-be philosophers and saints, not strictly creative artists.)

After Poe, Melville, and Hawthorne, the second rank of antebellum literature (omitting some interesting one-book authors) is formed up by Cooper and Irving. Both of them achieved sufficient recognition abroad early enough that they could not be buried under Massachusetts obloquy. Both were at odds with the New England spirit. Read Cooper on the nasty lower-class Yankees (in the original precise ethnic meaning of that term) who swarmed into and defaced his ancestral region in upstate New York (*Homeward Bound and Home as Found*) and in opposition to abolitionists (*The American Democrat*). And recollect that one of Irving's most popular stories concerns the disgrace of an absurd canting New Englander, Ichabod Crane, who presumed too much on the good manners of the Hudson Valley Dutch.

Perhaps the most egregious remaining uncorrected legacy of bias from these old literary wars is the long-continued obscurity and misunderstanding that surrounds the Charleston romancer William Gilmore Simms (1806-1870), who just possibly, when accurately appreciated, will rank shoulder to shoulder with Cooper and Irving. He was the premier antebellum writer of the South, after Poe, and the premier interpreter of the West, after (or perhaps with) Cooper. One of the most prolific, talented, multifaceted, and wide-ranging of American authors in the 19th century, Simms was recognized everywhere before the Civil War (except in the most chauvinist Boston circles) as a major force in the creation of an American literature. Today he is almost unknown in any serious way except to a few specialists.

A measure of the neglect is that the first and last biography of Simms was published in 1892, and that a superficial and badly misconceived one. An excellent six-volume edition of his letters has been produced in South Carolina. but this has been little used by literary scholars and even less by historians, few of whom have awoken to the fact that Simms was the most articulate intellectual in the South in the late antebellum period and thus is, or ought to be. of considerable interest to general as well as literary history.

There are, it is true, some formidable obstacles to an appreciation of Simms. One of the contributors to *Long Years of Neglect*, James E. Kibler, Jr. (with an essay on Simms's poetry), has said elsewhere that Simms must have written steadily with both hands all his life. He published about 70 or so separate titles—poetry, plays, novels, short stories, history, essays—and probably an equal amount of material, often anonymous or pseudonymous, in the numerous Southern journals of which he served as editor and chief contributor. (In his spare time, Simms was a planter, a public man, and the chief literary talent scout and critic of the South.)

Not only is the volume and diversity of his work so daunting as to encourage most scholars to pass him by, but much of the vast output is hard to find. *The Cassique of Kiawah*, possibly Simms's best novel, was until recently virtually unobtainable. *Woodcraft*, the other possible best, is a little more available, having been reprinted in South Carolina in an annotated edition along with Simms's other Revolutionary War novels during the American Revolution bicentennial. By a strange fate, Simms's best-known and most available novel, *The Yemassee*, the one which most people are likely to have read if they have read anything, is far from his best.

   Added to these logistical obstacles are the ideological problems. As an unapologetic and explicit defender of the regime of the Old South, Simms is a highly unsympathetic and nearly incomprehensible figure for most modern scholars. Even so, the main reason that Simms's writings are relatively unknown and undervalued is scholarly inertia—the tendency to repeat old errors generation after generation rather than do the hard work of real exploration and reassessment.

   In fact, in the past half-century or so, there has been a very large accumulation of specialized scholarship on Simms, in books, articles, and theses, exploring specific aspects of his oeuvres and life. The net result has been a gradually rising estimate of his literary standing. This considerable literature has never been formulated in a way that has had much impact on general history; however, the present volume of essays does not come out of the blue, but is an expression of a long—gathering movement. In the book are a dozen essays by both literary scholars and historians on Simms's major works and aspects of his career. It remains to be seen whether the insights and judgments presented here will be integrated into a more general understanding.

   I do not want to claim too much. Simms possessed a high order of talent, not genius. He did not write *Moby Dick, or The Scarlet Letter*, Any author as prolific as he was, is bound to suffer from unevenness. He is sometimes careless and melodramatic, not, as in the conventional Parringtonian account, because his art was undermined by a romantic and extroverted Southern society, but because a restless temperament led him ever onward to new material. However, at his best, Simms could tell an important story well, with great dramatic conviction and a serious confrontation of moral and social issues.

   I do not want to put down Cooper, whom I admire and who has an essential place in American literature. Moreover, Cooper preceded and made possible Simms's literary exploitation of the materials of the

American Revolution and frontier. Nevertheless, comparison with Cooper is the most telling that can be made for Simms. I would contend that in his best works Simms was a better storyteller than Cooper, a better plotter, a better psychologist. Moreover, he had a much ampler historical and social imagination as well as a vast fund of something Cooper lacked entirely—humor. Most readers have found Simms's frontiersmen and Indians superior to the more famous characters of Cooper. Moreover, Simms truly anticipated many of the great achievements of 20th century Southern literature, whereas Cooper has no real progeny.

Most of Simms's major work, and much of the lesser, is found in the three series of novels, or "romances" as he called them, that he produced more or less simultaneously from the 1830s to the 1850s: those set in the colonial Southeast (*The Yemassee, The Lily and the Totem, The Cassique of Kiawah*, and others); those concerned with the American Revolution in South Carolina (*The Partisan, Mellichampe, The Scout, Katharine Walton, The Forayers, Eutaw, Joscelyn*, and *Woodcraft*; and the "border romances," set in the newer Southern states (*Guy Rivers, Richard Hurdis, Border Beagles, Beauchampe*, and others).

In these books Simms created an all-encompassing, Balzacian panorama, from the 16th to the 19th century, of the history and society of the region south and west of Virginia, a region that is, after all, large and authentically American, even if seldom noticed, except negatively, in Boston. In the process he explored as extensively as anyone ever has the great dramas of colonial settlement, Revolution, and the conquest of the frontier, and portrayed fully every social class—the aristocracy, lesser gentry, yeomen, poor whites, frontiersmen, slaves, Indians. At their best these books display drama, humor, robust realism, large and complex historical themes, and a sophisticated treatment of manners.

By a twist of fate even more curious than the popularity of *The Yemassee* there is a lingering impression that Simms was a prudish, stilted writer, full of wooden figures of Southern ladies and gentlemen. Though he did pay some allegiance to ideal aristocratic types, as models for a society that was emerging from the lawlessness and crudity of the frontier, the impression of artificiality is far from just. In fact, in his own time and later, Simms was usually subjected to the opposite criticism. The New Englanders thought that he was too graphic and realistic in dealing with the hard facts of sex, violence, and human drives. Later, when Victorian standards were being abandoned for "realism," he was dismissed as a mere romanticist. He was, thus, first condemned for not being genteel enough, and then for being too much so.

It is closer to the truth to say that Simms, like Faulkner and the other Southern greats, dealt with a full range of characters well, especially vividly and convincingly with the middle order of Southern society, the non-aristocratic whites, and that his most predominant characteristic and greatest virtue as a writer is a robust and often sophisticated realism. Contrary to an oft-repeated judgment also, Simms's women are as close to flesh and blood as those of any contemporary male writer, as Anne M. Blythe shows in discussing the range of female characters in her essay herein on *The Cassique of Kiawah*. The same can be said about the strong and shrewd widow Eveleigh in *Woodcraft*. The essay by Blythe on *The Cassique of Kiawah* and that on *Woodcraft* by James B. Meriwether, the scholar who has been responsible for bringing a number of Simms's books back into print, are the most important perhaps of a number of good essays in this collection, focusing as they do with considerable depth and insight on Simms's two more enduring books. *Woodcraft*, as Meriwether shows, is a study, at the same time profound and humorous, of the difficult process of restoring social order in South Carolina after the guerrilla civil warfare of the Revolution, told through the experiences of Captain Porgy, a Rabelaisian member of the lesser gentry. Any Southerner will recognize Captain Porgy as an archetypal character of high authenticity. *Woodcraft* displays Simms's historical and social perceptions at their most complex.

Another aspect of Simms's work usefully explicated in this collection is his relationship to the genre known as backwoods humor. In this connection are the essays by Linda E. McDaniel on *Paddy McGann* and Mary Ann Wimsatt on Simms's short fiction. *Paddy McGann*, one of Simms's late creations, was a South Carolina river boatman, candid and self-assertive in the tradition of the frontier, who by a series of fantastic adventures is transported to New York where he observes the literary society of the day and undergoes haunting experiences of the supernatural reality of evil. Among the short stories, "Sharp Snaffles: How He Got His Capital and His Wife" is surely a neglected masterpiece of 19th century American writing. It is the story of a landless North Carolina mountaineer's struggle to establish himself as a man and a member of his community. As the essayists show, these works contain seriously conceived and crafted elements of the exuberant fantasy and humor of the American tall tale, interwoven with moral struggle and social criticism and a mature understanding of the human condition. No one who is familiar with these works can dismiss Simms as a mere shallow defender of the aristocracy.

Among the biographical essays, the more noteworthy are Miriam J. Shillingsburg on Simms's last lecture tour in the North in 1856, an eye-opening account of the literary politics that have been previously mentioned, and an analysis by David Moltke-Hansen of the development of Simms's understanding of American history. Simms's achievements in the realm of history are certainly another area of unjust neglect.

Much of Simms's fiction was profoundly historical. He also wrote history and biography, and he thought deeply and originally about the stormy relationship between historical fact and literary art, as may be seen by perusing his collected essays *Views and Reviews in American Literature: History and Fiction* (1845). In the collection under review new ground is broken in Nicholas C. Meriwether's essay on *The Lily and the Totem*, a failed but interesting attempt by Simms to combine history and fiction in a new genre. It is perhaps not too much to say that in his theory and practice Simms anticipated some of the most creative historical writers of our own time—John Lukacs, Solzhenitsyn, George Garrett, Shelby Foote—in a testing of the frontier between fact and art and a realization of the dead end of so-called objective history.

I have made some rather sweeping assertions about the rightful place of William Gilmore Simms in American letters which the 12 essayists, or many of them, will not necessarily endorse. They are a good deal more circumspect, modest, and scholarly in putting forth his claims than I have been, though most would agree that his standing ought to be higher than it is. You are free to disagree with me, but I will not take you seriously until you have read Woodcraft, *The Cassique of Kiawah, Paddy McGann,* "Sharp Snaffles," and *Views and Reviews in American Literature.* If you have not, you do not know Simms. You do not really know 19th century American literature.

The writers of the essays would not necessarily agree, either, with the description of 19th century literary politics with which I introduced my discussion. Yet surely Simms's neglect, if such it is, reflects more than an accidental overlooking of one writer. It reflects a particular partisan heritage of ideological, not literary, judgments which ought to be exposed and re-examined.

The title of the introductory essay by the editor of this collection, John C. Guilds, makes a statement and poses a question: "Long Years of Neglect: Atonement at Last?" The statement is undoubtedly true. The question remains to be answered, though this volume marshals a powerful and pertinent case for reparations. (1989)

Literature in the Old South

Foreword to *The Adventures of Captain Simon Suggs,* by Johnson Jones Hooper (1845), Nashville, Tennessee: J.S. Sanders, 1993, 201 pages.

In an ideal world the separate studies of history and literature would enlighten one another. A historian—whether of republican Rome, 17th century France, the Old South, or any other subject—would gain insights into an era from its imaginative literature. Insights of a kind to be found nowhere else, for the best imaginative literature is created by the most acute consciousnesses and closest observers of a society. A good knowledge of history, on the other hand, can illuminate an author's text and mind for the literary scholar, saving him from countless misleading assumptions that he inevitably brings to a work from the unavoidable fact that he himself is the product of a different age.

Unfortunately, in the real world, rather than cross-fertilization, we have an ever-narrowing specialization of scholarship. Even worse, where controversial subjects—like the Old South—are under consideration, historians and literary scholars tend to consume one another's most superficial generalizations, thus denying themselves obvious truths and compounding the distortions that pass for established knowledge.

This explains why the predominate literary scholarship has been such a long time reaching a proper appreciation of the merit of the writings known as "Southwestern humor," writings of which Some *Adventures of Captain Simon Suggs* is a fine example.[44] Told by literary scholars, inaccurately but persistently, that the significant American writers of the 19th century came out of the vicinity of Boston, historians naturally assumed that the "Southwestern school" was of minor importance. Since the historians already "knew" that the Old South was characterized by excessive romanticism, obviously such realistic and even bawdy and rollicking writers as the "Southwestern humorists" must, by definition, be a minor and transient phenomenon of the frontier and not a major clue to the history of the Southern people.

On the other hand, literary scholars, assured by historians, inaccurately and persistently, that the Old South was an intellectual wasteland, wedded to the hopeless defense of evil institutions and incapable of

---

[44] Hooper's original title was *Some Adventures of Captain Simon Suggs, Late of the Tallapoosa Volunteers: Together with "Taking the Census," and Other Alabama Sketches.*

the creative art and critical thought that characterized the enlightened North, were confirmed in their decision to dismiss the writers of the Old South without any serious examination.

These assumptions about antebellum Southern literature long governed the scholarly consensus, although there were always a few dissenting independent minds. But in truth every implicit assumption catalogued above was a falsehood. The historians, consciously or unwittingly, were upholding the results of the Civil War. The Civil War was and still is the central event in American history in terms of the scale of bloodletting and revolutionary change which it occasioned. To justify the postbellum state of affairs, historians had to postulate the Old South as a peculiar anomaly, an unnatural, unlovable society that had offered an intolerable obstacle to the inevitable upward sweep of middle class Northern democracy—which was assumed as the normal condition of the universe. The victorious side required not only that the South be defeated and conquered; it had also to be discredited, demonized, and downgraded.

The literary scholars who assumed the inconsequence of the literature of the Old South were not only misled by historians; they were also unconscious heirs of the logistical triumph of Boston in American letters. In the literary politics of the antebellum period, a host of well-organized, industrious, mutually-admiring New England scribblers pursued a calculated policy of personal and sectional self-aggrandizement, presenting their peculiar insular culture to the world as all that counted in America and ignoring or slandering the rest of the country. After the Civil War they lacked any strong opposition and had the field pretty much to themselves, except for sporadic populist rumblings from the Midwest.

The hegemony they created persisted well into this century. Anyone who will look at the "mainstream" literary history and criticism of the late 19th century and early 20th centuries will see a host of second and third-rate New England writers celebrated as the perihelion of American letters, with only an occasional slighting reference to the Southerner Poe or the New Yorker Melville. This incredibly mean-spirited and petty Bostonian warp to the understanding of American literature has even now not entirely disappeared, though a great deal of painstaking scholarship has slowly loosened its grip.

It was not until the widespread recognition of the high achievements of 20th century Southern writers—a recognition largely forced upon reluctant Northeastern savants by European critics—that it began to register that the triumphs of Faulkner and the other Southern greats could not have been created in a vacuum—that they must have had antecedents. The stage was now set for the perceptive to discern that the writers lightly dismissed as "Southwestern humorists" were not outdated curiosities, but, rather, among the most creative and original and fruitful pioneers of the real American literature. Viewed in this new light, the "Southwestern humorists" begin to look like the forebears of a great tradition. Not merely *infra dig* purveyors of popular humor—a notoriously perishable literary commodity—but realists, skilled portrayers of authentic life below the level of the genteel, often profound social observers.

And, as research has shown, the "Southwestern humorists" were not oddities. In their own time they were mainstream, wrote for a large audience, were widely popular, and were considered very normal and characteristically American. Further, honest examination reveals that crippling over-gentility was a Northern problem—it has left the once celebrated occupants of the sacred circle of literary Massachusetts—Whittier, Longfellow, Lowell, Bancroft, and many others—dated and irrelevant. It was the South that produced realistic and anti-romantic writings, and New England sentimental and genteel. Most of the American literature of first-rank and of enduring interest was produced in the "benighted" regions. Among other things, this might lead us to suspect that the "mind of the Old South" was not "closed" at all but quite lively and creative.

A closer look at the context in which antebellum writers flourished will reveal another erroneous postulate. The regional dividing line in literature was not, as we might think, at the Potomac (North vs. South), nor at the Appalachians (East vs. West). It was at the Hudson River (New England vs. America). The chief magazine outlet for the stories of the "Southwestern humorists" was *The Spirit of the Times*, published in New York City and read by the rural gentry everywhere except New England. Those regions of the North that had not been Puritanized by New England infiltration were closer to the South than to Boston, culturally.

Far from being only a frontier product or a localized and transient form of literature, the picaresque and rollicking stories of the "Southwestern humorists" were a new variation on a very traditional form of rural literature quite familiar in eastern America and in the English and Irish county press. Thus, while it is quite true that the frontier provided material, even in a sense the underlying theme, for the writers of which

Hooper is so fine an example, it is wrong to dismiss them as merely Western "local color."

Unlike such New England saints as Emerson and Thoreau, none of the Southwestern writers set up to be professional men of letters, full-time social critics, and gurus. All were deeply involved in the quotidian life of their communities and in pursuing other professions. Their writings began as occasional, leisured contributions to local papers—"at first designed," as Hooper says in his Preface, "to amuse a community unpretending in its tastes."

Their books usually appeared as afterthoughts to satisfy popular demand. And almost all the writers of the school—Hooper, A.B. Longstreet, George Washington Harris, William Tappan Thompson, Thomas Bangs Thorpe, Henry Clay Lewis, Joseph G. Baldwin—limited themselves to one or two books. They were widely scattered across the South and never were a self-conscious clique. They were aware of each other, obviously worked out of the same traditions and reacted to similar conditions, and wrote for the same audience. But they did not pursue literary politics.

Hooper is in almost every respect a typical case study of the antebellum Southern writer of humorous sketches, in background, motives, and career. He always refused to subordinate the man and citizen to the author. A gentleman could express his talents, amuse and instruct his neighbors, enjoy the celebrity of his accomplishments, but he could not be merely a writer. He had to be an amateur, in the old and honorable sense of that term. Longstreet was a clergyman and college president, Harris a steamboat captain, Hooper a lawyer and newspaper editor.

In fact, Hooper, like Longstreet, became impatient with his literary fame and went on to other activities. We are told that in 1856, when Hooper was a delegate of Alabama to a Southern commercial convention, sitting next to Albert Pike of Arkansas, poet and future Confederate general, there was a call from the platform for a speech by "Simon Suggs." Hooper glowered in his seat and refused to answer the call or confound his own identity with that of his character. The exception to this Southern style was Poe, a landless orphan with a drinking problem, who had to eke out a short and meager existence as a magazine writer and editor. And, partially, William Gilmore Simms, who, although he married a plantation, was driven by restless talent and ambition to production of more than seventy books in every genre.

Here, too, the dividing line between gentlemen amateurs and careerists is evident at the Hudson. Melville had to put in his years at the customs house, and Cooper was, in his primary identity, the New York equivalent of a Southern planter. Only the Bostonians had the wealth and the alienation from everyday America to proclaim themselves primarily "intellectuals." Thoreau's father owned a factory, and Emerson cleverly married the terminally ill daughter of a banker.

Hooper fits the pattern of his group, too, in that he was born in the older and settled parts of the South to a family of station and encountered at an impressionable age the crude contrast of the newly settled frontier, which provided him literary matter and stimulus. Johnson Jones Hooper was born in 1815 in the seaport of Wilmington, the largest town in North Carolina, into a line of prosperous planters, merchants, and physicians. On his mother's side he was directly descended from Jean Antoine DeBerniere, a heroic leader of the Huguenots, and (for those who believe in the literary gene) from Jeremy Taylor, the eloquent 17th century English preacher. On his father's side were several of the leading Revolutionaries of North Carolina, including great-uncle William Hooper, signer of the Declaration of Independence.

Hooper's father had literary interests and turned out occasional essays and articles about state history. In fact, according to his friend, the North Carolina historian Griffith J. McRee, it was Archibald Maclaine Hooper's "fondness for polite letters," along with a too easygoing temperament and failing eyesight, that made him a worldly failure. Unsuccessful as a planter, lawyer, newspaper editor, and customs collector, the father allowed the family fortunes to dwindle away. Johnson, the youngest of six children, was denied the advanced education received by his older brothers, one of whom became a distinguished professor of classics at Chapel Hill.

Instead, he received much of his education and his first literary experience in the shop of a newspaper his father edited for a time, the *Cape-Fear Recorder*, which again is a familiar pattern for a "Southwestern humorist." At fifteen he published a humorous poem about the pompous local British consul who fell into the water during a ship-christening ceremony. Such humor was a staple of the tidewater South and rural Britain, as well as the frontier, which should remind us not to overemphasize the "western" in "Southwestern humor." Southern humor was Southern humor, taking all of life and not just the raw conditions of the frontier for its province.

At the age of twenty (1835) Hooper joined a lawyer brother in Alabama, in order to prepare himself, in the customary way, for practice. It was a newly settled region not yet entirely redeemed from the Choctaws and Creeks. The move west was not at all unusual since, in 1860, half the people then alive, white and black, who had been born in North Carolina were living beyond the mountains. Except for a youthful sojourn in Texas and the final year in Richmond, Virginia, where he died, Hooper spent the rest of his life in east central Alabama, living at LaFayette (Chambers County), Dadeville (Tallapoosa County, the home of "Simon Suggs"), Wetumpka (now Elmore County), and Montgomery.

In Alabama Hooper practiced law, edited newspapers, and held occasional minor public offices. When a lady whose hand he sought turned him down, he immediately married her younger sister, broadening an already extensive network of kin throughout the region. To Mrs. Mary Brantley Hooper was dedicated "The Rose of Alabama," a then famous poem of Hooper's friend, Alexander Beaufort Meek. Johnson J. Hooper was an integrated member of the world he wrote about, not a disdainful outside observer.

Again, in the typical pattern, Hooper's first writings were casual contributions to local papers to amuse his neighbors and give the dignity of literature to the early history of his state. His sketch, "Taking the Census," came to the attention of William Trotter Porter (to whom *Some Adventures of Captain Simon Suggs* is dedicated), editor of the New York *The Spirit of the Times*. Porter promptly requested material from the Alabama writer.

The Spirit of the Times had already become the chief outlet of Southern humorists and remained so throughout the antebellum period. It was filled with stories, both factual and imaginative, of hunting, fishing, horse racing, and other traditional and rural matters, with slices of realistic life at all levels of society, with rollicking high spirits and good times, and with a strong but not exclusivist or offensive American pride. That is, it appealed to American readers wherever the secularized Puritan prophecy and sentimental poesy of New England (so assiduously peddled as "American" culture) did not flourish.

The Spirit of the Times published a natural literature, written by men with the spontaneous inclination to formulate and share their observations and reflections on life, not to pursue personal fame and literary politics. This is the best kind of literature. After all, Shakespeare began writing plays not with the intent of being the world's greatest dramatist but because he needed material for the theatre of which he was actor-manager. And doubtless Homer started out as shared entertainment of comrades-at-arms around the campfire.

In 1843 Porter began publishing Suggs stories, some of which had already appeared in Alabama papers. They were immensely popular and were reprinted in newspapers everywhere. Porter, who had already discerned that the "Southwestern writers" constituted an important school of American literature, included Suggs in the collection he published in 1845, *The Big Bear of Arkansas*.

In that same year, the book here republished, the first edition of *Some Adventures of Captain Simon Suggs*, appeared, in obvious response to popular demand. The book went through eleven printings and editions during the author's lifetime. Meanwhile, Suggs was widely anthologized in humor books on both sides of the Atlantic, including a book published in London in 1853 called *Yankee Humour*, the English editor not understanding that in America "Yankee" meant a New Englander.

Hooper wrote other books of stories and a hunting book, *Dog and Gun* (New York, 1856), which had some popularity, though Simon Suggs was his great creation. He grew less interested in writing and more interested in politics during the 1850s, being an unsuccessful candidate for office, a homeless Southern Whig, and finally a secessionist.

He was appointed Secretary to the Provisional Congress of the Confederate States, and moved with the Congress from Montgomery to Richmond. Never in good health, Hooper died in June 1862, two days before his forty-seventh birthday, while McClellan's army was in sight of the church spires of the city. He was buried in an unmarked grave in Shockoe Hill, Richmond's Catholic cemetery, having converted shortly before, to the surprise of his associates, to the Roman Church.

With the appearance of "Simon Suggs," Hooper became "almost at a bound," as the great scholar of Southern literature Jay B. Hubbell put it, one of the most popular writers in the country. And Captain Simon Suggs himself became a household familiar, deeply fixed in the imagination of Americans. The Captain is utterly reprehensible, but also likable. In his high spirits, his irrepressibility, his irreverence, his capacity to adapt and to triumph over circumstances, he taps something deep and essential in the American spirit.

The Captain's most famous saying captures it: "It is good to be shifty in a new country." It summed up his philosophy of life but also spoke deeply to the necessities of the New World. There were other famous sayings: "Mother-wit can beat book larnin' at *any game*." "There is no telling which way luck, or a half-broke horse will run."

Suggs's adventures begin when he is able to escape his Georgia home with some capital by outwitting his execrable father at cards. He heads west. His subsequent escapades, cast satirically in the form of a campaign biography for a sheriff's election, give Hooper a chance to look at many aspects of the life of the time. Suggs appears as a land speculator, a bank agent, a captain in the Indian "wars," a courtroom defendant, and a would-be evangelist. The view of the shortcomings of society in the newly settled Alabama country is harsh but all in fun and not mean-spirited.

Some Adventures of Captain Simon Suggs continued to be reprinted and anthologized now and then during the later 19th and early 20th centuries. Hooper was the subject of occasional scholarly commentary, as well as imitation and pastiche. Perhaps something of a revival of serious interest was achieved when Bernard DeVoto pointed out in *Mark Twain's America* (1932) how much Twain owed to Hooper. The debts were numerous, the most striking being the similarity of the famous camp meeting in Chapter XX of *Huckleberry Finn* to "The Captain Attends a Camp-Meeting."

From then on Hooper received fairly steady scholarly attention, including a 1952 biography, *Alias Simon Suggs*, by the Alabama scholar W. Stanley Hoole. But it is perhaps more interesting that Hooper continued to have readers. In 1950 a band of eleven of Suggs's admirers, some Alabamians and some Northerners, bought and erected a memorial over Hooper's remains in Richmond.

The scholarly attention that Hooper and his humorist colleagues received when the 20th century began to recognize their literature was focused upon the idea of the "frontier," largely because it was stimulated by the connection with Twain.

The frontier (an imprecise and mobile designation, remember) is most certainly an important consideration in understanding this literature, which most immediately was the response of educated Southerners from the older settlements to crude and unformed new communities. But the "Southern" is as essential an ingredient as the "Western," a point often lost. The rollicking view of life that the stories reflect had its roots in the older South, where it had been transplanted from England and Ireland. The subtitle of Porter's *The Big Bear of Arkansas was and Other Sketches, Illustrative of Character and Incidents in the South and South-West.*

But a deeper and more essential point is that a division between the South and the West is illusory. Both identities are essential and inseparable. As Andrew Lytle puts it, "pioneering and settling are successive stages of one movement." Donald Davidson wrote, in introducing the works of Simms, that the great theme of Southern literature (and history) is "the interaction of civilization and the frontier." Or as more recently David Moltke-Hansen has written; in summing up Simms's views, the South came into existence "out of the dialectical interactions of plantation and frontier." That is, the South is that combination resulting from the civilized given of the established plantation regime extending itself over and being influenced by the frontier. This is indeed true of America at large and is the core meaning of the famous Turner thesis on "the significance of the frontier in American history." Even the New Englanders, the exception who lived out of artificially imported European categories, had to pretend to a frontier. Which is why Emerson declaimed about "Self-Reliance" and Thoreau memorialized his adventures at his little frog pond barely out of sight of the smokestacks of Boston. There was not an East and a West but a New England and an America.

Among the Southwestern humorists we can see certain differences that reflect deeper currents of change in society. Longstreet in *Georgia Scenes*, writing a decade or more before Hooper, is more didactic. He portrays the crude conditions of the newly settled and backwater regions with the understanding that they are transient. Though able to move well in that society, he remains something of the outside agent of civilization and morality. He is a critic of the failings of the backwoods, but also a critic of the failings of polished society.

Hooper is without obvious moral teaching. He lacks perhaps some of Longstreet's social complexity and sense of literature as the portrayal of manners. His social criticism is there but is illustrated rather than stated, as is the assumption of the gradual progress of civilization. George Washington Harris, writing in the late antebellum period a decade later than Hooper, created "Sut Lovingood," an even more untamed and unredeemable character than Suggs. Harris verges upon despair and nihilism in his view of society because, I would suggest, he was writing at a time when the intransigent hostility of the North and therefore a daunting crisis for the South were inescapable. And when what had been the opportunity of the frontier was becoming the hopelessness of the backwater, and the alienation characteristic of the modernized consciousness was beginning to make headway.

Though drawing on the same tradition, Twain, after the Civil War, goes several steps further toward the abyss. He is a product of the South, but there has been a radical break. He is a self-selected exile, writing not within his community but for the gratification of their conquerors. He has achieved nearly complete nihilism in his view of the unregenerate nature of life as molded by the American frontier. The tensions inherent in his role as a traitor may account for Twain's oft-noted underlying ambiguity, angst, and aggression. The great Southern writers of the 20th century have kept a hold on their traditions. They suffer from the burden of a modern consciousness and sometimes have one foot over the abyss, but they have remained, in the final analysis, within the community and the tradition of what M.E. Bradford has called the "corporate bond" of the South. We might even suggest that their greatness lies in the balancing act.

The critic Kenneth S. Lynn deals with Hooper and his comrades at length in his influential *Mark Twain and Southwestern Humor* (1959) under the interpretive theme of "Whiggery." He develops an elaborate view of "Suggs" as a political-social satire by a displaced aristocrat, disgruntled at his loss of standing and deference from the crudities of "Jacksonian democracy." There is a grain of truth there, but to make it the main theme is to go too far and to misunderstand the context.

Hooper does indeed take an occasional swipe at the vanity of Jackson and the disreputability of some of his supporters. However, the concept of "Whiggery" is extremely elusive at best, and Lynn's sense of it is drawn from a Northern context. In the South, the social divisions between Whigs and Democrats were very fluid and varied considerably from state to state and decade to decade. Hooper himself was at times a Democrat and at times a Whig.

The gentleman who has withdrawn from a society too crude for him, to ridicule it at a distance is a Northern phenomenon. It is impossible for men to be more deeply engaged in their society than were Hooper, Longstreet, Harris, Simms, and their like. While they are most certainly social critics, they are not alienated outsiders. Hooper is an Alabamian and Suggs is his neighbor. Hooper's poking of high-spirited fun at his state is also a form of allegiance to and celebration of Alabama, a part of the recognition of its history, identity, and life.

Several of the modern commentators on Hooper have claimed Suggs explicitly as the direct ancestor of Faulkner's Snopeses. While it is true in a broad sense that Faulkner worked out of the tradition of which Suggs was a part, it is a mistake to draw the connection so closely. It is less a matter of direct literary influence than of Faulkner's having taken his bucket to the same cultural reservoir. That is, Faulkner's imagination was formed by the same Southern heritage of manners, temperament, experiences, conditions, impulses, and views of life as was Hooper's. As far as I am aware, Faulkner never mentioned Suggs, though he did on at least one occasion, in casual response to a question, mention as an influence Harris's "Sut Lovingood." The phenomenon of Faulkner is a miracle of creation, but also a product of the distinct chain of Southern culture (which numerous savants have denied exists).

There are other reasons to draw the family connection loosely between Snopes and Suggs. Suggs is, though a reprehensible character, also highly likable and delightful. We would not at all mind spending an evening in the tavern listening to him, as long as we kept a good grip on our wallet. No Snopes that I am aware of was ever agreeable company.

More important, in the world of Captain Suggs, the War is not yet lost. Suggs is the product of "a new country" which is in the process of being civilized. Simon himself seems to have settled down and to be on the point of achieving some degree of respectability when his "biography" appears. We don't doubt that his children will be respectable, perhaps even leading members of the community, when the "new country" is no longer so new. But with the Snopeses the War is already lost and so there is no possibility of civilization. The South has been traumatized and truncated. As Allen Tate, the poet, wrote at about the same time that Faulkner's Snopeses were created: "All are born Yankees of the race of men." Suggs was the product of a stage of social development that will be surmounted. The Snopeses are the end of the line—a local manifestation of the alien conqueror. In Faulkner there is no possibility of social redemption. The only redemption will be individual and will have to be earned over and over again.

Furthermore, Suggs, for all his cruelty and selfishness, is not without his virtues. His depredations are not motivated by the relentless inhuman greed of the Snopeses, but simply by the desire to get along with as little honest toil as possible. He makes his famous raid on the believers' collection plate (in "The Captain Attends A Camp-Meeting") only after his wife informs him that "the sugar and coffee was nigh about out" and there were not "a dozen j'ints and middlins, *all put together*, in the smokehouse."

And a lot of Simon Suggs's misbehavior is simply hell-raising, not unattractive even if it does usually lead to cheating the cheater and shearing the lambs, who, after all, are born to be cheated and sheared. He does not take himself too seriously, enjoying self-satire, and he seems to delight as much in the foibles of humanity as in the opportunities for profit that these foibles present to the shrewd.

Furthermore, he has a very human weakness—an addiction to "the tiger," that is, the game of faro, which he persists foolishly in believing he can beat. No Snopes ever gambled on less than a sure bet or just for the hell of it. And Simon Suggs loves his children. In "The Captain Is Arraigned Before A Jury Of His Country" we learn that Suggs "was really an affectionate father," something that as far as I recall was never said about any male Snopes. These qualities lend a nice touch of complexity to a character who might otherwise come close to a caricature. Perhaps I am wrong, but I am inclined to believe that under less harsh conditions Suggs will evolve not into a Snopes but rather into a good old boy, something close to V.K. Ratliff.

Readers who have not met "Southwestern humor" have a treat in store, and Simon Suggs makes probably the best slope for a beginner. Go on to Longstreet's *Georgia Scenes*, William Tappan Thompson's "Major Jones," Harris's "Sut Lovingood," Henry Clay Lewis's "Louisiana Swamp Doctor," and William Gilmore Simms's "Sharp Snaffles" and "Paddy McGann."

As a historian I find this literature not only enjoyable in itself and consoling in the associations it makes with a lasting Southern tradition, but also valuable because for students it constitutes a very healthy antidote to the abstractions and distortions that are commonly retailed about the South and its history. I do not see how the summing up of the contributions of "Southwester humor" that appeared in the January 1860, *The Spirit of the Times* can be bettered. The commentary (written probably by Thomas Bangs Thorpe, as Porter had died in 1858) was directed at the hostility of Northerners toward the South, an attempt to bring back the brotherly spirit that was necessary for the preservation of the true Union. *The Spirit* wrote:

> Some of the best things, always the most original, produced in this country, are the results of Southern pens. For more than a quarter of a century the columns of the "Spirit" have teemed with the finest specimens of writing, overflowing with wit and sentiment, playful and profound, a large part of which is destined to become permanent specimens of real American originality, which we have been largely indebted to Southern correspondents.

The True Fire Within

A review of *Henry Timrod: A Biography*, by Walter Brian Cisco, Madison, New Jersey: Fairleigh Dickinson University Press, 2004, 168 pages.

Henry Timrod died in 1867 at the age of thirty-nine from tuberculosis—his end aggravated and hastened by inadequate food and the rigors of eking out a living amidst the charred ruins of South Carolina's capital city. The newspaper which had provided the only income for himself, wife, child, and widowed sister's large family, had gone up in Sherman's fire. He described the last period of his life as "beggary, starvation, death, bitter grief, utter want of hope," and added: "I would consign every line I ever wrote to eternal oblivion for one-hundred dollars in hand." The man who spoke thus may well have been America's greatest poet living at the time.

Consider the first and last stanzas of his "ode" sung in 1866 as ladies brought flowers to the otherwise undecorated graves of 600 Confederates killed in the long siege of Charleston.

> Sleep sweetly in your humble graves,
> Sleep, martyrs of a fallen cause—
> Though yet no marble column craves
> The pilgrim here to pause....
> Stoop, angels, hither from the skies!
> There is no holier spot of ground,
> Than where defeated valour lies
> By mourning beauty crowned.

For my money, no better lines of verse came out of the great American bloodletting of the 1860s. The experts, of course, would say that we should prefer as a dirge the lines from the, shall we say, flamboyant Whitman in "O Captain! My Captain!":

> But O heart! heart! heart!
> O the bleeding drops of red,
> Where on the deck my Captain lies,
> Fallen cold and dead.

Perhaps the experts are right in their preference for the most representative if not the best American poet.

Timrod was well recognized from the 1850s onward as a powerful, profound, versatile, and subtle poet, though he is best known for the poems that expressed the deepest sentiments of the
Southern people during and after the War.

Whittier described Timrod's verse as "very powerful & impressive.... He had the true fire within." The Gentle Quaker poet looked forward to the time "when no sectional feeling will interfere with the recognition of his genius. Longfellow concurred, predicting that in the future Timrod's verse "will have a place in every cultivated home in the United States." These were generous sentiments, especially as Timrod had a greater range and depth as poet than either of the New England laureates.

Their predictions did not come true. A volume of Timrod's collected poems was never published in his lifetime and not until six years after his death, and then only because of the extraordinary efforts of friends. The popular anthologies are hardly aware that he ever existed.

Timrod has had to wait even longer for a biographer, but the wait was worth it. Cisco has written extensively on South Carolina notables. (He has a new biography of the neglected military and political giant, General Wade Hampton, in press.) He gives us the life of the man and poet straightforwardly and from primary sources. This is a proper biography without any of the distorting theorizing (actually dime-store Marxism) that pervades so much historical writing these days. We have the opportunity to recover Timrod and some lost elements of American culture as well. (2004)

Thomas Nelson Page

Introduction to *In Ole Virginia, or Marse Chan and Other Stories*, by Thomas Nelson Page (1887), Nashville, Tennessee: J.S. Sanders, 1993, 201 pages.

In Ole Virginia is a memorable portrait of the Old South before its destruction and one of the small company of truly enduring achievements in 19th century American literature. Its author, Thomas Nelson Page, was the most popular and most representative Southern writer of his time and one of the few Southern writers of any time to achieve the fullest measure of recognition and worldly success in his own lifetime.

Page was born in 1853 at Oakland plantation in Hanover County, Virginia, the same county in which Patrick Henry and Henry Clay had been born. Four obvious influences can be seen in his origins.

First, an ancestral pedigree that reads like a roster of the First Families of Virginia. Second, a childhood spent in a region north of Richmond during the War Between the States that was one of the most heavily fought-over areas of the continent. Third, reduced family circumstances, which gave a spur to industry and ambition. Fourth, a spinster lady relative (remembered in Page's sketch, "My Cousin Fanny," in the 1894 collection *The Burial of the Guns*) who introduced him to literature and determined the direction of his aspirations.

Turning twelve two weeks after Appomattox, Page experienced the War at the most impressionable age, so that the heroism of the men in gray and the women who sustained them, and the hardships of the "Reconstruction" peace which followed, formed the central theme of his experience and thus of his writing. He is the premier interpreter in fiction of those Southern experiences for his generation.

Page knew directly the fall of fortunes entailed by defeat for Southerners, especially those of his class, in an irregular education, interspersed with periods as a tutor. He was able to attend Washington and Lee (then Washington College) for a time when General Lee was president, but could not stay long enough to graduate. After a while, he was able to attend the University of Virginia Law School. Again, he had to leave without graduating, although he enjoyed at Charlottesville a stimulating literary fellowship.

In 1872, he began a law practice in Richmond that was moderately successful and which he continued for some years, even after his literary career had begun to prosper. In 1886 he married Anne Seddon Bruce, whose pedigree equaled his and who is perhaps the model for Anne in "Marse Chan." She died suddenly a year and a half later at age twenty.

"Marse Chan," Page's first significant published fiction, appeared in 1884 in the popular *Century Magazine* of the Scribner publishing family. The editors liked the story but delayed publication for two years, apparently because of misgivings about the readability of the dialect. The doubts proved unfounded. When published, the story was immediately popular, and thereafter demand for Page's work on the part of the Northern reading public never ceased.

In 1887, his first book, *In Ole Virginia*, a collection of his earliest stories, appeared to critical and popular acclaim. It remained his most popular and characteristic book. "Marse Chan" has always been his best-loved story, and Page considered the second story in the volume, "Unc' Edinburg's Drowndin'," to be his best-crafted and most technically perfect tale.

By 1893 he was able to give up law practice and lecturing. He married into a very wealthy Northern family and established a home in Washington, a gentleman of means free to mingle in the highest society, enjoying fame, a Maine seaside cottage, membership in the best New York clubs, and extended European travel. He was a friend of Theodore Roosevelt and Woodrow Wilson.

From 1913 to 1917, during most of the World War I era, Page was, on Wilson's appointment, the American ambassador to Italy, a difficult assignment well-performed. He died in 1922 at Oakland where he had begun.

Even after achieving fame and prosperity, Page continued writing—stories, novels, dramas, poetry, history, social commentary. The collected "Plantation Edition" of his works, published by Scribner's, ran to eighteen volumes. *In Ole Virginia* was Volume 1. This continued productivity, along with occasional efforts to break out of his successful formula and topics, are sure signs of serious literary craftsmanship and dedication. Page must be taken as a serious writer, in spite of the fate of immense popularity in his lifetime followed by neglect afterward.

When asked about his literary career, he wrote, in what is surely a remarkably accurate and guileless writer's confession: "I think the principal thing after my liking for books, was my desire to see myself in print. Emulation of others, the desire to add to my poor income, and ambition afterwards played their part; but I think ... the first motive was, to use a term for want of a better—vanity."

The fact that a Southern writer, an unequivocal defender and celebrator of the virtues of the South and its people, could enjoy such a successful career is a commentary, of course, on the period of American history in which Page flourished. To put a fine point on it, he could not have achieved such recognition, as Southern writers have learned the hard way in less hospitable eras, had he not been perceived to be performing a service for the North.

Page was fortunate to begin writing at a time when the North had become disillusioned with the failed and misguided crusade of Reconstruction and was experiencing a widespread if not universal impulse for reconciliation and healing of old wounds. Such a reconciliation was necessary if American society was to go on to a higher level of unity. Thus, it was a period in which Southerners could receive some encouragement on the national literary scene, and there was an audience willing to believe that there had been, after all, some honor, heroism, and sincerity in the Lost Cause.

Page did not pioneer the fiction of sectional reconciliation, which had already become a familiar mode when he began to publish, but he did become its most successful practitioner. Reconciliation by inter-sectional marriage was a popular theme, holding out the promise of a restoration of pre-War civility, and nowhere more happily treated than by Page in "Meh Lady: A Story of the War."

For Northerners Page provided reassurance that sectional conflict was not intransigent, that the South had accepted restoration of the Union in good faith. For Southerners, he satisfied the desire to establish that they had not been dishonorable in their motives and conduct in the War and that the South had not really been the domain of diabolism of lurid abolitionist and Black Republican propaganda. Both sections got something from the bargain. Page is thus a central cultural figure in American history, in the restoration of that real Union that must rest, as John C. Calhoun had always argued, on consent rather than conquest.

It is customary in recent commentary to dwell impatiently on the alleged disservice Page did the South in casting its history into an attractive and comforting myth. But he performed an equal or greater service for the North, where the preponderance of his readers were, by assuaging its guilt—not guilt over abandonment of the blacks at the end of Reconstruction, as modern liberal historians urge, because there was no guilt about that—but guilt over having indulged in excesses of political fanaticism in the War against erring but honorable countrymen.

A central part of the reconciliation bargain was the North's willingness to leave the problem of race relations to the Southern States. The most recent school of historiography sees this as a kind of moral betrayal of a previous commitment to equality. But it is doubtful if there ever had been such a commitment, except on the part of a very small minority, and hatred of Southern whites had always been a stronger motive for reform than sympathy for Southern blacks. It might be more accurate to say that the North had concluded that it had been wrong-headed to seek anything more than the original war aims—preservation of the Union and economic hegemony.

What is likely to be most unsatisfactory to egalitarian readers of the later 20th century is the skill and success with which Page incorporated the black people into his Southern myth (and I mean myth here as an imaginative conception formulating a social truth in a way that is not counter-factual but supra-factual).

In Ole Virginia is Virginia before and during the War, as remembered fondly by its black bondsmen after its destruction. Here Page showed his real skill as a writer and a defender of the South, for he portrays the plantation gentry through the eyes of its faithful retainers. He was not the first or only Southern writer to do so—Joel Chandler Harris and others were about the same mission—but he perhaps did it best.

Much can be said about this before we dismiss it as no more than an imposture upon black Americans. The bardic voice, the survivor of a vanished regime who remains to tell its story—a role which Page ascribed to the blacks—has been a post of honor in Western literature from time immemorial. The virtues of Page's white Virginians are not imaginable or possible without the context of black Virginians.

Further, a bit of historical perspective might remind us that Page's attitude toward the black people, if paternalistic, was admirable and moral given the parameters of his time For the choice in late 19th century America. as unpalatable as the historical truth may be, was not between old Virginia paternalism and social and political equality. It was between old Virginia paternalism and the hard racism that can be seen, for instance, in the works of Thomas Dixon.

If it is true that race relations are today better in the South than in other parts of the United States, and many would agree that they are, then surely it has something to do with the world that Page portrayed and the realities that lay behind it. For Southerners white and black the South has been a place they have to live in, and a place that is on the whole worth preserving—not a political abstraction to divert attention from the contradictions and hypocrisies of American society at large.

Given the long record of the crimes, follies, and misfortunes of mankind, and the realities of his era, Page's position is eminently moral and constructive. He reconciled the South to a failed sacrifice that was as great as any ever undergone by a large group of Americans. The War killed a quarter of the white men in the southeastern states and set the South back three generations economically.) And he also provided some of the grounds for future incorporation of black and white in a once-more viable Southern society.

The South had to come to terms with the greatest bloodletting in American history and the defeat of cherished hopes. And with potential for racial conflict such as was unknown in the northern and western states until the 1960s. Page in response created an ideal fictional world, but faced with the circumstances of despair and insoluble conflict, idealism was a heroic and constructive response.

In a literary sense he kept alive the reality of black characters in mainstream American literature, and therefore kept open a vital line that stretches on to William Faulkner's Lucas Beauchamp in *Intruder in the Dust* and Dilsey in *The Sound and the Fury*, Faulkner's characters were created in a literary age that was "realistic" rather than "sentimental" like Page's, but the line of descent is real, nonetheless.

The voices that Page creates in his work, black and white, are authentic Southern voices. Public voices, perhaps, that do not say everything they know and feel, that tactfully treat some troublesome subjects, and that consciously dramatize themselves—all of which are things that Southerners, black and white, are wont to do in real life. But they are authentic voices, in their own terms.

No writer can entirely escape his age. Page's age was one of sentimentality, something which his audience and editors expected. As Jay B. Hubbell, one of the leading students of Southern literature, has put it, Page's picture of Ole Virginia is a painting, not a photograph. If he did not escape sentimentality, he did at times surmount it. Often his effects are not so much sentimental as truly poignant. How skillfully he surmounted the cheaper forms of sentiment can be proved by a comparison with some of the now-forgotten popular literature of the time, and by the fact that he created a painting that, though unmistakably of a certain period, will endure in its interest to later generations.

Southern writers that followed him inevitably rebelled against Page. One thinks, for instance, of his fellow Richmonders, James Branch

Cabell and Ellen Glasgow. But the next generation rediscovered the path.

The plantation society presented by such 20th century writers as William Faulkner in *The Unvanquished*, Caroline Gordon in *Penhally*, or Shelby Foote in *Jordan County*, is a tougher and more realistic and earthy and ambiguous world than Page's. But like Page, these writers surmount the limitations of their own period ("realism") to redeem rather than reject Southern history. They create a world that is essentially admirable, that offers us in place of cynicism and despair a glimpse of heroism and honor that is a model for later generations of Southerners. This, surely, owes something to the trails blazed by Page.

It is difficult to judge Page fairly because it is difficult to recover a clear view of the plantation, which has been subjected to so much positive (*Gone With the Wind*) and negative (*Roots*) romanticism, and which has become politicized as the abode of the ultimate horror of American history, slavery.

The plantation already had a long literary tradition when Page began to write, developed by such writers as John P. Kennedy and William Gilmore Simms in the antebellum era. The literary convention of the plantation was as old as American literature, because the plantation was as old as American history.

Despite the tendency of scholars to mistake literary traditions for life, the plantation was far more than a scene for fiction—it was a historical reality of immense importance, central to American history and a characteristically American institution. It was not a remote quaintness or peculiar evil on the fringes of society. It is quite safe to say that without the institution of the plantation, the whole first two centuries of American development would have been retarded and the course of American history would have been quite different. And not necessarily better if we eliminate all the positive benefits that accrued to American society from the class that produced Washington and Jefferson.

Strictly speaking, the plantation is defined as a large agricultural unit with a dependent labor force, engaged at least in part in the production of staple crops, such as tobacco, cotton, or sugar, for the world market. The plantation was already well established in Latin America and the Caribbean before it appeared in 17th century Virginia and Carolina. In North America it took on Anglo-Saxon and Protestant features and existed in the midst of a largely yeoman society, which gave it distinguishing characteristics.

The amount of attention historians have paid to the plantation and the moral and ideological passions that it has aroused belie their frequent tendency to minimize its importance or deny its centrality. For some modern historians, like Kenneth Stampp, the plantation was only a particularly ugly form of capitalism. Here we find a failure of historical imagination, an inability to conceive of a different society in its own terms of to understand any other way of life except as a defective form of Americanism.

Most historians, however, whatever their value judgments, understand that the plantation world was a unique form of society. One convincing formulation is given by the Italian historian Raimondo Luraghi in *The Rise and Fall of the Plantation South*. The South was a seigneurial society, neither feudal nor capitalist, with its own social reality and its own ethics—and not merely a debased form of bourgeois society. It is this world that is the locale of Page's fiction.

Antebellum Southern writers who used the plantation as a scene for fiction had been romantics to a degree, but had never lost a certain earthy realism. In keeping with his era and the elegiac nature of his mission, Page progressed further along the road to sentiment. We should remember that this was what the Northern audience wanted. (Southerners were too poor to buy enough books to make any writer a success.) Even so, Page, like his predecessors, never quite loses touch with the reality that the plantation is first and foremost a working farm. We always know that crops have to be planted, flooded creeks crossed, provisions put up for the winter, horses cared for. In real life the ending does not always work out so happily as in "Meh Lady," but the hardships portrayed in that story were very real and intimately known.

There is no need to over-emphasize Page's sentimentality. The seemingly improbable plot of "Marse Chan," for instance, is, as Page explained in his introduction to the Plantation Edition, based on the real story of a soldier whose sweetheart had told him to come home only with honor, and who was killed shortly after. The real story involved a Georgia private and not an FFV, however.

Readers who want to read more of Page after *In Ole Virginia* might look at the story collection *The Burial of the Guns*, where they will find deft and realistic treatments of social issues. The title story concerns the War—heroism and pride in defeat. But the other stories are more contemporary: social hypocrisy and triumphant spinsterhood in "My Cousin Fanny"; alcoholism and post-war demoralization in "The Gray Jacket of No. 4"; deception and disappointed love in "Miss Dangerlie's

Roses"; and the sufferings and courage of the poorest class of white Southerners in "Little Darby." None of these stories would satisfy an exponent of French naturalism, but given the standards and tastes of the time, they deal with social issues in an unflinching way.

Superficially, Page fits perfectly with the prevailing historical stereotype of the Southern Bourbon. As misleadingly described in the works of C. Vann Woodward, the Bourbon was a member of the antebellum gentry who made his peace with Northern capital, uniting with the most exploitive elements of American society for his own profit, while diverting the South from its real problems by sentimentalizing its past.

Though this historical interpretation is widely accepted, it is not strictly true, in regard either to Page or to the politics of the leading class in the South after the War, Rather than aiding and abetting the vested interests of the age, Southerners quite often provided a leavening influence of old-fashioned liberalism in a rapacious, utilitarian society—which was a heritage of the plantation class and its preference for honor over profit, its distaste for ruthless individualism, and its purchase on the ethics of an earlier American republicanism that had been forgotten in the North.

Page's novel *Gordon Keith* (1903), though it is not a successful work of fiction, deals with the shallowness and vanity of modern New York society and its pursuit of wealth. And in *John Marvel, Assistant* (1909), he exhibits sympathetic interest in the plights of labor and of Jews. In the larger sense, he is a critic, not an abettor, of the abuses of the Gilded Age. Indeed, the planter class had always been the seat of American liberalism, ever since Mr. Jefferson had stood up to General Hamilton and his schemes.

The idea of the plantation rests most uneasily in the American consciousness. On the one hand, it has been determined to be the seat of all horror. On the other, it is inextricably tied to some of the highest moments and grandest personalities of American history. One suspects that most of the thousands of tourists who throng Mount Vernon and Monticello imagine them to be something like Ohio farms. But, of course, they are nothing of the kind; they are plantations, examples of the very society with which Page is concerned.

Americans are unable to deal with the plain fact that eight of our first twelve Presidents were the masters of plantations, not marginally but in their primary social identity, and resort to all sorts of subterfuges to thrust the fact from mind. But the essence of American nationality and American institutions lies in the plantation quite as much as in the New England town meeting, or more so. How do we reconcile this to the images that appear in *Roots* and a host of other less celebrated works?

It may be true that the plantation is something of another age and that it embodied evils that have now been happily surpassed; but that is not the whole story. Is it not better and truer to view the society that produced Washington and Jefferson and Lee in the light provided by Page than in the lurid colors of neo-abolitionist melodrama?

And why is it, if the plantation is a place of horror, that even today its relics give us a sense of peace and order, of communion with the roots of our society and a better past, while the vast expanses of modern urban democracy and egalitarianism give us only a sense of unease? We approach here some profound regions of the American soul, however strenuously denied, of which Page is the artistic medium.

Page's world is indeed an idealistic world, not likely to satisfy such modern types as the pragmatist, the utilitarian, the ideologue, or the cynic. And it is true that at times in his work such qualities as honor, duty, courage, and sacrifice approach an unpersuasive abstraction. But not always.

For Page does present human qualities and aspirations and behaviors that really did exist at one time. We know that people with the virtues he portrays did live. The heroism in adversity, the tragic deaths by battle and fever, the extravagant chivalric gestures, the sensitive pride, the aristocratic ethics, the unswerving loyalty, the affections between masters and servants, all really did exist, no matter how much moderns may choose to disbelieve them. They can be abundantly documented, to the satisfaction of any honest observer, in the hard documentary record of thousands of Southern families. It is just that now historians prefer to emphasize other things.

For us Page has made, in fiction, a number of satisfying human characters, characters who give us hope in the potential of our nature and who are models that we badly need of grace, courage, and honor. They are far more persuasive and useful than any number of politicians' and social scientists' paeans to democracy and progress, In that sense. Page is not so outdated as some think, and in fact will never be outdated. And, as well, *In Ole Virginia* is full of just plain good tales, well told, which is what a book of stories should be. (1991)

A Mirror for Artists

Cleanth Brooks on Faulkner

A review of *On the Prejudices, Predilections, and Firm Beliefs of William Faulkner*, by Cleanth Brooks, Baton Rouge: Louisiana State University Press, 1987, 162 pages.

The present belongs to the rich, the powerful, and the famous. But the past and the future belong to the powers of imagination. Some centuries, hence, the celebrities of our day—like Dan Rather or Michael Jackson—will be as utterly forgotten as the famous courtesans and gladiators of ancient Rome. Minor presidents will be but a name in the history books, like the forgotten triumvir Lepidus, while more important presidents will rate a few lines that will strike a pale glimmer of recognition among the better educated, as do Marius and Sulla today.

But at that future time intelligent men and women will, quite possibly, speak and write of Faulkner's America in somewhat the same fashion as they do now of Shakespeare's England or Virgil's Rome. Faulkner cast the consciousness of our time and country into the enduring form of great literature, and in the long run it is by literature that a people and an era are known.

In a dozen major works, out of which anyone may make his own choice of half-a-dozen masterpieces, the Mississippi storyteller recorded a vision of man's experience on this continent in the 19th and 20th centuries and placed that vision in a juxtaposition with God, nature, and history that will compel attention and generate meaning as long as civilization exists in anything resembling the form that we know it.

A great literary achievement is self-evident, or nearly so. It becomes itself a historical event, a benchmark for an era. It differs from public and collective historical events, however, in a significant respect. Historical events take on a certain inevitability and factuality. A great artistic achievement, on the other hand, though indispensable in understanding an era, is intrinsically improbable. Masterworks of the imagination, in the final analysis, cannot be explained by reference to the conditions of the time or the artist's experience or personality. They represent in some sense a stunning and unexpected intervention of the gods, an inspiration in the original signification of the term—the creation of something valid and true that did not exist before.

Surprised, we tend to doubt even the plain and self-evident aspects of a great piece of literature and to cast into unnecessary mystery and confusion those parts of the artist's life and work that are fairly easily understood. We make complications out of simple matters and simplifications out of mysterious ones. Consider all that has been said about Shakespeare, and how much of it has been sheer foolishness.

While the greatness of a literary corpus may be self-evident, it is not self-explanatory, and is bound to create a large and continuing commentary. A figure that looms as vast as Faulkner's will create around it the inevitable concomitants of commerce, in the same way that souvenir salesmen always appear on the outskirts of a tragedy or a miracle. Thus, Faulkner's home may be toured at times, for a fee; literary hacks who met him once in New York or Hollywood can sell their anecdotes to the Sunday supplements; and his works are peddled in lurid covers from drugstore racks and are turned into awful movies.

At a slightly higher level, Faulkner furnishes endless raw material for the flourishing industry of academic non-books. Any university press that puts out a tome with Faulkner in the title can hope to break even on library sales alone, and any petty scholar can win his modest day of glory (and tenure) by hacking and cutting at some small corner of the corpus until it fits, or seems to fit, whatever current intellectual fad is going the rounds. Faulkner is particularly appealing to a certain type of Southern pedant, ashamed of his origins, who hopes to put them behind him by positioning himself vis-à-vis Faulkner. Some have demonstrated to their own satisfaction that Faulkner was a renegade Southerner exactly like them. Others have demonstrated with equal conviction, to themselves, that Faulkner fell short by not being a sufficiently satisfactory renegade, unlike them.

Even if we limit ourselves to that commentary and criticism which is serious and valuable, we still have a large literature, international in scope. Indeed, it has often been the foreigners who have sooner and better understood what Faulkner told. The French did so early on. Remoter cultures, for instance Japan and the Islamic world, have produced valuable readings, as have some of the smaller nations of Europe, perhaps because during this century the smaller nations have lacked the comfortable illusions of security that the larger states have enjoyed, and thus have been closer to the primal experiences of life endured by Faulkner's white, black, and red Mississippians.

Not, however, the British. In an amusing essay, Cleanth Brooks shows how the hothouse literary criticism of Great Britain, with a few exceptions, has been and continues to be somehow incapable of understanding what Faulkner was about. Distinguished British critics are unable to apprehend the difference between Mississippi and Missouri and have dismissed as unrealistic and impossible passages of Faulkner dialogue the likes of which any Southerner has heard a hundred times before he was twelve.

To make sense out of his work, to set it in its just proportions and bounds, to cut through the confusions and complications that accrue from a proliferating commentary, a great writer needs what is as rare as himself—a great scholar. This is especially true if the body of work is large and complicated enough that the whole must be known before the main themes can be differentiated from the minor ones. And even more true if the writer himself did little to facilitate understanding and sometimes deliberately threw out fake scents, as Faulkner did when faced with unworthy or unseemly inquiries.

A great scholar Faulkner has found in the person of Cleanth Brooks. In addition to a large and varied contribution to other aspects of literary understanding in America, Brooks is the author of the definitive *William Faulkner: The Yoknapatawpha Country (1963) and William Faulkner: Toward Yoknapatawpha and Beyond* (1978). Still going strong in his eighty-second year, Brooks has just published a collection of twelve essays, originating as lectures, that take up various aspects of Faulkner which have proved troublesome to interpreters.

As Brooks well knows, a great literary achievement is vision, not opinion; art, not argument. The question of the writer's opinions or views is indeed a secondary, sometimes even a misleading, question. But it is nonetheless one we must ask: What did Shakespeare *really think* about royalty, religion, women, Jews? Such questions are inevitable, and even if at times they tend to divert our attention from the fruitful ambiguity of an artist's vision to the less important question of his opinions, they deserve answers.

These answers Brooks undertakes to provide for Faulkner. He does so out of a knowledge of Faulkner's discursive statements—his essays, speeches, interviews, letters, where he was speaking for himself and not for a character, but also, and more importantly, out of the text of his novels and stories. Out of these the sensible reader, like Brooks, who does not bring too many preconceptions, who knows the whole work, and who knows the context of the life and society out of which Faulkner came, can construct convincing answers to questions about Faulkner's beliefs.

To think of what Brooks is about as "criticism"—a bad word—is misleading because it brings to mind an esoteric exercise of expertise. There is nothing esoteric whatsoever about this book or anything else that Brooks has written. "The New Criticism," of which he is said to be a leader, is not a problem for Brooks, only for those who have made it into a straw man to attack or who have taken too literally and bureaucratically what it proposes.

Like all of the critics of the English-speaking tradition—Johnson, Lamb, Hazlitt—Brooks is simply a careful and honest reader who never loses sight of the connection between literature and life. There is no mystery or anything exotic about the process. Brooks is, in fact, though it has been little noted, not so much a literary critic as one of our great essayists. One has to read him on subjects that are not precisely literary matter—Southern religion, Southern speech, or the Episcopal prayer book controversy (a few examples)—to fully appreciate this.

Perhaps to place the truest value upon Brooks's achievement in the explication of Faulkner, one had best have some idea of the immense pile of errors and nonsense that exists in print on the subject. To have ploughed through this debris and rendered the essential points into plain sense is an accomplishment. Any intelligent reader, however, can appreciate the clarity, charity, sweet reasonableness, and profound but lightly worn learning evident in Brooks's style and matter.

Among other things, Brooks's latest book provides a good short course on how to read a serious novelist, and thus is an antidote to much silliness. Brooks's style is easy and conversational. While never condescending to the reader, he can make complex theological and philosophical points clear and relate them to Faulkner's vision with ease, As a result, the beliefs and ideas and "prejudices" that lay, in part, behind Faulkner's novels and stories emerge as clearly as they are ever likely to, and thus provide an indispensable basis for understanding those works.

The twelve essays are of two types. A few, like "The British Reception of Faulkner' mentioned above, take up secondary aspects of Faulkner's career. Another of this sort is the piece on the relationship between Faulkner and his Southern contemporaries, the Fugitive-Agrarians, a relationship that has been much puzzled over and often misunderstood. It is not true, as has frequently been suggested, that the Fugitive-Agrarians failed to recognize Faulkner or underrated or regarded him with hostility. Brooks delineates where their views and his displayed correspondences, and where they did not.

A larger group of essays consider separately aspects of Faulkner's views on such subjects as women, the family, the chivalric tradition, Christianity, community, history, and the American experience. With

Brooks's insights we learn as much as we are ever likely to know about how Faulkner thought and felt, and we build toward a picture not of Faulkner the artist, but of Faulkner the man, citizen, thinker, and commentator on public life.

In this respect perhaps the most interesting essay is "Faulkner and the American Dream." Here Brooks discusses the nonfiction work that was projected by Faulkner in his last years as "The American Dream: What Happened to It?" Some unconnected fragments of this were finished and a certain amount may be cautiously postulated about what the unfinished part might have contained. For Faulkner, the American Dream was an ancient Jeffersonian vision of individual freedom and virtue in community, not a slogan for the Wall Street Journal. It is a vision that we have moved so far away from that it is no longer recognized, even as an antiquity, but for Faulkner, it was a real though beleaguered ideal. To contemplate with Faulkner this ideal may teach us things about our present society that we are not likely to learn from our politicians, publicists, and pundits.

While there is nothing sacred about a great writer's public and political (in the broadest sense) opinions, an artist whose historical vision achieved the breadth and profundity of Faulkner's deserves at least as much of a hearing as a citizen as most of the persons whose opinions fill the print media and the air-waves. It is a little surprising that Faulkner's public statements, collected and published as long ago as 1966 by James B. Meriwether in *William Faulkner: Essays, Speeches, and Public Letters*, have not received more attention.

Anyone who wants to see how Faulkner applied his vision to contemporary affairs should read his speech to the Delta Council in Cleveland, Mississippi, made in 1952. On that occasion Faulkner expressed his fear that the noble postulation of the Declaration of Independence of the right to life, liberty, and the pursuit of happiness was in danger of becoming no more than a shorthand for material security and of losing its spiritual dimension and thus its nobility. Part of the value of Brooks's exposition is that he makes us aware of the roots and the applications of the vision of courage, honor, and community that suffuses Faulkner's fiction.

If Brooks's previous work on Faulkner provides the best introduction to one of the great literary achievements of our century, then his latest work provides the best preface to that work. It is perhaps the commentary with which the novice reader of Faulkner should begin. And the work he will want to come back to when everything else has been read. (1988)

Faulkner and Thomas Wolfe

A review of *Faulkner's Search for a South*, by Walter Taylor, Urbana: University of Illinois Press, 1987, 242 pages.

Posthumously, William Faulkner has achieved a celebrity that, if we take him at his word, he despised and eschewed, but which seems inseparable from modern commercial culture. Every second man in the street, who can't remember who is currently Vice-President, recognizes Faulkner's name as that of a famous writer. Every lumpen intellectual who once read *The Sound and the Fury* in a sophomore lit class feels qualified to "explain" Faulkner. Worse, Faulkner has become an industry. His home can be toured, at certain times, for a fee. Minor literati who met him once at lunch in New York or Hollywood can, with but slight embroidery, sell their recollections to the Sunday supplements. An academic press that publishes a book with Faulkner in the title will probably break even on library sales alone. Faulkner supports a whole scholarly phalanx, and there are undoubtedly people around who have made more money explicating and analyzing him than *he* ever made creating works of genius. (Admittedly, it is also true that several great scholars, who are perhaps as rare as great writers, have devoted careers to him, in both Europe and America.)

When a cultural phenomenon becomes as large as William Faulkner, liberals must be equipped to orient themselves to it. They must know what liberalism is supposed to say about the phenomenon, a process not unlike the way adolescents learn about Jordache jeans and members of fraternal orders acquire passwords and intricate handshakes. This need has created an entire school of literary criticism, of which *Faulkner's Search for a South* is an example.

The easiest tactic would be simply to postulate that Faulkner was a liberal. Aren't all wise and good men? Walter Taylor has taken a more honest, difficult, and sophisticated path. He admits that, after all, Faulkner was not a liberal. He flunked the ultimate litmus test—his attitudes toward Southern history and the race question never quite coincided with the attitudes decreed by liberal convention. But since these are the only possible attitudes for wise and good men, their absence in Faulkner presents an interesting phenomenon for scholarly description and explanation. Faulkner failed to find the South described by liberal convention. It is inadmissible that he may not have been looking for it. Therefore, that he did not find it is an interesting "failure" to be accounted for.

Thus, the "failure" that Faulkner himself sometimes spoke about, which generally has been interpreted as a felt failure of artistic realization, has metamorphosed, for Taylor, into a "failure" to find the right South. He kept searching for it but could never quite find it, according to Taylor, because of his commitment to the condescending, paternalistic outlook that turn-of-the-century Mississippi "aristocrats" developed as a counterweight to the unabashed racism of the "poor whites." This commitment was all the more poignant and ambiguous because of Faulkner's family's dubious position within the "aristocracy." Taylor makes his case with considerable skill and enterprise. However, to too great a degree one has to be willing to he persuaded by speculative biographical evidence like the following:

> The Faulkners *would never know* whether they were Cavaliers or rednecks, and not knowing would affect them profoundly.... For thirteen-year-old Bill Faulkner, trying to understand the family heritage *must have been* frustrating.... As Faulkner grew older, he *must have* grown increasingly aware that Vardaman's victory [over the "aristocrats" in Mississippi politics] was a pivotal event in his life....To twenty-five-year-old Faulkner, on the threshold of his career as a novelist, the episode [a scandal involving a politician who was once his grandfather's law partner *must have* spoken volumes. [**emphasis added**]

The trouble is, those of us who are not liberals feel restricted to writing biography from documentary evidence and to criticizing literature from a text. Further, Taylor's interpretation works only if we accept a simplistic scenario of Southern history as a conflict between "aristocrats" and "poor whites." (Any of Faulkner's works which cannot be made to conform to this scenario, like *The Unvanquished* or *The Reivers*, must be dismissed as "a mire of paternalistic propaganda," or "smug nostalgia," or "a parrotlike recreation of the Old Order's official rationale.") But one of the things that can he learned from Faulkner—or from anywhere else in Southern literature or history that one wants to look—is that the South has *always* been made up of a variety of middle classes as well as "aristocrats" and "poor whites." This is the beginning of all wisdom as far as the South is concerned, and it can be denied only under the strongest ideological imperative.

The effort to construe Southern history entirely in terms of the bipolar conflict of aristocrat and redneck leads to sonic strange twists in this work. For instance, we must accept that "aristocrats" have been "Cavaliers" and "poor whites" have been "Puritans." Southern poor whites traditionally have been blamed for every sin in the decalogue, but to find them characterized as the chief repositories of American "Puritanism" (a tortured term, here undefined), especially when construing a text, *Light in August,* which clearly deals with Northern Calvinists, is bizarre.

But at a more fundamental level, it seems to me, this treatment of Faulkner hopelessly blurs the line between a writer's life and times and his work. It is true, as Taylor quotes Ralph Ellison, that there is an "inescapable connection between the writer and the beliefs and attitudes current in his culture." But isn't the point of great literature that the connection is not simple, but rather complicated and original? One cannot understand any great literature until one understands that it is, in the first instance, vision and not opinion, description and not argument. Taylor is a Mississippian who has put the shame of his Southern origins behind him by adopting the conventional liberal view toward them. For him, Faulkner "failed" because he did not take the same route. But why must we assume that Faulkner ever wanted to find the South that Taylor has found, or that we would remember him if he had? May we not be forgiven for preferring the South that Faulkner did find, painful and ambivalent as it was for him and for us, to the more comforting but far less instructive one that he failed to find?

In essence, then, this work is merely another exercise in labeling that tells us more about the labeler than the labelee. It is one more installment in the Southern confession of sin, of which too much has already been inflicted upon the world. (1983)

***

A review of *Welcome to Our City: A Play in Ten Scenes*, by Thomas Wolfe, Baton Rouge: Louisiana State University Press, 1983, 132 pages.

Thomas Wolfe might be taken as the pioneer practitioner of the Southern confessional, but that would be only superficially true. While Wolfe wrote works that could be called confessional and his content was in part Southern, there was nothing intrinsically Southern about his confessional style. It was, rather, personal, and he often managed to turn his pain into artistic vision rather than political platitude, Secondly,

Wolfe's confessional could not be fully Southern because he was not. Like Mark Twain, Wolfe was a fringe Southerner. The Asheville of his boyhood was an unrooted tourist haven. He knew the South the way one knows a city that one has passed through on a highway. Ever after, the city looms in your mind characterized by the first glimpse of grimy industries and slums. You do not know how it really is to the people who belong there. That was pretty much Twain's and Wolfe's relation to the South—a gypsy one. Twain knew the South by the ugly backsides of river towns, under the bluff. Wolfe could never entirely separate the idea of the South from mountain boarding houses for tubercular tourists and the villas of rich interlopers. His idea of the South was not so much wrong as incomplete. Which is not to say that it could not achieve at times a compelling power and interest.

Welcome to Our City was performed twice at a Harvard workshop theater in 1923, to local acclaim. A text of the script of that performance is here published for the first time (an abridgment of a different version, which Wolfe failed to market on Broadway, was published in 1957 in *Esquire*). This publication thus fulfills a scholarly purpose, enlarging the available knowledge of Wolfe and of the literature of the 1920s.

The title of the play is ironic. Superficially, the play is a conventional 1920s attack on boosterism, a theatrical *Main Street* with a Southern setting. It is, in effect, about a scheme of politicians and real estate men in a small Southern city to snatch the central district from its traditional black residents.

Attacks on boosterism have rather faded with time and with the restoration of the notion that the decades hated by liberals (the 1920s and 1950s) were actually good times for us common folk. And intelligent people no longer take seriously reformers who believe that all would he right with the world if only we could clear the slums and suppress the fundamentalists. What makes Wolfe's play more than a dated, conventional attack on boosterism is its Southern setting. He has explosively wedded the race question to the genre. Further, the Southern context renders the elements of conflict ambivalent in another way. In Sinclair Lewis's *Midwest*, we find a clear confrontation between boosterism (greed and convention) on the one hand, and enlightenment (idealism and cosmopolitanism) on the other. But in the South, not only does the conflict of black and white complicate matters, but boosterism is itself complicated by an alliance—conflict with the remnants of the Old Order. (The Midwest has no Old Order.) In this situation, enlightenment is at times an ally of boosterism. Wolfe wrote before the stereotypes, in the South at least, had achieved finality. Thus, a progressive professor appears as a member of the booster coalition, and idealism, albeit a flawed and compromised version, is at least partly represented by an "Old Colonel" character, the remnant of a regime older and perhaps better than boosterism. Main Street was never this complicated.

Wolfe's treatment of the confrontation of races also preceded the hardening of stereotypes that began to take place in the 1930s and had become inviolable orthodoxy by the end of World War II. His blacks, like his Southern whites, are not sentimental heroes but tragically flawed characters. Neither blacks nor Southern whites will find themselves portrayed in a way that promotes a glow of warm contentment. Wolfe keeps his distance from both, and many of his characters are cruel caricatures. True, each one is a genuine and recognizable Southern type, but there is such an absence of positive types that a rounded picture does not emerge. Nevertheless, there is a brutal integrity in his observations.

Wolfe perhaps comes closer to a tragic, rather than a satiric, effect in his rendering of the interior racial dialogue of the South, a centuries-old phenomenon that has almost always been sentimentalized in American lore and literature. In the last scene, following the inevitable violent climax, an aging patrician and a reluctantly radical black patriarch are left to confront each other. "I belong to a day that is past!" laments the patrician. "An' wheah do I belong?" responds the black man. Wolfe's bitter detachment and lack of easy sentimentality doubtless explains why the play was never produced on Broadway and why it has remained largely unknown. (1983)

A Mirror for Artists

Homage to George Garrett

A review of *Poison Pen; Or. Live Now and Pay Later*, by George Garrett. Winston-Salem, North Carolina: Stuart Wright, 1986, 258 pages.

The conditions of modern culture involve us in painful but inescapable ambiguities. Politics, the noble pursuit of harmony and justice in community, cannot be separated from expediency, greed, fanaticism, and the vulgarities and superficialities of mass communications. Education, a high and essential calling, is entangled beyond recall with a bureaucracy of immense power and dubious social utility, Literature, which has traditionally enjoyed the allegiance of some of our best minds and most human aspirations, cannot be extricated from the imperious requirements of publicity and marketing.

Thus, in a society of immense wealth and population, anything that our forefathers would have regarded as a serious book is, at best, of marginal profitability. Publishing, once both a culturally esteemed and practically useful enterprise, now concerns itself largely with Jane Fonda exercise books, the memoirs of Lee Iacocca, the social reflections of Nancy Friday, and the art of Harold Robbins. A serious literary culture exists, or rather several serious literary cultures, within the increasingly imaginary borders of the United States, but in a fragmented and compromised state.

In fact, what usually passes for our serious literary culture, though it likes to think of itself as in perpetual heroic revolt against commerce and Establishments, prospers chiefly as a function of the business of publicity and itself constitutes an Establishment which ruthlessly enforces cultural and political conformity. With few exceptions (Bellow and Percy, for instance) those "serious" current writers who come readily to mind do so not because of their intrinsic superiority but because they are the ones selected, from among many others, to be published by the major New York houses, celebrated by the New York (it used to be Boston) critics, promoted by the major bookstore chains, studied in the prestigious Northeastern universities, and, as a simple reflection of the above, recognized as "important" by the federal public broadcasting and arts bureaucracies. (The proclivities of the last mentioned, as far as a somewhat distant observer can tell, have been little affected by the Reagan Revolution.)

It is no great exaggeration to stipulate that nearly every American writer of the last half century who is of any standing in the perspective of the ages has, at least at times, been "unknown" to the New York literary Establishment or has (like Faulkner) related to it in a state of barely suppressed outrage. And it is no accident that George Garrett, the author of *Poison Pen*, has been an active critic of the Establishment and in an "unknown" essay has written a devastating expose of the arts bureaucracy."[45] ("Unknown" = anything that is officially unrecognized in New York, although it may be "known" to thousands or even millions of people who don't count.) Writes Garrett in *Poison Pen*, referring to certain critics: "They are a tough bunch, Christie [Brinkley], and, like the rest of the Establishment, they pay only a pursed and puckered lip service to the battered old concept of free speech. Free speech is when *they* want to say something. Get it?"

These prefatory remarks are necessary for the uninitiated. For how else can we explain that this book, published by a small house specializing in limited editions of established Southern greats, is by a writer of major stature (though relatively an "unknown" to celebrity) and that it may well prove to be (though that remains to be seen) one of the most significant American novels of social commentary in our century.

Had George Garrett stopped writing at the age of forty (about 1970) he would have already established a big space for himself, in any objective canon of American literature. He could not reasonably be excluded from any list of the dozen or so most important poets of the post-war period. He had a secure place in the short story anthologies. He had achieved some critically successful screenwriting. And he had published several novels that were masterful treatments of the social and moral ambiguities of the New South and post-war American society. (Black comedy would be a handy and not entirely misleading label for their genre.)

Such versatility is an impressive achievement, both of character and skill, considering the commercial and psychological pressures that must propel any moderately successful writer to make his current work resemble his last successful one. Beginning in the 1970s, however, Garrett broke more barriers. He established himself as an able teacher of writing at Princeton, Bennington, Michigan, South Carolina, and most recently Virginia—to the degree that he has been a mentor to a considerable portion of the best young writers of the day. In addition, he

---

45 "Southern Literature Here and Now," in *Why the South Will Survive, by Fifteen Southerners* (Athens: University of Georgia Press, 1981).

produced an amazing and unexpected literary, cultural, and historical feat: his novels *Death of the Fox* (1971) and *The Succession: A Novel of Elizabeth and James* (1983).

It was thought that the historical novel had long ago exhausted its possibilities. Yet Garrett, in these two books, brought to life Elizabethan England in a way that was at the time audaciously innovative in technique, intensely modern in consciousness and profoundly traditional in values. In so doing he demonstrated that it was still possible for a modern American writer to make contact with the pristine English language, the authentic religious belief, and the terrible immediacy of both glory and disaster that marked Shakespeare's England.

Though formally distinct from *Poison Pen*, these novels provide, implicitly, a key to understanding the import of *Poison Pen*. Unless seen in the light of these earlier works, Poison Pen's devastating parody of contemporary America could be mistaken for a product of nihilistic despair, despite its sustained hilarity. But seen in that light it takes on the coloration of social conservatism (in the profoundest sense) and Christian affirmation that marks great satire in the English tradition.

One notable characteristic of Garrett's work, particularly evident in the Elizabethan novels, is its masculine voice. Our intellectual culture has, since the first third of the 19th century, become increasingly feminized. There have been occasional revolts. Hemingway and Mailer essayed a masculine voice, though what they often achieved was an unintended parody. By a masculine voice is meant not technique or subject matter but, in a profound sense, the tone and perspective of the writer. James Jones, to whom Garrett was a friend and biographer (1984), had it, though, I would suggest, at a lower level of talent than Garrett's own.

Our historical fiction tends at its worst toward soap opera and in its better manifestations toward tapestry weaving—both feminine pursuits. Faulkner's voice was a masculine one—that of the country lawyer-hunting camp raconteur. Garrett's is that of an old soldier. An old soldier telling tales in a tavern—bawdy, skeptical, ready for anything. An old soldier who has buckled on his harness and gone over the top more times than he can remember; who has seen all of the best and worst that is to be seen in man and woman, leader and comrade; who has accepted as reality and come to terms with the terrifying moral ambiguity and physical contingency of individual human existence.

Old soldiers are disillusioned with all that passes for commonplace virtues and everyday securities; yet at the bottom they have not nihilistic despair but a lean belief in the essential realities of courage, hope, love, and the simple affirmations of the Book of Common Prayer. One of Garrett's Elizabethans comments that the bravest and most sacrificial act he ever witnessed was that of the man on his way to the gallows who cursed his wife and children and kicked his dog.

The masculinity of Garrett's voice reveals itself also in its striving, its audacity, and its irreverence. His work embodies the joyous testing of skills on new frontiers, a restless dissatisfaction with what has already been accomplished. *Poison Pen*, in more than one respect and in its own way, is as daring as the feats of Evel Knievel or Chuck Yeager. And Garrett's old soldier, though capable of a profound dignity and respect for that which deserves it, is at the same time subject to fits of irrepressible and high-spirited aggression against conventions and pieties that he sees as serving pretense and privilege rather than truth and order.

The protagonist of *Poison Pen* is one John Towne. Towne is a full-time con artist, misanthrope, and lecher. He is a sometime porn writer, mercenary, impersonator of black Southern Protestant clergymen, and professor of English. Towne, arguably, could hold his own with the best of Evelyn Waugh's creations. He expresses his misanthropy and anti-social destructiveness (or his clear-sighted realism and just indignation, if you wish) by writing letters, from a variety of adopted personae, to American celebrities—letters that commence with a certain plausibility and develop into masterpieces of comic insanity (or sanity, if you wish).

Structurally, it is all a little confusing. We know Towne, except for his letters, only through Holmes, a lazy and befuddled English professor at an obscure women's college in Southwest Virginia, who is Towne's somewhat unwitting and unwilling literary executor. The author, George P. Garrett, Jr., occasionally intrudes with evident embarrassment and awkwardness into what may be loosely called the narrative, since no better term occurs to me. He, too, writes letters to celebrities. To make matters even more confusing, Towne is the author of two unpublished novels, *Life with Kim Novak Is Hell* and *Realms of Gold*, the latter of which concerns one R.C. Alger, a descendant of Horatio Alger, who also writes nasty letters under assumed names. *Poison Pen* obviously and deliberately stretches the conventions of the novel. Whether or to what degree it is successful in a technical sense can be left for the literary gents and ladies who concern themselves with that sort of thing. They will probably be some time working it out, and their answer will very possibly be negative.

For observers of society the meat is in the "poison pen" of John Towne—his letters to the likes of Bo Derek and James Farmer, Timothy Leary and Jimmy Carter, Teddy Kennedy and Truman Capote, Mrs. De Lorean, and many others. Letters by which a great many of the inanities, outrages, and immoralities of American life are brilliantly uncovered for those who have eyes to see (or, if you will, by which cherished institutions and noble persons are subjected to brutal and unfair assault). Imagine a sincere convert to the "Playboy Philosophy" writing to Hugh Hefner for advice—a convert who, we gradually learn, is a victim of cerebral palsy and is at a loss how to implement his newfound but hard-won and deeply felt philosophy. Or imagine the president of the South Texas Pancho Villa Club inquiring politely of Lyndon Johnson about the terms of compensation for non-citizen multiple voting. I will give away no more. That is enough for anyone to determine for himself whether to regard John Towne as the funniest man to come along in years or as a menace to human decency. Possibly he is both.

In *Poison Pen*, Garrett can be compared most obviously with Waugh. But that does not go far enough. Mix in some Juvenal and a dash of Lucius Apuleius, some Swift and Sterne, some of the more bawdy and cynical passages of the Elizabethans and Jacobeans. And there appears to be something of the rank flavor of "Sut Lovingood," a character of the antebellum Southern writer George Washington Harris, of whom Huck Finn was a pale derivative.

Bring this style to the subject matter of contemporary America in order that we may see it in a way it has never been seen (in print) before—its cults of celebrities and sex goddesses; the preposterous propensity of its intellectual classes to honor and reward the destructive and anti-social and despise the normative and honest; the incredible (considered from the point of view of their private characters and talents) poltroons and mediocrities who have achieved the highest public office and influence in the last half century. Add to this our tendency to commercialize or bureaucratize every creative insight and decent instinct, as well as our progressive incapacity to distinguish between public image and private reality. Mix in also the bathos of the middle-aged author coming to terms with frustrated ambitions, and the middle-aged male facing the sad realities of declining physical powers.

Of course, it has been fashionable and safe for a century to bash American society. But Garrett's John Towne definitely does not suffer from "selective indignation." He bashes Goldwater and Reagan, the FBI and the IRS, fundamentalists and the corporate culture. But, alas, he has no decent respect toward those other and better things of which no man can speak except in tones of hushed reverence—John Kennedy, the civil rights movement, progressive clergymen, sex therapists, the political and ethnic pieties of the civics text, and the most distinguished authors of the day.

On the face of it, *Poison Pen* is an egregious exercise in bad manners—in every conceivable sense and to such an extent that we might easily be misled as to the author's intentions. Misled if we did not know that Garrett has written earlier, in an essay on Southern literature:

> Manners represent a formal obligation to one's neighbor (who is always Everyman) and the ritual recognition of the love of God and for the presence of the Holy Ghost in all of one's fellow creatures. Therefore an act of bad manners may well be, to the Southerner, an act of violence. A violation of the code of manners may well be taken as at least meaning the same thing as a fist in the face or a blade between the ribs.[46]

Seen from the standpoint of antique courtesy, we may begin to suspect that *Poison Pen* represents not a capitulation to bad manners but an outrage, expressed by parody, at a society that has not bad manners but no manners at all. *Poison Pen* merely reveals the logic of that large segment of America in which all distinctions of age, sex, condition, achievement, and virtue, all dignity and ceremony, have been washed into an immense cesspool of egalitarianism, superficiality, puerile candor, and image-mongering.

A similar point may be made about the language of *Poison Pen*, which is pervasively obscene, yet employed by an author whom we know to be steeped in the Elizabethans and the Southern oral tradition and to be capable of the most skillful and creative employment of that noble instrument the English language (called by Waugh "incomparably the richest of languages, dead or living"). An author who we know also has defended that language in ringing terms against the contempt shown by a leading member of the New York Establishment, the poet-critic Robert Bly, who referred to it as a vestige of colonialism and as "the alien English element" in America that needed to be cast aside. What is going on here? The pervasive obscenity of Poison Pen is the artist's parodic response to a society in which the once manly and creative art of swearing has given way to a compulsive, repetitive, filthy-mouthedness

---

46   *Ibid.*, p. 138.

of both sexes among a people lost to imagination, courtesy, and a sense of fitness and occasion.

If Garrett's voice is masculine, it is also Southern, a characteristic that must be pointed out because, though it is acknowledged by the author and evident in our remarks on manners and language, it is not necessarily obvious. Recently Garrett publicly reiterated his debt to the Fugitive writers for their example and encouragement. In fact, his earlier novels can be likened in some respects to Warren, and the Elizabethan novels carry echoes of Andrew Lytle's *At the Moon's Inn* and *Alchemy*, But, Garrett admitted, he was not always a lawful disciple, because he was "sassy and irreverent and indifferent to ... certain standard rules and regulations of Fugitive fiction."[47]

The Fugitives and their "lawful" disciples, whatever their subject matter or private persona, maintained a certain decorum of public discourse and deference to the classic unities that Garrett most certainly does not observe in *Poison Pen*. Very possibly, had he done so, he might have written a more effective and enduring book. But possibly also, he decided correctly that the cultural metastasis at work in the postwar world is so fast-acting that only the most radical treatment has any hope of arresting it and that the patient is so distracted from his true condition that one must go to the extremest lengths to get his attention. (1986)

***

A review of *Entered From the Sun*, by George Garrett, New York: Doubleday, 1990, 349 pages.

It would not be entirely wrong, I suppose, to describe George Garrett's most recent novel as a murder mystery or detective thriller, for the investigation of a violent death (that of the poet and playwright Christopher Marlowe in 1593) is the focus of the plot of *Entered From the Sun*. However, that description would be a little like saying that *Moby Dick* is a story about a boat trip or that *King Lear* is about the hardships of old age before Social Security.

In *Entered From the Sun*, Garrett continues the stunning fictional exploration of Elizabethan England begun in his *Death of the Fox* (1971) and continued in The Succession 1983). *Death of the Fox* tells of the downfall and execution of Sir Walter Raleigh in 1618,

---

[47] *Dictionary of Literary Biography Yearbook 1985*, edited by Jean W. Ross (Detroit, Michigan: Gale Research Company, 1986), p. 184.

and *The Succession* centers on the rise of James I to the English throne in 1603. *Entered From the Sun*, though published last, precedes the other two books chronologically. In the trilogy, it is a kindred and distinct performance, yet a prologue rather than an equal partner, because *Entered From the Sun* is shorter and of lesser historical scope than the other two.

Garrett's Elizabethan novels have, unexpectedly, breathed new life into what many thought of as the exhausted and trivialized genre of the historical novel by bringing vividly home to a modern audience one of the great ages. Elizabethan England saw, with respect to literature, statecraft, religion, and the embrace of the terrible burden of freedom for the individual human conscience, the birth of the modern world, or at least that part of it made up by the English-speaking peoples. (Though Garrett does not make a point of this, it was in addition the age of the births of Virginia and Massachusetts and thus of the United States, so that the author has made a profound though indirect contribution to understanding of American history.)

But this does not exhaust what Garrett has done in these books. He has not only recovered the historical age at the core of the modern English-speaking world. He has also, this time through the emblematic mystery of Christopher Marlowe, plumbed the even greater mystery of human existence itself in a way that will leave no serious reader unmoved.

Though dead before he was thirty, Christopher Marlowe attained a permanent place in English literature. As a lyric and dramatic poet, he was the author, among much else, of the enduring poems that begin "Come live with me and be my love" and "Whoever loved that loved not at first sight?" And those lines (from *Doctor Faustus*) of Helen of Troy that commence, "Was this the face that launched a thousand ships / And burned the topless towers of Ilium?"

Marlowe was the first great playwright of the Elizabethan stage. In him we see the transition from medieval drama to the great poetry, tragedy, comedy, and history, the unmatched exploration and evocation of human experience that made the Elizabethan stage one of the greatest ages of literature. In a series of dramas composed in quick succession in the 1580s (*Doctor Faustus*, *Tamburlaine the Great*, *The Jew of Malta*, and *Edward the Second*), Marlowe anticipated almost every range and nuance of Shakespeare's greatness. Indeed, in *Entered From the Sun*, Shakespeare is still a promising newcomer, known more as a player and manager than a playwright, and considered a skillful borrower rather than an original genius.

Marlowe's genius is a given. The matter at hand is the mystery of his life and of his death. There seems little question that he was a rake, drunkard, and brawler—all behaviors commonplace for his time and situation and not the least unusual in any age for those touched by the glory and burden of poetic genius. But what about the charges of perversion and atheistic blasphemy? Were these slanders circulated by political and literary enemies or was there substance to the charges?

Was Marlowe, during his sojourn in France and at other times, a government spy gathering information about those Englishmen who retained the Roman faith? Or was he, perhaps, himself a secret adherent of that faith and thus a potential rebel and traitor to the English throne and church? For this was the age, we can never forget, when England maintained a desperate and ruthless position between the great Catholic powers of Europe on the one hand and Puritanism and other forms of domestic dissent on the other.

The sudden, violent, and early death of such a man can but heighten the mystery. Thus, Garrett has put at the center of his book a genuine mystery that touches all the complicated strands of the age. It is a real mystery, not like the pseudo-mystery of Shakespeare's authorship or non-authorship of Shakespeare's plays. The mystery allows Garrett to explore the ambiguous relationship between appearance and reality, play-acting and "real life." They are not all that easy to tell apart at any time, the author seems to be saying, but at no time less so than England in the reign of Elizabeth I.

Marlowe's death occurred in an unlicensed suburban London inn not far from where the queen was temporarily in residence. He was killed at the end of a day of relatively quiet drinking, dining, and gaming with three companions, all of whom were well known as unscrupulous pursuers of gain and occasional secret agents. What was Marlowe doing there? What actually happened in that room where he met his death from a knife into the brain? And why? A coroner's jury, on the evidence of the only available witnesses, his three companions, found that Marlowe's killer had acted in self-defense, in fear of his own life, after being attacked and cut by Marlowe, who, it was well known, was subject to fits of violence. But was this all there was to it?

In Garrett's novel, various ambitious lords and politico-religious factions, the struggle among whom for preponderance in the kingdom makes up so much of the politics of Elizabeth's reign, become interested in the answers to these questions. Interested enough to pursue prolonged, ruthless, and secret investigations into the matter of Marlowe's death. It is the fictional device of multiple, parallel, and secret inquiries into the Marlowe mystery that make up the novel and allow Garrett to bring in historical figures like Elizabeth, the Earl of Essex, Sir Walter Raleigh, the Walsinghams, and the playwrights Thomas Kyd, Robert Greene, and William Shakespeare.

The device allows Garrett to deploy and explore various lesser, fictional characters whose fates give us insight into the age. Three of them are unforgettable: Captain William Barfoot, scarred soldier and scion of the Catholic Northern gentry ruined by rebellion in the previous generation; Joseph Hunnyman, handsome and ambitious and ambiguous part-time stage player; and the Widow Alysoun, one of those women one meets once or twice in a life-time-beautiful enough to have her way with the world, and what is much rarer, with a masculine will and ambition strong enough to actually try it.

We are alternately stunned and elated by Garrett's knowledge of Elizabethan England in all its aspects, tangible and intangible—its everyday life, class structure, customs, opinions, beliefs, fears, assumptions, technology, politics, religion, dress, and literature, as well as its larger complexities and tendencies. To the knowledge of a superior historian Garrett adds the imaginative power of an artist. Even before the Elizabethan novels, Garrett had a secure place as a poet and short story writer. The trilogy lifts him to even greater status among American writers.

History serves Garrett as it served Shakespeare, as the enveloping action for exploration of the eternal mystery of human consciousness and fate. All of the fictional characters are mysteries, to the reader and to themselves. They are inhabitants of the age in which manners and outward appearances are brought to their greatest power—when appearances are reality. The high manners of Elizabeth's reign grow out of, represent, mask, and try to make bearable a world in which every day and every night is a gamble against deadly violence, the caprice of rulers and great lords, and the ruthlessness of religious absolutes. It is an age in which the Black Plague descends repeatedly. It is an age well suited to reveal the terrible moral and physical ambiguity and contingency of human existence.

Although both a murder mystery and a historical novel, *Entered From the Sun* is also a drama—a tragedy—though in the form of a novel. Characters enter and depart and reenter. Scenes shift constantly.

The story is told in scenes, with just enough stage direction to give the players—and the reader—context.

In spirit, *Entered From the Sun* approaches an Elizabethan drama within the forms of a modern novel. Garrett's language is not blank verse or strictly Elizabethan, however; it is Elizabethan in spirit, not in form. We should remember that this was the age in which life was most like drama and drama most like life. Drama is an ideal form for conveying horrifying juxtapositions of glory and despair, the relentless immediacy of a fall from grace and death, and burdensome ambiguities of motives, actions, and fates.

Garrett's view of the world is totally without illusion. It does not shrink from acknowledging the worst and lowest that is in mankind. It is subject to fits of boisterous irreverence against the everyday consolations of bourgeois existence. Yet, at bottom, his vision is not nihilistic but indomitable and redemptive. It is the voice of a very tough yet fundamentally Christian outlook, hardened and uninnocent but not defeated, accepting the mystery of God's handiwork in this world even under an unflinching knowledge of the tragedy of man's lot. The voice in *Entered From the Sun* is also an aristocratic voice—a remnant of a tradition in which the aristocracy was still involved in the perils of risk, decision, and leadership as well as the comforts of privilege.

Richard M. Weaver wrote in *Visions of Order*: "The more man is pressed with the tragic nature of his lot, the more he dramatizes his relation with the world." This captures the center both of Elizabethan drama and Garrett's writing. In an essay on the failings of modern drama, published in *The Reactionary Imperative*, M.E. Bradford amplifies by reminding us what drama is and where it comes from: "To begin with, we must remember that all theatre has its primordial origins in religious feeling, in some sense of the providentially given features of our condition as contingent beings, of human limits—and their source." *Entered From the Sun* is a tough, irreverent (to many things, though not all), and raw portrayal of life. It is also an antique act of devotion that brings the reader through terror and despair into a glimpse of the sun.

Though an essential part of the trilogy, *Entered From the Sun*, exciting as a story and as an exercise of fictional craft, seems to me the least of the three books—perhaps because its theme is of smaller historical scope; perhaps because Garrett's achievement, like any great act, is now so established, so much with us, so obvious that it seems too easy and we expect too much. And we cannot experience again the stunned amazement that we enjoyed with the first reading of *Death of the Fox.*

Nevertheless, we now have in this completed trilogy a masterpiece, as imperishable as anything can be in this flawed and transitory world of ours—a world whose apprehension has been highlighted and enhanced by the art of George Garrett. (1990)

***

A review of *Whistling in the Dark: True Stories and Other Fables*, by George Garrett, New York: Harcourt Brace Jovanovich, 1992, 225 pages.

Poetry, short story, novel, drama, screenplay, criticism, the teaching of writing: George Garrett has excelled across the entire spectrum of literary art. I can call to mind no other contemporary American writer who approaches this feat, though perhaps Garrett's friend Fred Chappell comes closest. But what is even rarer for a first-rank artist, Garrett also excels in the essay, in the explicit and direct examination of the world.

As the American novel became more and more solipsist in style and trivial in subject matter, Garrett went in the opposite direction. If he had stopped writing at 40 (more than 20 years ago) he would already have had an enduring space in the poetry and fiction anthologies. But rather than coast along comfortably repeating himself, Garrett leapt new and higher barriers, producing the stunning and unexpected achievement of his Elizabethan novels: *Death of the Fox* (1971), *The Succession: A Novel of Elizabeth and James* (1983), and *Entered From the Sun* (1990).

In so doing, Garrett brought to life a critically formative period of the world we live in, and did so in a way that was audacious in technique, intensely modern in consciousness, and profoundly traditional in values. He demonstrated also that it was still possible for an American writer (or at any rate an American Southern writer) to make creative contact with the pristine and vigorous English language, the authentic religion, and the terrible contingency and ambiguity of human life that marked Shakespeare's England. And since out of Shakespeare's England was founded Virginia, the restoration was a part of American history as well.

More recently Garrett the essayist has taken for his field contemporary American life and letters. So along with two collections of literary comment— *My Silk Purse and Yours and The Sorrows of Fat City*—he has provided us with a sort of memoir, *Whistling in the Dark*, which allows us to begin to understand something of where his great books came from. Of course, art of this stature comes from God—the original and root meaning of inspiration—but we still need to understand the human and historical means by which the divine plan was worked out in the writer George Garrett.

This is not a book about literature per se and certainly not a sordid and self-serving account of cash advances gained, prizes won, and celebrities met. When Garrett writes about literature he does one of three things: tells a good story; gives generous praise where it is deserved, especially to the under-rewarded (and no writer is more generous to his contemporaries); or gets in a couple of quick devastating punches to the solar plexus of over-rated Northeastern literary celebrities.

Whistling in the Dark is a collection of the meditated experiences that made the writer. For instance, we learn how the "selfish intensity" of his youthful conditioning as boxer and footballer helped to shape a literary career and point of view. And we see Garrett the young soldier in the heart of Europe in the intense early days of the Cold War, standing in a weeping crowd of Austrians to greet a trainload of broken POWs returning from Russian captivity years after the war is over. "I stand there knowing one thing for certain—that I am seeing our century, our time, close and truly."

The recollections flow from a Southern sense of family as the essential unit of society. So that Garrett's Confederate great-grandfather is an integral part of his experience, along with all the generations in between and now—a proliferating connection centered in old hardscrabble prewar Florida. In Southern life there are no alienated individuals; there are families living, for better or worse, in real time and place. Therefore, American history is not a reservoir of officially approved slogans and abstract propositions, but a living experience. For this reason, Garrett can in three-and-a-half pages say more that is original, true, and significant about the Civil War than any number of pompous pseudo-intellectuals in 15 hours of government-subsidized TV.

The writer who emerges from this rich context is not the logistical manager of a career; he is a child of history and a part of it. If we are going to have cultural relativism, Garrett observes, let's really have it. Let's forgive other generations for the sin of not being like us, as well as other cultures:

> Much was probably wrong with old America… and eager historians are busy telling us as much about their sins and follies as they

can find out or imagine. But somehow ... the old Americans created the place and above all the climate of social hope and political liberty....This was their intention. This was their triumph. It cannot be revised away by anyone except a liar.

And it must be forgiven by anyone who is a Christian. After all, they were our people.

Garrett's view of the world is tough, irreverent, and unillusioned. Yet we find, at bottom, not the cheap nihilistic despair of contemporary fiction but a lean residue of belief in the essential realities of faith, hope, courage, truth, and love. It is a perfect expression of Richard Weaver's "sentiment not sentimentality." One of Garrett's Elizabethan characters comments that the most heroic action he ever saw was that of a man on his way to the gallows who cursed his wife and children and kicked his dog.

So, we find in the works of Garrett the consciousness that marks Christian civilization still alive in high art and in a time of troubles and a century of horrors. From this we can take some hope, though not fatuous optimism. As Garrett writes, after looking over the photo images of our Civil War forebears:

> Something has happened to the American face.... Somehow the standard-issue American face has changed over from its apparent material of cut stone, poured bronze, or whittled hardwood into something else, something much like molded plastic or (on a bad day) Silly Putty. And smiling. Almost always smiling.

This mingling of artistic imagination and empirical observation, which penetrates at once to the heart of matters, is what we have come to expect from our most consummate man of letters in this late day. (1993)

A Mirror for Artists

A Bow to the Ladies

A review of *Understanding Mary Lee Settle*, by George Garrett, Columbia: University of South Carolina Press, 1988, 187 pages.

One useful way to distinguish between types of novelists is to characterize them as either intensive or extensive. An intensive novel, much the more common variety in modern times, deals with a small segment of individual experience and consciousness, wringing from it the maximum psychological meaning. Though it may encompass intensive experiences, an extensive novel, more common in earlier times, paints with a broad brush and achieves social and historical complexity.

When a writer does both of these things at a high level, and can even combine them successfully into a seamless whole, then one begins to think in terms of "great" and "enduring." This characterization fits Faulkner, Conrad, Hardy, Dostoyevsky, and Solzhenitsyn. And, according to the novelist and poet George Garrett, our relatively unknown contemporary American and Southern writer, Mary Lee Settle, will, in the long view, find a place in this company.

Writing of Settle's, *The Beulah Quintet*, which makes up the largest part, but by no means all, of her work, Garrett says, "No other serious American novelist of Settle's generation—that generation which came to literary prominence in the years following World War II—has chosen to attempt anything so large and ambitious.... Settle's remarkable accomplishment stands alone in its time."

Garrett, in the little handbook to Settle's work called *Understanding Mary Lee Settle*, displays in detail why he thinks this is so, in terms of both technical literary achievement and social significance. Though this judgment may not have yet found a home in the most fashionable circles of organized literary culture (there were protests from New York when Settle won the National Book Award for *Blood Tie* in 1978), Garrett does not stand alone. The critic William F. Ryan writes: "Mary Lee Settle may well be determined as the 20th century American novelist who most splendidly recorded the passion and ideals of our history." Writes Roger Shattuck: "The crucial scenes of the series [*The Beulah Quintet*] give mythic scope to the classic American pioneer story."

Official modern taste is definitely existential and prefers the intensive to the extensive. It is uncomfortable with fiction that achieves a complexity of social and historical vision. Why this is so is an interesting realm for speculation—perhaps because historical complexity always introduces ambiguity and thus undermines the most fashionable liberal clichés. Just to deal with recent Southern writers, one thinks immediately of the popularity of Flannery O'Connor and Eudora Welty, who plow a narrow segment of human experience for all it is worth, with great artistry but without any social or historical breadth, except perhaps inferentially. Among the men, Walker Percy and Reynolds Price fall into the same intensive category. Percy portrays the consciousness and circumstances of the contemporary South perceptively, but nowhere does he achieve much historical depth, at least not without a great deal of exegesis outside of the books themselves. If he did, he would be as good as or better than he is, and much less popular. In *The Killing Ground* Mary Lee Settle takes up Percy's theme, the consciousness of the 20th century Southerner buffeted between heritage and modernity. Because she does so against a deep historical background and without Percy's intimations of the supernatural, it is possible that she does so more successfully, though in a way that is less accessible and has less broad appeal.

By both the nature of her work and her uneven reception, Settle cannot be likened to O'Connor or Welty. A closer analogy, perhaps, would be Katherine Anne Porter. But a nearer likeness can be drawn to Elizabeth Maddox Roberts, a now almost forgotten giant from the early part of this century and the grandmother of modern Southern writers. Like Settle, she combined the intensive and the extensive into a seamless whole. In *The Great Meadow* Roberts rendered the American pioneer experience into art as well as it has ever been rendered, and in *The Time of Man*, which deals with the poorest of white Southerners on the land, she achieved an experiential intensity of such heartbreaking lyrical beauty that, were Americans a people who really valued literature, she would today be a cult figure.

Another likeness can be made to Caroline Gordon, a Southern writer who, like Settle, combined existential intensity and historical vision. As does *The Great Meadow*, Gordon's novels of the 19th century South, like *Penhally* and *None Shall Look Back*, anticipate parts of Settle's *Beulah Quintet* in their portrayal of the imperatives and ambiguities of Southern history. *None Shall Look Back* appeared at about the same time as *Gone with the Wind* and dealt with the same subject: the experiences of Southern families, especially the women, in the Civil

War. Now forgotten, Gordon's work encompasses ten times the truth and beauty of the popular classic.

Settle, who in speeches and interviews has had a good deal to say about the nature of literary reputation, would probably prefer to be forgotten and under-rated like Roberts and Gordon than to suffer the fate of Marjorie Kinnan Rawlings, the last likeness that will be drawn to replace Settle in a developmental perspective. Rawlings resembles Settle in the clarity and unsentimental hard-headedness of her vision of contemporary life and in a career of heroic craftmanship and perseverance against non- and mis-recognition. Rawlings, a very serious writer, suffered from having her beautiful pastoral story, *The Yearling*, made into a lachrymose Disney movie, so that ever after she has been thought of, when remembered at all, as a sentimental juvenile writer, something very far from the truth. More recently, her semi-fictional memoir *Cross Creek,* a profound and honest appreciation of her struggles with nature and of the lives of her white and black neighbors in the Florida "cracker" country, also suffered the Hollywood treatment. The film version of *Cross Creek*, starring a ludicrously miscast Mary Steenburgen, turned the work into a weird and utterly unfaithful rendering of wimpish feminism meets Tobacco Road. One is thankful that Hollywood has not yet seen *O Beulah Land* or *The Scapegoat* (from *The Beulah Quintet*) as hot properties.

Settle's biography is complex, and is dealt with briefly and sometimes elliptically in *Understanding Mary Lee Settle*, as it relates to understanding her work. First, is her genteel Southern background (born 1918) centered in Charleston, West Virginia, which as "Canona" is the central place of *The Beulah Quintet*. This is followed by an incomplete education at Sweetbriar College, a brief stint on the stage, service in England during World War II, a journalistic career, and then a long period of laborious and unrewarded dedication to writing—punctuated by poverty, several marriages, long residences abroad in odd places such as Turkey, and a successful bout with cancer. Finally, in the 1970s, she received a National Book Award, a considerable though mixed critical recognition, and an appointment at the University of Virginia.

One of the things that first must be said about Mary Lee Settle is that her corpus of fiction is so large, so varied, and so good that it cannot be characterized in brief fashion. Like the best writers, or the best anything, she has continually set herself new challenges.

Her literary achievement could, however, be divided into two categories, one typified by the five novels of *The Beulah Quintet*, and the other by her international or cosmopolitan novels, *Blood Tie and Celebration*. A considerable portion of her other work can be loosely related to these categories.

Among these books, mention should certainly be made of her World War II memoir, *All the Brave Promises: Memoirs of Aircraft Woman 2nd Class 2146391* (1966). Settle was an early American volunteer for the Women's Auxiliary of the Royal Air Force. The book is first of all an account of this unusual experience. But Settle's gifts have made it much more, and it may not be too much to say that there is nothing like it in the literature of the war, certainly not in English. *All the Brave Promises* achieves a moving universality in plumbing the experiences of Western man (and woman) in the 20th century, as a cog in an immense, impersonal, and often incomprehensible machine. I can think of no other work of either fact or fiction from the war that succeeds so well on both levels: as vivid personal experience and as allegory. Charles B. MacDonald's *Company Commander* equals it in vividness but not in literary skill or philosophical depth. The fictional accounts of Anthony Powell, Evelyn Waugh, and James Jones tell us much about the meaning of the experience but lack the hard edge of reality that marks *All the Brave Promises* from the first to the last word.

The five novels of *The Beulah Quintet* constitute an epic of American history through the story of a group of interrelated families who settled in the mountain valleys of what became West Virginia in the 18th century. The books were not written in chronological order. Each stands alone as a novel and each reflects a different set of approaches and techniques. Garrett, himself an accomplished historical novelist, well describes the creative impulses that went into the series, its growth and development, and the array of devices, some of them "daring and risky," that are employed.

The epic stretches from the English Civil Wars of the 17th century almost to the present. One of the daring elements is that the books do not tell a continuing story in a literal sense, but drop into history at widely separated points. They are joined together (like real history) by a continuity of families and by an unbroken though largely unconscious chain of memory.

The families include what in Southern terms would be considered both the gentry and the yeomanry, perhaps as well some who could be considered "hillbilly" or "poor white." To these are later added other elements: 19th century Irish immigrants, and a mulatto branch of the central family, the Laceys. The novels vary in the degree to which they are intensive or extensive, but each has a rich range of interrelationships between families, generations, men and women, and surrounding society.

Prisons (1973), which could stand alone as an impressive feat of historical fiction, begins the story of several of the families in the midst of the English Civil Wars, the central figure being Johnny Church, a member of the Puritan gentry executed by Cromwell at the age of twenty for an excess of Dissent. There are many writers who can portray the lust, violence, and intrigue of the period well, as Settle has done. Few could so successfully interweave with them a vivid understanding of the ideas and idealism of liberty and Protestantism, as she has done.

O Beulah Land (1956) is the story of the building of Canona in the wilderness of western Virginia by settlers who range from Tidewater gentry to refugees from the London jails, an experience told at such a high level that it becomes truly epic. The opening scene, describing the long flight of Hannah Bridewell, alone, across the mountain wilderness after Braddock's defeat, is possibly one of the great passages of American literature. The central theme of O Beulah Land—and I venture this cautiously about so complex a work—is the nuances of successes, failures, and partial successes, in the transfer of the ideas and ideals of liberty from the Old World to the New.

Know Nothing (1961) re-enters history when the settlement planted in *O Beulah Land* is the fully developed society of the late antebellum South. Better pictures have been drawn of the Old South, as by Caroline Gordon, yet this one is fully elaborated and compelling and brings out many facets that are realized nowhere else. Most readers will find Hannah Bridewell alone in the wilderness the most moving scene, among many extended and compelling scenes that Settle has crafted into the *Quintet*. For me, the most stunning comes at the end of *Know Nothing* when, in the opening weeks of the Civil War, Southern volunteers of all classes and ages, gallant and disorganized, enthusiastic and deeply ambivalent, are plodding forward through rain and mud toward what we but not they know is a doomed effort to hold the Federals out of western Virginia. This scene says more about Southern history than a whole library full of historical "nonfiction."

In *The Scapegoat* (1980) we move forward again to the early 20th century. "Beulah Land" is now the coal mines. The mountain paradise of liberty is a gutted outpost of international industrialism. The gentry are in the process of being converted into mere agents of Northern and foreign capitalists. The yeomanry have been subjected to the mines or pushed to the periphery of society. New elements have been added: a world of immigrants, existing side by side with that of the natives but seldom interpenetrating, with its own elaborations and interior dialogues; outside labor agitators; modern pop culture; and stirrings of feminism and progressivism. In a story that takes place over a very short period, centered on a murder during a mine strike, Settle manages to portray all of these elements in depth, with sympathy and understanding and without sentimentality.

The Killing Ground (1982) is, as Garrett explains, a daring exercise of semi-autobiographical fiction that draws together the past set forth by the other four books into a modern consciousness facing its own complexities—existential, spiritual, familial, and societal. As I have argued above, nowhere has a modern Southern consciousness been plumbed so deeply and significantly. And thus, we have a case study for us all in the pain and difficulty of relating traditional impulses to the historical, institutional world that man has created for himself in the later 20th century.

Like most great works of art, there is nothing esoteric about *The Beulah Quintet*. It can be understood to a degree and enjoyed by any sensible reader. But it should not be confused with the costume dramas that make up the bulk of popular historical fiction. It encompasses an artistry, an authenticity, and a multi-layered breadth of vision that is not found there.

To outline the plots of the quintet and to describe it generally does not, of course, tell us all that it means. Like any work of art, it is best grasped in its own terms rather than in description. It advances us to consider carefully, as Garrett does, how the work as a whole gradually grew out of Settle's own background, thought, and experiences. We can add that it is certainly a deep meditation on human life, an existential quest for meaning shaped by a powerful historical sense.

One aspect of the meditation is the recurrent theme of liberty. If Settle gives allegiance to anything throughout her work, it is to those people who, to her, represent a recurrent striving for freedom, a resistance to restraints that are unchosen and indefensible. She (and here she resembles Faulkner) is a democrat in a profound and old Jeffersonian sense that has almost disappeared Never is her insistence on liberty sentimental or self-indulgent. It is always put forward in the context of candid knowledge of the costs. Settle has through most of her life appeared to be a kind of liberal. She went abroad in disgust when Nixon was elected in 1972. To apply terms of liberalism and conservatism from contemporary political discourse, however, is to distort a view that comes from a different and profounder realm. Her liberalism has never been conventional. Nowhere is there in print a more telling exposure of the hollowness of the Kennedy phenomenon of the sixties and the delusions of those who participated in it than appears in *The Killing Ground*. And in her public statements she has acknowledged that threats to liberty may not all come from the stereotyped demons of the right. They may well come, in a more insidious form. from the commercial and cultural clannishness of the urban liberal publishing oligarchy, for instance.

All of this does not exhaust what might be learned from *The Beulah Quintet*. "The place of the whole extraordinary quintet, and the place of *The Killing Ground* within it." Garrett observes, "remain to be fully known and understood. Time will tell " Exactly. and it is a measure of the importance of the work that those who have read it closely have not clarified and exhausted all its possibilities.

The other grand division of Settle's work is in remarkable contrast to *The Beulah Quintet*. Besides the epic of her own people and country, she has made a substantial contribution, in *Blood Tie* (1977) and *Celebration* (1986), to the literary portrayal of a major phase of modern life, the interaction of Western and non-Western cultures.

The interpenetration of the West and the Third World at the individual level may be the most significant phenomenon of our era, larger than the world wars of the struggle between communism and constitutionalism. Our period, unlike any since the later Roman Empire, is one of intermingling and universalization of culture. This was the subject of Conrad and Kipling at the beginning of this century, and it has continually attracted both great and lesser writers. On the lesser side one thinks of the soap operas of *A Passage to India* and Paul Scott's novels, from which the popular television series *The Jewel in the Crown* came. At a somewhat higher level are Lawrence Durrell's *Alexandria Quartet* and George Orwell's *Burmese Days*. And cultural interaction has been the ground for the major work of V.S. Naipaul.

Among these writers, Settle belongs in the higher and serious group. With an intensely modern consciousness, she renders a candid and objective vision that explores the nuances of the phenomenon. Neither the Westerners nor the "natives" receive disdain or sentimentality. She is neither a "colonialist" nor a ritualistic egalitarian.

Blood Tie is set in a coastal Turkish town, and is an immensely complex exploration of the circumstances and minds of modernizing locals and a variety of American and European exiles. There is a large cast of well-realized characters, all of them caught in a timeless tragedy of illusions and misapprehensions. *Celebration* has a smaller cast of characters—a young American widow, a CIA man, a black African Jesuit, a British homosexual, a Muslim doctor, and a few others. The setting moves from London to Hong Kong to Turkey to Africa. As the title suggests, the book moves, in the end, to find, among all these troubled and strange characters, an affirmative celebration of what Faulkner would have called "the old verities."

Garrett suggests that these two novels represent "the most successful and serious *international* fiction written by an American in our time." Even more than *The Beulah Quintet*, however, these books have yet to be fully assimilated and assessed. But undoubtedly, anyone who has not become familiar with the works of Mary Lee Settle has not exhausted the potentialities of American literature. (1988)

A Mirror for Artists

Tom Wolfe: Two Between the Ribs

A review of *Hooking Up*, by Tom Wolfe, New York: Farrar, Straus, and Giroux, 2000, 293 pages; and *The Lecturer's Tale*, by James Hynes, New York: Picador USA, 2001, 388 pages.

How does he get away with it? Ever since *Bonfire of the Vanities*, I have wondered at Tom Wolfe's success. The success itself is well deserved: Wolfe is a dazzling writer, without peer as an observer of contemporary American life. But can't the brilliant social and literary critics of New York figure out what he is up to? Have they ever actually *read* his books? (A suspicion I have long held about some professors is that they discourse pompously upon classic works that they know only by the labels pasted on them by others.) In *Bonfire*, Wolfe exposed the warts beneath the expert makeup on the shining countenances of every institution and nearly every major ethnic group in New York City, revealing the self-appointed, supreme American beauty for what she is—a decayed, pox-ridden harlot. The novel is a rollicking good story that one does not have to be a *New York Review* of Books reader to enjoy. But as George Garrett has pointed out, coming from a Southerner like Wolfe, such an attack is a breach of manners equivalent to a dagger between the ribs.

When the movie version of *Bonfire* (a deserved flop) came out, my puzzlement was not satisfied. Every major character in the book—every telling point in the book—was transformed. In the novel, the Southern belle who catalyzes the plot is unscrupulous, but intelligent and forceful; in the movie, she is a simpering idiot. The unsympathetic Jewish judge is changed to a sympathetic black one. Had Hollywood caught on and deliberately blunted the dagger? Or was it simply another case of the usual vulgarization of text?

Then came *A Man in Full*. Surely they could see it now? They could, of course, pass the novel off as an exposé of the always despicable South (the repulsive world of New South businessmen, racism, college athletics, and phony commercial religion) if they hadn't read the book. But the most telling mask-snatchings in *A Man in Full* reveal the proletarianization of the white working class in California, the social wreckage left behind by the flower children, and a less-than-complimentary view of upwardly mobile blacks and immigrants. One is ordinarily allowed to write about none of these—except in the style of Pollyanna.

Maybe some of them are catching on? In "My Three Stooges," Wolfe hilariously recounts the efforts of Mailer, Irving, and Updike to damn *A Man in Full*, up to and including spluttering obscene harangues on television that were intended to convince the world that Wolfe is not, like them, a real writer and that his works really don't rank as American literature, at least among "us" (the New York intelligentsia who really count).

The essays (if that is the right term) and one fiction story in *Hooking Up* are, without exception, gems of observation, understanding, and style. They bring Wolfe's laser beam further into forbidden territory, revealing still more unfashionable facets of American life. The catastrophic collapse of culture and morals is the overriding motif. Wolfe, in his reportage, traces significant phenomena, the kind that "intellectuals" always miss? the engineers and entrepreneurs who created Silicon Valley and the revolution it symbolizes; the thinkers (including Edward O. Wilson) who have brought the attention of the world, for better or worse, back from nurture to the centrality of nature; the deplorable state of American art, architecture, education, and the novel.

Beneath the motif of decadence lies another, softer one: that of a society living on the remnants of Christianity—the Midwestern Protestant background of the pioneer computer geniuses is a case in point. And in the story "Ambush at Fort Bragg," Wolfe exposes—beyond mercy—the dishonesty, ignorance, and egotism behind the production of television "news." If they don't get the message now, they never will; and I expect the television celebrities are too far gone in self-worship and empire-think ever to see themselves in the stark light of truth.

Anyone concerned about the state of education in America will do well to heed Wolfe's treatment of academia and "intellectuals." Another one, right between the ribs! Intellectualism—the cult of ignorant indignation—amounts to the seeking of sainthood by revolting against a society that is, supposedly, ignorant and clueless. For Wolfe, however, the self-appointed saints have missed the real point: How could they not notice and give credit to America's astounding successes—the innovation, the democratic spirit, the freedom, the unimaginable affluence of the common people?

Hilaire Belloc, who hated dons (he lost out on an appointment at Oxford), maintained that they all had something wrong with them—a stutter, a limp, the inability to chat up a mere slip of a girl. That is not entirely true anymore, thanks to the American fetishization of education and to Sputnik, which resulted in the pouring of billions of dollars into "higher" education, drawing to academia an infestation of well-groomed parasites far worse than those fumbling dons—con artists, rakes, bureaucrats, politicians.

James Hynes's *The Lecturer's Tale* plunges delightfully into that world, via the English faculty of the fictional (but representative) Midwestern University of Minnesota. The Lecturer is a naive academic whose career is going down the plumbing system because he really loves and believes in literature and wants to impart his knowledge to the young.

In the course of a plot that includes supernatural elements reminiscent of C.S. Lewis's fiction, Hynes lays bare, with only slightly heightened caricature, all of the successful types in present-day institutions of "higher" education, where reputation bears not the slightest relationship to either scholarship or the wellbeing of students, much less the transmission of Western civilization. These characters are only slightly heightened by caricature: After all, we live in a country where Stanley Fish is paid more than a quarter-million dollars a year as a professor of literature to teach that literature has no meaning.

Evelyn Waugh once wrote that his novels could not properly be described as satires because satire involves pointing out the gap between standards and behavior, and he was writing about people who had no standards. By Waugh's rule, we can't call *The Lecturer's Tale* a satire. Besides, it's hard to satirize what is already its own parody. Yes, it really is that bad. As the Australians say: "Too true." (2001)

Bernard Cornwell's Starbuck Chronicles

A review of *Battle Flag*, by Bernard Cornwell, New York: Harper Collins Publishers, 1995, 356 pages.

In the middle part of the 20th century one of the main staples of the Anglo-American reading public was the historical novel, or romance. Such "swashbucklers" were not great literature, but they had their virtues. In the hands of skilled writers like C.S. Forester or Kenneth Roberts, they introduced a great many people to some decent history which they would not otherwise have encountered.

Of course, "historical" themes have often been employed by great writers—as in *War and Peace*, George Garrett's Elizabethan novels, or, in the case of the War Between the States, such works as Andrew Lytle's *The Long Night*, Caroline Gordon's *None Shall Look Back*, or Gore Vidal's *Lincoln*. But I am speaking of writers a cut below this level—though the dividing line between a great and a very good writer is not necessarily that sharply defined. Historical novelists like Forester and Roberts and many others flourished in a day when millions read them along with William Faulkner in the old *Saturday Evening Post*.

Forester's *Captain Horatio Hornblower*, Roberts's *Northwest Passage*, Rafael Sabatini's *Captain Blood* and *Scaramouche*, and Kathleen Winsor's *Forever Amber*, along with many others, became lavish movie productions that brought to the masses a not-contemptible elementary introduction to important epochs of the past (and managed to entertain them without gore, four-letter words, or onscreen copulation). Similar works that were excellent, but which did not make it into the movies were the Civil War and World War stories of John W. Thomason and James Warner Bellah, and the colonial novels of Inglis Fletcher. Though romanticized, such works were generally accurate in historical setting. Their fictional characters were genuinely representative, if somewhat unnaturally highlighted, persons, and they mingled with real historical figures who were authentically portrayed and brought to life.

If there is any merit in this genre of literature, we have indeed fallen on evil times. The staples of the reading public, and the viewing public, are now such pseudo-historical fictions as the works of the execrable John Jakes and the faker Alex Haley. The trouble with such books and the sordid television docudramas that are made from them is that, while they claim to be historically researched, they lack any connection with or understanding of the spirit of the times and peoples, the social and psychological context, they are allegedly portraying. They are historical soap operas, pandering to the most superficial sentimentalities and concupiscences of our own time rather than educating us to the far and unknown country of the past.

What such a decline reveals, of course, is what everybody already knows, that the powers-that-be in American cultural logistics have essentially lost (or rather never had) any connection with the fabric of American history and society or indeed of Western civilization: they live in a multicultural world of ephemeral slogans and stimulations. The English are not quite so degenerate, in this respect at least, as measured by the fine set of historical romances about the American War Between the States that have issued in rapid succession from the pen of Bernard Cornwell.

The recently published *Battle Flag* follows, in *The Starbuck Chronicles, Copperhead,* and *Rebel*, which are already in mass paperback editions. Cornwell, who before he turned to our war was already well-known for his Sharpe's Rifles stories of the Napoleonic wars, has the virtues of those older historical romancers mentioned above.

The hero, Nate Starbuck, is the scapegrace son of a Boston abolitionist preacher who finds himself in Richmond at the outbreak of the war and is adopted into the Southern community and army. Starbuck is a convincing character, with depth of personality, and Cornwell includes with him a panoply of other characters who, unlike Jakes's or Haley's, actually think, talk, and act like real 19th century Americans. The characters sometimes verge on caricature, but they are authentic and well-drawn caricatures; that is, they are genuine representative types.

As Starbuck participates in the fate of the Confederate Army of Northern Virginia in Falconer's Legion—*Battle Flag* concludes with Second Manassas—he encounters a host of real Southerners, and some real Northerners as well. There is the supercilious blueblood, the tough mountaineer sergeant, the country schoolmaster who develops an unexpected taste and capacity for warfare, the born-again slave trader, and many others. These characters ring true as real types from our past. And on each side there is the ambiguous mixture of good and evil, honor and vileness. For instance, of the Southern Unionists, one is a sincere abolitionist and the other a plundering opportunist. Real historical personages—in *Battle Flag*, John Pope and Stonewall Jackson—are integrated skillfully by Cornwell and portrayed authentically. His battle narratives are as well done, as vivid, moving—and wrenching—as they can be.

It is important that Americans regain a real sense of our history that transcends the slogans and cartooning of the mass media. We will not get it from the vast establishment of academic historianship which has bureaucratized itself into irrelevance to the public discourse. Historians, increasingly and for the most part, speak only to each other (and even then they don't listen). If we do begin to recover some sense of the past, it may be from writers like Cornwell. *The Starbuck Chronicles* is a pleasant and easy place to start your reeducation on the War Between the States. (1995)

A MIRROR FOR ARTISTS

Styron's Bad Example

A review of *This Quiet Dust and Other Writings*, by William Styron, New York: Random House, 1982, 305 pages.

The materials in *This Quiet Dust and Other Writings*, collected from between 1953 and 1982, though ordered by neither logic nor chronology, constitute an autobiographical account of William Styron's experiences and ideas. They also present Styron's direct political and social polemics rather than his indirect artistic commentary. The picture that emerges of Styron as social and political commentator is that of a Virginian, sprung of what once would have been referred to as "good stock" and blessed with not inconsiderable literary gifts, who caters to the tastes of the New York intellectual community. At the same time, with a kind of aristocratic capriciousness, he occasionally flaunts his refusal to be absorbed completely by that community.

To grow up and find a place in the world is difficult. It is more onerous for the intelligent and sensitive youth who feels the urge to create and express, to make his way as a writer. The greater the intelligence, the more authentic the desire, the harder the way is in an age when the path to cultural success is strewn with commercial barriers and ideological land mines. The plausible, the adaptable, and the opportunistic can quickly find the way to preferment, while those who bear the genuine burden of the gods approach awestruck and encumbered. Make the young person a Southerner and the difficulty is multiplied Even if he is as pliant and ambitious as a PR man or a ward heeler, there is probably something in his experience that will put him out of step. And there will certainly be something in the reaction of the gatekeepers of the great world of cultural success that will add obstacles to his approach. The Southerner's insight may be no more profound than others; but it will be in some indefinable but real sense sadder, less exuberant. He will find himself both inwardly and outwardly a negative reference point, a counter-version of the American impulse.

Several strategies can be taken by the Southern writer who aims to succeed. One is to be so good that the world must meet him on his own terms. Another is to adopt an adversarial posture. Both of these approaches are very difficult, perhaps too tough, for the pedestrian writer. However, those who take up the challenge often reap benefits. The pain and effort involved may enhance the vision that the writer brings to his work, enabling him to fulfill the burden of his creative urge in a high manner.

One other strategy is possible. The writer can go over to the enemy with the zeal of a convert. Confirm with firsthand testimony the truth of all of the enemy's conclusions about his own folk. In this approach, liability can be turned into an asset. One can mouth the accepted clichés with an exotic panache. Liberals like nothing better than to have all the angels on their side, to co-opt both sides of the argument. Consequently, in the 1960s there was a spate of books by liberals attempting to prove that "true conservatives" agreed with liberals about everything important. People who disagreed with liberals could only be pseudo-conservatives. What could be more reassuring to the intellectuals of New York than to know that all "good Southerners" agree with them about the South and nearly everything else?

Thus, Styron. Or at least, so we can dispose of Styron the political and social commentator, though I confess to be a little less sure about Styron the artist. One of his pieces herein is a defense of the license of the historical novelist. In a kind of reply to both the militant black and the academic critics of *The Confessions of Nat Turner* he argues convincingly that the novelist should not be too tightly bound to literal historical fact, that it is his duty to find new meaning in historical events by applying imaginative vision to them. Quite true. The problem is that what Styron finds in history is not a new meaning but a liberal convention. The paucity of his artistic vision is evident when *The Confessions of Nat Turner* is compared to Faulkner's *Absalom, Absalom!* or Andrew Lytle's *Velvet Horn*. Faulkner and Lytle convey a sense of history and a moral vision of majesty and complexity. Styron's history is flat, and his morality is superficial. Could it be that the too-easy accommodation Styron has made between the New York intelligentsia and his real self has forestalled his highest development as a writer, deprived him of the profounder vision that others have achieved with perhaps no greater gifts?

The substitution of narrow, fashionably politicized views in *This Quiet Dust and Other Writings* is compounded by the fact that here he obviously aspires to be seen as a social and political thinker. The subjects are typically conventional, and the conclusions crafted to guarantee predictable responses. Few writers have run the gamut of fashion so wide and so well: blacks, Southern guilt, the Holocaust, the military, environmental pollution, the 1968 Chicago riots, "Lollipops" (the title of one section of his book, referring to prematurely despoiled young women), capital punishment, Christ-like felons suffering from a bad environment and a callous public, the tawdriness of everything American, normal, and average.

It is not so much the conventionality of his subject matter that palls as the conventionality of his response to it. Styron's mastery of language does not redeem the flatness of his perception. He is at his best when his vision is not strained through the filter of fashion. His pieces on other writers (e.g., Fitzgerald and Thomas Wolfe) are shrewd, sincere, and often generous. When he doesn't attempt to make social judgments, he can be eloquent and moving, as in his description of his native Tidewater. And in his musings on war, he makes one of his occasional dissents from liberal shibboleth. He eschews, if I understand him correctly, a blanket condemnation of the American military, accepts the inevitability of wars, and insists on adherence to old-fashioned codes of civilized warfare. But then one remembers that these occasional dissents are only a kind of spice to dress up the blandness of the fare, idiosyncratic personal gestures that in no way compromise ideological conformity.

Faulkner drew on the vestigial aristocratic aloofness of his Southern background for a catholic magnanimity to humanity; Styron uses it for purposes merely cavalier and self-indulgent. Nowhere is this self-indulgence more evident than in the author's flirtation with the criminal, which he recounts at length and candidly in a section entitled "Victims." The "victims," of course, are the perpetrators, not the objects of criminal acts. Styron and George F. Will led a successful movement to save a confessed murderer from execution by the State of Connecticut. Some years later, when this individual was about to be paroled into Styron's care, he escaped prison, kidnapped and raped a suburban housewife, and terrorized three children. Styron admits that he was glad it was not his daughter who was raped, but declares that he feels no guilt for his role in the matter. His special vision of service to the oppressed and neglected and redeemable criminal cannot be deflected by the sufferings of a few accidental victims.

However, Styron's self-examinations on crime and punishment can be candid, deeply probing, and they sometimes contain a redeeming remnant of Christian compassion. What they lack is the great artist's (and the great believer's) *encompassing compassion*. Ultimately there is an irresponsible moral posture that takes up the criminal out of disdain for the ordinary. Witness this description of two policemen: neither "are vicious men; they are merely undiscerningly obedient, totally devoid of that flexibility of mind we call imagination." Styron is less a chronicler of human suffering and injustice than he is one of a band of self-anointed nobles whose mission is to thwart an America that, in their eyes, routinely oppresses the weak, convicts the innocent, cheats, swindles, pollutes, and wages war. Styron and his readers see themselves as lifted above that mundane run of humanity who think that murderers should be punished, who sense that to excuse a criminal because of a bad environment is an injustice to every person who has surmounted a bad environment without wielding a bludgeon on a helpless victim. (1983)

Chapter Eight

The Agrarian Vision

Up From Menckenism

A review of *Serpent in Eden: H.L. Mencken and the South*, by Fred C. Hobson, Jr., Chapel Hill: University of North Carolina Press, 1974, 242 pages.

As all the world, or at least every lettered Southerner, knows, in or about 1920 Mr. H.L. Mencken, then the undisputed high arbiter of American culture, proclaimed his discovery of the "Sahara of the Bozart." The vast territory between the Potomac mudflats and the Gulf, large enough to swallow up France and Germany, was, according to Mencken, as sterile of art, intellect, and culture—of the beaux-arts—as the great desert. It was a "gargantuan paradise of the fourth-rate," ungraced by a single picture gallery, orchestra, or theater worthy of attention, a single writer who could write, or a thinker worthy of "Portugal, Serbia, or Estonia." The South, in sum, was a land of lynchers and primitive fundamentalists, a humid *ultima thule* where the subhuman peasantry who merely threatened civilization elsewhere in the United States had actually succeeded in extinguishing it.

By Mr. Hobson's lights, Mencken's clanging *alarum* was, for better or worse, a galvanic event in the history of the New South, startling into activity two contentious movements—Southern Liberalism and the Southern Renaissance in literature. Both movements would have come without Mencken, but their advent was hastened and the particular forms they took were irreparably shaped (or warped) by Menckenism. With an admirably impartial temper for what is obviously a regional *devoir*, Hobson has tracked down the ramifications of the Menckenian assault on the Southern mind.

Mencken's slashes against the South, which he saw as benevolently surgical, were fraught with the ambivalence of what the psychoanalysts identify as a love-hate relationship. His outrage at the degradation of the New South was, in part, a product of his admiration for the Old. This will surprise many, but the Mencken of the "Sahara" thought of the

Old South as "a civilization of manifold excellences. undoubtedly the best that these States have ever seen." And it was Mencken who wrote that the Civil War was "a victory of what we now call Babbitts over what used to be called gentlemen." Again, it was Mencken— and this was a first-hand and convincing recollection and not simply mythifying, as Hobson, a son of the New South and therefore skeptic of the Old, would have it—who said that his Baltimore was less corrupt than other large American cities because of the honorable influence of ex-Confederate émigrés, "many of whom arrived with no baggage save good manners and empty bellies."

From the "Sahara" until he was diverted by F.D.R., Mencken continued to concentrate on the benighted South, particularly on what he considered its stultifying subjection to a fundamentalist theocracy. Despite his pose of detachment, Mencken in the 1920s and 1930s, it is apparent, played recruiting officer and chaplain for the guerilla forces of Southern Liberalism. He identified and counseled emergent Southern Liberals, published and praised their works, and exhorted them to lay about them hammer and tongs. The Southern Liberals, in turn, revered and emulated Mencken, although with the exception of that venomous scribbler W.J. Cash, his disciples were unable to match the savagery of his attacks. It is an ironic sidelight on the restless urbanite conservatism of the era: Mencken, the scorner of uplift, the pitiless castigator of do-gooders, he who more than any other unmasked the aggression and vacuity that often underlay the reforming impulse, became, where the South was concerned, a crusader for redemption. In mitigation, it must be said that the Southern Liberalism that Mencken nourished was still unformed, that it might have become, had men like the sociologist Howard Odum realized their best, something other than a rag-tag camp follower of urban progressivism.

Mencken's relationship to the Southern Renaissance, more specifically to the Fugitive-Agrarians of Nashville, is more problematic, and vividly exhibits, as Hobson shows, his defects as a literary critic. Mencken slighted both the literary and social significance of the Agrarian writers and of their undercover collaborator William Faulkner. That is to say, when the resurgence of Southern high culture he had hoped for appeared, he failed either to recognize or comprehend it. The Agrarians spoke out of portions of the Southern tradition he was not equipped to appreciate. Yet Hobson believes, and perhaps he is right, that Mencken, in the "Sahara" and even more by his cruel cavortings at the Dayton "Monkey Trial," was the indispensable antagonist for the

Agrarians, that it was he who sent them back to their roots for that periodic renewal Mr. Jefferson had recommended and thus catalyzed *I'll Take My Stand.*

Being gentlemen, the Agrarians, unlike the Liberals, were repulsed rather than exhilarated by the savagery of the public Mencken. Constituting most of what remained in America of articulate Jeffersonian democracy (my notion, not Hobson's), they could not join him in dismissing the yeomanry as *boobus americanus.* To the essentially German Mencken the artistic elite realized itself in destructive rebellion against the surrounding social fabric. The Agrarians, inheritors of a not completely attenuated English patriarchal tradition (not to mention their archaic classical educations) conceived of art as in harmonic tension with its environment. Certainly, the burden of their renewal carried them far away from Mencken's premier nostrum for Southern ills—destruction of the prevailing religious orthodoxy. Mencken, they saw, failed to discern the genuine and indispensable *pietas* beneath the evangelical excesses. To Mencken's indictment then, the Agrarians had no choice but to bring in a verdict of "Guilty, and proud of it!" In so doing, they affirmed what Babbitt and More had already discovered in their own manner: Menckenian conservatism was diverting, it was often useful in a negative way, and its strenuous audacity commanded a certain respect, but in the long run its sustenance was thin. (1974)

Uncle Sam's Other Province

A review of A Band of Prophets: The Vanderbilt Agrarians After Fifty Years, edited by William C. Havard and Walter Sullivan, Baton Rouge: Louisiana State University Press, 1982, 190 pages; and *Regionalism and the South: Selected Papers of Rupert Vance*, edited by John Shelton Reed and Daniel Joseph Singal, Chapel Hill: University of North Carolina Press, 1982, 353 pages.

The intellectual history of the South is yet to be written. By this statement I am bootlegging in two premises. First, that there is such a thing as the South with a distinctive history. Second, that Southern history includes an intellectual life worthy of study. Though persons can be found to controvert the first premise, they can easily be dealt with: their position—that there is no distinctive South—is essentially either perverse ideological reasoning (the South is bad, therefore its existence must be discounted as a temporary aberration) or materialist reductionism (the South doesn't exist because it can't be counted).

Concede, then, a distinctive Southern history, but what about its intellectual life? Here it is harder to make headway. That the South has, throughout its existence, had a life of the mind important enough for historical attention is not an uncontested thesis. Even many who are aware of the importance of 20th century Southern literature are not aware of or not willing to concede anything of importance before this century. This scholarly consensus is mistaken. Richard Beale Davis, in his immense work *Intellectual Life in the Colonial South*, proved both the presence and the distinctiveness of a life of the mind in the colonial era South. The 19th century Southern intellect still awaits its great historian, but he will appear. That intellect is underrated simply because it is unknown. Everyone thinks he already knows what the writers and thinkers of the Old South had to say, so nobody has ever bothered to read them. Sooner or later, someone will: Jefferson and Poe, George Washington Harris and Joel Chandler Harris, William Gilmore Simms, John C. Calhoun and others will be woven together into a meaningful picture. When that is done, at least two things will be established. First, that there was no great discontinuity in values between the Jeffersonian generation and the Confederate generation of Southerners, contrary to what has so often been declared. Second, that the 19th century Southern mind was quite the opposite of its currently popular image—that it was classical rather than romantic, critical and ironic rather than simple and hyperbolic. But that is another story.

The South is different. Even when Southerners do the same things as other Americans, it is often for different reasons. They sympathized with Richard Nixon, for instance, not because they thought he was any good, but because they thought he was no worse than his enemies. The South is America's Basque provinces—a region which has always contributed more than its share to the nation, yet one that is not quite a respectable part of it; it is the most conservative part of the nation, yet it is particularist and runs athwart the mainstream even when the mainstream flows conservative. The Agrarians of *I'll Take My Stand* would seem to fall to the right of any American center line, but one wonders if they fit into the national left/right dialectic at all. When William F. Buckley, Jr. edited an anthology of American conservative writing a few years ago, he did not include any of the Agrarians, nor even so relevant a follower of theirs as Richard Weaver; yet he included a number of writers and themes that could not seriously be considered "American."

Southern liberals have almost as much difficulty fitting in as Southern conservatives. In fact, one may safely maintain that no Southerner can ever be fully respectable as a liberal. No matter what excesses he may indulge in to expunge his taint, he will never succeed.[48] Jimmy Carter knew the things one had to say and do, and he said and did them. But many Americans simply could not accept his performance. (The same thing happened to Truman and Johnson, which indicates the degree to which liberalism embodies ritualistic role-playing rather than substantive issues.) Unwittingly, by his frantic effort to live up to the role expected of him, Carter exhibited how mechanical and formalistic and empty liberalism had become and thereby rendered a great service.

If it were not already a cliché, I would be tempted to suggest that American conservatives are largely 19th century bourgeois capitalists (though never quite as consistent in practice as in theory) and American liberals are 20th century social democrats (except that whereas European social democrats are fueled by class antagonism, American ones are driven by puritanical fury and hypocrisy). Southerners, on the other hand, whatever side they might come down on in national politics, are still 18th century republicans in their basal political instincts. They have always had—and still have—by and large a different sense of the dividing line between the public and the private, a different sense

---

48   48 Bill Clinton has proved me wrong here.

of the range and purposes of the state. This outsider viewpoint has its uses. George Wallace was hated by both liberals and conservatives, but by coming, as it were, out of another league, he was able to upset the convenient and self-serving way the game was being played by the major teams and to restore some competition to the contest. His smashing of the phony consensus of the early 1960s by his success at raising neglected issues during the Northern primaries was a decisive element in establishing current political dialectic. Its power, for example, is forcing the Republican Party toward a grassroots conservative position that it would never have adopted on its own and against which it struggles.

Rupert Vance was, in the terms of his time, a Southern liberal. He believed that his land, the South, was in critical respects benighted and that the knowledge and techniques of social science could be employed to illuminate some of that darkness. This put him, in Southern terms, on the left, and made him, at least superficially, an American liberal. Yet one need only compare Vance's approach with the direction sociology has taken in recent decades to grasp the significance of the "Southern" in "Southern sociologist." For one thing, Vance always maintained an aristocratic aloofness, and his sense of his discipline was a high, rigorous and demanding one. For another, his critique of the South was from the inside, which is why his essay "Is Agrarianism for Farmers?" is the most effective as well as the fairest of the many contemporary attacks on *I'll Take My Stand*. Vance was as much a Southern patriot in his own way as the Agrarians. It was, after all, his life's work (unsuccessful in the judgment of his editors) to establish a *regional* sociology.

Thus, given the perspective of time, the gulf between the Vanderbilt group and the Chapel Hill "liberals" appears narrower today than it seemed to them in the 1930s and 1940s—almost a *tactical* rather than a fundamental parting. (What is said for Vance in this regard goes equally for at least some other Southern liberals: his Chapel Hill colleagues Howard W. Odum, another sociologist, and W.T. Couch, a publisher, for example.) Alas, Southern progressives fit almost as poorly into the national dialectic as Southern conservatives.

It is well known that Southern writers can write. Less well known is that Southern historians can write. Not known at all, but true, is that Southern *sociologists* can write. Vance's thought was always in focus and his prose always lucid. He could explicate methodological problems, statistical findings, or philosophical points with equal clarity and ease. He was no piker as an old-fashioned social commentator either, as one can see by perusing his two satirical pieces on late 19th century

Southern politics, "Tennessee's War of the Roses" (about the feuding Taylor brothers) and "A Karl Marx for Hillbillies" (about Arkansas's Rabelaisian Governor, Jeff Davis). Vance was not alone. Humanistic sociologists are a Southern tradition. That was true of Vance's colleague Odum, and it is true of his successor at Chapel Hill, John Shelton Reed, co-editor of the Vance essays and one of the contributors to *A Band of Prophets*.

A Band of Prophets is a collection of some of the papers given by the cream of Southern scholarship at a conference held at Vanderbilt University in observance of the 50th anniversary of *I'll Take My Stand*. There is some irony in Vanderbilt's sponsorship of this respectful celebration. The university and the Nashville business community, until quite recently, were anxious to be modern and progressive and were deeply embarrassed by the only two things they had that were of interest to the outside world—"country" music and the Agrarian writers. Both prejudices have been overcome, but one fears for the wrong reasons. Despite the irony, these papers are the most significant commentary to appear yet on the Agrarian work; they are, themselves, important contributions to the still-to-be-written history of the life of the mind in the South. Reed's paper is concerned with the degree to which the Agrarian statement and movement adumbrated a Southern nationalism analogous to European movements. It is the most original and groundbreaking of the essays, although they are all richly varied and worthy of attention. Charles P. Roland describes admirably the Southern historical background of the 1920s out of which *I'll Take My Stand* emerged Lewis P. Simpson considers the Agrarian cast against the intellectual history of Western man and concludes that they were a part of the Republic of Letters engaged in artistic revolt against modernity and its solvents. George Core presents an astute history of the New Criticism and its relation to the Agrarian movement. Robert B. Heilman gives a Northerner's carefully considered appreciation of the prophetic power of the work. Louis D. Rubin celebrates the success of *I'll Take My Stand* as a piece of literature, as a poetic work in the tradition of Christian humanism. The least satisfying part of *A Band of Prophets* is the transcribed discussion between the three living Agrarians: Lyle H. Lanier, Robert Penn Warren, and Andrew Lytle. Disappointing is a relative term here, since the discussion was skillfully led by Cleanth Brooks, certainly one of America's most inspired scholars. (Brooks, indeed, should be awarded the title Thirteenth Southerner. He was just too young by a hair to be in *I'll Take My Stand*.) As the editors of *A*

Band of Prophets point out, the surviving Agrarians have maintained a remarkable stability of viewpoint; their discussion takes up almost as if *I'll Take My Stand* was a conversation left off yesterday.

But perhaps that is what I find disappointing. Lanier and Warren have long been cut off from the day-to-day life of the South. Only Lytle is still rooted there. One gets the sense that the former two are fighting yesterday's rather than today's battles. Warren's pre-occupation with Nixon leads him at times very near the banality of any conventional Northeastern university professor. (As if a politician lying were something new, or of very high priority for a social commentator in a country where millions of peoples' incomes are disappearing before their eyes, where nearly half the families are broken, and where as many as 150,000 children were kidnapped, raped, enslaved, and murdered in one year.) Lanier, quite rightly, is still concerned about preserving a humane scale against gigantism in business and finance and about protecting the natural world against destruction and pollution. That is all well and good, and the continuity is consoling, but these threats to the humane order do not loom quite so large, proportionately, as they once did. I would argue that the plain people of the South and perhaps of America have succeeded to a remarkable degree in humanizing the city and the factory—not completely but to a remarkable degree. The problem of economic and political gigantism is secondary, a problem solvable given sufficient will and intelligence. Our pressing crisis is not industrial pollution but cultural pollution (though, of course, the two are related, which was a large part of the burden of the Agrarian message). What threatens us most is not the unintended disruption fostered by urban-industrial life, but the intentional destruction wrought by morally and intellectually corrupt policies—the deliberate discouragement of religion, family, community, and tradition.

That is why I find Lytle's comments the most rewarding. He still has the old fire, still keeps the original enemy in view, but seems to realize that the enemy may wear more than one face. Lytle is concerned with the peril posed by the progressive Western loss of the sense of the sacred, of place, of craftsmanship, of family, of political genius. His remarks, archaic and anecdotal in style (they were referred to playfully by Brooks as "Rutherford County metaphysics"), are still as relevant as eternity. (1982)

Andrew Lytle

A review of *From Eden to Babylon: The Social and Political Essays of Andrew Nelson Lytle*, edited by M.E. Bradford, Washington, D.C.: Regnery Gateway, 1990, 260 pages.

Sixty years ago, Twelve Southerners published a book of essays called *I'll Take My Stand*.

Because of its startlingly unfashionable affirmation of the South over the North and of traditional agrarian ways over the life of modern America, and because of the major literary stature of some of the writers, the book has remained a subject of commentary, controversy and interpretation to the present day.

With the recent death of Robert Penn Warren, only Andrew Lytle remains of the Twelve Southerners. He is still active at 87 on his mountain farm at Monteagle, Tennessee. It is known to many, and will become more so with the passage of time, that Lytle is one of the major American writers of our century. The author of three world class novels— *The Velvet Horn, The Long Night,* and *At the Moon's Inn* —and of several classic short stories including "Alchemy," Lytle was also for many years a writing teacher and editor of *Sewanee Review*.

In the past few years, publishers have been bringing out new editions of his books, so that now nearly all are once more in print, not only the novels and stories, but also his biography of Bedford Forrest and his memoir *A Wake for the Living*.

In 1988 Professor Lewis Simpson of Louisiana State University edited *Southerners and Europeans*, a collection of Lytle's scattered literary criticism and essays on the craft of writing. From Eden to Babylon, M.E. Bradford's collection of Lytle's social and political commentary over 60 years, completes the compilation of Lytle's work. It also provides a necessary way of interpreting that work. Unlike some modern authors, Lytle's opinions on politics, economics and history are not fashionable sidelines but are an integrated part of his artistic vision.

This collection includes essays on a great variety of subjects and occasions: the earliest agrarian essays on farming as a way of life and an economy; later reflections on the cause represented by *I'll Take My Stand*; explorations of Southern history and its heroes, such as John

Taylor of Caroline, Robert E. Lee and John C. Calhoun; and commentaries on craftsmanship, religion, education, and modern life.

It is clear that Lytle's view of the world has remained the same, though growing in sophistication and complexity until it has reached, in the more recent writings and interviews, a theological dimension. Even at his most theological, as in a piece on the myth of the Garden of Eden, Lytle keeps an earthy sense of human nature and man's everyday life, full of charm and humor. In this he exhibits the relationship between Southern literature and such English writers as C.S. Lewis and J.R.R. Tolkien.

Lytle's vision of the good life is one abandoned by modern man: a life of families independent and self-sufficient on the land, with a harmonious relationship between generations and men and women, where work is carried on with a sense of divine vocation.

It is a profoundly conservative view, though having little in common with the Hollywood conservatism of Ronald Reagan, the preppy conservatism of William Buckley and his host of imitators, or the capitalist conservatism of Wall Street. It is very far from the way of life of the urban, pluralist, modern American Empire (thus the title, From *Eden to Babylon*). But it can't hurt us to be reminded that Lytle's vision was once what was meant by America. (1990)

Allen Tate

A review of *Allen Tate: A Recollection,* by Walter Sullivan, Baton Rouge: Louisiana State University Press, 1988, 117 pages.

    Inferior minds are interested in things. Average minds are interested in personalities. Superior minds are interested in principles. The lower categories are excluded from the higher, but the reverse is not true. A superior mind also exists in the worlds of things and personalities.

    Allen Tate's was a mind of the third category, but this memoir by Professor Walter Sullivan of Vanderbilt University, who was a member of Tate's "circle" from the 1940s until Tate's death in 1979, is concerned with the realm of personality. Tate's character flaws, weak moments, very active sex life, and senescent infirmities are graphically remembered in this unquestionably well-crafted and powerful biographical document. It is an example of the now familiar genre of revelation about the personal lives of authors, setting at naught Faulkner's dictum that the important thing about a writer is his work. The tone is established by a remark of Brainard Cheney, an intimate of most of the Agrarian-Fugitive group, in regard to Tate, as rendered by Sullivan: "He's a monster! Goddamn it, he's a monster! But I love him."

    The central members of the Agrarian-Fugitive group—Davidson, Warren, Lytle, Ransom, and Tate—loom large in the creative literature and criticism of the 20th century, and almost as large in social thought, as is testified by their ever-widening rings of disciples, now into a third generation, and by the continuing output of literature on them. Why this is so is not yet fully explicated, though the ultimate answer will probably lie in the region suggested by Tate himself in a few brief, casual, and crucial essays on Southern literature as the product of a uniquely pregnant moment of transition from tradition to modernism.

    The centrality of these writers to intellectual life in the West is an amazing phenomenon when you consider that they lived most of their lives and did most of their work (with the partial exception of Warren) in a world that was alien and inhospitable to them—in its prosperity, utilitarian manners, bureaucratization of art and scholarship, innocence of guilt and sin, and triumphant materialism. They were marginal men in nearly every respect except the most important—their personal integrity, their dedication to craft, and their crucial purchase on the disintegrations of modernism.

None was more marginal than Tate, who alone among this group pursued the life of the unrooted Bohemian artist—intellectual on both sides of the Atlantic, who literally lived by his wits for much of his life, and who flouted many of the traditional conventions. Not the greatest artist among the Agrarians; not, contrary to Sullivan (like Tate, a Roman Catholic convert), the best theologian (a distinction that belongs to Andrew Lytle), Tate nevertheless combined the highest skills of poet, critic, and essayist to become, as M.E. Bradford has put it, "the most complete example" of "the man of letters in the antique European sense" among contemporary Americans.

For this reason, it is possible that Tate will find his place among the small company (after Yeats and Eliot) who will be looked back upon by intellectual historians as exemplary figures of our age, as Erasmus was for the 16th century and Goethe for the 18th. If so, he will be exemplary both in his poetic vision and intellectual formulations and in his disordered private life, which is so thoroughly and skillfully examined here.

As an historian I can by no means approve the suppression of the record, but one wonders why Professor Sullivan did not deposit this recollection in the Vanderbilt University library for the use of future biographers. The decision to publish at this time, when a number of the persons portrayed are still living, is especially puzzling because Sullivan has been an eloquent opponent of the graphicness of modern literature. To advocate reticence in art while publishing ugly stories about one's friends seems to me exactly the opposite of the course that would be pursued by a proper disciple of the Agrarians, who advocated and displayed integrity in art and good manners in private life.

Sullivan's treatment is not and is not intended to be a contribution to intellectual history or an examination of Tate's place in letters. Its intent is biographical context, a cause it serves forcefully. But the most important thing about a writer, or probably about any man (except for that part best known to his Creator), is indeed his work, which this book illuminates only marginally, if at all. In fact, we are not yet at the point where Tate and his confreres can be assessed with true historical perspective, though perhaps we soon will be. This book, as the author probably knows, is a document of the transition.

© 1989 by *National Review*, Inc. Reprinted by permission

Family Reunion

The cream of Southern writers and thinkers gathered this spring at Converse College in Spartanburg, South Carolina, for a literary reunion. Present were Andrew Lytle, Cleanth Brooks, George Garrett, Peter Taylor, and Eudora Welty, who regaled a large and enthusiastic audience of students and townspeople with readings from their works and informal discussions of Southern literature.

The highlight of the two-day gathering was a roundtable discussion between all of the principals except Miss Welty, on the South. Peter Taylor, one of America's greatest short-story writers, recalled how William Faulkner's *Absalom Absalom*, considered by many today as *the* American novel, was first received by New York critics: it was officially opined that the book had been written by a crazy man. Taylor went on to describe what he feels Southern literature is all about: it is a struggle to humanize modern life by understanding it and reconciling it with the Christian tradition of the West. No small task, but one which Southern writers have mastered.

Cleanth Brooks, one of America's greatest literary scholars, commented on today's culture. The students of today are, he fears, outside Western civilization. They are equally cut off from both the old traditional oral culture of the West and from the written high culture. According to Brooks, the three bastard American muses hold sway in literature. These are Sentimentality, Propaganda, and Pornography, the latter a billion dollar industry predicated upon the unwillingness or inability of Americans "to see reality as a whole." And only the writers of the South still have the cultural base to see the present situation for what it is, rather than to be a part of it.

The key to Southern literature, Andrew Lytle (perhaps the greatest living practitioner of Southern literature) told the assembled audience, is that it is still Christian and still has a Christian grasp of the reality of evil. The Southern tradition is squarely at odds with the Puritan or Northern tradition.

The Puritan puts evil in the object—whiskey, a gun, a bad environment, etc.—rather than in the human heart. Once evil is projected into the object, the Puritan is able to justify to himself his right to attack and reform others in the name of his own sanctity. This reduces to a disguised form of a will to power. What the Puritan wants is not salvation but power. He is, in the final analysis, a minion of the Devil.

George Garrett, poet and novelist, described with some relish the economic and cultural decay of the once powerful Northeast and declared his belief that, judging from the youngest writers just coming on the scene, Southern literature is still great and still Southern and will continue to be for a long time. (1982)

French Agrarian Cinema

The French are among the least noticed and celebrated of the contributors to what has become the United States. But at one time New France covered a good part of North America. The two most interesting provinces on the continent, Quebec and Louisiana, are remnants of that empire. Huguenot refugees contributed talents to the British colonies far out of proportion to their numbers.

When the 13 colonies confirmed their independence at Yorktown, there were more French than American soldiers present and a French fleet on the coast. But soon a promising alliance ended when the French got up to mischief with guillotines and military emperors, giving our Northeastern elite the excuse to return to their natural Anglophilia. When, more than a century later, General Pershing landed in Europe and declared "Lafayette, we are here," it was a nice touch. But everybody knew we had come to save the Brits and not the Frogs.

Those of us who are interested in tradition, regionalism, preserving authentic rooted cultures and who know that "small is beautiful," can learn something from the French. Despite their highly centralized government and a streak of avant-gardism, the French remain the most tenaciously regionalist, traditionalist, and culturally conservative of Europeans, and maintain a strongly rooted Catholic faith.

The best way to learn this, other than a long sojourn, is from their film. The French are the best filmmakers in the world. (The Germans are the worst, their film reflecting the brutish nihilism of their language, philosophers, and history.) And for French film the best place to start is with the rich heritage of Provence. The popular book and television series "A Year in Provence" was full of insider references to previous triumphs of Provencal filmmaking dating back to the 1930s. The episode about a runaway baker's wife harked back to Marcel Pagnol's wonderful 1938 movie, *The Baker's Wife*.

Pagnol, a novelist as well as a screenwriter and director, created a Provencal world that raises the movies to the level of literature. Though he died in 1974, his legacy is still working. Pagnol's stories were the basis for two marvelous pairs of recent films: *Jean de Florette* and *Manon of the Spring* (1987); and *My Father's Glory and My Mother's Castle* (1991).

Provence and neighboring Languedoc were the original home of the medieval troubadour and thus the source of the great Western invention—romantic love. Despite the mild Mediterranean climate, which is responsible for such fleshpots as Cannes, Nice, and Monaco, most of Provence is rugged and not well watered. In pastoral and agricultural times, it provided what Arnold Toynbee would call an optimum challenge for those who had to live off the land. The need for human ingenuity and endurance and the moral conflicts that come with the struggle for survival made for prime literary territory, like Ireland or Mississippi. (This also has something to do with why Arles, in Provence, has attracted more great painters than any other spot on earth.)

Among the strengths of Pagnol's stories are a long time perspective—generations rather than a weekend; a sense of real people in real places. There is tragedy and evil but in a context that affirms family, community, decency, and a Christian civilization. Not much more can be asked of film.

Interestingly, Pagnol's first work was urban. The trilogy *Marius*, *Fanny*, and *Cesar* (1929-36), although based on Marseilles, has all the Christian virtues of his rural stories. The trilogy formed the basis for the American musical *Fanny*, an adaptation that had little to recommend it other than Leslie Caron's legs. Among other titles either written or directed by Pagnol are *Harvest* (1937), *The Well-Digger's Daughter* (1941), and *Letters from My Windmill* (1954). At this late stage of the millennium and Western culture, this body of art remains a solid consolation to those who care to see. (1998)

James Kibler

A review of *Our Fathers' Fields: A Southern Story*, by James Everett Kibler, Columbia: University of South Carolina Press, 1998, 444 pages.

Professor James Kibler has written an instant classic that ought to be on the shelf of every Southerner. *Our Fathers' Fields* ranks easily among the handful of most important Southern books published in the last several decades. It was many years in the research and writing, but on publication has arrested attention and won praise even from Southern liberals. The first printing has sold out, but more will be available.

Dr. Kibler, a very distinguished scholar of Southern literature at the University of Georgia, acquired in the 1980s ownership of a decaying antebellum plantation house in his native Newberry County, South Carolina. For some years he has been personally working to restore the residence and its garden to the elegant simplicity of their antebellum days. (Elegant simplicity, not ostentatious splendor, for the author points out that the life of this antebellum plantation was abundant, but close to the soil and to the Christian and classical heritage, not ostentatious in the style of the Yankee rich.)

Years of research and contemplation (and work) have given Dr. Kibler an intimate and detailed knowledge of the place. He knows all that can be known about the building and furnishings, every native plant of the garden and farm, and details of the everyday life of the plantation family, white and black. This, along with more conventional historical research into the Hardy family, who were the creators and owners of the plantation, has allowed the author to present a beautiful and sympathetic picture of 200 years of a place and a family. As Shelby Foote has written in a comment on the book, *Our Fathers' Fields* is the history of a Southern family "seen from the inside ... that brings us home to who we are by showing us where we came from." Foote adds that Kibler's work "resonates for all of us [Southerners, that is] in the very core of our being."

There is nothing quite like this book in Southern (or any) literature. May it last forever as a beautifully written, thoughtfully distilled presentation of the goodness of Southern life over many generations. And that this work, which absolutely pulls no punches in its loyal Southernness, could be published and promoted today by a "mainstream" press may well be an indication of times changing for the better. (1998)

* * *

Foreword to *Poems from Scorched Earth*, by James Everett Kibler, Charleston, South Carolina: Charleston Press, 2001, 109 pages.

The scholar and the poet are different sorts of men, so it is thought, though both are necessary to a healthy culture. To find high accomplishments of both in the wielder of one pen—while not unknown in the long span of Western civilization—is rare. James E. Kibler is of that rare company.

Long established as a leading scholar of the literature of the South, Kibler as poet brings his scholarly skills to bear on our history, and particularly that trauma of invasion and conquest endured in the middle of the last century.

Anyone can cite historical "facts," but a higher faculty is necessary to teach us their meaning and significance for humanity. History at its best is a rendering of human experience, something very different from the pasting on of labels that passes for historical understanding too often in our day. History is a story, and a story must be somebody's story. As Kibler says, "We learn each other's stories / Or kill each other off." So, the artist and the scholar, in their higher reaches, are not so different after all. As our great novelist/historian Shelby Foote has said, they both hope to tell us the same truth, though by different methods.

Kibler brings yet another faculty to these lines, what our poet Donald Davidson called "knowledge carried to the heart." Descended from a long line of Newberry District folk farming on the same land, Kibler knows the meaning of Place. That is something that is vouchsafed these days to very few Americans. No mere Agrarian of the book, he knows the land and its hard-won favors. And he knows the opposite of Place. Not No Place (Utopia) because even rootless people must live somewhere. The opposite of Place is Empire.

Those earlier Americans, the Romans, made a splendid Empire, but when too many of them forgot or never knew the *lares et penates* and the *genius loci*, they lost it. And long before they lost it, it had become a burden rather than a boon to mankind. One of Kibler's themes is the American Empire, the birth of which was announced by Sherman's and Sheridan's fires, the savagery of which shocked even the Prussian

The Agrarian Vision

General Staff. Instead of song and story the Empire lives by abstractions: "Abstraction sanitizes all / And welcomes encore of the scene."

But the earth may be scorched in more than one way. It may be impoverished and poisoned by the acts of men without Place—clear-cutting, strip malls, golf courses, chemicals—the Empire in its utilitarian phase. The natural result is Kibler's "The Land Wedded to Waste." Wasted land means a wasted people, the scorched earth of the spirit. "Use without love is abuse":

> Consume. Consume.
>
> Don't bother with outdated Liberty.
>
> Empire contains the seeds of its own destruction.
>
> An empire wedded to waste
>
> Shall perish from the earth.

The Empire suffers under the poet's curse, and as Donald Davidson put it, the poet's curse seldom fails. But the true poet must also give us hope, and Kibler does. "Dark blood":

> Cries from the ground
>
> And will itself at last be heard.
>
> It runs in living veins And gives us tongue
>
> To free us from a dragon's curse.
>
> Do we hear, even now,
>
> ... the call to rise
>
> To voice the course of force-bound empire into Homes,
>
> ....
>
> From out the fire-scorched land
>
> To place and hearths particular.

From death-dealing abstraction to the well-loved particular place—it is a journey we must make, if we are to survive. (1999)

Russell Kirk's "Southern Valor"

M.E. Bradford, who departed this vale of tears one year before his friend Russell Kirk, published an appreciation of Kirk in the pages of *The Intercollegiate Review* eighteen years ago. He likened Kirk, aptly, to his neglected predecessor in American thought," Orestes Brownson. Brownson was a widely learned and deeply earnest conservative democrat of the 19th century, who (like Kirk) "settled in Michigan, and ended up a Roman Catholic and a traditionalist. "[49]

Brownson was also a disciple of John C. Calhoun, an advocate of federalism, and a defender in the North of the Southern people both before and after the War between the States. Brownson's twenty volumes of collected works reflect a lifelong engagement in defense of the public order of Christianity, tradition, and genuine social justice. His likeness to Kirk is indeed compelling in every respect, not the least in that these two men of letters from the Deep North appreciated the necessity of encompassing the South in any persuasive and viable traditionalist vision of American society.

Privately, Bradford liked to tell the story of how his Vanderbilt mentor, the poet and unreconstructed Southern Agrarian Donald Davidson, had met the young man Kirk sometime in the early fifties before Kirk had burst on the scene with the first edition of *The Conservative Mind*. "Dr. Don" instructed Bradford that Kirk was a man whose friendship and collaboration were to be cherished—and so they were for three decades.

Davidson's admiration for Kirk was reciprocated. In a late piece Kirk wrote:

> Browsing in 1939 in the library at Michigan State College, an earnest sophomore, I happened upon a new book ... entitled *The Attack on Leviathan*, and subtitled *Regionalism and Nationalism in the United States*. It was written eloquently, and for me it made coherent the misgivings I had felt concerning the political notions popular in the 1930s. The book was so good that I assumed all intelligent Americans were reading it.[50]

---

49 "A Proper Patrimony: Russell Kirk and America's Moral Genealogy," in M.B. Bradford, *A Better Guide Than Reason: Studies in the American Revolution* (LaSalle, Illinois: Sherwood Sugden, 1979), p. 215. It was first published in *The Intercollegiate Review*, vol. 12, no. 1, fall 1976.
50 50 "Donald Davidson and the South's Conservatism," in Russell Kirk's *The Politics of Prudence* (Bryn Mawr, Pennsylvania: Intercollegiate Studies Institute, 1993), pp. 99-100.

Only later did Kirk learn that Davidson's book had been ignored by the intelligentsia and pulped by its publisher not long after it appeared. Many years after, Kirk put *The Attack on Leviathan* on his list of the ten most important conservative books, along with Burke, Adams, Brownson, Tocqueville, Roepke, Eliot, and others. And he saw to its republication in his Library of Conservative Thought. "Both before and after the Civil War," Kirk wrote in drawing up his list of ten, "half the important conservative books of America have been written in the South."[51] He might have added that many if not all of the Northern conservatives he celebrated in *The Conservative Mind*, like Cooper, Melville, and Brownson, had a Southern tinge and Southern sympathies.

In his characteristically charming style, which eschewed the journalistic, polemical, and pedantic, and hearkened back more than any other writer of our time to the graceful, gentlemanly communication of 18th century Britain, Kirk observed, in another late piece:

> More than sixty years ago, when I was a fourth-grader in the very northern town of Plymouth, Michigan, twelve Southerners published a book entitled *I'll Take My Stand: The South and the Agrarian Tradition*. That same volume, a heartfelt defense of the permanent things in the South's culture, has been discussed ever since.... Young men and women who come to study with me in my northern fastness discover this literature even without my having commented on any of it—and read the books, night upon night, even to the witching hour of three.[52]

On many other occasions Kirk praised the Southern Agrarians, who he likened to the "Celts of the Twilight," going often to battle but seldom to victory. "The authors of *I'll Take My Stand* did not propound a rigorous ideology or display a model of Utopia; the principle purpose of it was to open eyes to the illusions of Modernism." Their position was "not the only mode of conservative thought, but it is an important mode."[53]

The aims that Kirk correctly ascribed to the Southern writers were, of course, his own; and the same is true of their disciple Richard Weaver and of every other 20th century thinker worthy to wear the colors of traditionalist. They were engaged in a common struggle—a fight, as Bradford put it, against "discontinuity, rupture, and drastic

---

51 "Ten Conservative Books," in *The Politics of Prudence*, p. 54.
52 *The Politics of Prudence*, p. 107.
53 Ibid., p. 112.

innovation."⁵⁴ That is to say, they stood against that strong current of Americanism that regards our country as a notion, an unfinished infinitely malleable proposition for progress and democracy.

America was, rather, though a new land in the wilderness, a fabric of culture stretching back to Jerusalem, Rome, Athens, and London. Which is, of course, self-evidently true and yet ignored in most of our public discourse, including the words of many who fancy themselves "conservatives." As Bradford described it in his essay on Kirk's achievements: "Kirk's amiable but unremitting determination is to require of our generation a grudging admission that America has a religious, a moral, and therefore a political genealogy; a patrimony that could be called unrevolutionary and not at all modern."⁵⁵

Russell Kirk was invariably "amiable," as Bradford put it, as well as eclectic and generous. His conservatism was never an ideology but a wide net that captured all who gave allegiance to "the permanent things." ("The permanent things" and the "moral imagination" were two of Kirk's favorite phrases.) Only very rarely was he provoked into a mild irritation with those he felt were not true defenders of the permanent things, such as libertarians and neo-conservatives.

Thus, while Kirk did not like to emphasize differences, being a student of history, he understood perfectly well tensions and incompatibilities between different ways of being conservative. The incompatibility, for instance, between the tradition represented by Randolph, and Calhoun, and Brownson, on the one hand, and that of Alexander Hamilton, on the other hand, that dubious conservative who "fascinates those numerous Americans among whom the acquisitive instinct is confounded with the conservative tendency.⁵⁶ This Kirk in *The Conservative Mind*, put very gently, but it is clear which side he was on in the division that runs all through American history and makes even today a gulf dividing those who call themselves "conservatives."

Irving L. Horowitz, Kirk's publisher in recent times, in a moving and very insightful memorial tribute, commented that "for Russell, what ought to be is at least as important as what is in the conduct of human affairs." And "he understood that our world was comprised, if not shrouded, in mystery and paradox; and hence in need of dispositions and not dogmas."⁵⁷ This is quite far from that often prevailing

---

54 *A Better Guide Than Reason*, p. 208.
55 Ibid., p. 29.
56 Russell Kirk, *The Conservative Mind, From Burke to Eliot*, 4th revised edition (New York: Avon Books, 1968), p. 80.
57 Irving Louis Horowitz, "Remarks Delivered at a Memorial Service for Russell Kirk at St.

progressive and pragmatic side of the American spirit, which prefers results to mysteries.

Horowitz describes in his reference to "disposition" what was one of Kirk's main themes always: the moral imagination, that Western man at his best reflected and was guided by spiritual apprehensions and historical wisdom, not by the abstractions of social improvers and their little pamphlets and party platforms. This is the chief lesson Kirk drew from Burke and Kirk's chief legacy to us. "Moral" because only in such a fully mythopoeic role can man, made in the image of God and not merely a culture-bearing animal, fulfill his real ethical nature. "Imagination" because the employment of that faculty leads to understandings liberated from the material and animal and because most of the really important wisdom of the race is preserved in imaginative and not rationalistic form.

Patrick Buchanan, in his tribute to Kirk, put the same lesson in slightly different words. He summarized Kirk's primary message as the truth that ideology, the curse of our sad century, is merely a sham religion that takes possession of a soul that is empty. Whether it is fascism, Marxism, democratic capitalism, "the end of history," or any other secular utopia."[58]

This rejection of ideology is a mode of thinking, and living, that Kirk shared with the Southern Agrarians and with the subject of his first book, *Randolph of Roanoke: A Study in Conservative Thought* (1951). For many years I have asked persons at various conservative gatherings what books have most influenced their thinking. A surprisingly large number, over three decades or more, have pointed to Kirk's *Randolph*, more than have mentioned *The Conservative Mind*.

That a conservative of Kirk's stamp should value the South should not shock anyone. It was, after all, Randolph, the quintessentially Southern statesman, who said: "I love liberty and hate equality," thus summing up the American traditionalist's creed as well as it has ever been done. Where else in America than the South could Kirk find substantial and continuing traditions to oppose egalitarianism and utilitarianism, to affirm the American link with British culture and a propertied order, a preference for local liberties and prescriptive rights, and a distaste for abstract schemes and rationalistic progress?

Joseph's Catholic Church, Washington, D.C." Typescript, pp. 1-2.
58 Patrick J. Buchanan, "Russell Kirk: Giant of American Conservatism," in *Putting America First*, vol. 1, no. 5 (June 1994), p. 2.

For in fact, as Kirk recognized in the section of *The Conservative Mind* which he entitled "Southern Valor," the South, for reasons historians have long contended about, has retained more firmly than elsewhere a kind of primal, telluric connection with the tradition of Old Western Man, both self-consciously in political revolt and unconsciously in its folk fabric. All of which is evidenced clearly by the statistics on Christian orthodoxy, personal and local loyalty, and willingness to fight. (Since this is providential it can be a source of satisfaction but not of self-satisfaction for Southerners.) What Kirk called "Southern Valor" and what Richard Weaver described as the "older religiousness of the South" is simply Burke's "the cheap defense of nations," "the nurse of manly sentiment and heroic enterprise," and "unbought grace of life." (This is also the reason, to quote a title by Davidson, "Why the Modern South Has a Great Literature.")

Kirk's Southern alliance is not surprising then, any more than was Brownson's. Nevertheless, at the time he published *Randolph of Roanoke* it was daring to choose as his exemplary American conservative and Burkean the most intransigently Southern of all American statesmen. This Kirk well realized, because he addressed that very matter in the book's opening passage. What relevance could the ideas of the eccentric Randolph have for post-War America?

> America, which presently finds herself the chief protector of the traditions of Western society and therefore a conservative nation, has suffered from a paucity of men of conservative intellect. She needs to re-examine her first principles, if she is to withstand the social atomization which most of the world is experiencing.[59]

Here Kirk was not only explaining his attention to Randolph of Roanoke, but describing his own life's work, which was then at its beginning. And the words are perhaps truer now, getting nigh on half a century after they were written, than ever before.

In response to this felt need of the early 1950s, Kirk pointed out that Calhoun was at last receiving the attention he deserved, which indeed he was, from conservative and moderate scholars like Peter Drucker, Margaret Coit, Clinton Rossiter, Felix Morley, and others. The study of Randolph was even more justified then; his thought "was an appeal to tradition, and against the god Whirl, and it has its disciples yet."[60]

---

59 Russell Kirk, *Randolph of Roanoke: A Study in Conservative Thought* (Chicago, Illinois: University of Chicago Press, 1951), pp. 1-2.
60 *Ibid.*, p. 2.

At this date, when we take for granted the learning that Kirk, Weaver, Bradford, and others have made conventional in regard to the Southern aspect Of American conservatism, it is easy to forget how bold was Kirk's strategy. The received wisdom of American conservatism, such as it was at that time of its intellectual nadir, followed Henry Adams's nasty writings in which Randolph was presented as a crazed genius, "the sable genius of the South." The South was regarded, and nowhere more so than among the acquisitive Hamiltonian conservatives, as the most radical and, indeed, evil part or America, least of all a repository of essential values. When it was not ignored entirely.

In a chapter called "Change Is Not Reform," Kirk felt compelled to argue down the prejudice that Randolph was not a statesman at all. For too many Americans, a statesman was not he who preserved the ancient constitution, shaping when necessary, but he who hacked it down to clear the ground for ever newer and grander constructions. Wrote Kirk:

> Truly conservative statesmen—leaders whose chief desire is the preservation of the ancient values of society—have been rare here; often men called conservatives have been eager for alteration of a nature calculated to encourage a very different kind of society—Hamilton most conspicuous among them. Professed devotion to the cause of undefined progress and innovation has been virtually a prerequisite for political advancement.[61]

In this Kirk was strictly in the tradition of Southern politics.

Like the Founding Fathers and the Southern writers, he admired, Russell Kirk was a genuine man of letters, effortlessly combining the wisdom of history and literature with the needs of the daily world—a rare thing in our time of journalism and "social science." The man of letters, though broadly learned and capable of a scholarly exposition or a philosophical argument, is not a pedant.

Able to turn out a craftsman-like story or poem, yet he is not a self-conscious artist. Willing, if the times are so disjointed as to demand it, to pen a scathing political polemic, he definitely is not an ideologue.

American culture and public life are in a perilously low state, but how much worse off we would be if it had not been for Russell Kirk and his valorous life in behalf of the moral imagination that is the essence of our civilization. We have no better example of resourceful defense of unchanging principle, through bad times and worse. (1994)

---

61 *Ibid.*, p. 134.

Belloc as Historian

Foreword for the new edition of Charles I, by Hilaire Belloc, Norfolk, Virginia: Gates of Vienna Books, 2003, 286 pages.

Warning. Belloc's writings are highly addictive. Fortunately, the craving they create can be readily satisfied. He wrote so much and so well that the supply never runs out, and the best of his works can be reread endlessly.

Belloc was one of the very best writers of nonfiction English prose in the 20th century, which is simply another way of saying that he had a virile, independent mind which expressed itself—archaically—through the written word.

I like Belloc most when he is retelling, in inimitable fashion, his own experiences, as in *Hills and the Sea, The Cruise of the "Nona," The Four Men,* or *The Path to Rome*. His verse, which I suppose would be classified by the misleading label "light," is always a delight:

When I am dead, I hope it may be said
His sins were scarlet, but his books were read.

Belloc was also one of the few courageous souls who was able to view his own times without the facile optimism that characterizes most contemporary thinkers, especially in the English-speaking world. In *The Servile State* (1912) and many other works, he warned that vaunted modern "progress" was undermining the Western spirit and conditions of freedom, and leading the masses of us back into serfdom. Not much has happened since to contradict his foreboding.

The West that Belloc admired was not the West of great cities, immense accumulations of capital, ignorant and hysterical mass media, and "democratic" politicians with oil on the tongue and both hands in the till. It was rather the once (and future?) West of a gentry and yeomanry free and independent in mind and property, presided over by personally responsible rulers and informed by the true Faith. In this respect he and his few but dauntless comrades-in-arms found allies in the Southern Agrarians and a few other thinkers on the western side of the great water.

Given this view of the world, Belloc's numerous biographies and histories are guaranteed to irritate pedants, positivists, Whigs, and other enemies of the human race. The fact that Belloc can think, write lucid narrative, portray historical personalities convincingly, and reach conclusions that have not been pre-digested by others opens an immense gap between his histories and the writings of the great bulk of bureaucratized, "professional" historians that flourished in his time and since.

Historical writing for more than a century has been dominated by Whigs. People who assume that the history of mankind is a tale of "progress." The latest point in time is the highest and best point in time, and all has been tending toward this, our moment. Such has been the implicit assumption of our times, even on the part of those who were not aware that such an assumption controlled their thinking. Such mindsets have made history very dull by removing from it the drama of contingency and human choice. In Whig history, Evil is no longer a permanent force in the world, and human nature does not remain the same in all times. Rather, enlightened policies and proper education will eradicate evils and mould the plastic human world into proper shape. One would think that the 20th century would have disabused even the most sanguine publicists of the Whig philosophy of history, but not so. The most rabid of its current practitioners are even proclaiming "the end of history" in a perfected world of "democratic capitalism."

In Belloc's own time and place, the Whig philosophy carried specific implications: Protestantism is better than Catholicism; capitalism is better than what went before; "science" is better than "superstition." Proponents of this historical trajectory usually believed, though they did not always avow, that what was inevitably to come, socialism and "rationalism," would be even better.

In such an intellectual milieu Belloc wrote very iconoclastic history. His biographies concentrate in the late-Middle-Ages and Reformation eras of the European past. This was the germinating time for Whiggery, and Belloc portrays the downsides of "progress" powerfully. Today, for those of us occupationally doomed to function as historians, dipping into Belloc's biographies is like a refreshing swim after a long, hot day plowing through desert sand. Here is real grappling with important human experience, instead of what flourishes today—largely a weird combination of deterministic "social science" and uncritical, romantic endorsement of favored causes.

In his life of *Charles I*, Belloc comments that the duty of a historian is to help us understand ourselves and our situation, and that the true method of the historian calls for examination of Circumstance and Character. If that be so, Belloc does his duty in the highest degree. (2003)

Their Children's Children

There are a large number, possibly a majority, of people who call themselves conservative. But the more they are examined, the less conservative they will appear. —G.K. Chesterton, Outline of Sanity

A review of *The Rebuke of History: The Southern Agrarians and American Conservative Thought,* by Paul V. Murphy, Chapel Hill: University of North Carolina Press, 2001, 351 pages.

Chesterton, an English Catholic version of a Southern Agrarian, once remarked that Yankee tycoons—Rockefeller, Ford, Morgan—all had the same face. (A face, he added, that any decent man would relish rearranging with a fist.) Similarly, of American "Liberal" academics it can be said that they all have the same *mind* —to the extent that it is absolutely possible to predict what they will say before they say it. I have been testing this for 40 years and have a 100 percent success rate.

In such a situation, an academic becomes celebrated and distinguished when he can say the same thing in a different way, present the familiar tune in a new arrangement. This latest investigation of the Southern Agrarians of *I'll Take My Stand* and their legacy and disciples fills the bill. The author of this doctoral dissertation has dug into the careers of such familiar second-generation Agrarians as Richard Weaver and M.E. Bradford, and the third generation which includes the esteemed editor of this journal and other writers quite familiar to *Chronicles* readers. It should be flattering, I suppose, that "the Chronicles group" are taken so seriously as to become moderately significant historical figures, except that Professor Murphy regards us more as laboratory specimens of deviancy than as serious thinkers. After all, you can't easily predict what we will say before we say it.

When dealing with the South, the pattern is even simpler and more predictable. Everything Southern is by definition evil and wrong. I know one historian who achieved celebrity with a biography that showed that a Civil War era Southern spokesman was a rake and a misanthrope, not a real discovery since it has long been well known. QED, a fresh proof of the evilness of the South. The purveyors of this merchandise are never asked the simple question: "Compared to what?" That a Southerner can be shown to be humanly flawed is all we need to know and damns the whole society. It would be bad manners to mention, say, General

Hooker or Henry Ward Beecher, or to point to the quite extraordinary number of personally admirable characters who flourished in the South at the same time. Ken Burns's notorious Civil War "documentary" is an extended exercise in this kind of thinking.

There is obviously something more going on here than historical analysis. I am reminded of the brilliant intellectual who blamed Timothy McVeigh and the Unabomber on the "atmosphere of violence" created by "the Southern gun culture," though neither one had anything to do with the South nor guns. Or the recent movie in which a Southern character (he had a battle flag plate on his truck) beats his wife and other women and children, hates Jews but is a fundamentalist, hates blacks but practices voodoo. These are rituals of exorcism. The base line is anything "American" is always good and wise and righteous. No proof is needed. Anything bad that shows up in the 50 states must be "Southern."

I'll Take My Stand has always presented a problem for this type of "scholarship," because of the literary eminence of some of the contributors and because it has been continuously attractive to considerable numbers of people. One response is to dismiss it as harmless metaphor, a literary exercise rather than the radical critique of American society that it is. Another is to bury it as hopelessly reactionary, nostalgic, and irrelevant.

Professor Murphy has invented a new tune for the old song. Yes, he agrees, *I'll Take My Stand* really was an expression of radical conservatism. The trouble is, he has discovered, that the second and third generations of followers and even some of the original Agrarians themselves have abandoned or distorted the true Agrarian principles! Some of us have betrayed the true message of radical critique of capitalism by becoming just regular "conservatives." Others of us have betrayed the universality of the teaching by becoming involved in what could be called Southern identity politics.

Southerners can't do anything right, it seems. If we seek allies we are abandoning our best values. If we remain purists we are isolated and futile. If we try to adapt to radically changed circumstances we are abandoning principle, etc. You see the game. If we accommodate to the world that exists we have again betrayed our principles, but if we make a practice of not shopping at chain stores then we are simply figures of fun.

There are a number of things wrong with this. I do not know of any serious Agrarian who has become a Buckleyite conservative. It is true that some of us once thought we had allies there but have long since learned that we were badly mistaken. If we had really sold out to the conservatives, your esteemed editor would be ensconced in the Beltway, drawing a fat salary and writing punditry for the *Wall Street Journal* and *National Review Online*. Besides, there is nothing in Agrarianism fundamentally incompatible with free markets and private property. What the Agrarians criticized was the excessive gigantism, concentration and abstractness of wealth. If we are not "radical conservatives" then what can we be?

The author can get away with this only by carefully defining the Agrarian message to suit himself and carefully selecting the figures to be examined. Thus, in his book, Donald Davidson and those who have followed him went astray by emphasizing the Southernness of the Agrarian message. But this is no deviation, as the author would have to admit if he had paid attention to Owley, Lytle, Wade, Young, and Fletcher rather than just Tate and Ransom. If he had acknowledged the full amplitude of the work, he would have to admit that it is rich enough to inspire many different movements. Besides, he might, if he were inclined to be generous, have concluded that the direction of identity politics was an unavoidable path for Southerners, the only pariah group of the multicultural American empire, the only people who are required to disown themselves to be "good Americans." (Unlike, say, Muslims and pederasts.)

Professor Murphy, to give credit where credit is due, has done a good deal of research and covered things that have not been previously treated. He has grasped the significance of the early writings of "the Chronicles group" in *Why the South Will Survive* and *The New Right Papers*. However, his attempted intellectual biographies of Thomas Fleming and Samuel Francis, for instance, are journalistic—episodic and superficial. They do not achieve substantial or accurate accounts of the development of their ideas, much less of the relationship of such development to "American Conservative Thought" (itself never defined). One would never guess at the originality and power of these two thinkers and the followers and admirers they have found. Murphy wishes only to exorcise them away in pigeonholes he has pre-selected, whether they fit or not.

In these larger things, *The Rebuke of History* does not, in my opinion, achieve a useful account of the Agrarian legacy. And it sometimes goes astray on smaller things as well. The history of the Chapel Hill Conservative Club is garbled. Murphy on the vicious neoconservative attacks on M.E. Bradford and the Rockford Institute is but a mouthpiece for the official neocon cover story, when what was most important about these events was their clandestine aspect. I find myself claiming that "the Southern way of life" transcended history and geography, when I wrote exactly the opposite.

But for what I consider the greatest flaw in Murphy's understanding of the Agrarian view he has many precedents: making Allen Tate the central intellectual figure of the movement. All bad interpreters of the South love Tate for the same reason that all bad interpreters of the Constitution love James Madison—he was a lightweight thinker who can be molded into any shape desired.

Tate has been taken repeatedly to be the definitive interpreter of Southern history. In fact, he was ignorant of history and as far as one can tell never did any primary research. He was a speculative theorist, proposing grand ideas that seemed plausible to many. His biography of Jefferson Davis was written in Paris without any significant sources yet presumed to be profound critique of Confederate military strategy. It was nothing of the sort. He did not know what he was talking about. It was the second worst book written by any of the Twelve Southerners, the worst being his silly, misconceived, badly written novel *The Fathers*.

Tate was fond of portraying the Old South as if it were the New, which he did know something about—as an enervated, incomplete regime doomed to failure. Compared to what? In fact, the South in the 1850s, even in the older states, was highly dynamic, productive and optimistic. How else could it have sustained four years of warfare against a much larger power? Despite Tate's theorizing, the Old South never was, never claimed to be, and never wanted to be "a feudal society."

Tate's most often cited theory is that the South failed because it lacked a coherent theological worldview. But the South did have a unifying theology, if not an established church. Comparatively, the South has been and still is the most solid Protestant Christian society in the world, and that unity has sustained the region under suffering and preserved its uniqueness.

The Rebuke of History gives us a new but essentially predictable narrative of the Agrarian legacy. The author's considerable talents as an intellectual historian do not result in a satisfactory work. No real answer is given to the question of the place and influence of Agrarianism in "American Conservative Thought." This may be in part because the battles are still going on. (2001)

Chapter Nine

In Justice to So Fine a Country

What is a Southerner?

Expert testimony in several federal court cases:

Scholars in every field in the humanities and social sciences have long recognized that Southerners have formed a distinct people within the body of Americans from the earliest colonial times to the present. Authorities in history, political science, economics, sociology, folklore, literature, geography, speech, and music, have recognized and studied the significance of this distinctiveness. The distinct identity of Southerners has also, of course, been a commonplace of everyday life in the United States, and distinctive Southern manners, customs, attitudes and behavior have been material for our greatest creative artists in song, story and movie-making.

Nearly every college in the United States and many in Europe (as well as Japan and Australia) offer courses in Southern history, literature, and other subjects. A number of universities have special institutes devoted to study of the South. (The University of North Carolina at Chapel Hill, the University of South Carolina, the University of Mississippi, John Hopkins University, and Cambridge University are a few examples.) Thousands of scholars around the world are studying Southernness. Thousands of books and dozens of popular and academic journals and websites are available today that are devoted specifically and exclusively to the South. It cannot be credited that this activity would be devoted to something unless it were real and significant.

Many explanations and descriptions have been offered in scholarly literature as to the origins and nature of a distinctive Southern people, beginning with the ethnic origins of the American colonial population and coming up to recent date in studies of public opinion and voting behavior.

An important, recent and authoritative study is *Albion's Seed: Four British Folkways in America* by David Hackett Fischer, prize-winning Professor of History at Brandeis University, Boston (New York: Oxford

University Press, 1989). From exhaustive study in Britain and America, Fischer has identified four different cultural groups from the British Isles that formed differentiated cores of cultural development in what has become the United States. These groups came from different regions of Britain and were separated by religious denomination, economic activity, dialect, manners, and customs.

1) Puritan settlers of New England who came from the East Anglia region of England and formed an identifiable religious and cultural group, which spread to other parts of the Northern states.

2) Settlers from the English Midlands and Wales who settled the Delaware River Valley, belonged to a variety of dissenting religions such as Quakers and Baptists, and pursued economic activities and goals different from those of New England and the South.

3) Gentry and servants from the English southern counties who settled Virginia and the Carolinas in the 17th century, largely Anglican, engaged in plantation agriculture. and displaying manners, customs and attitudes very distinct from groups 1 and 2.

4) Borderers, sometimes loosely described as Celtic, who came from Ireland, Scotland, and the Scots-English border region. They were largely Presbyterian living were markedly different from those of the ordinary English. They settled the piedmont regions of the Southern colonies and spread across the Appalachians in the late 18th century.

Fischer piles up convincing data that these groups formed different cultural centers in the evolution of America. Groups 3 and 4 merged in the early 19th century, to become the Southern people. The distinctiveness of a Southern people was well recognized by everyone by that time—by Southerners, by Northerners, and by foreign travelers. The famous English writer Charles Dickens observed after a trip to America that the Americans formed two distinct peoples. Fischer also provides extensive and convincing evidence that these distinct American cultures persist to this day, a distinctiveness, which can be seen in attitudes, political behavior, and daily life. An interesting example he provides is the startlingly different actions and methods of leadership of two American generals in the Pacific theatre during World War II, both named Smith, one from the North and one a Southerner. Countless other examples can be cited showing such differences in recent history.

Historians have also identified as keys to Southernness climate and a historical experience that differs markedly from the general American. The South was warmer than the North and the regions of Europe from which settlers of America came, giving it a different kind of agriculture and crops (cotton, rice, tobacco, sugar), and thus a different kind of economic activity and a different relation to the marketplace than the rest of the United States. When the U.S. Department of Agriculture decided in the 1920s to commission a definitive history of American agriculture, it found that it required two distinct studies to cover the subject: Percy W. Bidwell, *History of Agriculture in the Northern United States, 1620-1860* (Washington: 1925), and Lewis Cecil Gray, *History of Agriculture in the Southern United States to 1860* (Washington: 1933).

Southerners have, unlike other Americans, more than 350 years of living in a biracial society, in which whites and African-Americans have reciprocally influenced each other's development. It should never be forgotten that the number of African-Americans outside the states of the South was statistically insignificant throughout American history up to World War I. In evidence of a distinct Southern culture, it should be pointed out that Southern African-Americans share with Southern whites nearly every aspect of Southern culture except ethnic origin and political behavior, and differ from general American attitudes in the same direction as do white Southerners.

Undoubtedly the most decisive historical event in firmly establishing a Southern people was the failed War of Independence of 1861-1865. Unlike all other Americans, Southerners have suffered military defeat and occupation and massive destruction by invading armies on their soil. The Confederate States of America was characterized by a mobilization and casualties far beyond that ever experienced by any other Americans at any time in their history. (Gary Gallagher of the University of Virginia, *The Confederate War*, Cambridge: Harvard University Press, 1997.) It is estimated that 85 percent of the eligible male population was mobilized in the War of Independence and one of every four Southern white men was dead at the end of the War. (Comparison: Northern losses were 1 in 10; and the loss was simultaneously made up by immigrants. American losses in later wars are trivial percentages in comparison.) The experience of total war, invasion, conquest and defeat had effects, both tangible and psychological, that have lasted for generations and that mark Southerners now living. War is the single greatest solidifier of a nationality, and it is hardly credible that Southerners would have fought to such an extremity for independence if they had not been conscious of being a separate people.

C. Vann Woodward, Pulitzer Prize historian of Yale University, in his famous study *The Burden of Southern History* (Louisiana State

University Press, 1960), has emphasized this distinctive experience as giving Southerners a heritage of defeat and sorrow. Coupled with long-standing guilt and frustration from the difficulty of race relations, this burden of history has made Southerners a sadder, less optimistic, but perhaps wiser and more realistic people than other Americans whose history has been one of uninterrupted success.

Woodward points also to another consequence of the War. In contrast to America in general, which has been a land of opportunity, progress, and prosperity, Southerners, both white and African-American, have a long experience of poverty. The most prosperous region of the United States in 1860, the South was from 1866 to at least World War II the most impoverished. An estimated 60 percent of the region's capital was destroyed by the War, leaving it economically helpless and subject to exploitation of its resources and peoples as a colony of the United States. In 1860 nearly all white Southern families were independent landowners. In 1900, forty percent of white Southerners were tenants or sharecroppers. And 60 percent of African-American Southerners were in this position, though in absolute numbers there were more white sharecroppers than black. In the 1930s, President Franklin D. Roosevelt famously referred to the South as "the nation's No. 1 Economic Problem," and public discussions were full of references to the South's colonial economic status.

The South has long been known as a source of cheap labor. As well as African-Americans, hundreds of thousands of white Southerners have moved to the North and West in the 20th century, as industrial labor. In the North and West, they were treated as and understood themselves to be a distinct ethnic group, referred to negatively as "hillbillies" and "Okies." Evidences of this can still be seen (like "Little Dixie" neighborhoods in Chicago and country music in Bakersfield, California). It is impossible to over-estimate the effects of generations of poverty within a prosperous country in forming a distinct Southern identity. Even in currently prosperous and growing areas of the South today, the better jobs are largely occupied by newcomers from other parts of the country and the blue-collar jobs by native Southerners.

Southern differences in manners, speech, recreations, religious beliefs, cuisine, and music are commonplace observations in everyday life in the United States. These differences do not have to be absolute. Scots and some Irish and Welsh speak English and are like Englishmen in various way, but they are still obviously distinct nationalities, as are the French-descended Canadians. Speech, religion, music, manners, and cuisine are the universal markers of ethnic distinction. The proof of distinctive Southern characteristics in these areas is easily established by the well-known negative (and sometimes positive) reactions that Southerners receive from other groups.

Contemporary markers distinguishing Southerners as a distinct group have been given systematic scientific study, in the works of John Shelton Reed, Kenan Professor of Sociology at the University of North Carolina at Chapel Hill, especially *The Enduring South*.

Besides differences in lesser matters such as names of children, places, and businesses, Reed demonstrates that public opinion surveys have consistently shown statistically significant differentiation from the American average, especially in three areas:

1) Southerners are the most consistent believers in basic orthodox Christianity as measured by their belief in the Bible, a future state of rewards and punishments, and the reality of Evil, as well as in their church attendance. They even outscore Roman Catholics in other parts of the country on these factors.

2) Southerners are more local and family oriented, less interested in distant events and celebrities than Americans in general.

3) Southerners, for better or worse, live by a different definition of the line between private and public. They are more conscious of giving and receiving offense and tend to deal with such things in person rather than call in public authorities. For instance, in the South murders most commonly occur between persons who are acquainted. In the North there are more commonly attacks by strangers.

Reed has also demonstrated through scientific attitude surveys that Northern and Southern students at the cosmopolitan University of North Carolina at Chapel Hill recognize themselves as having different thoughts, feelings, and behavior. The distinctions discovered by Reed are not absolute—there is some overlap—but they are statistically significant (as well as readily confirmed by empirical observation). See the attached article by Reed from the *Encyclopedia of American Ethnic Groups*.

Another relevant work is The South and the Sectional Conflict by Davia M. Potter of Stanford University, generally recognized as one of the outstanding historians in the United States in the 20th century (Louisiana State University Press, 1968). Potter affirms the separateness of the Southern people and describes how that difference has been created by distinct folkways (thinking, feeling, behaving in ways common to members of the same social group) and separate political experiences.

The hallmarks of a living national culture are its production of arts both at the folk level (arising spontaneously from the people) and at the level of high culture. Southerners have produced several original styles of music, and it is hardly to be doubted that Southern writers have produced a distinct (and highly regarded by the world) literature. The acclaimed novelist George Garrett has demonstrated that distinctive Southernness persists in the most recent generation of outstanding writers. And he has interestingly related Southern literary prowess to the distinctive manners of the region. George Garrett, "Southern Literature Here and Now," in Fifteen Southerners, *Why the South Will Survive* (Athens and London: University of Georgia Press, 1981).

The history of a distinctive Southern speech has been examined by the world famous literary scholar and critic Cleanth Brooks (Yale University) in *The Language of the American South* (University of Georgia Press, 1985). Brooks has demonstrated how distinctive Southern speech has contributed to the success of Southern literary efforts. The distinctiveness of Southern accents was part of the lifelong study of the greatest American scholar of English dialects, Raven I. McDavid of the University of Chicago, author of *Linguistic Atlas of the Middle and South Atlantic States* (Chicago, 1980 and later editions) and *Sociolinguistics and Historical Linguistics* (University of Odense, Denmark).

That Southerners can be distinguished by differing voting behavior is a commonplace calculation of politicians and news media and is the subject of much continuing study by political scientists.

Establishing the reality of the Southerner is akin to proving that Iowa grows corn or that Hollywood is located in California. When the term "Southern" is used, there is not a mind in America that does not immediately reference impressions, favorable or unfavorable, of particular history, literature, music, cuisine, manners, and political and religious tendencies.

I would like to conclude my expert testimony with a personal statement derived from a speech I made at the annual meeting of the Southern Historical Association in New Orleans in 1995, parts of which were published in the journal *Southern Cultures* (University of North Carolina). It refers not to the "Civil War" but to Southern identity today:

The Confederate Battle Flag:
A Symbol of Southern Heritage and Identity

I remember my own father and uncles returning from World War II with stories of how Southerners, particularly rural and working class ones, were denigrated and ridiculed by urbanites for their speech, manners, and attitudes. There was a general cultural attack at the time on "hillbillies." This was the beginning of my consciousness of belonging to a separate people from other Americans. It was at that time that we began to display the Confederate battle flag at times from the front porch and to observe Lee's birthday and Confederate Memorial Day. It is relevant, too, that my grandmother was the daughter of a Confederate soldier and had a fund of stories of the family in the War. Our identification with the Confederate battle flag was nearly a decade before *Brown vs. Board of Education* and it had nothing to do with segregation, the Dixiecrat movement of 1948, or football, contrary to what has been stated by several scholars who have claimed to study the matter impartially.

My Southern identity had thus been brought to my attention before I entered school, and the battle flag was the obvious symbol of that identity, and a beautiful and hallowed object as well. Time, and the success of the civil rights movement and other great changes in the South, have done nothing to diminish this. Rather, to the contrary. The fact that the United States is increasingly a multicultural empire rather than a federal republic, will make ethnic identities, including the Southern, even sharper in the future, which bodes well to see symbolic struggles among Northerners, Latin Americans, African-Americans and Asians. Southerners, the oldest and largest minority in America, have a right to claim their heritage and its symbols. The South is larger in territory, population, economic strength, and history and more distinct in culture than many of the separate nations of the earth.

In recent years, I have spoken often to meetings of the Sons of Confederate Veterans, the United Daughters of the Confederacy, Civil War Roundtables, local historical societies, and other groups. These groups of good citizens are full of defenders and displayers of the battle flag. For most of these good Americans the flag is not a symbol of white supremacy, but an identification with their own ancestors and heritage and an affirmation of their own identity. (2003)

The Rev. Mr. Longstreet and the Nine Dwarfs[62]

You may have missed the teapot tempest of PC hysteria that inaugurated the campaign for the 2004 Democratic presidential nomination. The nine announced candidates gather today (May 3) in Columbia, South Carolina, to unveil their charms in a public forum. The show was scheduled to take place at the Longstreet Theatre on the campus of the University of South Carolina.

Then someone discovered that the building is named for the Rev. Augustus Baldwin Longstreet, one time president of the University's predecessor institution, South Carolina College. And Horrors! Mr. Longstreet in the period before the War for Southern Independence defended slavery and advocated secession! Of course, the august aspirants for World Emperor could not be expected to meet on such unhallowed ground, so the gathering was shifted to another building, about which more in a moment.

Let's set aside the fact that the Longstreet Theatre has been the scene previously of numerous public occasions in which at least two Presidents of the United States, the current Pope, and numerous other world dignitaries have appeared. Even William F. Buckley used to televise his orchestrated debates from that very place since it is not too far from the family winter palace in Camden. No one ever complained about the name before.

What strikes most is the astounding ignorance of and contempt for American history that the political leaders and the press exhibit on this and similar occasions. They act as if some dark and terrible secret had been discovered. It is true that Longstreet, who was a Methodist minister, newspaper editor, college president, and author, believed, accurately, that the Scripture, while it condemned bad masters, did not condemn servitude per se. There was nothing surprising about this—every member of the clergy in the South at that time—Methodist, Baptist, Episcopalian, Lutheran, Presbyterian, Catholic, and Jewish—said the same thing. So did orthodox clergymen of the North (those opposed to evangelical hysteria and the overturning of society according to the alleged divine revelations of individuals). A number of distinguished Northern clergymen wrote learned treatises against the abolitionists.

The defenders of slavery were, unfortunately, forced into making these unseemly statements because their society was under attack by

---

62 Dwarf (noun): a little devil. Webster's New World Dictionary.

abolitionists. Let's be clear about this. Abolitionists were not people with rational and moral objections to slavery who were anxious to find measures to get rid of it, as the previous generations, including many Southerners, had been. They were secularized post-Christian Puritans conducting a malicious, slanderous, hate-filled, totalist propaganda campaign against every aspect of Southern life with the ruthless irresponsibility of religious zealots. (Remember, Lincoln was always careful to claim that he was not an abolitionist!)

Abolitionists proposed no practical steps for the end of slavery, an institution inherited from early colonial times and intricately intertwined in very basic ways with economics, society, and everyday life. Emancipation, however desirable, posed problems for which not even Lincoln could propose a real solution. Abolitionists were not concerned about the welfare of black people. They wished to expunge their sinful Southern fellow citizens from the earth, which they believed would lead to a pure and heavenly America. Their leading egghead, Ralph Waldo Emerson, said he was less concerned for the fate of a thousand blacks (whom he expected to disappear with the end of slavery) than with one white man corrupted by slavery. Daniel Webster, the greatest man of the North no less, said that the abolitionists were solely responsible for destroying the prospects for eliminating slavery.

During the brief press furor over the Rev. Mr. Longstreet, there were two interesting (to me at least) facts about the situation that did not come out. No one knew or bothered to mention that in spite of his sins, Longstreet was the author of *Georgia Scenes*, one of the classics of early American literature. And that the Longstreet building, built in the 1850s as a gymnasium, was used as a stable by the U.S. Army during the War and Reconstruction (which saved it from being torched).

Also, most people, if they think about it at all, think the building was named for the Rev. Mr. Longstreet's nephew, General James Longstreet.

But it gets funnier. The carnival has been moved to the theater in a nearby campus building, Drayton Hall. I do not know for which member of the Drayton family Drayton Hall is named. I do know that the Draytons, who produced prominent leaders from the Revolution to the Southern War, including a Confederate general, were for generations among the largest slaveholders of South Carolina.

Drayton Hall is bordered by College Street, Main Street, Greene Street, and Sumter Street. Greene Street is named for General Nathaniel Greene of the American Revolution, who was awarded a large Georgia plantation for his services (the plantation on which, by the way,

Eli Whitney perfected the cotton gin). Sumter is named for General Thomas Sumter, one of the heroic South Carolina partisan leaders of the Revolution. He was also a large slaveholder and as an old man in the late 1820s advocated the secession of South Carolina from the Union.

In fact, it is not easy to find a building built on the campus before the 20th century, or a street in the central area of the capital city of South Carolina that is not named for a slaveholder or a secessionist! Obviously, we have not gone nearly far enough in expunging the evils of the past. While we are at it, let's make a clean sweep. Why should we wait for the civil rights groups and the press to pick off these abominations one by one? Why should our national capital, Washington, be named for that old slaveholder, and the District of Columbia named for a dead white male exploiter and genocidist? For that matter, does not the "States" in United States suggest evil, exploded notions of State rights? It is long past time that these matters be attended to. (2003)

Harvard Goes South

A review of *Tombee: Portrait of a Cotton Planter*, by Theodore Rosengarten, New York: William Morrow, 1986, 750 pages.

This curious big book is an amalgam of left-wing scholarship and commercial panache. On the one hand, the author, a Harvard Ph.D. in American Civilization and a missionary to South Carolina, seems to have enjoyed extended foundation support during the production of this book, as well as a good deal of paid assistance in the drudgery of transcription and research. And his work has received respectful attention in both the *New York Times* and the *New York Times Book Review*. On the other hand, a generous publisher has secured for *Tombee* a book club selection and has allowed the author an indulgent 750 pages to present the biography and diary of a relatively obscure and historically insignificant planter on the Sea Islands of the South Carolina coast.

The chain bookstores, in my portion of the Union at least, were piled high with copies of *Tombee* for the Christmas trade, suggesting a hope of capitalizing on the century-and-a-half-old preoccupation of the American reading public with the Old South that made best-sellers out of Uncle Tom, Uncle Remus, "Marse Chan," *Gone with the Wind* and *Roots*.

Contained within these bulging covers are two potentially good books, each about a third the size of the artifact that exists. The author seems to have discovered, or rather to have had pointed out to him, the existence of an intimate journal of Thomas B. Chaplin, kept over a period of many years. Chaplin was a planter in the isolated region between St. Helena and Port Royal sounds inhabited by a few dozen planter families and some thousands of slaves. Leave aside the fact that among those few white families were a number of remarkable men (and women)—Elliotts, Rhetts, Seabrooks, and others, of whom Chaplin was probably the least interesting. Leave aside the fact that there are dozens, possibly hundreds, of other planter diaries in existence that are equally or more important than Chaplin's. (One sometimes gets the sense that this one has assumed immense importance among the Intelligentsia of the Northeast because it was the one read by someone from Harvard.) Leave aside the fact that there are certainly dozens of scholars equally qualified to present this material to the reading public as Mr.

Rosengarten. Still, Chaplin's diary is an extended, intimate, and candid record of real life in a vanished part of America. And it is always good to have historical sources made readily available. Thus, the publication of Chaplin's diary, appropriately introduced and annotated, would have been a valuable scholarly contribution.

Unfortunately, while it remains valuable, the value is compromised by the author's statement that he cut out a third of the original material. While he describes in several pages himself going about constructing the "published diary" out of the original, his discussion of his editorial procedures is so subjective that he never really meets the basic scholarly requirement of indicating fully the nature of the omitted material.

On the other hand, one might have made use of the diary and other sources and written an interesting short biography of Chaplin, which would have been more useful than the author's decision to present both an abridged diary and an over-extended biography. Like most of his neighbors, Chaplin was an able sportsman and Confederate soldier. Unlike most of his neighbors, he was not a successful agriculturalist. His fortunes declined even before the War, and he engaged in a protracted tedious litigation with his stepfather. After the War, like many other 19th century Americans who lacked non-addictive pain-killers, he became a dope fiend, which perhaps explains part of his presumed appeal to the contemporary reading public. One might argue that some of his more significant neighbors would have made a better study, should one want to examine in depth the society of the Sea Islands, which was somewhat peculiar by Southern or even by South Carolina standards. But there is a great historical value in studying the more ordinary level in any situation, and I have no quarrel with the selection of subject. Rosengarten's approach is in the familiar genre of the psychosocial, by which we have learned that beneath their stern exteriors our 19th century forefathers were quite often as human (i.e., screwed up) as we are. That is fine and well worth knowing, so long it is kept in perspective with other historical considerations.

A good deal of value and interest emerges from the biographical treatment. Its flaws are two. First, there is no true historical perspective. The reader never quite escapes from the awareness that he is being lectured by a superior modern observer on the political, social, moral, and character shortcomings of other men of another day and place. Though his actions and comments are described fully, one will never understand, from this source alone, what made Chaplin tick. His political beliefs, for instance, are never made meaningful because the author cannot really believe that they were real, serious, inherited, and rational in Chaplin's world and not just a smoke screen to fool observers.

Secondly, the author felt impelled to frame his biography with an extended and digressive history of the Sea Island region and of South Carolina from early colonial times through Reconstruction. Where first-rate secondary sources exist, as for the Reconstruction period, this is fairly successful. On the whole, it is not. John C. Calhoun dies in the wrong month. Robert Barnwell Rhett, foremost of the fire-eaters, is described as a "provincial." Rhett was a Southern nationalist, and Rosengarten is free to disapprove of him; however, he was not a "provincial," as any rudimentary perusal of his correspondence or career will indicate. To characterize a complicated historical figure in this way is little more than sloganeering. At another level, the author tells us, "On the eve of secession, the great majority of white people in South Carolina did not own any slaves." From this statement he proceeds to an extended discussion of the beliefs and motives of the nonslaveholding farmers, about whom he surely knows less than I know about Paraguayans. But the whole discussion is pointless. The most salient fact about antebellum South Carolina was that nearly one-half of the body of citizens were slaveowners and that, unlike any other American state, there was no "great majority" of nonslaveholding farmers.

Such missteps are trivial taken alone, but cumulatively they suggest a level of historianship somewhat lower than *Tombee* aspires to. Should you wish to learn something about the Sea Island planters, let me suggest you pass up *Tombee* and turn to a book by one of their number that is a classic expression of their *spirit—Carolina Sports by Land and Water* (1846) by William Elliott, which is a good deal more than its title suggests. Or you might turn to the letters of the Jones family from the adjacent region of Georgia, letters published a few years ago as *The Children of Pride*.

There is little in *Tombee* that the specialist cannot find more reliably elsewhere. Nevertheless, the book has already achieved the critical acclaim which it sought, and which was doubtless fore-ordained. I am not apprised of the degree of its commercial success. Presumably, there are still some thousands of "general readers" tucked away in odd corners across that great forest of satellite dishes that make up American culture. But I suspect, *Tombee* will prove a bit too heavy and too cynical for them, and too bulky for the Hilton Head tourist trade. (1987)

Keeping Up with the Joneses
(Southern Style)

A review of *The Children of Pride: A True Story of Georgia and the Civil War*, edited by Robert Manson Myers, New Haven, Connecticut: Yale University Press, 1984, 671 pages.

In retrospect, the publication and public reception (as measured by sales and critical attention) of *The Children of Pride* must be seen as a minor but significant event in the cultural history of America in the 1970s—one of those peculiar counter currents that history always throws up against the prevailing trends of a time to remind the thoughtful of the ambiguities of existence and historians of the perils of generalization.

During the 1970s the popular, and indeed to an unacknowledged but considerable extent, the scholarly idea of the Old South was formed and sustained by television docudramas. The readers of *The Children of Pride*, however, could not loll in their chairs and be effortlessly entertained by facile imitations of history. They had, instead, to grapple with 1,800 pages of closely-packed eight-point type. The story they found was not a diversion concocted by the brightest talents of Hollywood, but rather, from first to last, was authentic documentation of the mundane existence of persons who really lived in the same time and place as the fictional characters of *Gone with the Wind* who had once captured vast public attention.

The real persons who emerged from this effort were not stock characters of the Old South. That is to say, they were not drawling, vicious, sometimes charming degenerates; languid, feeble-minded women in low-cut gowns; or noble, cardboard blacks suffering patiently until the day of jubilee: all designed to titillate, divert, and arouse comforting feelings of superiority and righteousness in the beholder. Instead, the family of Colonel Charles C. Jones, Jr., of Liberty County, Georgia, were remarkably devout, ethical, conscientious, and intelligent men and women. The blacks emerged, in many cases, not as stereotyped victims but as authentic human beings, living lives of meaning as members of an extended plantation family.

Nor could the readers of *The Children of Pride* be stimulated by the insinuations of easy and illicit sex that have always, since the time of abolitionist propaganda, formed a backdrop to portrayals of the Old South. That is, unless the readers were so rarely unjaded as to be stimulated by chaste expressions of affection between married or soon to be married men and women. Violence, too, could not be vicariously enjoyed, except in after-the-fact letters of men who recounted their experiences of battle with subdued realism and a consciously-imposed, classical restraint.

Nor, in a decade of dissent and reform, fanatically pursued, could the reader even find any straw men of fire-eating reaction. Southern sentiment and social conservatism could be found aplenty in the musings and communications of the Joneses—but equally evident were a stern sense of duty, a discerning and socially responsible patriotism, and a reluctant but firm response to what was matter-of-factly perceived as foolish and intolerable provocation. Far from allowing indulgence in a vicarious sense of righteousness, any serious attention to the behavior and sentiments of the Joneses was more likely to induce a sense of moral inferiority and social decline.

It is difficult to tell to what extent the numerous readers of *The Children of Pride* were provoked to larger historical generalizations. Most, perhaps, like the majority of reviewers, concentrated upon the fascination and poignancy of the story told. Yet anyone who is familiar with the primary sources for the history of the Old South would have little trouble in finding many other families who differed only in incidentals from the Joneses. For few families is the documentary record so complete. Many were less articulate than the Joneses. The religion and ethics of most had a more Anglican and less Calvinist cast than that of the Presbyterian Georgians. Still, the Joneses were not unique, and their essential characteristics could easily be documented in many hundreds of other families in every state of the Old South were anyone inclined to collect, transcribe, and publish the record. They present not an individual story but a social picture.

This social picture of the Old South is not, of course, a total picture. No one view can encompass all the realities of any complex society. But it does constitute a substantial reality. Given that, *The Children of Pride* is not merely a curious cultural artifact; it is also a permanent object lesson in the difference between history as the search for truth, which enriches, and history as amusement or as a mine for ideological ammunition, which debases. No part of the historical experience of Americans has received more of the latter kind of attention than the Old South. Yet, despite this, there has always emerged, often unexpectedly, a counter-trend, which perhaps can be taken as evidence of the recurring human need for the truth and inspiration of the authentic.(1984)

Confederate Rainbow

Books reviewed: *The Jewish Confederates*, by Robert N. Rosen, Columbia: University of South Carolina Press, 2000, 517 pages; *Clear the Confederate Way!: The Irish in the Army of Northern Virginia*, by Kelly J.O. Grady, Mason City, Iowa: Savas Publishing Company, 1999, 348 pages; and *Fire and Roses: The Burning of the Charlestown Convent, 1834*, by Nancy Lusignan Schultz, New York: Free Press, 2000, 317 pages.

As we all know, in the Civil War an expansive, democratic, progressive, multi-ethnic North defeated a bigoted and reactionary South so that government of the people, by the people, and for the people should not perish from the earth. Like so many of the common beliefs about the War (which are now being enforced as official indisputable truths) the picture is not true. (In this respect it is like many other official untruths: that the War was fought for the benefit of the slaves, or that Andersonville was worse than Northern prisons, or that, according to current Hollywood, Confederates were vicious barbarians who made war on women.)

Everyone knows about Meagher's Union Irish brigade and their heroic charge at Fredericksburg. Mr. O'Grady sheds some interesting light on this: General Meagher never exposed himself to fire; rather than an exhibit of Irish-American adherence to the Union cause, the Fredericksburg debacle caused a great falling off in Irish support for the War.

Meagher was not much of an Irish patriot, unlike John Mitchel, a true Irish nationalist, who served the Confederacy and gave it the lives of two sons. Pius IX, at the instigation of the heroic Confederate priest John Bannon, strongly condemned and curbed Union recruiting. As a Dublin newspaper observed in 1861, "we cannot but recollect that in the South our countrymen were safe from insult and persecution, while 'Nativeism' and 'Knownothingism' assailed them in the North."

In fact, the Northern cause was big on WASP supremacy. There was a strong Puritan, Cromwellian streak in the North which decried Catholicism and non-WASPs in general. (German Protestants were OK.) And this sentiment was strongest in Northerners who tended toward abolitionism and the harshest anti-Southern attitudes. One of the reasons many people disliked Southerners, as is evident in the sources of the time, was that they were considered not WASP enough! More people disliked slaveholders because of their close association with Africans than because of the evils of slavery. In fact, the most fundamental goal of the War and Reconstruction was to keep blacks out of the North.

This aspect of Northern society is illuminated in *Fire and Roses*. We see how economic and religious tensions were projected onto Catholic newcomers—leading to the spreading of malicious rumors, the sacking and burning of a convent, and the refusal of local authority to punish the perpetrators. (Such things went on in Philadelphia as well as sacred Boston.) In fact, the destruction of the convent reminds one in all sorts of ways of Sherman's progress. Catholic churches and convents in the South went up in flames as readily as any other religious buildings. Probably Mary Surratt would not have been executed if she had not been hated as a Catholic.

Now, this was happening when Catholics and Jews were being honored and elected to office in the South by Protestant neighbors. Bishop John England of Charleston was the leading prelate in America, on friendly terms with all the clergy of the community, and invited to address the legislature. There were two Jewish, and several Catholic Senators elected from Southern states before the War, nearly unthinkable at that time in the North.

All immigrants, from whatever quarter (including the North) who had resided in the South for any amount of time before the War, were loyal Confederates. In fact, the antebellum South, far from being narrow and bigoted (whatever may be said about later times) had a tremendous power to bind the allegiance of diverse elements.

This is nowhere clearer than in the case of the Jews. It will surprise many, though it should not, because the truth has always been there, that the South held the allegiance of its Jewish citizens, who fought and sacrificed, as loyally as any other group. Later Jewish immigrants knew nothing of the War and adopted the Union viewpoint to be good Americans. So, the story of Jewish Southerners, probably a greater number percentage-wise than in the North, has not been told until now.

Mr. Rosen, a Charleston attorney and amateur historian has given us a really valuable work that brings to light the lives of a forgotten though interesting and worthy group of Americans. And I mean "amateur" in the best possible sense. It is the amateurs who are able to see things the conformist academics never think of, and who will in the future compose the real historical works.

Jewish Southerners perceived, rightly, that abolitionists were strongly anti-Semitic. The abolitionist Theodore Parker believed that Jews were "lecherous" and sometimes did kill Christian babies. The abolitionist William Lloyd Garrison described a New York newspaper editor as "a miscreant Jew," "the enemy of Christ and liberty," and a descendant of "the monsters who nailed Jesus to the cross." The catalog of such sentiments among the most fervent abolitionists and supporters of the Union war effort is a large one, headed by John Quincy Adams. A whole book could be written on the subject.

Americans' historical understanding is in a peculiar state. While honest and sincere historians are always bringing to light new and interesting nuances to the central events of our history, these new discoveries make no headway with the academic establishment (and the political forces which claim historical justification) and never affect in the slightest the accepted understandings, which for the academics as well as the politicos are becoming more and more groupthink slogans indifferent not only to nuance, but to all evidence and argument.

These fine works shed new light on antebellum and wartime America and its diverse peoples. The next great subject that needs definitive and exhaustive treatment (some starts have been made) is the story of the tens of thousands of black men who were part of Confederate armies. Hundreds, probably thousands, went with Lee's army to Pennsylvania and back and took their wounded or dead masters home. In fact, the Southern soldiers who survived the famous attack at Gettysburg, I am told by a close student of the subject, came back to the Confederate lines which were marked by a multitude of black faces. (2004)

In Justice to So Fine a Country

The Assault on Tobacco

The assault on tobacco continues. The recent phenomenon of federal and state governments levying reparations on the tobacco industry for health care costs is unprecedented, and it presents much food for thought. It is likely that the companies, already diversified. will not suffer much, or at least a good deal less than they would if subject to endless class action suits. Other health-endangering corporations— Seagram's, Anheuser-Busch, the makers of the Corvair and the Pinto, have never been singled out in this way. In fact, they would more likely be candidates for bailout than prosecution. It is an easy bet that if the tobacco industry was as important to New York, Massachusetts, or Michigan as it is to the Carolinas, we would be seeing a rather different federal policy. South-hating, almost as old as American history, can always be called into play. A recent wire service story, datelined Tokyo, told how the evil tobacco growers of the Southeastern United States, facing declining domestic markets, are cruelly addicting unfortunate Japanese teenagers to cigarettes.

With all the talk of reparations these days, we ought to extend our thinking a little beyond the usual victim groups. The Indians (excuse me, Native Americans) owe us for the damage tobacco has done. The Europeans who first came to the New World were happily innocent of the Stinking Weed, but they soon caught on (and their governments soon recognized a great opportunity for monopolies and tax revenue). There were arguments all across Europe as to whether it was a good or a bad thing, but it was a major and ineradicable habit by the time the novelty died away, and tobacco quickly spread to the rest of the world. So, the Native Americans, now flush with casino money, owe not only us poor white and black Americans, but the Europeans, the Chinese, and everyone else for having thrust this terrible addiction on us.

There are other curious features: the government suing for the recovery of healthcare costs, for instance. The tacit assumption seems to be that government is the main provider of healthcare—an idea I thought we defeated back in 1993. Is the government in fact grabbing for itself compensation that is potentially due to thousands of individual sufferers?

The tobacco saga also illustrates the sad ignorance of history that afflicts American bureaucrats and media. We ought to have a little more sympathy for tobacco. (I confess to being descended from a long line of tobacco farmers, one of the most skilled and intensive forms of agricultural endeavor.) Tobacco was the most important product of North America in the 18th century. It vastly aided the economic growth of America and was the mainstay of North Carolina, Virginia, and Maryland. Without tobacco, development would have been retarded, and the colonies would not have had the strength to fight a War of Independence. Possibly tobacco did not do our ancestors much harm, and may even have offered them considerable comfort in a world with fewer comforts and more dangers than ours—as it did the fighting men in World War Il. Our forebears constantly breathed air infused with the smells of coal and wood fires, tanning, soap-making, manuring, animal slaughtering, weaving, dyeing, and the like. A good pipe or dip of snuff was a pleasant change for them.

Before this century, people enjoyed tobacco in pipes, cigars, chewing plugs, and snuff. It appears that cigarettes, a strange modern invention, do the most harm. The older forms of tobacco were produced by craftsmanly efforts. The cigarette is a typical industrial product, mass-produced for the lowest common denominator. It is the emblem of our century, with its excessive urbanization, centralized governments, indiscriminate global warfare, uniformitarian culture, and frantic tempo. Smoke 'em if you got 'em. (1998)

In the Land of Cotton

A review of *Breaking the Land: The Transformation of Cotton, Tobacco, and Rice Cultures Since 1880*, by Pete Daniel, Urbana: University of Illinois Press, 1985, 352 pages; and *As Rare as Rain: Federal Relief in the Great Southern Drought of 1930-31*, by Nan Elizabeth Woodruff, Urbana: University of Illinois Press, 1985, 203 pages.

When we write of Southern rural life (as when we write of Southern speech, manners, history, or literature) we essay a phenomenon significantly different from that which would normally be suggested were the modifier "Southern" to be replaced by "American."

In the beginning, Southern agriculture laid the foundation for America. It was Southern tobacco, and to a lesser extent rice, indigo, cotton, and naval stores, which provided the economic incentive and *raison d'être* for the British settlement of North America. Aside from the fur trade, the Northern colonies had no function in the British Empire except as a haven for Dissenters. The adherence of the South to the War for Independence was an act of sheer political idealism, against self-interest and without the economic and religious motivations of New England.

Even through the first half of the 19th century, the Southern staples were the core of American agriculture. During most of that period cotton made up more than half the dollar value of exports of the United States. It therefore provided the wherewithal for our imports, and since the Federal government was chiefly financed through the tariff on imports, cotton provided the government's revenue base. The commercial greatness of New York was built to a considerable extent on the cotton-carrying trade. Alabama was a flush outpost of a vital international commodity when Indiana, at the same longitude westward, was still a backward world of subsistence farmers. It was not until the last decade before the Civil War that the great Midwestern breadbasket came into its own, with the construction of railroads to the Northeast and the production of machinery that could cultivate the virgin prairies and plains and harvest on a grand scale, including the reaper invented by the Virginian Cyrus McCormick.

The great agricultural historian Lewis Cecil Gray has written that the plantation system constituted the scenic highlands of the antebellum

Southern economy, though most of the land area was occupied by small, independent farmers. Though rice, sugar, and hemp required the large capitalization of a plantation, cotton and tobacco were democratic crops that could be grown and sold for a profit as readily by the small farmer as by the planter. A considerable portion of the population, as has recently been re-emphasized, lived in the Old South on the large-scale open-range raising of livestock, an American adaptation of traditional British border economy and the direct, legitimate sire of what is thought of as "Western" ranching.

The South of the late antebellum period was prosperous and stable. The Southern population, including blacks, except in the less developed areas, lived snugly in rough abundance, content with the Jeffersonian ideal of independence and relatively immune from the tremendous religious and economic stresses of modernization being endured by Northern society. During the panic of 1857, when Northern banks and mercantile houses experienced a landslide of bankruptcy and the Bank of England saved itself by extraordinary measures, Southerners were hardly touched. It was at this juncture that an over-cocky Southern spokesman told the world that "Cotton is King!"

As always, hubris extracted its price. The failed War of Southern Independence left the antebellum infrastructure in ruins. There was immense destruction, confiscation, and theft of property, without any post-war Marshall Plan. The slaves were freed, itself a vast liquidation of capital which at the same time drastically lowered the value of land in the most productive parts of the South. The freedmen were of interest to the North chiefly as political pawns. They had few economic alternatives except to remain on the land as a dependent labor force. Somehow, a considerable number of black people acquired land and achieved some independence. How this happened is not understood, because, while liberal historians have devoted billions of words to the black experience, they have shown little interest in how this truly constructive feat was accomplished.

The planter had few economic alternatives either. His capital, if he was lucky, consisted of the land and a cache of Confederate bonds. He had to borrow to supply and feed his labor force through the year; his survival depended on a network of credit that led ultimately to Yankee capital. The crop was already mortgaged before it was planted. There was no cash for wages; and anyway, too many Southerners, white and black, were endowed with the Jeffersonian ideal of Independence to submit to wage labor. A system of sharecropping and tenantry grew up, leaving thousands of farmers at the mercy of distant forces of supply and demand over which they had no control. Except for flush periods, like World War I, the price often did not meet costs, and vast numbers sank into an inescapable pit of debt. A majority of the black population remained in a condition that cannot be called peonage because it was too vagrant. Startlingly, large numbers of formerly independent white families were reduced to similar status. In fact, by the end of the 19th century, the number of white croppers and tenants exceeded the number of black (though a higher percentage of the black population was in this condition). No Southerner ever suffered from the strange delusive assumption, encountered repeatedly in conversation with upper-middle-class Northern liberals, that most poor people are black and that poverty is chiefly the result of racism.

Although this brief sketch oversimplifies the history of Southern agriculture, it does provide the necessary context for FDR's famous statement that the South was the nation's Number One Economic Problem. The profitability of cattle and later oil in Texas and Oklahoma modified the picture, as did industrialization in some areas and the partial survival of the independent small farm class. But the bleak pronouncement remained broadly true. Meanwhile, Southerners continued to hold on to a militant Jeffersonianism, both as political program and folkway, for which the economic base had disappeared, while the North was swept along by that combination of open-ended material progressivism and social democracy which for most people constitutes the American way. Pete Daniel, in *Breaking the Land*, recounts that the Southern way of life began to change in the 1880s, with the arrival of agricultural colleges and extension agents, quintessential progressive American institutions, which generated a new sense of technical prowess and profit motive and thus began the slow transformation of Southern agriculture to its modern scientific and capitalist form. Daniel's work provides a sound and welcome amendment, but does not alter the larger story, for the real change came in the 1930s with mechanization and farm subsidies. This corrective commentary, by way of background, brings us to more recent history, and to the books in hand.

As Rare as Rain, the less important of these works, is concerned with the question of rural relief as it presented itself during the Depression year 1930, when the rainfall fell to as low as one-third of normal in parts of the South and pushed many people over the line between normal hard times and disaster. to relieve localized suffering without a government apparatus of permanent relief. The author sees the case as another proof of the failures of Hooverism. Woodruff may well be right, for all I know, that a public and more permanent system of welfare was needed. However, I am not sure that the evidence presented proves the point. To begin with, the rural and urban problems of the Depression were different. It is not at all self-evident that a welfare system designed for industrial relief was the best answer to rural distress.

Woodruff's treatment falls into a recognizable genre of liberal complaint. Relief must not simply relieve distress, it must get to the root of "the problem of poverty"—that is, it must be political. The charitable institutions which assisted in the Southern crisis must, by definition, be judged failures. They did not try to use their leverage to alter the social structure which enlightened urban thinkers considered to be the fundamental cause of the problem. Heaven forbid, relief was even administered through local landowners and officials, who also were not political.

At the root of the analysis, though here expressed in a very mild and temperate form, is the urban intellectual's hatred and fear of the landowner or any rural person above the dependent class. Not sharing the urban liberal scale of manners and values, such persons represent a threat. The fear of the countryman is a persistent theme in American manufactured popular culture from the time of Sinclair Lewis. In television drama, the humane sensitive urbanite is always violated by the vicious small-towner, never the other way around (despite what statistics tell us about comparative crime rates). At present, thousands of the best minds of the East and West Coasts lie awake nightly into the wee hours, fretting in fear that primitive Christians from the boondocks may actually rise up and put a crimp in the drug traffic and pornography industry. This attitude, in a much more virulent form, accounts for the worst excesses of the Bolshevik Revolution. The Bolsheviks did more than adopt a mistaken farm policy; they deliberately set out to exterminate or enslave all independent and productive farmers, for whom they had an irrational hatred built upon feelings of vulnerability and inferiority.

It is not clear to me that Woodruff's evidence demonstrates that the old ways were completely hopeless, and it certainly does not demonstrate that the welfare and farm subsidy programs that have since grown up were the best or only alternatives. The most serious distresses seem to have been localized, like the credit crunch in the Arkansas delta, for instance, or to have involved a marginal lumpenproletariat of the sort that had always existed in the Kentucky mountains. It is not at all clear that the farmers who reluctantly asked for help in extremis were in the least interested in political revolution.

And the landowners and small-towners whom the author finds controlled by their own narrow interests seem to me to have been, for the most part, decent, public-spirited, and commonsensical folks who were doing the best they could, and whose moral concern for their fellow man far transcends that of most Federal officials or college professors.

If *As Rare as Rain* is a political tract masquerading as an academic monograph, *Breaking the Land* offers a pastoral lament cast in the form of social history. Daniel tells the story of how the South moved from its 19th century way of life (and it was a way of life and not simply a way of business) to modern commercial agriculture. It is a transformation in human affairs which he considers (with only slight exaggeration) "as significant as the enclosure movement that revolutionized the Old World." For anyone who knew the South as recently as the 1940s, there has indeed been a revolution. Any early-middle-aged South Carolinian can remember when almost every available patch of land was aglisten with cotton in the summer, and the mule and wagon was a common moving sight on the roads. One has to look hard today to find a cotton field, and mules are about as numerous as zebras.

Millions of Southerners, white and black, have moved to the North, the West, and the Southern cities. They have left behind them in the country a mechanized commercial agriculture employing only a fraction of the population; the remnants of a yeoman class which gets most of its income out of day labor in the city, though it still clings to the land; and sizable pockets of black communities which have not yet been integrated into the modern economy except insofar as it is represented by the Federal welfare system. Daniel is less interested in the economics of Southern rural life in the last century than he is in the human story of the replacement of a way of life. The human experiences of the revolution are presented in *Breaking the Land* with vivid detail, without sentimentalizing the old way of life but with a sympathetic awareness of the genuine loss involved in the destruction of its more consoling features.

The author has another theme that will strike a responsive chord for all of those who are not willingly enfeoffed to the gospel of limitless material progress. The course of the changes that overtook the South was dictated, as portrayed by Daniel, by the decisions of large capital and government policy, decisions which often involved deliberate choice from an ideology of gigantism and maximum productivity. Indeed, it is quite fair to give the New Deal farm policies in the South the greatest share of credit for the pockets of dependency (as opposed to merely poverty) in the South, and as a second consequence of the same dislocations, the Northern urban nightmare. But there were indeed other alternatives, alternatives that, had decisions been made from a different scale of values, might have worked toward the preservation of the viable small farm, owned or tenanted, and toward an optimum rather than a maximum productive relationship with the land. Such policies were, in fact, suggested in the 1930s by Southern Agrarians and others who were enamored neither of big government nor big business. Among the many appealing proposals, none was more drastic than the suggestion that unemployed or underemployed families be staked to a homestead, even subsidized, to remain on the land and produce.

This is doubtless a shocking proposal to the coterie of sophists and calculators, calling themselves conservatives, who have recently discovered that the production of the stuff of life is just another form of corporate enterprise, that our farm support programs represent a nonsensical nostalgia, and that we must let the "marginal" farmer go to the wall so that the market can wisely redistribute resources. But even many who hold no particular brief for the present government price system recognize that every enlightened and prosperous nation on the globe makes special provision for its farmers, and not from an obsolete affection for the yeoman ideal. The truth is that the agricultural market is the great unsolved problem of the modern economy. No one has as yet devised more than a makeshift solution to the cycles of overproduction and underproduction and price fluctuation that have beset agriculture since at least the 18th century. Whatever due obeisance we give to the market, and much is due, there is something wrong with the approach of the sophists and calculators.

Leave aside the ad hominem argument that some of these gentlemen were socialists until a few years ago and that they have never been nearer to a real farm than the Chicago futures market. What is more to the point, we do not start with a clean slate. The free market is a grand ideal, but from the founding of the United States government until at least the 1930s, public policy was not laissez-faire but planned industrial growth by subsidy and favorable legislation for the industrial sector at the expense of farmers and consumers.

Today's agricultural support can be seen as a redressing of the balance. Today we have a government which builds and maintains waterways and airports for the yachts and private planes of the rich;

which subsidizes illegitimacy on an immense scale; which bails out billion-dollar corporations; which pays untalented and obscene poets to write gibberish. Under the circumstances, it should not shock our free enterprise sensibilities too much to hope that policies can be devised that will not only allow the small farm to survive but to increase in numbers.

The goal of encouraging families to flourish on the land is both more attainable and more desirable than most of the ends for which public money is spent. I for one am willing to forego a good deal of the theoretical virtue and actual efficiency of the free market for such an end. I suspect that in the long run even the economic effect would be favorable, but I have no doubt that the social effect would be entirely to the good. For the life of nations, like the life of persons, is more than a balance sheet. (1986)

Dixie Dystopia

How easy it is to make people believe a lie, and how hard it is to undo that work again.—Mark Twain

Books reviewed: *The Last Confederate Flag*, by Lloyd E. Lenard, Baltimore, Maryland: America House, 2001, 432 pages; *Bedford: A World Vision*, by Ellen Williams, Belleville, Ontario, Canada: Guardian Books, 2000, 299 pages; and *Death by Journalism?: One Teacher's Fateful Encounter with Political Correctness,* by Jerry Bledsoe, Asheboro, North Carolina: Down Home Press, 2002, 275 pages.

Just in case you haven't heard, we are in the midst of a Culture War. Death by Journalism? is a battle report from the front lines. *The Last Confederate Flag* and *Bedford: A World Vision* are fictional near-future projections, in the spirit of Orwell, of how the war is going to end. Coming all at the same time, these books give a grim view of our prospects. The war is heating up and Culture is losing.

Fortuitously, these authors tend to support my understanding of what the war is all about: a totalitarian-minded drive to impose a uniform public non-culture on the American people. Despite optimistic statements to the contrary, America has never been, culturally, all one thing. (I mean by culture here something like widespread folk attitudes and articulated and unarticulated assumptions about private and public things.) There is a Jamestown-Robert E. Lee country music America. Let's call it Confederate America for short. Conquered, impoverished, and despised, Confederate America remarkably maintains a continuing vigor, mostly below official radar and fashionable discussion.

Then there is Plymouth Rock-Abraham Lincoln-General Motors America. I am talking here about "culture," not economics.) For short let's say Yankee America. Yankee America never really had much folk culture except a kind of leveling out of distinctions and what John Lukacs has aptly described as a genuine but peculiarly materialistic idealism. Yankee America has had and continues to have lots of power, prestige, and wealth, but its chief strengths have been technology and productivity. Next came Ellis Island-Catholic-Perry Como America, which we can call Catholic America. It mostly acquiesced in such aspects of Yankee

America as it liked or was forced to accept, while adding a little spice to the Boston pot roast.

Now we have Frankfurt School-Martin Luther King-MTV America. It was invented by European totalitarians and imported into the United States in the 1930s. It is aggressive, mean-spirited, bent on conquest, and, on the evidence in these books and all around us is already in control of much of the American arsenal of cultural power. Let's call this phenomenon, though the label is not really accurate, Multicultural America. It is this America that has initiated the Culture War and is spearheading its offensives. They take no prisoners and do not spare the weak and innocent.

Yankee America is culturally and demographically moribund. The victories of the Multiculturalists are a result mostly of the Yankee elite's intellectual shallowness and moral cowardice and continual appeasement. In fact, the Yankee elite and the Multicultural elite can barely be distinguished anymore. Though it has temporarily rallied its masses by an appeal to abstract "America," with the help of Limbaugh radio demagoguery, the Yankee elite is really holding on to its wealth and some of its prestige by drawing taxes, votes, and fighting men from Confederate America and Catholic America. Two Connecticut Bushes have become President by pretending to be Texans and pretending to represent the concerns of traditional Americans for whom they never have and never will do anything. (Ford, Dole, Kemp, etc., could not pull off the trick.) All the while surrendering everything but money to The Huns. It is Little George, the preferred candidate of sincere Christians, who has changed the American motto from "Protestant, Catholic, Jew" to "Protestant, Catholic, Jew, *and* Muslim." Clinton took money from the Buddhists, but even he did not promote them into the Pantheon.

As I see it, Catholic America is very uneasy about the advances of the Multicultural Huns but has developed no widespread resistance. Its allegiance is to "America" and it has not quite grasped that the map of America has been redrawn by the Multiculturalists and that it is next on the list of targets after Confederate America has been disposed of. Pat Buchanan has tried to tell them, but so far has not had much success.

The fact is that Confederate Americans (wherever they live) are the only numerous block of the American populace that have so far resisted (largely reflexively rather than reflectively) the multicultural dispensation. (The South was the only region that voted a majority against the recent outrageous mass amnesty for illegal aliens, for instance). Confederate America is also the only American culture that can keep and recruit individuals into its ranks at the folk level without and even in opposition to government education and patronage. In fact, it has been continuously gathering recruits from the ranks of Yankee and Catholic defectors.

The Number One objective of the Multiculturalists in their current offensive is to quash and eliminate Confederate America by Soviet style propaganda and suppression. This task is made much easier by the fact that much of Yankee America and Catholic America disdain Confederate America, harbor many old prejudices against it, and are not averse to giving us traitors another thrashing now and then.

Those who don't live in Dixie may have missed the pervasiveness of attacks against the culture and history of Confederate America that have been going on. In a small way, this can be seen as a late, as well as ugly and gratuitous, mopping-up campaign of the Civil Rights Revolution. It is certainly fueled by the prospective raid on the Treasury known as "reparations for slavery." But there is more to it than that. It is a major offensive of the Multiculturalists. It is being abetted by the short-sighted leaders of Yankee America who are hoping that Confederate Americans (still demographically numerous) will keep voting Republican and be pacified into resembling Yankee America. Unfortunately, becoming more like Yankee America is merely a stage on the way to multiculturalism. As a great 19th century Southern thinker, Robert Lewis Dabney, observed, Northern "conservatives," in the entire course of American history have never conserved anything.

I don't want to give away too much of the plots of two fine novels; but *The Last Confederate Flag* is a story of an upright, respected citizen who, by speaking publicly in favor of Confederate symbols and resisting a murderous armed attack on his home by militant minorities, ends up with his family slaughtered, himself in prison, and a demon figure in the media. In *Bedford: A World Vision* we get a taste of the New World Order. "World Vision," totalitarian, therapeutic, and pseudo-tolerant, is the pervasive ideology, enforced at every level.

What used to be Alabama is now a numbered district of the World Order. Non-Liberal Christians are confined, except during work hours, in camps where their intolerance will not damage the public. And there is much more. Both books are well-told, attention-holding, thought-provoking stories.

Are the circumstances these authors have laid out fevered fantasies, unthinkable in good old quotidian America? Here are some things that have really happened in recent months. A boy doodles a Confederate flag in his notebook at school and is suspended. In another state a boy checks out a school library book with the same offending symbol. He is beaten to the point of hospitalization by black and Hispanic students. The victim is suspended from school. The thugs remain untouched by any authority.

During the Presidential primary in South Carolina, candidates McCain and Bush declare that the status of the Confederate banner is a matter for the people of the State. After the primary, Bush's henchman illegally remove, in the dark of night, two harmless plaques put up years ago by Confederate widows, from the Texas supreme court building. McCain makes a special trip back to South Carolina to declare that he lied for advantage and really thinks the flag must be banished.

A peaceable old gentleman stands up to ask a question of a famous "Civil Rights" personality after a speech at a public university. In accord with prior instructions by the speaker, the old gentleman is hustled out of the chamber and roughed up by three burly young policeman before he has said a word. The policemen make no reply and seem embarrassed when onlookers ask what he had done wrong.

A longtime much respected Congressman dies, leaving a request that "Dixie" be played at the gathering of his mourners. The Vice President of the United States demands that the offending tune be suppressed as the price of his attendance at the funeral.

Distinguished clergymen and scholars who have spoken publicly against the official Totally Evil version of Southern history, are characterized as an extremist conspiracy by low-level employees of a "Civil Rights" organization, people without any credentials or moral standing to pass judgments on either history or other people's character. The libels, however, are taken as fact by media and registered by law enforcement agencies.

I could catalog a hundred more such instances. Don't think that only the useless nostalgic sentiments of misguided Southerners are at stake here. The Yankee or standard version of American history is also an obstacle for the conquering forces. I know of a university professor who teaches that colonial Virginians (Washington and Jefferson) were similar to the Taliban. (Presumably because they were not feminists and sometimes carried weapons.) I'll bet your children are learning the same.

All this should tell us several things, besides the truth that *The Last Confederate Flag* and *Bedford: A World Vision* are not fantasies but merely logical extensions of present trends. They also tell us that local initiative and decision-making and (almost) local thought have disappeared. Law enforcement and education and information media have been imperialized to the point where every public school principal in every place in the land is conditioned to act in exactly the same way to enforce policies from Washington, however unreasonable or in defiance of common sense or community sentiment they may be. Every newspaper reports (and ignores) the same stories the same way, and every police and sheriff's department take instructions from the FBI. We should also be made aware that history, as a humane, intellectually liberating study, is being replaced by an officially-enforced party line.

In his Foreword, Bledsoe explains that he was prompted to write his careful investigation in *Death by Journalism?* because he had come to realize that "political censorship had become a very real possibility" in his own neighborhood. And the dustjacket copy for once is precisely true: "*Death by Journalism?* raises important questions about free speech, academic freedom, racial politics and news media integrity."

Jerry Bledsoe, a maverick investigative reporter and best-selling author of true crime books, tells in *Death by Journalism?* the sad true story of Jack Perdue, who became a national media demon and was literally hounded to death when he was picked to be the innocent target of a Multicultural advance man in the heart of North Carolina. That is my native country and Bledsoe's, and the author's account rings true. Jack Perdue was a year or two ahead of me in Greensboro High School (which incidentally was the first school in the state to be integrated, while we were there).

Jack was an engineer by trade and a lifelong, published, amateur (in the best sense) historian, with a vast knowledge of all aspects of local lore. He was also a benevolently active citizen, respected for integrity and service, who volunteered to teach for free an adult education course on "North Carolina in the Civil War" at a branch of the Randolph County Community College. Randolph County is a largely rural region, partly absorbed into the Greensboro southern suburbs.

Enter from the left, Ethan Feinsilver, son of a D.C. psychiatrist, University of Chicago graduate, recently hired as a reporter for the *Greensboro News & Record*, and assigned to the Randolph County beat. Mr. Fensilver, whose press associates found him to be a disagreeable loner, found Randolph County to be the domain of despicable rednecks and his reportage of local affairs reflected his attitude even before he heard of Jack Perdue.

Then in 1998 he discovered Jack Perdue's course. Perdue was giving a balanced account of conditions and events in his beloved area during the War, which included the fact, well-established, that some black people served the Confederacy. He taught nothing that is not being taught in a hundred places at this moment or that has not been taught for the last hundred years. The trouble was, Jack Purdue had not had advanced study, where he would have learned that evidence must be re-interpreted according to current dicta.

No Civil Rights group had complained. Students in the elective course, some of them Northern immigrants, have been extensively interviewed by Bledsoe. None found anything biased or offensive in the course. They also found Jack Perdue to be a fair and good teacher, resisted repeated attempts by Mr. Feinsilver to provoke negative comments from them, and were amazed by the baseless and outrageous assertions reflected in Feinsilver's questions and in his subsequent news stories.

The News & Record now reported that Randolph County Community College was sponsoring the teaching that antebellum blacks were happy as slaves and was serving as a front for a "neo-Confederate hate group" (the Sons of Confederate Veterans). The story was soon seen worldwide on the AP wire, provoked an investigation by the U.S. Civil Rights Commission, and became a topic for national TV news and talk show attention. It was now accepted as "fact" that a Southern college was teaching the old, evil, exploded fiction that slaves were happy. Across the country papers carried headlines like "Sugar-coated Slavery," "A Rosy View of Slavery," and "College Course Opens Old Wounds," reporting that a Southern college was promoting slavery.

The college officials and students all emphatically denied the substance of Mr. Feinsilver's now worldwide "news" stories. Here is a telling point: the newspaper executives stonewalled and upheld Feinsilver's accuracy (though curiously he was put on probation and, apparently, dismissed six months later). After months of the stress of international demonization, Jack Perdue died suddenly of a heart attack. He had always been healthy and was barely 60. His family and friends believe that he was literally murdered by the media. The same news executives refused to run an obituary of a local who had been made an international figure a few months before by their own efforts, and refused to be interviewed by Bledsoe, who is himself a former prize-winning reporter for the paper (which twice offered me a job as editorial writer long ago in my misspent youth).

We learn from this the awful evil power and lockstep thinking of the media, of course. We learn that the local press dances to the tune of the Multiculturalists and heeds not its own community.

But we already know those things. I am more interested in the role of History in all of this and what it tells us about the state of American thought and discourse. Why was the college allowing him to teach false ideas, Feinsilver demanded to know of Jack Perdue?

I have my own questions. What was a newspaper reporter doing in a classroom uninvited investigating the orthodoxy of what was being taught? Can you imagine this happening say in an Afro-centric or Gay and Lesbian Studies course? Set aside that the reporter is a hostile outsider who seems to believe that his orthodoxy should be enforced on other people with a different heritage by the methods of media lynching.

Where does Feinsilver's orthodoxy come from? What authority or knowledge does Mr. Feinsilver possess to make his version of history unquestionable truth and someone else's false and dangerous? Obviously, because he considers himself a representative of the Multiculturalists who are endowed with divine right (if they only believed in the divine) to impose their interpretations on all of society.

Is there now an established official version of history from which dissenters can be punished? We are all required to accept the official summing up of several centuries of complex American history in a few vulgar slogans? Are historical interpretations to be eternally static in keeping with the attitudes of official "experts" rather than fields for weighing evidence and debating conclusions?

Of course, none of this is really History. It reflects a mentality identical to that which created official Soviet history, in which dogma and slogans are substituted for study of the immense complexities of human experience. The latter can perhaps make us a little wiser. The former serves only the purposes of conquest. The prevalence of the Soviet style seems to be where we are now. Don't expect the too-numerous cohorts of credentialed academic historians to put up any opposition to the reduction of investigation and understanding to propaganda and conformity. They will acquiesce in, where they do not actively abet, the official orthodoxy. (2002)

Tar Heel Dead

In my honest and unbiased judgment, the Good Lord will place the Garden of Eden in North Carolina, when He restores it to earth. He will do this because He will have so few changes to make in order to achieve perfection.— Sam J. Ervin, Jr.

In Justice to So Fine a Country

A review of *Dictionary of North Carolina Biography*, edited by William S. Powell, Chapel Hill: University of North Carolina Press, 1979 onward, the first three of six volumes.

William S. Powell's magnificent portrayal of an American state through a collective biography of its men and women of eminence or interest has reached midpoint in its publication. I will try to explain why it is worthy of serious notice by readers of the magazine of American culture.

One of the great virtues of this collection is an old-fashioned scholarship that is at once skillful, thorough, aware without being trendy, and pious without being blind. The editor has spent a lifetime exploring every facet of the history of his state and mastering it with a thoroughness seldom matched today. The result is a grand and comprehensive design that leads to an inclusiveness, accuracy, and insight that is of permanent value.

Let's face it: the libraries are full of biographical dictionaries. Many of them, even some bearing the names of famous scholars as editors, are merely publishers gimmicks, cut-and-pasted together by people who were unable or unwilling to see their subject freshly and comprehensively and full of articles written hastily by clock-watching "scholars" who merely compile and rewrite old mistakes of fact and judgment. Not so in this remarkable work.

Another consoling feature is the collaboration of hundreds of authors on some four thousand sketches, with professional scholars and amateurs (in the old and honorable sense of that term) appearing shoulder-to-shoulder without embarrassment. The collaboration is reminiscent of that golden age of American culture around the turn of the 20th century, when history and all other endeavors were dominated by gifted amateurs, the last great promising moment before "experts" and "progressives" took government and learning away from the people and ruined them forever. We North Carolinians have always been behind the times in many ways—and glad of it.

Pardon me if I talk about "we." Though I have been in exile south of the Catawba for some years,

I'm a Tar Heel born
And a Tar Heel bred.
And when I die,
I'll be a Tar Heel dead.

Unlike some neighbors I will not mention, we don't like to brag. Our motto is "*Esse Quam Videri*": to be rather than to seem. But I will point out to a world whose perspective is slanted by New York and Hollywood that we make up a pretty big slice of America, both in size and history. For instance, we are the tenth most populous state (1980 census), a position we have not deviated far from throughout this century. We are six times bigger than New Hampshire, twice as big as Iowa or Oregon, considerably bigger than Indiana or Wisconsin Yet for some reason our presidential primary, which has been competitive for decades now, is never noticed like those states' by the media moguls. (Could they be *prejudiced*!??)

At the time of the American Revolution, we were bigger than any of the 13 colonies except Virginia and Pennsylvania (that is, bigger than New York or Massachusetts) and growing fast. And unlike some states I won't mention, our influence was always heavily on the patriot side, especially after we broke the Scotch Tories at the Battle of Moore's Creek Bridge, which, if American history were ever told right, would be as famous as Bunker Hill.

And we have a pretty long history, by American standards, and including three rebellions *before* the Revolution, going back almost four centuries now. We have always made up our own minds, and always been American re-publicans. Not democrats, not progressives, not liberals, not conservatives in your Wall Street sense, but American republicans. Our Revolutionary heroes chronicled here, to name just a few—John Ashe, Richard Caswell, William Richardson Davie, Cornelius Harnett, James Iredell, Willie Jones—were fully the equals, as patriots and statesmen, of some of the better-advertised chaps from other states.

Perhaps our most representative leader of all time was Mr. Macon.[63] As I said, we think for ourselves. Consider Sam Ervin or Jesse Helms. You will have a rather hard time fitting them into any categories devised by the newspapers or the Stanford political science department. (Ervin appears herein. Senator Helms does not. The DNCB's one discrimination is against the living, who are not included.)

Not only are we a large state with a history a good deal older than the United States and an independent spirit, but we are an empire within ourselves. A coastal (plantation) region, a piedmont (yeomen and industry) region, and a mountain region, each one distinct and bigger

---

63 See Clyde N. Wilson, *From Union to Empire: Essays in the Jeffersonian Tradition*, Columbia, South Carolina: The Foundation for American Education, 2003), pp. 61-65.a

than the similar regions in any other Southern state. You can find within our broad bounds anything that you can find in any Southern state, most of anything that you can describe as generally American, and a great deal that is not found anywhere else.

When it came time for the Civil War, we did not want to rush into things. But when others had fouled it up beyond help, we did not hesitate. We told Mr. Lincoln what he could do with his troop requisition and voted 120-0 for secession. We provided 45 generals to the Confederacy (Civil War buffs will find in the DNCB a host of familiar heroes like Gilmer, Grimes, Hoke, Pender, Pettigrew, Ramseur, and many others) and nearly a fourth of the men who carried General Lee's bayonets for four years. But we also produced George W. Kirk, who fought a guerrilla war against the Confederacy from the mountains; General John Gibbon, who commanded some of the federal troops on Cemetery Ridge; and Solomon Meredith, who moved off to Indiana and ended up in command of the Iron Brigade, the best outfit in the Northern army. As I said, we do our own thinking.

We have always exercised an undue influence inside the Congress, where smarts count more than publicity. Consider, in the 19th century, James I. McKay, chairman of the House Ways and Means throughout the Jacksonian era, or Willie P. Mangum, president pro tem of the Senate, or William A. Graham, the Whig candidate for Vice President in 1852, men who in their own day were as famous as Clay or Webster. Or in the 20th century, Claude Kitchin, Woodrow Wilson's floor manager in the House, or Carl T. Durham, first and for many years chairman of the joint Atomic Energy Committee. Or outside the Congress, Josephus Daniels, probably the most powerful Democratic editor in the country, who was FDR's chief when he was Assistant Secretary of the Navy and who always referred to FDR as Franklin, even after he was a fourth-term President.

Maybe your taste runs to the bizarre—people who did not hold public office but who did something unusual. How about the assassin Thomas C. Dula, who is immortalized in the folk song "Tom Dooley" and who was in the same Confederate regiment as my great-grandfather and his brothers? Or how about Eng and Chang Bunker, the original Siamese twins, who, after they made their pile on Barnum's circuit, lived the rest of their lives alternately on adjacent plantations near Andy Griffith's Mount Airy, the prototype for "Mayberry"?

Or maybe you don't care much for politicians but like business and professional types. How about industrialists like the Dukes, Haneses, and Reynoldses? Or James K. Hall, the Southern Karl Menninger? You want writers? How about Thomas Dixon, who was not only a fabulously successful evangelist in New York and Boston but sold millions of copies of *The Clansman*, which formed the basis for *The Birth of a Nation*? Or Johnson J. Hooper, not only the grandnephew of one of our Signers of the Declaration of Independence and secretary of the Confederate Congress but also creator of the fictional Captain Simon Suggs, the true ancestor of Faulkner's Snopeses? You will find in the DNCB significant figures from literally every field of human endeavor—entrepreneurship, education, religion, all the arts, sciences, and professions.

Nor would I have you think that the women, and the blacks, and the Native Americans have been neglected. They are very well represented. How about George Moses Horton, the black poet who taught the children of prominent families in antebellum days? Or James C. Jones, the free black man from Raleigh who was President Davis's coachman and trusted confidential messenger during the War? I could go on, and on.

Throughout the 19th century, to an even greater degree than most of the Older states, we drained off most of our population increase to the heroic endeavor of settling the West. Mr. Powell has recognized this as an important part of our history, and has included not only those who played a significant role in our state but the Tar Heel-born who built up newer commonwealths. We played, as is obvious, a major role in every Southern state to the West, all the way to Texas—providing them with governors, congressmen, clergymen, editors, educators, and soldiers—Presidents Jackson, Polk, and Johnson, and the famous Senator Benton of Missouri, just to mention the top of the list.

But what is less well-known, our natives played almost as big a role in the old Northwest, the region north of the Ohio and east of the Mississippi. Consider Abraham Lincoln's mother. Or William Allen, who walked to Ohio as a boy and was for years in the antebellum period a senator and boss of the Democratic Party in that state. Or "Uncle Joe" Cannon, who as a child left the Quaker settlements near Greensboro, moved to Illinois, and grew up to be the most powerful Speaker the House of Representatives has ever had. Or Richard J. Gatling, who left the family plantation in Hertford County to go off to the Midwest and invent and manufacture the Gatling gun. In fact, if you are a WASP whose family settled the Midwest before 1860, you have a one-in-three chance of having North Carolina blood in your veins. This is not to mention later and less systematic Tar Heel immigration—Richard Weaver of the Ingersoll Foundation's Weaver Award, for instance.

The Far West? How about Kit Carson, the famous mountain man of New Mexico? A longtime Chief Justice of Washington State? Joe Lane, one of the great pioneer figures of Oregon? Or O.P. Fitzgerald, who not only founded Methodism in California but was a contemporary of Bret Harte and Mark Twain in developing California literature?

Why am I so enthusiastic about the DNCB? Not only because of the quality of the scholarship and the masterful inclusiveness of the design in every respect. Not only because of the tradition and civic heritage that is represented by the pietas of its conception and broad collaboration of its execution, both so rare and unexpected in this day and age. But because it contains vast stores of material on the real life and real deeds and real thoughts and motives of a large slice of real Americans. In a dark time when our culture is reduced to trashy novels and MTV, our politics to whining and smugness and hypocritical platitudes, and our history to Hollywood docudramas and warped ahistorical interpretations of our great documents and events, this is something for which we can be truly thankful. (1990)

South and West

American historians often write of a contrast between the South, a closed reactionary society, and the West, free and open and characteristically American. The dichotomy thus presented is a false one. The West is the South. That is, to the extent that the West is a theater for heroic action, rather than just a place to start a new business, it is the Old South transmitted to a new environment. The cowboy, to the degree that he represents the embodiment of a code of life rather than just a person who tends animals, is nothing more or less than the Southern gentleman on the plains.

It is no accident that the most famous Western novel, written by a Pennsylvanian, Owen Wister, and set in Wyoming, was called *The Virginian*; nor that the most memorable character in Robert Service's Alaska poems was from Tennessee; nor that John Wayne's best Western movie, *The Searchers*, begins in 1865 with the hero riding up to his prairie home in tattered gray.

But the Southernness of the American West is not just in the realm of romance. The romance in this case merely reflects the facts. Boone, Crockett, Lewis and Clark, the heroes of the Alamo, Kit Carson, Jim Bridger, Jesse James, nearly all the epic heroes of the frontier were Southerners. The "cowboy humorist" Will Rogers was the son of a captain in the Confederacy's Cherokee brigade. You will hear nothing except Southern accents today on America's only remaining frontier, the North Shore oil fields.

We repeat: The West is only Western because it is Southern, because it bears the impress of the culture of the Old South rather than the Old North. That is why Oklahoma produces cowboys, oil wildcatters, country music singers, writers and scholars, evangelists and outlaws, and Kansas produces wheat and an occasional communist.

Many know J. Evetts Haley as a Texan, a rancher still active in his eighties, and a politician of the Southern conservative stripe. He is best known, perhaps, for his audacious 1956 campaign for the governorship of Texas and for his 1964 book, *A Texan Looks at Lyndon: A Study in Illegitimate Power*, a work that was accurate in both its history and its prophecy. Many fewer people know Haley as an historian of the American Southwest. As a historian, Haley has been so prolific and skilled in portraying the heroic frontier of the Southern Great Plains that it takes nearly 60 pages just to list his books and articles and a whole book has been devoted to them.

Haley the historian explores that cultural nexus where the South and the West come together. Thus, the history of the Southwest becomes a phase of the Southern literary Renaissance. (1982)

The South and the American Empire

A reply to Harry W. Crocker III:

This discussion began with Mr. Crocker's column in the *Southern Partisan* which disparaged my disparagement of "the Cowboy in the White House," Teddy Roosevelt. Mr. Crocker argues that imperialism is well within the Southern tradition, citing the Louisiana Purchase, and many other examples of expansionism under Southern leaders in early national history. I do not consider the expansion of American settlers into nearly unoccupied lands adjacent to the existing States to be imperialism. When Jefferson thought of those vast lands to the west, he thought of future generations of free men in free states and free confederacies, not of an empire like the British. All Americans regarded the British Empire with hostility until the late 19th century when the British and American plutocratic classes merged.

Remember that the territories acquired in the 19th century were for the most part peopled thinly by nomadic Indian tribes. At the acquisition of Texas and California, Americans already outnumbered Mexicans in those areas. Usually, the U.S. government got involved only after private enterprise Americans had already occupied an area. And the U.S. government was mostly motivated by the desire to prevent British imperialism occupying the power vacuum on our borders.

Surely there is a qualitative difference between the kind of migration and colonization that I am describing and the kind of imperialism advocated by Teddy Roosevelt, Lodge, Hay, or Wilson. Sending fleets around the world and trying to dominate ancient, heavily-populated lands like China and India; or bringing the supposed benefits of the American Way to the Philippines by fire and sword in the interest of bullying nationalism and Big Business; or getting involved in the insane mayhem of the Great War, is not the same thing as American pioneering. Teddy Roosevelt wrote silly books picturing great pioneers like Boone as precursors of his own brand of imperialism (which, incidentally, rested on racist assumptions). Qualitatively, the two things are the opposite poles of American tradition—Southern frontiersmen and Northeastern elites.

I cannot agree that imperialism is a good and seemly thing, nor a necessary thing, nor that it is a Southern thing. No Southerner should equate Teddy Roosevelt with Confederate heroes or the present crop of federal "leaders" with the great Southern statesmen of earlier times. The South and everything it embodies and represents is incompatible with empire. The South is and will continue to be the first victim of the U.S. government's substitution of empire for constitutional republicanism. If the last century is any guide, in the future wars of empire Southerners will shed more blood proportionally and receive less reward than any other group.

One needs to keep always in mind the ancient distinction between nationalism and patriotism. Patriotism, love of one's land and people, does not require aggression against other peoples. Nationalism expresses the love of power, not of the land and people. What better examples of this do we need than the neoconservative chicken-hawks who fill the media these days? Mr. Crocker and I both want an America that stands tall, is respected, and not afraid to assert its just rights. Our difference is over what is more likely to achieve this. In my book, restraint from imperialist adventure does not necessarily mean that a people lack dynamism, nor does it require economic autarky.

Mr. Crocker admires the British Empire and its spreading of civilization around the world. So, do I. It is one of the most striking phenomena in history. However, civilization and democratic forms took root mostly in the lands that were colonized by British people, the Commonwealths, rather than among the foreign peoples that were dominated. There is rather a considerable difference between a colony of the home country and an imperial possession.

Heaven knows the world is dangerous, always has been, and always will be. But is exercising imperial power really the best way to preserve America? Insular Sparta lasted longer than imperial Athens. Doesn't empirical history suggest pretty strongly that empire leads to over-extension, exhaustion, and decay? All the greatest Americans have emphatically warned against going abroad in search of demons to slay.

And I might say that carefully limited punitive strikes against real threats need not require the creation of empire. Effective response to 9/11 doesn't necessarily mean occupying Afghanistan and Iraq. The latter is supported mainly by imperial cant. How can we take seriously a world power that imports and nurtures enemy terrorists and defends foreign borders with more effort than it does its own? Chesterton, a writer I am sure we both admire, in a brilliant essay, "The Empire of the Ignorant," described this sort of thing as the "fairy tales" that were used to justify the imperialism of his own time.

That Mr. Crocker's style of imperialism is different from and better motivated than that of the Carter and Clinton administrations and the neoconservatives I readily grant. But what reason do we have to think that the U.S. will be governed in the future by the "right kind" of imperialists? It is more likely that the policies of our empire would be set by the Bushes and Liebermans who never saw a shot fired in anger and who are devoted, not to a realistic exercise of national interest, but to the childish vision of America as moral policeman of the world.

The Romans and the British had for a time a real aristocracy to run their empires—a leadership class that was smart and tough and was sometimes even seen leading the charge from the front. Americans haven't elected aristocrats to power since 1865. The top military brass look more like agile bureaucrats than heroic leaders in war. The debacle of the Iran rescue mission, the Beirut Marine massacre, the Moscow Embassy betrayal, the tragic quagmire of Vietnam, the Somalian disaster—none of this gives us much faith in the leadership of the U.S. military. Winning wars against third-rate powers by the overwhelming expenditure of advanced hardware does not prove military prowess.

Mr. Crocker also doubts the conventional wisdom that imperialism means the end of republican freedom. I wonder why empires are ruled by emperors and why our presidents seem more and more like emperors? The last election was not much more dignified or expressive of democratic rule than the Praetorian Guard changing emperors in Rome. In both cases the candidates have little qualification to rule except that they came from ruling families, like Bush and Gore. It may be true that in an empire power is spread thin and is sometimes less onerously centralized than in insular governments. This seems to have been the case at some times in some parts of the Roman Empire, but the long-term trend goes the other way. The point is that imperial rulers are not responsible; they do whatever they want, including denying the rights of and murdering their own citizens.

The reason empire is incompatible with republican self-government, a truism to our Founding Fathers, is that empires don't have citizens—they have subjects. Subjects are expected not to have much self-motivation but to take their cues from the center. More importantly, subjects are interchangeable serfs and cannon fodder for an empire. What do we mean when we say we are going to save the United States? As Paul Craig Roberts has been demonstrating in a series of columns recently, American citizenship has all but disappeared. Anyone is an American, which tells us that American is now a meaningless concept.

At this very moment, by the design of our aspiring imperial ruling class, historic America is being transformed into something else by Third World immigrants who have more legal privileges than I do, and my family on both sides has been here since the early 1600s and played a real if humble role in making "America." I suspect that Mr. Crocker intends to belong to the future ruling class. I don't expect that I or my descendants will.

Who will make the sturdy legionnaires of the future who will police and expand the empire? As in Rome, the core nation is dissolving into wastrels and proletarians. Where is the sturdy yeomanry that poured from the fields and factories to meet the challenge in World War II? Will the legionnaires come from the affluent Hindus who are right now colonizing my neighborhood or from the Mexican and Vietnamese gangs who are fighting a turf battle in a town just down the road? From the devotees of heavy metal and promiscuity? From sheltered sensitivity-trained suburbanites?

Mr. Crocker seems to think that multiculturalism is something that happens to countries that fail to exercise their imperial muscle. I draw an opposite conclusion: multiculturalism is obviously a by-product of empire. I take the present sad state of Britain as evidence. Isn't it more reasonable to assume that Britain has been exhausted by the inevitable effects of imperialism, rather than that it fell into a sorry state by giving up imperialism?

Men may sometimes be willing to die in defense of their land and people. Nobody dies for an empire unless he is paid to do so. Sacrifices are sometimes required to preserve civilization, but the value of civilization is, as C.S. Lewis pointed out, exactly in the degree which it allows us to quietly enjoy our own family and friends and pursuits, undisturbed by the phony dreams and real dangers of imperial power and glory. (2002)

Lost Causes Regained:
The Works of M.E. Bradford

No people has ever existed wholly without a meaning.
—James Warley Miles, Charleston sermon, 1863

The South was dead, and buried, and yet she rose again.
—Thomas Nelson Page, The Old South, 1892

How can the traditional society be preserved as the model of the right conduct of mind in the face of the modern shift to the vision of mind as the proper model of society? This may only be accomplished, to be sure, by mind's assertion that society is its model.
—Lewis P. Simpson, Mind and the American Civil War, 1989

Books reviewed: *The Reactionary Imperative: Essays Literary and Political*, by M.E. Bradford, Peru, Illinois: Sherwood and Sugden and Company, 1990, 230 pages; *Against the Barbarians, and Other Reflections on Familiar Themes*, by M.E. Bradford, Columbia: University of Missouri Press, 1992, 268 pages; and *Original Intentions: The Making and Ratification of the United States Constitution*, by M.E. Bradford, Athens: University of Georgia Press, 1993, 165 pages.

Strange to say, there have been those who have denied the reality of the South. Earlier in this century some "social scientists" refused to recognize a Southern identity or a Southern tradition, although they acknowledged a regional cluster of certain quantifiable social pathologies. This position was wrong because, in fact, a Southern identity is verifiable by the methods of social science, as has been demonstrated by John Shelton Reed.

The doubting viewpoint was based less on empirical observation than on wishful thinking. Since the South was evil, it was best to treat it as spurious and unreal, a kind of temporary shortfall from the norm of a progressive American universe. Some who were too historically grounded to deny the existence of the South yet confidently predicted its imminent disappearance. An abundant rationale was provided by the thesis that any distinctiveness that had characterized the South was the product of a racial caste system that was an irrational survival of colonialism. When this had disappeared, so would such other relics as poverty, religion, and tradition, and the South would be indistinguishable from Ohio. Slavery and segregation have now disappeared, yet the South, though undoubtedly much changed, has shown a remarkable capacity to maintain a perverse distinctiveness in behavior and values.

Denial of the reality of a Southern tradition, though earnestly proselytized, does not hold up, having been put forward by people whose careers were built upon what they alleged did not exist. Indeed, hundreds of presumptively sane scholars around the globe are devoting careers to the study of "the South," which suggests that it must in some sense be a reality.

More importantly, millions of people through many generations have found "Southern" a compelling badge of identity. That has been going on for about three centuries now: the South is older than the U.S.A. Not only natives but outsiders have observed something distinctive, and often attractive. It is said that the bloody St. Andrew's cross of the Confederacy was displayed as a symbol on both sides in the Spanish Civil War. Southern music, white and black, is known to almost all of mankind. The South is larger in population, territory, historical import, distinctive folkways, and literary presence than many of the separate nations of the earth. We do not have to agree on a definition to accept "the South" as a reality about which we may have useful discourse. I can't define romanticism, or faith, or poetry, but I know 'em when I see 'em. A good definition is given by Francis Butler Simkins and Charles P. Roland in their classic *A History of the South*: "not quite a nation within the nation, but the next thing to it."

M.E. Bradford has defined the South as "a vital and long-lasting bond, a corporate identity assumed by those who have contributed to it." It is a celebration of that bond to go on in good Southern fashion and follow definition by illustration:

> In the field the Confederate army was an extension of the region's social character, not the embodiment of a separate and antiseptic military profession or martial juggernaut.... When I think of the regional Gemeinschaft, I always think of ... Lee in the Wilderness that day when his men refused to let him assume a position in the line of fire and tugged at the bridle of Traveler until they had turned him aside.

Then there are skeptics who acknowledge the reality of the South but deny it any life of the mind, any cultural or intellectual quality beyond a sterile and reactionary defense of evil institutions and a delusionary Lost Cause. But in recent years intellectual historians of the highest caliber—not only Bradford but Michael O'Brien, Eugene D. Genovese, Lewis P. Simpson, David Moltke-Hansen, Richard Beale Davis—have given us the wherewithal to discern a Southern life of the mind that runs uninterruptedly from Robert Beverley to the present. A mind distinct from those of old New England and modern New York that are taken to be "American." A life of the mind not only continuous and unique but important, for how can anyone deny the significance of a line that is anchored near one end by Jefferson and near the other by Faulkner?

Being the product of an almost-nation-within-the-nation has imposed peculiar burdens and also perhaps special advantages on the Southern man of letters, whether literary artist or scholar. He has had to make his way in a society in which political and economic power, cultural prestige, and basic premises are foreign and often hostile to his native situation and instincts.

Southerners have adopted various strategies to meet this problem. There is the familiar example of the Southern liberal who conspicuously repudiates his heritage in the view of the larger world, though he may retain a few external characteristics that have market value. (The type is numerous, but I think one is hard pressed to find any first-rate artist or thinker who has adopted this stance unequivocally.) A more common and often successful strategy involves a seeming or partial critical distance from the Southern tradition or parts of it. This is the course taken by the first rank of Southern literary artists—Faulkner, Percy, Warren, Porter, Foote, Garrett, Chappell, Tom Wolfe—and also many among the first rank of scholars, Howard Odum, Cleanth Brooks, Simpson, and Reed. A concession is made, often ironic or minimal, in apparent acceptance of outside judgments and prejudices. This is necessary to establish communication with those, potentially hostile, who control the cultural patronage of American society.

One never finds in any of these first-rank figures a complete repudiation of Bradford's "corporate bond" of the South, however, but rather some affirmation, more or less overt, of allegiance. This appears even with C. Vann Woodward, the most successful of Southern liberals, who seems to repudiate the South, but always stops just short with a retreat into irony. It is obvious that for such Southerners the outsider situation has been turned into an advantage, not because it gives them a critical distance from the South, but on the contrary because being Southern gives them a critical distance from the complacent assumptions of mainstream American culture.

There is another strategy open to the Southern man of letters—an explicit defense of Southern quasi-nationality. Indeed, it would be surprising if so large a historical phenomenon as the South, important to many people over many generations, did not produce a continuity of defenders, though the explicit affirmation of the Southern corporate identity usually involves sacrifice of a degree of worldly recognition. I think of Andrew Lytle, Caroline Gordon, Allen Tate, and Donald Davidson among the artists, and among the scholars, Francis Butler Simkins, Richard M. Weaver, Douglas Southall Freeman, Thomas Fleming, and M.E. Bradford.

Those who hoped that the Southern tradition was moribund have received a stunning setback in the career of Bradford. No scholar of our time has described the corporate identity of the South on a broader canvas or with profounder insight. No man of letters has affirmed the positive value of that bond with greater energy, ingenuity, and persistence. Bradford's deliberate confrontation of the modern "vision of mind as the proper model of society," by a defense of the traditional ground of the South, has been carried out for three decades now with great skill on the unfriendly terrain of modern academic discourse.

Remarkably, the campaign has been waged within the disciplines of literature, history, and political thought simultaneously, as well as on other fronts. If, as has been said, genius is identified by the ability to create one's own vocation, then Bradford's career has been the expression of a unique genius. He has created for himself the role of a multifarious scholar of Southern traditionalism within the American intellectual dialectic—with an audacity against overwhelming odds which must be called heroic, and which has slowly but surely drawn admirers and disciples.

Among admirers, the Northern conservative Jeffrey Hart has written that in his "essays, some of them among the most important of our time, Bradford provides us with a master phenomenology of the American and Western spirit." Genovese, celebrated historian of the mind of the South, affirms Bradford's importance, as does Forrest McDonald, the leading constitutional historian of the day, who provides the foreword for *Original Intentions*. Bradford's trenchant performance of "mind's assertion that society is its model" has immediate forebears in

Davidson and Weaver. But he has enlarged the battlefront with learning that resonates profoundly through the last three centuries of British and American life and thought, while being unflinchingly engaged with the relevancies of the present.

Those who hope to hold their own against superior numbers must have skill and audacity. Francis Marion and Bedford Forrest are good Southern examples that come readily to mind. The measure of Bradford's achievement is the headway he has made against impossible odds—an unexpected feat of intellectual virtuosity that has guaranteed the survival of the intellectual defense of Southern tradition into the 21st century.

One reason for the slow recognition of this feat is that Bradford's books, such as the latest, have consisted of collections of essays, scholarly articles, and public addresses. The dispersal of insight through several hundred distinct pieces retards understanding unless one is able and willing to see the pattern. Whether Bradford's topic is a Faulkner short story, Patrick Henry at the Virginia ratifying convention, the strengths and weaknesses of Reaganism, Lincoln's speeches, the colonial South, Lyndon Johnson, or the latest works on Cromwell and Sir Walter Scott, the pattern is there. Whether the form is an article in a scholarly literary journal, a talk at the public library dedication in a small Texas town, or a lecture at a German university, Bradford's discourse constitutes a single corpus with a consistent and deeply thought out standpoint, one remarkable life's work.

He confronts directly not only ascendant liberalism but also the older and powerful orthodoxy of American nationalism. His essays on Lincoln, spread through several books, are as brilliant as any ever written on the subject, and unavoidably unpopular. Bradford argues that Lincoln's influence was baneful—the substitution of a heretical style of speaking for the gods in place of the reason and consensus of the Founders, with unfortunate consequences for America ever after. The position is irrefutable but also provoking because it challenges the most unexamined and therefore most fervent part of American mythology.

But these are not the only orthodoxies Bradford has bearded in their lairs. In an era of scholarly specialization his learning has ranged across fields in a way that is remarkable and defiant. He has not only mastered large fields, he has creatively related them and audaciously put them at the service of a social purpose, communicating not only across disciplines but to a larger public. This runs the danger of forfeited attention in an age of specialties.

Though it makes access to his discourse not too easy, it is a virtue because it recreates the ancient discipline of rhetoric. As a traditional rhetoric, Bradford assumes that form and substance, knowledge and ethics are inseparable, that communication is a function not only of the expertise but of the character of the speaker. Thus, the communication itself validates the social and political reality of the South about which it communicates and the pre-existent bond of those to whom the communication is addressed in the fullness of their being. It is an ethical and communal and not merely a utilitarian act. It thus speaks to a social life that pre-dates the rule of the expert and assumes a body of citizens who share a community of values and ideas. This manner of proceeding by its nature rejects the premise that the man of letters is or should be alienated from the society that produced him. Anyone who has read with understanding the lectures of Simms, the speeches of Calhoun, or Faulkner's talk to the Delta farmers will understand the point.

American scholars as a rule value intense analysis of small questions and effect a "scientific" neutrality. But small questions often lead to insignificance, and neutrality to unconscious enslavement to fashion. This leaves public discourse to crude and superficial popularizers. Bradford's breadth of learning and old-fashioned eloquence, informed by allegiance to a living community of people, is grandly anomalous. An example is "The Festive Spirit of Andrew Lytle" (*Against the Barbarians*), which makes us see the intimate and compact relationship between one of the great writers of the day and the Southern heritage of manners and temperament, and thus restores the broken bridge between life and literature.

Another example is "The Great Convention as Comic Action" (*Original Intentions*), about the miscalculations of young James Madison at Philadelphia. To the equipment of an historian deeply learned in the primary sources and a student of political thought with a brilliant grasp of the intellectual milieu, Bradford adds a playful, unexpected awareness of the literary conventions of the day and turns the familiar account of events into a new and dramatic story. In a brief and charming narrative, he makes us question conventional wisdom about things with which we thought ourselves familiar and see them in a way unimagined before.

Perhaps my favorite of the many essays is "Franklin and Jefferson: The Making and Binding of Self" from an earlier collection, *A Better Guide than Reason* (1979). In examining Franklin's autobiography and Jefferson's *Notes on the State of Virginia* together, Bradford brings to bear history, political thought, literary criticism, and social psychology, not in any self-consciously "interdisciplinary" manner, but in an effortless and masterful distillation. Laying out the differences between the two Founders, often thought to be on the same wing of the Revolution, liberals and cosmopolitans together, Bradford is at his most subtle and profound. They were, he demonstrates, very different kinds of cosmopolitans and radicals. One can never look at the relationship of North and South or American history itself in the same light again.

One aspect of Bradford's work is his commentary on Southern literature, almost all of which, both fiction and poetry, comes within his purview. (And also, American Western literature, as befits a Texan.) With much subsidiary critical insight, Bradford's largest persistent theme is the affinity of Southern literature with the great tradition of letters, a theme expounded in *Generations of the Faithful Heart* (1983) and continued in many pieces in The *Reactionary Imperative* and *Against the Barbarians*. The man of letters need not be, and in the South has not been, alienated from the social matrix that made him, but in fact should be its bardic voice. If the argument is carried for Faulkner it is sufficient for all, and the interpretation of Faulkner as predominantly the bard of the South and not the alienated modern is made persuasively in essays on many aspects of that giant's works in many of Bradford's books. The argument should be heard even by those disposed to dispute.

The continuity of Southern history is a theme that is developed not only in literature but in essays that deal with politics and history, a series adjacent to but distinguishable from the literary criticism. For a few samples, I recommend "A Long Farewell to Union" (*Against the Barbarians*), "Where We Were Born and Raised" (*Reactionary Imperative*), "The Colonial Origins of the Southern Tradition" (*A Better Guide Than Reason*), and much of *Remembering Who We Are: Observations of a Southern Conservative* (1985).

Still another aspect of Bradford's work has been a problematic endeavor to establish a Southern voice within the movement of American conservatism, renascent in recent decades but resting upon a different and shallower base than the Southern corporate bond. Along with literary and historical essays, the books contain commentaries on public events and political philosophy. Woodward and Norman Podhoretz, federal arts policy, modern conservatism, Eric Vogelin, Russell Kirk, Michael Oakeshott, Roman history, and much else come under Bradford's purview.

Another spacious portion of Bradford's corpus is devoted to the history of the American Founding. This is the subject of Original Intentions as well as other current and earlier works. A Worthy Company (1982) is a set of Plutarchian portraits of the Framers, which Against the Barbarians supplements with similar treatment of leading members of the ratifying conventions. These portraits, with the essays on other aspects of the Founding in *A Better Guide than Reason* and elsewhere, have rescued a vital part of American history from the misunderstandings piled up by succeeding generations of conflict.

Under Bradford's direction we can recover the pristine identity of the American people at the Founding. We see clearly the intellectual and moral assumptions that governed the process by which the scattered inhabitants of British North America articulated themselves into a federal republic. It is a full-blooded and dramatic account of what our forefathers were like, what they really believed and why, what they intended and what they did not intend in the great cause to which they pledged life, fortune, and sacred honor. Whether he agrees or not, no student of the events can refuse to come to terms with Bradford's account. And only those emotionally committed to the élan of the French Revolution can fail to find it persuasive. Interestingly, Bradford's treatment of the Northern Founders is as good as or better than his treatment of the Southern, a recovery of many neglected aspects of Northern history and identity.

Here too the ability to surmount barriers of disciplines and alienation between the man of letters and society is vital. For Bradford, as for the Founders, politics, history, and literature are not separate, mutually exclusive, and merely technical activities. They are, rather, ethical pursuits, the final end of which is the cultivation of good men. And since the quality of men is expressed in the quality of their citizenship, politics and learning and literature should be a seamless fabric. Bradford's work not only reminds us of this lost truth of the humanities but shows us how the fabric can be restored.

James Warley Miles, a talented theologian of the Old South, comforted his fellow citizens during one of the endless bombardments of Charleston, with the thought that the Almighty is not frivolous, he does not create a people without a purpose. Put another way, a culture thrown up by history has an intrinsic value in the scheme of the universe. That problematic thing we know as the South is such a culture. I am tempted to venture the argument that Providence has chosen that the South not disappear, at least not yet. Rather, it has allowed the appearance of a compelling restatement of its significance. That is what has been achieved by M.E. Bradford. We have here more than a scholarly career, we have a cultural phenomenon of extraordinary import. (1992)

What to Say about Dixie?

What to say in brief compass about the South?—a subject that is worthy of the complete works of a Homer, a Shakespeare, or a Faulkner. The South is a geographical/historical/cultural reality that has provided a crucial source of identity for millions of people for three centuries. Long before there was an entity known as "the United States of America," there was the South. Possibly, there will still be a Southern people long after the American Empire has collapsed upon its hollow shell.

One fine historian defined the South as "not quite a nation within the nation, but the next thing to it." The late M.E. Bradford, whose genial spirit watches over us even now, defined the South as "a vital and long-lasting bond a corporate identity assumed by those who have contributed to it." This is, characteristically, a broad and generous definition. He proceeded to illustrate that when visualizing the South, he always thought "of Lee in the Wilderness that day when his men refused to let him assume a position in the line of fire and tugged at the bridle of Traveler until they had turned him aside..." This was clearly a society at war, not a government military machine.

The South is larger and more salient in population, territory, historical import, distinctive folkways, music, and literature than many of the separate nations of the earth. Were the South independent today, it would be the fourth or fifth largest economy in the world. Citizens of Minneapolis consider themselves cultured because of their Japanese—conducted symphony that plays European music, and assume that the Nashville geniuses who create music all the world loves are rubes and hayseeds. New Yorkers pride themselves on their literary culture. Yet in the second half of the 20th century, if you subtract Southern writers, American literature would be on par with Denmark or Bulgaria and somewhere below Norway and Rumania.

Southerners are the most regionally loyal citizens of the United States. But paradoxically—or perhaps not—they have traditionally been the most loyal to the country at large, ready to repel insult or injury without the need to be dragooned by any ridiculous folderol about saving Haiti or Somalia for democracy. Southerners have given freely to the Union and generally avoided the demands for entitlements that now characterize American life. But their loyalty has been severely tested, especially considering all they have ever asked in return is to be left alone.

Southerners have less reason to be loyal to the collective enterprise of the United States than does any group of citizens. The South was invaded, laid waste, and conquered when it tried to uphold the original and correct understanding of the Declaration of Independence and the Constitution. It took 22 million Northerners, aided by the entire plutocracy and proletariat of the world, four years of the bloodiest warfare in American history and the most unparalleled terrorism against civilians, to subdue five million Southerners—all followed by the horror of Reconstruction. During this entire period, "the Northern conservatives" never opposed the smallest obstacle to the devastations of the radicals. In fact, the Northern "conservatives" have never, in the course of American history, conserved anything.

Since the War, the South has been a colonial possession, economically and culturally, to whatever sleazy elements have been able to exercise national power. A major theme of the American media and popular culture is ridicule and contempt for everything Southern. A major theme of American historical writing is the portrayal of the South as the unique repository of evil in a society that is otherwise shining and pure.

A severely condensed but essentially accurate interpretation of American history could be stated thusly: There are two kinds of Americans. There are those who want to be left alone to pursue their destiny, restrained only by tradition and religion; and those whose identity revolves around compelling others to submit to their own manufactured vision of the good society.

These two aspects of American culture were formed in the 17th century, by the Virginians and Yankees, respectively. The Virginians moved into the interior of America and carved their farms and plantations out of the wilderness. Their goal was to re-create the best of English rural society. They merged with even more vigorous and independent people, the Scots-Irish, to form what is still the better side of the American character.

The Yankees of Massachusetts lived in villages with preacher and teacher. They viewed themselves as a superior, chosen people, a City upon a Hill. As far as they were concerned, they were the true Americans and the only Americans that counted, ignoring or slandering other Americans relentlessly—a sentiment persisting to this day.

The days of Jefferson and Jackson illustrate the freedom and honor underlying America when ruled by the South. During their eras, Virginians gave away their vast Western empire for the joint enjoyment of all Americans, (thus making possible the Midwest and West) and labored to erect a limited, responsible government. The New Englanders, during the same periods, demanded a reserve of lands for themselves in Ohio; instituted a national bank and funding system by which their money-men profited off the blood of the Revolution; passed the Alien and Sedition laws to essentially enforce their own narrow ideological code on others; opposed the Louisiana Purchase; and demanded tariffs to protect their industries at others' expense. All of which was done in the name of "Americanism."

This profiteering through government, which John Taylor of Caroline called the "paper aristocracy," has always been accompanied by moral imperialism and assumptions of superiority that are even more offensive than the looting. It is from this that the South seceded. It is this combination of greed and moralism which constitutes the Yankee legacy, gives the American empire whatever legitimacy it can claim, and fuels the never-ending reconstruction of society. That is why we use Marines for social work, so that our leaders can congratulate themselves on their moral posture. That is why every town in the land is burdened with empty parking spaces bearing the symbol of the empire, so that the Connecticut Yankee George Bush can posture over his charity to the disabled. That is why, right now, wealthy Harvard University receives from the treasury a 200 percent overhead bonus on its immense federal grants, while the impoverished University of South Carolina receives only 50 percent of its much smaller bounty.

The term American is an abstraction without human content—it refers, at best, to a government, territory, standard of living, and a set of dubious and dubiously observed propositions. It refers to nothing akin to values or culture, nothing that represents the humanness of human beings. It could be reasonably argued that there is no such thing as an American people, although we have persuaded ourselves there was when shouldering the burdens of several wars. There was perhaps a time earlier in this century when an American nationality might have emerged naturally. But that time has passed with the onslaught of new immigrants.

Unlike the term American, when we say Southern, we know we imply a certain history, literature, music, and speech; particular folkways, attitudes and manners; a certain set of political responses and pieties; and a traditional view of the proper dividing line between the private and the public. Things which are unique, easily observable, and continual over many generations.

The bloody St. Andrews cross of the Confederacy is a symbol throughout the world of heroic resistance to oppression—except in the U.S., where it is in the process of suppression. Southerners are democratic in spirit, but they have never made a fetish of democracy and certainly not of what Mel Bradford called "Equality." With T.S. Eliot, Southerners intuitively recognize that democracy is a procedure and not a goal, a content, or a substitute for an authentic social fabric. However free and equal we may be, we are nothing without a culture, and there is no culture without religion.

The South, many believe, still has a substantial authentic culture, both high and folk, and it still has a purchase on Christianity. That is, the South is a civilizational reality in a sense which the United States is not, and it will last longer than the American Empire. For a long time we have been asking what the South can do for the United States. A proper question to now ask is what can the United States do for the South? The Union is nothing except for its constituent parts. The Union is good and just to the degree that it fosters its authentic parts. That is precisely why our forefathers made the Constitution and the Union and gave consent, voluntarily, to them—to enhance themselves, not the government.

As the Southern poet Allen Tate pointed out, the wrong turn was taken in the War Between the States when the United States ceased living by the Southern conception of a limited partnership and became instead a collection of buildings in Washington from which orders of self-justifying authority were issued. The great classical scholar and Confederate soldier Basil Gildersleeve remarked that the War was a conflict over grammar—whether the proper grammar was "the United States are" or "the United States is." We have been using the wrong grammar.

The South's lost political legacy was laid out by Rev. Robert Lewis Dabney, Presbyterian theologian and Stonewall Jackson's chief of staff, several years following the War. Echoing Calhoun he said:

> Government is not the creator but the creature of human society. The Government has no mission from God to make the community, on the contrary the community is determined by Providence, where it is happily determined for us by far other causes than the meddling of governments—by historical causes in the distant past, by vital ideas, propagated by great individual minds especially by the church and its doctrines. The only communities which have had their characters manufactured for them by

governments have had a villainously bad character. Noble races make their governments. Ignoble ones are made by them.

The United States was created to serve the communities which make it up, not for the communities to serve the government. That is what the South and all authentic American communities need to recapture from a ruling class bent upon constantly remaking us. If we recapture that, we will again be citizens giving our consent to the necessary evil of a limited government, and not the serfs and cannon fodder of the American Empire. (1994)

Confessions of a Neo-Confederate[64]

My title is a little tricky. I do not consider myself a "Neo-Confederate," though I have been labeled as such, with malice forethought, by self-appointed snarling watchdogs of orthodoxy.

I am a Southerner who dwells not in the past (which is like a foreign country: we can learn a lot from it but can't live there) but is looking forward to a new millennium.

Yes, I am proud of the struggle of our people for independence in 1861-1865, which was truly heroic and produced deeds and leaders that won the admiration of the world. But my people have a history of three and a half centuries. I am also proud of Captain John Smith and Pocahontas and Eliza Lucas Pinckney; of George Washington and Thomas Jefferson and Old Hickory; of Edgar Allan Poe, William Gilmore Simms, William Faulkner, and Caroline Gordon; of Will Rogers, Richard Petty, Hank Williams and Louis Armstrong; of Sam Ervin and the Shag; of Cajun cuisine and barbecue; of Magnolia Gardens and the Alamo; of good manners and strong, quiet faith. Not as marketing opportunities but as precious possessions. I admire Ralph David Abernathy's humor and candor and Jesse Jackson's ability to upset self-righteous people.

Without my people, civilization in America would lack most of what is good about it and would be an even more shoddy, shallow and pathetic operation than it is, with nothing to recommend it except its former free institutions and an increasingly insecure material prosperity. Such a people as mine deserve to govern themselves and not be the economic and cultural whipping boys of the "American" regime. Not to be, as they are now, living under a moral regime dictated by Sodom and Gomorrah (i.e., San Francisco and New York).

I do not wish to take Fort Sumter or Cemetery Ridge. I do not wish to reinstate slavery or Jim Crow, though I would like to restore the U.S. Constitution if that were possible. What I want is for my people's unique and admirable culture to flourish and decide its own future. This is a happy and positive mission in tune with a changing world. If we don't

---

64 The propaganda term "Neo-Confederate" was created in direct obedience to V.I. Lenin's instruction: "We must write in language which sews among the masses hate, revulsion and scorn toward those who disagree with us." Neo-Confederates harbor dangerous ideas which must never be allowed a hearing, such as 1) the official party interpretation of American history is questionable; 2) a return to Constitutional principles and devolution of power are worth considering in response to overgrown federal power.

About the Author

DR. CLYDE N. WILSON was Professor of History at the University of South Carolina from 1971 to 2006. There, among other work, he completed the editing of the 28-volume edition of *The Papers of John C. Calhoun,* which has been praised for high quality, and he directed 17 Ph.D. dissertations, a number of which have been published.

Dr. Wilson is the author or editor of 40 other books and more than 800 articles, essays, reviews, and lectures in scholarly and popular journals and online.

He is founding co-director of the Society of Independent Southern Historians; former president of the St. George Tucker Society for Southern Studies; recipient of the Bostick Prize for Contribution to South Carolina Letters; winner of the John Randolph Society Lifetime Achievement Award; and was for many years a contributing editor to *Chronicles* magazine.

Professor Wilson has received the Robert E. Lee Medal from the Sons of Confederate Veterans and was founding dean of the Stephen D. Lee Institute, educational arm of the SCV; He is the M.E. Bradford Distinguished Professor of the Abbeville Institute, and co-founder of Shotwell Publishing.

Dr. Wilson resides in the Dutch Fork of South Carolina, not far from the Santee Swamp where Francis Marion and his men rested between raids on the first invader of Carolina.

Best Sellers and New Releases

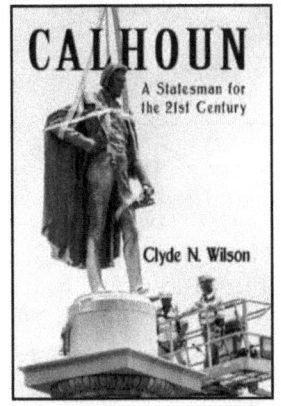

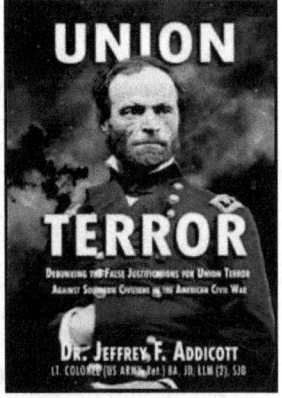

Over 100 Titles For You To Enjoy

SHOTWELLPUBLISHING.COM

THE SOUTH'S FINEST CONTEMPORARY AUTHORS.

Shotwell Publishing is proud to be called home by many of today's most respected Southern scholars and literary greats.

JEFFERY ADDICOTT
Union Terror: Debunking the False Justifications for Union Terror

Trampling Union Terror: Riders of the Second Alabama Cavalry

MARK ATKINS
Women in Combat: Feminism Goes to War

JOYCE BENNETT
Maryland, My Maryland: The Cultural Cleansing of a Small Southern State

ISAAC C. BISHOP
Defending Dixie's Land

GARRY BOWERS
Slavery and The Civil War

Dixie Days: Reminiscences of a Southern Boyhood

The Ultimate Primer for the Southern Outdoorsman

JERRY BREWER
Dismantling the Republic

ANDREW P. CALHOUN
My Own Darling Wife: Letters From a Confederate Volunteer

JOHN CHODES
Segregation: Federal Policy or Racism?

Washington's KKK: The Union League During Southern Reconstruction

WALTER BRIAN CISCO
War Crimes Against Southern Civilians

DAVID T. CRUM
Stonewall Jackson: Saved by Providence

STEPHEN DAVIS
Confederate Triumph: How the South Won Its War for Independence 1861–1863 Vol. One:1861

JOHN DEVANNY
Continuities: The South in a Time of Revolution

Lincoln's Continuing Revolution: Essays of M.E. Bradford and Thomas H. Landess

JOSHUA DOGGRELL
Doxed: The Political Lynching of a Southern Cop

JON DRESSLER
Missouri Poems with a Touch of Wales

JAMES C. EDWARDS
What Really Happened?: Quantrill's Raid on Lawrence, Kansas

TED EHMANN
Boom & Bust in Bone Valley: Florida's Phosphate Mining History 1886–2021

This Hallowed Ground

JOHN AVERY EMISON
The Deep State Assassination of Martin Luther King Jr.

DON GORDON
Snowball's Chance: My Kidneys Failed, My Wife Left Me & My Dog Died...

JOHN R. GRAHAM
Constitutional History of Secession

PAUL C. GRAHAM
Confederaphobia

When The Yankees Come: Former Carolina Slaves Remember

Nonsense on Stilts: The Gettysburg Address & Lincoln's Imaginary Nation

JOE D. HAINES
The Diary of Col. John Henry Stover Funk of the Stonewall Brigade, 1861–1862

CHARLES HAYES
The REAL First Thanksgiving

V.P. HUGHES
Col. John Singleton Mosby: In the News 1862–1916

T.L. HULSEY
25 Texas Heroes

The Constitution of Non-State Government

JOSEPH JAY
Sacred Conviction: The South's Stand for Biblical Authority

JAMES R. KENNEDY
Dixie Rising: Rules for Rebels

Nullifying Federal and State Gun Control: A How-To Guide for Gun Owners

When Rebel Was Cool

Reconstruction: Destroying the Republic and Creating an Empire

Uncle Seth Fought the Yankees: Book 1

WALTER D. KENNEDY
The South's Struggle: America's Hope

Lincoln, The Non-Christian President

Lincoln, Marx, and the GOP

J.R. & W.D. KENNEDY
Jefferson Davis: High Road to Emancipation and Constitutional Government

Yankee Empire: Aggressive Abroad and Despotic at Home

Punished With Poverty: The Suffering South

The South Was Right! 3rd Edition

LEWIS LIBERMAN
Snowflake Buddies; ABC Leftism For Kids!

PHILIP LEIGH
The Devil's Town: Hot Springs During The Gangster Era

U.S. Grant's Failed Presidency

The Causes of the Civil War

The Dreadful Frauds: Critical Race Theory and Identity Politics

JACK MARQUARDT
Around the World in 80 Years: Confessions of a Connecticut Confederate

MICHAEL MARTIN
Southern Grit: Sensing The Siege at Petersburg

SAMUEL MITCHAM
The Greatest Lynching in American History: New York, 1863

Confederate Patton: Richard Taylor and The Red River Campaign

CHARLES T. PACE
Lincoln As He Really Was

Southern Independence. Why War? The War To Prevent Southern Independence

JAMES R. ROESCH
From Founding Fathers To Fire Eaters

KIRKPATRICK SALE
Emancipation Hell: The Tragedy Wrought By Lincoln's Emancipation Proclamation

JOSEPH SCOTCHIE
The Asheville Connection: The Making of a Conservative

Samuel T. Francis and Revolution from the Middle

ANNE W. SMITH
Charlottesville Untold: Inside Unite The Right

Robert E. Lee: A History for Kids

KAREN STOKES
A Legion Of Devils: Sherman In South Carolina

The Burning of Columbia, S.C.: A Review of Northern Assertions and Southern Facts

Carolina Love Letters

Fortunes of War: The Adventures of a German Confederate

A Confederate in Paris: Letters of A. Dudley Mann 1867–1879

Bessie in Love and War

JOSEPH R. STROMBERG
Southern Story and Song: Country Music in the 20th Century

John Taylor of Caroline

Jack Trotter
Last Train to Dixie

John Theursam
Key West's Civil War

H.V. Traywick, Jr.
Along the Shadow Line

The Woke Revolution

Leslie Tucker
Old Times There Should Not Be Forgotten: Cultural Genocide in Dixie

John Vinson
Southerner Take Your Stand!

Howard R. White
How Southern Families Made America

Understanding Creation and Evolution

Mark R. Winchell
Confessions of a Copperhead: Culture and Politics in the Modern South

Joe Wolverton
What Degree of Madness? Madison's Method to Make American States Again

Walter Kirk Wood
Beyond Slavery: The Northern Romantic Nationalist Origins of America's Civil War

Clyde N. Wilson
Calhoun: A Statesman for the 21st Century

Lies My Teacher Told Me: The True History of the War For Southern Independence

The Yankee Problem: An American Dilemma

Annals of the Stupid Party: Republicans Before Trump

Nullification: Reclaiming The Consent of the Governed

The Old South: 50 Essential Books

The War Between the States: 60 Essential Books

Reconstruction and the New South, 1865–1913: 50 Essential Books

The South 20th Century and Beyond: 50 Essential Books

Southern Poets and Poems, 1606–1860: The Land They Loved, Vol. 1

Confederate Poets and Poems, Vol. 1 The Land They Loved, Vol. II

Confederate Poets and Poems, Vol. 2 The Land They Loved, Vol. III

Looking For Mr. Jefferson

African American Slavery in Historical Perspective

Defending Dixie

Titles We Think the Kids Will Enjoy:

Lewis Liberman
Snowflake Buddies; ABC Leftism For Kids!

Charles Hayes
The REAL First Thanksgiving

James R. Kennedy
Uncle Seth Fought the Yankees

Anne W. Smith
Robert E. Lee: A History for Kids

SHOTWELLPUBLISHING.COM

Green Altar (Literary Imprint)

CATHARINE SAVAGE BROSMAN
An Aesthetic Education and Other Stories (2nd Ed)

Chained Tree, Chained Owls: Poems

Aerosols and Other Poems

Partial Memoirs

RANDALL IVEY
*A New England Romance:
and Other Southern Stories*

The Gift of Gab

SUZANNE JOHNSON
Maxcy Gregg's Sporting Journals 1842–1858

JAMES E. KIBLER, JR.
Tiller: Claybank County Series, Vol. 4

The Gentler Gamester

*Beyond The Stone: Poems of
Tribute & Remembrance*

THOMAS MOORE
*A Fatal Mercy:
The Man Who Lost The Civil War*

PERRIN LOVETT
The Substitute, Tom Ironsides 1

Judging Athena

KAREN STOKES
Belles
Carolina Twilight
Honor in the Dust
The Immortals
The Soldier's Ghost: A Tale of Charleston

WILLIAM THOMAS
*Runaway Haley:
An Imagined Family Saga*

*The Field of Justice: Moonshine
and Murder in North Georgia*

CLYDE N. WILSON
*Southern Poets and Poems, 1606–1860:
The Land They Loved, Vol. 1*

*Confederate Poets and Poems, Vol. 1
The Land They Loved, Vol. II*

*Confederate Poets and Poems, Vol. 2
The Land They Loved, Vol. III*

Gold–Bug
(Mystery & Suspense Imprint)

BRANDI PERRY
Splintered: A New Orleans Tale

MARTIN WILSON
To Jekyll and Hide

Free Book Offer

Don't get left out, y'all.
Sign up and be the first to know about new releases, sales, and other goodies —plus we'll send you TWO FREE EBOOKS!

Lies My Teacher Told Me:
The True History of the War for Southern Independence
by Dr. Clyde N. Wilson

When The Yankees Come
Former Carolina Slaves Remember Sherman's March From the Sea
by Paul C. Graham

FreeLiesBook.com

Southern Books. No Apologies.
We love the South — its history, traditions, and culture — and are proud of our inheritance as Southerners. Our books are a reflection of this love.

www.ingramcontent.com/pod-product-compliance
Lightning Source LLC
Chambersburg PA
CBHW050546160426
43199CB00015B/2558